THE WORLD'S CLASSICS

PRINCIPLES OF POLITICAL ECONOMY AND CHAPTERS ON SOCIALISM

JOHN STUART MILL (1806–73), philosopher, political economist, bureaucrat in the East India Company (1823–58), and MP for Westminster (1865–8), was the dominant figure in English intellectual life in the latter half of the nineteenth century. In his childhood he received a rigorous utilitarian education from his father, James Mill, himself a disciple of Jeremy Bentham. At the age of 15, already a competent logician and political economist, he became an ardent Benthamite radical for about five years until his 'mental crisis' during the winter of 1826–7 precipitated a reaction against his Benthamite upbringing. Thereafter, he devoted himself to the project of reconstructing in a more satisfactory and a more liberal form the 'old' utilitarian philosophy he had inherited from his father, Bentham, and David Ricardo. In the course of pursuing this project, he produced treatises and essays on virtually all aspects of liberal democratic theory, for example, *Principles of Political Economy* (1848), *On Liberty* (1859), *Utilitarianism* (1861), *Considerations on Representative Government* (1861), *The Subjection of Women* (1869), and *Chapters on Socialism* (published posthumously in 1879). He had a long friendship with Mrs Harriet Taylor, whom he met in 1830 and married in 1851 about two years after the death of her first husband. She was the light of his life and, if his own testimony is accepted, a brilliant and original thinker who opened his eyes to the possibility of a much brighter future for the working classes, to wit, a far more egalitarian form of co-operative capitalism that might even evolve further, by a kind of spontaneous process, into a decentralized form of socialism. Long regarded as an eclectic and transitional thinker, Mill is interpreted in recent scholarship as a thinker of great power and imagination.

JONATHAN RILEY is an Associate Professor of the Murphy Institute of Political Economy, Tulane University, New Orleans. He gratefully acknowledges research support from the Murphy Institute during the period in which he produced this edition of Mill's

PRINCIPLES OF
POLITICAL ECONOMY
AND CHAPTERS ON
SOCIALISM

JOHN STUART MILL (1806–73), philosopher, political economist, bureaucrat in the East India Company (1823–58), and MP
for Westminster (1865–8), was the dominant figure in English
intellectual life in the latter half of the nineteenth century. In his
childhood he received a rigorous utilitarian education from his
father, James Mill, himself a disciple of Jeremy Bentham. At the
age of 15 already a competent logician and political economist, he
became an ardent Benthamite radical for about five years until his
mental crisis, during the winter of 1826–7, precipitated a reaction
against his Benthamite upbringing. Thereafter he devoted himself
to the project of reconstructing in a more satisfactory and a more
liberal form the 'old' utilitarian philosophy he had inherited from
his father Bentham, and David Ricardo. In the course of pursuing
this project, he produced treatises and essays on virtually all
aspects of liberal democratic theory, for example, Principles of
Political Economy (1848), On Liberty (1859), Utilitarianism (1861),
Considerations on Representative Government (1861), The Subjection of Women (1869), and Chapters on Socialism (published
posthumously in 1879). He had a long friendship with Mrs Harriet
Taylor, whom he met in 1830 and married in 1851 about two years
after the death of her first husband. She was the light of his life
and, if his own testimony is accepted, a brilliant and original
thinker who opened his eyes to the possibility of a much brighter
future for the working classes. He still, with more egalitarian form
of co-operative capitalism that might even evolve further, by a
kind of spontaneous process into a decentralized form of socialism. Long regarded as an eclectic and transitional thinker, Mill is
interpreted in recent scholarship as a thinker of great power and
imagination.

JONATHAN RILEY is an Associate Professor of the Murphy
Institute of Political Economy, Tulane University, New Orleans.
He gratefully acknowledges research support from the Murphy
Institute during the period in which he produced this edition of
Mill's Political Economy and Socialism.

THE WORLD'S CLASSICS

JOHN STUART MILL

Principles of Political Economy

and

Chapters on Socialism

Edited with an Introduction by
JONATHAN RILEY

Oxford   New York
OXFORD UNIVERSITY PRESS
1994

Oxford University Press, Walton Street, Oxford OX2 6DP
Oxford New York Toronto
Delhi Bombay Calcutta Madras Karachi
Kuala Lumpur Singapore Hong Kong Tokyo
Nairobi Dar es Salaam Cape Town
Melbourne Auckland Madrid
and associated companies in
Berlin Ibadan

British Library Cataloguing in Publication Data
Data available

Library of Congress Cataloging in Publication Data
Mill, John Stuart, 1806–1873.
Principles of political economy: and chapters on socialism / John
Stuart Mill; edited with an introduction by Jonathan Riley.
p. cm. — (The World's classics)
Includes bibliographical references.
1. Economics. 2. Classical school of economics. 3. Socialism.
I. Riley, Jonathan, 1955– . II. Title. III. Series.
HB161.M6 1994 330—dc20 93–28404
ISBN 0–19–283081–3

1 3 5 7 9 10 8 6 4 2

Typeset by Pure Tech Corporation, Pondicherry, India
Printed in Great Britain
by BPC Paperbacks Aylesbury, Bucks

CONTENTS

CONTENTS

INTRODUCTION

JOHN STUART MILL (1806–73), a man of brilliant intellect
and noble spirit, produced a large body of work that
constitutes an unusually powerful statement of what he
termed 'philosophical radicalism', or what today may be
termed 'democratic liberalism'. As his *Autobiography* (1873)
makes clear, he viewed his radical philosophy as a novel and
superior version of the older 'Benthamic type of radicalism'.
Jeremy Bentham (1748–1832) and his disciples, notably
Mill's father James (1773–1836) and, for a brief time in his
youth, Mill himself, emulated the eighteenth-century French
philosophes (including Voltaire, Helvetius, and Condorcet)
by glorifying reason as an instrument of reform, to the
neglect of cultivation of higher motives and noble character.
They tended to belittle existing customs and institutions as
irrational emanations of aristocratic class prejudice and religious superstition. At the same time, they took for granted
that conduct is motivated largely by self-interest. As a result,
they directed their reform efforts to improving the intellectual capacities of the masses and to establishing institutions
compatible with competitive pursuit of enlightened self-
interest. But they ignored ideal arrangements of which the
feasibility depends on development and intensification of
aesthetic and moral sentiments (including the desire for
justice, in the sense of equal rights for all): 'While fully
recognizing the superior excellence of unselfish benevolence
and love of justice, [they] did not expect the regeneration of
mankind from any direct action on those sentiments, but from
the effect of educated intellect, enlightening the selfish
feelings.'[1]

---

[1] All references to Mill's writings are to the *Collected Works of John Stuart
Mill* (33 vols.), gen. ed. J. M. Robson (Toronto and London, 1965–91),
denoted henceforth as *CW*. Moreover, the *Principles of Political Economy* will be
denoted as *POPE*; *Chapters on Socialism* as *COS*; *On Liberty* as *OL*; *Utilitarianism* as *Util.*; and the *Autobiography* as *Auto*. The present reference is to *Auto.*,
CW i 113.

This 'old' style of philosophical radicalism combined at least five leading elements: (1) a general Benthamite utilitarian point of view; (2) 'an almost unbounded confidence' in majoritarian democratic institutions and freedom of discussion; (3) rejection of any established church as incompatible with freedom of discussion; (4) a general presumption in favour of competitive capitalist markets, together with an emphasis on voluntary birth control as a means of permanently raising the wages of the working classes; and (5) a hedonistic psychology which, as developed by James Mill from a basis provided by David Hartley's *Observations on Man* (1749), viewed any person's sole ultimate goal as his happiness in the sense of pleasure (including absence of pain), and treated wealth and power as sources of pleasure inseparably associated with most persons' ideas of their happiness in contemporary civil societies.[2] For present purposes, the first and fourth of these elements require some clarification before we can appreciate how the younger Mill's political economy belongs to a 'new' style of radicalism with roots in the old.

Benthamite utilitarianism is central to the 'old' radicalism. According to Bentham, political and economic institutions should be designed such that predominantly self-interested persons, strongly motivated to acquire power and wealth, have adequate 'external' incentives to act so as to maximize the general happiness understood as the sum of the individual happinesses (enlightened self-interests), each to count for one and only one. He seems to have believed that the general happiness is in principle calculable in any situation because different individual happinesses are quantifiable and comparable. But he offered no general mechanical procedure for measuring or comparing individual happinesses. Rather, he claimed that the general happiness is comprised of certain concrete components (including security, subsistence, abundance, and equality) whose joint attainment should guide the design of social institutions. If majoritarian government promotes these concrete goals better than

[2] Ibid. 101–11.

alternative political institutions would in a given social context, for example, then that society ought to establish a democratic constitution together with suitable legal sanctions adequate to deter unconstitutional conduct.[3] Similarly, if competitive capitalist markets promote the goals better than alternative economic arrangements would, then the government ought to enforce suitable laws of private property and otherwise pursue a general policy of non-interference, or *laissez-faire*.[4]

Bentham himself proposed several institutions that he considered utilitarian in the context of contemporary English society, including the 'panopticon' prison, workhouses for the poor, schemes of taxation, and monetary systems. But he was mainly concerned to draft utilitarian legal codes (including constitutions), keeping in mind that such codes may vary across social contexts. He became an international figure as a result of his many proposals for legal reform (though most of his proposals were ignored). Despite his famous attack on natural rights, for example, he was elected an honorary citizen of France at the beginning of the Revolution for his advice to the new legislative assembly. He also proposed a number of times to codify the laws of the United States, writing to President James Madison in 1811, sending open letters to the Governors and citizens of all the States in 1817, and writing at last to

---

[3] Many different forms of political democracy are conceivable. For instance, Bentham claims, in his *Constitutional Code* (1830), that the US Constitution is utilitarian in the American social context. His view seems to be that its distinctive system of checks and balances establishes a government that is responsive to the enlightened interests of the majority. In other words, such a government best promotes the security, subsistence, abundance, and equality of the great body of the people. Even if this were so, of course, *unenlightened* individuals, motivated largely by the desire for power and wealth, are hardly likely to agree to establish or maintain any such democratic government. The requisite institutions must be established and defended (if at all) by the enlightened minority in the absence of mass education.

[4] Again, many different forms of capitalism are conceivable, depending on the legal definition of private property, the terms and conditions attaching to exclusive use of the things defined as property, the nature of the sanctions employed to enforce those terms and conditions, and so on. Moreover, it remains hard to see why *unenlightened* selfish individuals would agree to establish and maintain laws of private property.

President Andrew Jackson in 1830. But his offers were never taken up.[5]

As a close associate of James Mill, whom apparently he met in 1808, Bentham took an active interest in the remarkable education of Stuart Mill. He even offered to serve as a legal guardian so that the son's training might be continued in the event of the father's death. Both Mills were his frequent visitors in London, and the family (which he helped support financially until James Mill published his *History of India* in 1817 and parlayed its success into an appointment as Assistant Examiner in the East India Company as of May 1819) spent a good portion of each summer at one or another of his country residences from 1809 until 1817. He also arranged for Stuart Mill to gain some experience of French language and culture by living with his brother Samuel's family in France for more than a year (from May 1820 until July 1821). Once he returned to England, Mill became an ardent Benthamite for the next five years, until his so-called 'mental crisis' during the winter of 1826–7. In May 1823 he began his long employment with the East India Company, eventually rising to Chief Examiner of India Correspondence a couple of years prior to retiring in 1858 (when the Company itself was terminated as a Crown agency).

But Bentham's personal influence, both in Stuart Mill's education and in the character and conduct of the Benthamic school of radicalism, was secondary to that of James Mill. Unlike the reclusive Bentham, a lifelong bachelor who spent most of his time writing and was not much concerned to discuss views different from his own, James Mill was said by his son to be an admirable (if demanding) teacher and the driving force behind the Benthamic school, a leader whose animated conversation and rare moral qualities attracted various followers, including John Austin and his younger

[5] Whatever their other defects, US laws (constitution and statutes) are now codified, although judicial interpretation continues to be influenced by uncodified common law norms. For illuminating discussions of Bentham's works, see H. L. A. Hart, *Essays on Bentham* (Oxford, 1982); and Ross Harrison, *Bentham* (London, 1983).

brother Charles, Edward Strutt, Lord John Romilly and his son Edward, George Grote, Eyton Tooke (son of Thomas Tooke), Francis Place, Charles Buller, John Arthur Roebuck, Sir William Molesworth, and others: 'It was my father's opinions which gave the distinguishing character to the Benthamic or utilitarian propagandism of that time.'[6]

James Mill's best friend was David Ricardo (1772–1823), whom he met in 1808, the same year he met Bentham. After being banished from the family by his Jewish parents for marrying a Quaker, Ricardo had gone into business for himself as a stockbroker, becoming fabulously rich by the age of 25 and devoting more and more of his time after 1799 to the study of political economy. James Mill helped him to improve his writing skills, urged him to publish his great treatise *On the Principles of Political Economy and Taxation* (1817), and encouraged him to enter Parliament to make his views more widely known (Ricardo was MP for Portarlington, an Irish rotten borough, from 1819 until his death). The older Mill also published *Elements of Political Economy* (1821), a simplified account of Ricardo's theory 'fit for learners'. Stuart Mill was thoroughly familiar with its contents. It was based on the outlines he had prepared of his father's daily political economy lectures to him during 1819. His father also made him prepare (upon his return from France in 1821) a short abstract of every paragraph of the draft manuscript to facilitate the writing of the final product.

In addition to his father's series of daily lectures, Mill's 'complete course in political economy' at age 13 involved study of Ricardo's treatise ('the book which formed so great an epoch in political economy') and of his pamphlets on money (*The High Price of Bullion* (1810) and *Reply to Bosanquet* (1811) respectively), followed by a critical analysis of Adam Smith's *Wealth of Nations* (1776), a book said to be 'in many parts obsolete, and in all, imperfect'.[7] Moreover, Ricardo himself played an active role in the

---

[6] *Auto.*, *CW* i. 105.
[7] *POPE*, *CW* ii, p. xcii. Mill emphasizes that 'it was one of my father's main objects to make me apply to Smith's more superficial view of political economy,

course, frequently visiting the boy to discuss ideas. Mill's mature understanding of the Ricardian theory will be clarified shortly. For the moment, it is sufficient to emphasize that Ricardo and James Mill relied on the theory to argue for free markets and relatively modest reforms to the existing laws of private property. In his *Essay on Profits* (1815), for example, Ricardo advocated repeal of the Corn Laws to permit free trade in grains.[8] James Mill also proposed to tax any increments in rents gained by landowners as a result of government restrictions such as the Corn Laws. Moreover, both Ricardo and Mill emphasized that voluntary birth control was the only way for the working classes to avoid poverty and misery permanently. If the supply of labour was not suitably controlled, then, as Thomas R. Malthus (1766–1834) argued in his famous *Essay on Population* (1798), wages would tend to be driven by competition to a level that barely permitted physical survival. But none of these 'old' radical reform proposals (including free trade, taxes on land rents, birth control, abolition of primogeniture and entails, and so on) involves a fundamental departure from competitive capitalist institutions.

the superior lights of Ricardo, and detect what was fallacious in Smith's arguments, or erroneous in any of his conclusions' (*Auto.*, *CW* i. 31). Substantial portions of Mill's *Political Economy* are devoted to exposing Smith's errors. For examples, see *POPE*, *CW*, ii–iii. 116–30, 380–99, 456–7, 577–81, 587–617, 733–5, 829–30.

[8] Under various Corn Laws enacted during the period from the Norman Conquest until final repeal in 1846, the English market for grains (including wheat, oats, rye, barley, maize, malt, peas, and beans) was regulated. After 1660, the focus of regulation shifted from management of the internal trade for the benefit of consumers to protection of domestic producers from cheaper imports. In the well-known debates over the Corn Law of 1815, Ricardo argued unsuccessfully for free trade against protectionists including T. R. Malthus (although Malthus later abandoned protectionism). The 1815 law effectively banned imports (with exceptions for Canadian grains) unless average domestic prices reached very high levels. Import tariffs that varied inversely with domestic price levels were subsequently enacted in 1822 and amended in 1828. Beginning in 1839, strong agitation by the Manchester-based Anti-Corn-Law League (in which Richard Cobden and John Bright were prominent) eventually led to free trade 7 years later. For further discussion, see D. G. Barnes, *A History of the English Corn Laws From 1660–1846* (New York, 1930); and N. Longmate, *The Breadstealers* (London, 1984).

Stuart Mill's reaction against the 'old' type of radicalism associated with Bentham and Ricardo was precipitated by his 'mental crisis' at the age of 20, when for about six months he feared that critics might be right to dismiss utilitarianism as 'cold calculation; political economy as hard-hearted; [and] anti-population doctrines as repulsive to the natural feelings of mankind'.[9] The crisis passed as he came to realize that the critics were for the most part wrong. But it left behind a permanent legacy. As he explains:

I, for the first time, gave its proper place, among the prime necessities of human well-being, to the internal culture of the individual. I ceased to attach almost exclusive importance to the ordering of outward circumstances, and the training of the human being for speculation and action. I had now learnt by experience that the passive susceptibilities needed to be cultivated as well as the active capacities, and required to be nourished and enriched as well as guided. I did not, for an instant, lose sight of, or undervalue, that part of the truth which I had seen before; I never turned recreant to intellectual culture, or ceased to consider the power and practice of analysis as an essential condition both of individual and of social improvement. But I thought that it had consequences which required to be corrected, by joining other kinds of cultivation with it. The maintenance of a due balance among the faculties, now seemed to me of primary importance. The cultivation of the feelings became one of the cardinal points in my ethical and philosophical creed.[10]

In short, Mill now saw that no fundamental incompatibility exists between the basic tenets of radicalism and the cultivation of higher moral and aesthetic sentiments. Henceforth, he would be more open to ideas which were ignored by the 'official' radicals as antagonistic to their programme, for example, the insights of German idealists (including Goethe, Kant, and Schiller) and their British followers (notably Samuel Coleridge, Frederick Maurice, John Sterling, and Thomas Carlyle), of French socialists (including Claude Henri Saint-Simon, Charles Fourier, Auguste Comte, and Louis Blanc), and of feminists such as Harriet Taylor

[9] *Auto.*, *CW* i. 111-17, 137-45.   [10] Ibid. 147.

(whom he met in 1830 and eventually married in 1851, about two years after the death of her first husband).[11] But he would somehow combine their notions of noble character and egalitarian social utopias with the doctrines of Bentham and Ricardo. The real import of his passing depression, on this interpretation, is that it led him to formulate a better version of philosophical radicalism, a 'new' radicalism that retains what was 'permanently valuable' in the 'old' Benthamic school but at the same time makes more adequate provision for cultivation of the higher feelings and for ideal social arrangements founded upon them. Thus, a principal object of his conduct of the *London and Westminster Review* during the 1830s, he emphasizes, was 'to shew that there was a radical philosophy, better and more complete than Bentham's, while recognizing and incorporating all of Bentham's which is permanently valuable'.[12] Moreover, the great essays and treatises he wrote during the remainder of his life are properly seen to elaborate this 'better and more complete' radical philosophy whose coherence and appeal is still not generally recognized.

As I understand it, Mill's philosophy is a superior version of utilitarian radicalism in which the basic tenets of the old school are retained yet integrated with a broader perspective on human nature, a perspective that goes beyond self-interest (enlightened or otherwise) and takes account of the possibility that many individuals might develop higher moral and aesthetic sentiments. The 'new' radicalism is more cognizant of human capacities of imagination (including sympathy for others) and of mutual co-operation, more open to the possibility that individuals might form noble characters that reflect repeated acts of imagination and co-operation, and consequently less committed to institutions that presuppose the predominantly selfish type of characters observed hitherto. Without pretending to a fully adequate descrip-

[11] For discussion of these various influences on Mill's thought, see ibid. 137–272.

[12] Ibid. 221. See also ibid. 185–6, where Mill expresses affinity for the type of utilitarian radicalism espoused by John Austin during the 1830s (though Austin seems to have moved away from such an approach later in life).

tion, its leading features may be outlined as follows: (1) a more sophisticated utilitarian outlook which makes room for distinct kinds of pleasurable feelings and characters, including higher moral and aesthetic kinds, yet which remains Benthamite in the way it counts equally each individual's feeling or choice of a given kind to arrive at a social judgement of that same kind; (2) a less than boundless faith in majoritarian government and free discussion, reflecting a concern that the efficacy of democratic institutions depends on mass cultivation of certain moral feelings of co-operation and trust as well as on general intellectual improvement; (3) a commitment to universal equal rights to liberty with respect to one's 'purely self-regarding' choices, including choices of religious doctrine, of ideas on all other subjects, of sexual lifestyle, and so on; (4) a new awareness of the possibility that competitive capitalist institutions might gradually be replaced by a decentralized socialism, if the requisite moral sentiments and intellectual capacities could be developed; and (5) a version of psychological hedonism more subtle than that of James Mill, developed largely by Alexander Bain and by the younger Mill himself, which explains the higher aesthetic and moral sentiments as 'chemical combinations' that are produced from simpler feelings (including feelings of pleasure) in decipherable ways, through the principles of association.

What impact did Mill's 'new' radicalism have on his view of political economy? One important point is that he never abandoned his Ricardian approach to the abstract science. He let stand through all editions of his *Principles of Political Economy* (1848; 7th edn., 1871) the judgement that Ricardo was Britain's 'greatest political economist'.[13] Ricardo's theory admittedly required some clarification and even modification in view of subsequent contributions by various economists, including Mill himself. But Mill's 'pure theory' remained essentially Ricardian.

Despite his retention of Ricardo's scientific principles, however, Mill's 'mental crisis' led him to distance himself

---

[13] *POPE, CW* ii. 392.

from Ricardo's general Benthamic philosophy with its narrow focus on competitive capitalist institutions and its fixation on the predominantly selfish type of character moulded under such institutions. He looked to Smith rather than Ricardo when it came to practical application of the science in service of an adequate utilitarian 'Art of Life':

For practical purposes, political economy is inseparably intertwined with many other branches of social philosophy . . . Smith never loses sight of this truth . . . [A] work similar in its object and general conception to that of Adam Smith, but adapted to the more extended knowledge and improved ideas of the present age, is the kind of contribution which political economy at present requires.[14]

His aim in the *Political Economy* was to rework Smith's practical approach by applying Ricardo's advanced scientific principles in the light of a suitably 'enlarged' utilitarian philosophy that would go beyond narrow Benthamism to make room for a more complex psychology (admitting the possibility of higher kinds of pleasures and characters) and for improved ideas of social co-operation and equal justice. In particular, he wished to make clear that contemporary ideas and institutions of private property, and the highly inegalitarian distribution of wealth associated with them, were a matter of human choice and need not be accepted as 'natural'. By the time he published the third edition of his treatise in 1852, he and Mrs Taylor had firmly concluded that socialists were right to hold out the possibility of a radically egalitarian social ideal, even if any progress toward it must be gradual and difficult:

[O]ur ideal of ultimate improvement went far beyond democracy, and would class us decidedly under the general designation of socialists. While we repudiated with the greatest energy that tyranny of society over the individual which most socialistic systems are supposed to involve, we yet looked forward to a time when society will no longer be divided into the idle and the industrious; when the rule that they who do not work shall not eat, will be applied not to paupers only, but impartially to all;

[14] Ibid. pp. xci–xcii.

when the division of the produce of labour, instead of depending, as in so great a degree it now does, on the accident of birth, will be made by concert, on an acknowledged principle of justice; and when it will no longer either be, or be thought to be, impossible for human beings to exert themselves strenuously in procuring benefits which are not to be exclusively their own, but to be shared with the society they belong to. The social problem of the future we considered to be, how to unite the greatest individual liberty of action, with a common ownership in the raw material of the globe, and an equal participation of all in the benefits of combined labour. We had not the presumption to suppose that we could already foresee, by what precise form of institutions these objects could most effectually be attained, or at how near or how distant a period they would become practicable. We saw clearly that to render any such social transformation either possible or desirable, an equivalent change of character must take place both in the uncultivated herd who now compose the labouring masses, and in the immense majority of their employers. Both these classes must learn by practice to labour and combine for generous, or at all events for public and social purposes, and not, as hitherto, solely for narrowly interested ones. But the capacity to do this has always existed in mankind, and is not, nor is ever likely to be, extinct ... The deep rooted selfishness which forms the general character of the existing state of society, is *so* deeply rooted, only because the whole course of existing institutions tends to foster it ... These considerations did not make us overlook the folly of premature attempts to dispense with the inducements of private interest in social affairs, while no substitute for them has been or can be provided: but we regarded all existing institutions and social arrangements as being (in a phrase I once heard from Austin) 'merely provisional', and we welcomed with the greatest pleasure and interest all socialistic experiments by select individuals (such as the Cooperative Societies), which, whether they succeeded or failed, could not but operate as a most useful education of those who took part in them, by cultivating their capacity of acting upon motives pointing directly to the general good, or making them aware of the defects which render them and others incapable of doing so.[15]

The selections reprinted in the present volume display Mill's new radical approach to three grand economic issues, namely:

[19] *Auto.*, *CW* i. 239–41, emphasis original.

growth versus the stationary state, capitalism versus socialism, and the scope of government intervention in the competitive market. The selections are highly complementary
and deserve to be read in conjunction, despite the incomplete state and perhaps even ambiguous authorship of the
Chapters on Socialism (published posthumously by Helen
Taylor in 1879) as compared to the polished *Political
Economy* that went through seven editions during Mill's
lifetime. The fragment on socialism was drafted during the
winter of 1869–70. But Mill was apparently still working to
complete the draft 'to the last'.[16] Unfortunately, the original
seems to have been lost, raising fears that Helen Taylor,
John Morley, or others may have tampered with the manuscript prior to publication. I think that such fears should be
dismissed, however, in the light of the consistency of outlook (and even repetition of arguments) between the *Chapters* and the *Political Economy* (Book II, Chs. 1–2; Book IV,
Ch. 7).[17] As for the great treatise, it was 'rapidly executed'
in about eighteen months. Although 'commenced in the
autumn of 1845 and completed before the end of 1847', Mill
stopped working on it for some six months 'during the
winter of 1846–7, the period of the famine', to write (among
other things) forty-three articles in the *Monthly Chronicle*
'urging [unsuccessfully] the formation of peasant properties
on the waste lands of Ireland'.[18] Published in April 1848, the
first edition of 1,000 copies sold out within a year, leading
to a second edition in 1849, followed by a third (the most
extensively redrafted) of 1,200 copies in 1852, a fourth
in 1857, a fifth in 1862, a sixth in 1865, and the seventh in
1871. The treatise quickly became established as a text
in Anglo-American universities and was regarded as the
definitive statement of classical Ricardian orthodoxy until
it was supplanted by Alfred Marshall's *Principles of Economics* (1890), in my view, little more than a restatement of
Mill's ideas, making use of mathematical methods of calculus.
It also found a wide readership among the working classes.

[16] 'Helen Taylor's Continuation of the Autobiography', *CW* i. 625.
[17] See also *Auto.*, *CW* i. 237–41.   [18] Ibid. 243.

In addition to the seven library editions, an inexpensive people's edition was published in 1865 and sold more than 10,000 copies well before the winter of 1869-70 when Mill was drafting his *Autobiography*.[19]

The remainder of this introduction is organized as follows. The next section briefly summarizes Mill's Ricardian theory of exchange value and of the distribution of rewards among workers, capitalists, and resource owners. An understanding of the theory is needed to appreciate properly his arguments in the reprinted materials. Those arguments are then outlined in the following three sections. A concluding section evaluates the strengths and weaknesses of Mill's 'new' political economy and also gives some indication of its influence in the modern literature.[20]

Mill's Ricardian Theory of Value and Distribution

Some general features of the pure Ricardian theory as Mill interprets it are worth emphasizing.[21] First, exchange values of all commodities (including money) are invariably determined by market forces of demand and supply. But, for commodities whose production can be adjusted to satisfy whatever 'permanent' level of demand exists for them, market values tend to gravitate towards 'natural values' (or what Alfred Marshall called 'normal values') that are equivalent to (long-run marginal) cost of production. Even so, market values may never actually equal natural values for

---

[19] Ibid. 272.
[20] For a more detailed discussion, see Riley, 'Mill's Classical Political Economy', in J. Skorupski (ed.), *Cambridge Companion to John Stuart Mill* (Cambridge, forthcoming). See also the Select Bibliography for relevant readings on these topics.
[21] Mill's view of the Ricardian science more or less accords with that of Samuel Hollander, in my view. See the ref. to Hollander's work cited in the Bibliography. For discussion of the much different view of Ricardo's theory taken by the modern Cambridge school of 'neo-Ricardians', see e.g. P. Sraffa, *Production of Commodities by Means of Commodities* (Cambridge, 1960); G. Caravale and D. Tosato, *Ricardo and the Theory of Value, Distribution and Growth* (London, 1980); G. Caravale (ed.), *The Legacy of Ricardo* (Oxford, 1985); and E. Forget, 'The Ricardo Debates', *Canadian Journal of Economics*, 23 (1990), 434-45.

various reasons, including lags in the process of supply adjustment and shifts in the level of 'permanent' demand.

Second, non-optional laws and conditions of production, not the mechanisms of exchange and money, determine natural values in the context of any given stock of technical knowledge. Human beings have no choice in the matter. A produced commodity's natural value is set by the minimum rewards sufficient to call forth the physical inputs requisite to its production (respectively, labour, capital, and natural resources such as land). Unless workers receive a wage sufficient to enable them to raise a family at some customary standard of living, and unless savers are rewarded with a profit sufficient to induce them under existing social conditions to invest (rather than consume) their accumulated capital (proper allowance made for extraordinary risk or unusual managerial talents required of the investor), the requisite labour and capital will not be forthcoming in the long run. For production to satisfy any given level of 'permanent' demand, any commodity's market value must tend to compensate *at least* a subsistence wage and a minimum profit to the workers and savers who employ the least productive (zero-rent) natural resource inputs in its production. By improving labour productivity, technological advance may continually lower costs and thus natural values. But it cannot remove them entirely. Otherwise, commodities could be produced indefinitely without labour or abstinence, in effect, nature would freely supply the goods in abundance. In such a utopia, principles of political economy would cease to be of any interest.

Third, in a competitive capitalist context where separate classes of predominantly self-interested individuals own the respective inputs and compete over the distribution of the product, a subsistence wage and minimum profit are the *maximum* rewards that workers and savers respectively can reasonably expect in the long term. These distributive consequences of competitive capitalist institutions are as nonoptional as the laws and conditions of production. Given that profits are only made possible by the power of labour to produce more than the wages necessary to keep workers at their customary standard of living, what goes to the worker from production at the margin (that is, using the least productive natural resources) must come at the expense of his competitor, the owner of capital. Rent goes to those who possess superior types of natural resources. But such rent generally emerges as a result of the competition between capitalists and workers. It is equivalent to the additional product (profits and wages) made possible for capitalists and workers who use the superior resources: 'The superiority of the instrument is in exact proportion to the rent paid for it . . . Whoever does pay rent gets back its full value in extra advantages, and the rent which he pays does not place him in a worse position than, but only in the same position as, his fellow producer [at the margin] who pays no rent, but whose instrument is one of inferior efficiency.'[22] So, independently of the machinery of exchange and price, competition between the individual owners of capital and labour underlies the basic Ricardian principle of distribution. If the separate owners of the different inputs each bring their essential ingredient to the production process and then compete over the division of the product, then, whether or not they actually buy and sell anything at a price, an inverse relation exists between the ordinary rate of profit and the cost of labour to the capitalist.[23]

In addition to competition between different classes, competition between owners of the same factor also works its

---

[22] POPE, CW, ii. 429.

[23] 'The cost of labour' is distinct from the real commodity wage. What labour costs to the capitalist is 'a function of three variables: the efficiency of labour; the wages of labour (meaning thereby the real reward of the labourer); and the greater or less cost [in terms of labour and saving] at which the articles comprising that real reward can be produced or procured' (ibid. 414). If money may be assumed an invariable standard of value, then 'the cost of labour . . . is correctly represented by the money wages of the labourer' (ibid. iii. 698). The money wage level rises and the rate of profit falls if the commodity wage level rises and/or the natural cost values of the 'chief articles' comprising the commodity wage basket rise. 'But the opposition of pecuniary interest thus indicated between the class of capitalists and that of labourers, is to a great extent only apparent' (ibid. 700). This is because the real commodity wage may be high when the cost of labour is relatively low, the articles comprising the commodity wage basket being produced so efficiently that an ample supply can be provided to the workers at comparatively low cost. Thus, a high real wage may coexist with a high rate of profit.

effect. Consider workers. They seek wealth for themselves. But once their wage exceeds the level required to support a habitual standard of living, their aversion to labour and their desire for present enjoyment encourage them to pursue wealth for themselves through the efforts of others. Once above the customary minimum, in other words, they tend to have children on the expectation that these offspring will soon be capable of earning the same above-standard commodity wage as themselves. Given a sufficient number of children, each bringing in a surplus beyond what is necessary to her own support, the entire family (including the parents) might eventually be supported by the work and savings of the children alone. But if all workers pursue similar wealth-seeking strategies, then increased population (labour supply) tends in the long run to rapidly outpace the demand for labour (roughly equivalent to the stock of circulating capital). With due caveats relating to wage differentials across industries, the general level of wages is directly proportional to the ratio of (circulating) capital to population; and, therefore, in the absence of legal or customary checks on population, this wage level tends to be driven down to some habitual minimum. In short, if workers are motivated as political economists suppose, then Malthus is right that competition within the working classes tends to keep the workers at bare subsistence in the long run.[24]

Competition among the owners of capital also tends to enforce some uniform rate of return 'which is barely adequate, at the given place and time, to afford an equivalent for the abstinence, risk, and exertion implied in the employment of capital'.[25] The level of this minimum rate in a given society depends on the strength of the general desire to accumulate capital among those with wealth in that social context. But the strength of the desire in question is in turn ultimately

---

[24] If customary opinion denies an equal opportunity to acquire job skills and thereby impedes the free flow of workers between different employments, however, then different habitual standards may exist and the wage in each employment tends in the long run to be regulated by population increase among the class of workers customarily admitted into that employment (ibid. ii. 385–8).

[25] Ibid. 402.

determined by the degree of general security of property, and this may vary across societies. Now, actual profits are simply that portion of output which is produced by workers net of the real wages paid to support them. Given that the wages advanced by capitalists are roughly equivalent to the stock of circulating capital, the uniform profit rate is the ratio of net output to that capital stock. If capitalists are convinced that labour is sufficiently productive to generate the net output required to maintain at least the minimum profit rate, then capital will be forthcoming. But then competition among the owners of capital will tend to ensure that this minimum is also the maximum rate in the long run. Given that the effective desire to save has been triggered by net output expectations among most investors (including those with no unusual risk-taking proclivities or managerial skills), capital will tend to be invested until the ratio of expected net output to capital stock approaches the minimum rate.

Competition among resource owners will tend to ensure that the rents which flow as a result of the competition between capitalists and workers are also the maximum rents. But, in extraordinary cases where even the worst types of resources receive rents in the long term, competition is at best only partially operative. Resource owners in these cases have monopoly power to extract scarcity values from capitalists and workers for the use of resources, such values being a function of long-run demand and supply (taking for granted that resource owners may credibly threaten to further limit access).

Ceteris paribus, the competitive capitalist economy tends on this Ricardian view to gravitate towards a static long-run equilibrium in which market values converge on natural values (production costs), population is stationary with the working classes receiving a bare subsistence wage, capital stock is stationary with capitalists receiving no more than a minimum profit rate, and different qualities of natural resources are employed in production with owners of the superior qualities receiving rents from their mere possession. This rather 'dismal' equilibrium was commonly referred to as the 'stationary state'. Mill claimed that any 'opulent' economy such as Britain, with a large national product (gross and net) and more or less fixed supplies of superior natural resources, is habitually 'on the very verge of the stationary state' at all times.[26] Nevertheless, actual convergence is continually postponed because the stationary state 'itself flies before us' for various reasons, for example, technological innovations that prevent profits from falling to their minimum rate in a given social context.[27] Might it not be the case that consideration of technological advance and other sources of growth would fundamentally alter the Ricardian perspective as depicted so far? This is the first grand economic issue treated by Mill in the reprinted selections.

Growth and the Stationary State

Mill emphasizes that 'all the nations which we are accustomed to call civilized' exhibit a 'progress in wealth' which is likely to continue 'for some time' and eventually extend over most of the world.[28] Three general features of this growth process (which he also refers to as a process of 'civilization') are identified: (1) the continuous stream of

[26] Ibid. iii. 738. America is not an 'opulent' country because it has 'a large reserve of fertile land still unused' for production.

[27] Ibid. 752. Mill says that the usual rate of profits may not fall to the minimum for any of several reasons. In any given social context, for example, ordinary profits may be prevented from falling to the minimum rate by unproductive waste of capital as a result of rash speculation, by technological improvements, by cheap capital imports, by capital exports, and so on (ibid. 741–6). Moroever, the minimum profit rate itself varies across social contexts depending on the degree of general security of property. As security improves, therefore, the minimum rate may fall below its level in the earlier context, leaving ordinary profits to adjust accordingly. Finally, when different countries are at very different stages of progress, profit rates in the more opulent countries cannot fall to their respective minima because, below 'some practical minimum', their circulating capital would fly to the less opulent countries (ibid. 746).

[28] More generally, Mill speaks of a progress from savage states of economic society (gathering of vegetation, hunting, and fishing) to nomad economies (herding) to agricultural economies (cultivation of the land) to modern commercial and industrial economies, examples of all of which he thinks may yet be observed in the contemporary world (Ibid. ii. 10–20).

technological innovations; (2) 'a continual increase of the security of person and property', a security which when perfect would involve complete protection of equal rights of all persons in the community;[29] and (3) 'the continual growth of the principle and practice of cooperation', with the prospect of 'a great extension' of co-operative enterprises 'for industrial and other purposes', including joint-stock companies, voluntary philanthropic associations, and workers' co-operatives.[30] Political economy as he sees it makes no attempt to explain these three aspects of the growth process. Instead, it assumes for purposes of analysis that the process will continue and confines itself to investigation of the *consequences* for values and distribution.[31]

Concerning values, Mill argues that the forces of growth tend to cause the production costs of all commodities to fall, with the caveat that a uniform decline in values is impossible (because all things cannot decline in value relative to one another). Moreover, manufacturing products tend to fall in natural value and price relative to 'the products of agriculture and mines' because, for the latter products much more than the former, decreasing costs of labour and capital tend to be offset by increasing costs of raw materials. The growth process also tends to moderate 'the fluctuations of values and prices arising from variations in supply, or from alterations in real (as opposed to speculative) demand'. But it seems to exacerbate those 'conspicuous' business cycles 'beginning with irrational speculation and ending with a commercial crisis'. The reason for this, he indicates, is that the growth process tends to cause the rate of profit to fall. But 'a low rate of profits and interest

[29] Ibid. iii. 706. On the link between the vital general interest of security and justice in the sense of universal equal rights, see Mill, *Util.*, ch. 5 (*CW* x. 240–59); and J. Riley, *A Liberal Utilitarian Theory of Justice* (forthcoming).

[30] *POPE, CW.* iii. 708.

[31] The relevant variables (e.g. the growth of technological knowledge) are treated as 'exogenous' rather than 'endogenous' to the analysis. No attempt is made to explain changes in exogenous variables. Exogenous variables are 'outside' the analysis. Instead, the analysis seeks to explain changes in the endogenous variables, e.g. exchange values. Endogenous variables are thus 'inside' the analysis.

... makes capitalists dissatisfied with the ordinary course of safe mercantile gains' and encourages them to gamble on high-risk ventures promising extraordinary returns.[32]

With regard to the distribution of wealth, Mill offers what W. W. Rostow has called a 'rather remarkable' Ricardian analysis of five different growth scenarios, each involving a distinctive set of assumptions concerning the relative rates of increase of, respectively, population, capital stock, and technological knowledge.[33] The fifth scenario, in which all three rates are strictly positive, subsumes the other four cases. As Mill explains:

If during any period agricultural improvement [more generally, improvement in producing the commodities comprising the real wage habitually required by labour] advances faster than population, [then] rent and money wages [cost of labour] during that period will tend downward, and profits upward. If population advances more rapidly than agricultural improvement, either the labourers will submit to a reduction in the quantity or quality of their food, or if not, rent and money wages will progressively rise, and profits will fall.[34]

As a practical matter, he reaffirms Ricardo's conclusion that, in the absence of voluntary birth control, the growth process tends to further enrich the owners of natural resources without improving the lot of workers or capitalists: 'The economical progress of a society constituted of landlords, capitalists, and labourers, tends to the progressive enrichment of the landlord class; while the cost of the labourer's subsistence tends on the whole to increase, and profits to fall.'[35] In his view, population increase will eventually outrun agricultural improvement but workers must at some point refuse to accept a lower real wage (if only for physical survival). Prior to the workers' refusal, improvements permit profitable cultivation of less and less productive land without any increase of rents or labour costs (because workers offset the declining productivity by accepting lower

---

[32] POPE, *CW* iii. 718.

[33] W. W. Rostow, *Theorists of Economic Growth from David Hume to the Present* (Oxford, 1990), 115.

[34] POPE, *CW* iii. 729.   [35] Ibid. 731-2.

real wages). After the refusal, however, rents and money wages must progressively rise (because more labour is required to cultivate the same output from even worse lands). But then profits must progressively fall to their minimum rate, at which point capitalists will cease to make new investments (so that demand for labour stops growing). Whether this minimum rate is 'high or low, when once it has been reached, no further increase of capital can for the present take place' so that growth ceases.[36] Workers cannot accept a lower wage so that population (labour supply) also becomes stationary.

This Ricardian analysis suggests that technological advance may postpone but cannot fundamentally alter the gloomy stationary state that awaits the competitive capitalist economy. In short, an 'opulent' economy is, for any given state of technological knowledge, in the neighbourhood of a miserable stationary state where a stagnant mass of workers barely earns some habitual minimum wage, capitalists have no incentive to increase net investment because the ordinary rate of profits is at a minimum, and resource owners are receiving possibly large rents on more favourable (if not all) types of raw materials. Moreover, as technological knowledge advances, the stationary state does not tend to get any less miserable. Population and capital stock become progressively larger but the real wage still hovers at the same subsistence level and profits still gravitate towards the same minimum rate. Only resource owners benefit through larger and larger rents.

Despite this gloomy future held out by Ricardian theory, Mill goes on to emphasize the possibility of a much happier stationary state, a virtual utopia that might be attained under capitalism or socialism, where population is voluntarily limited by educated workers who thereby appropriate for themselves much of the net output that would otherwise be distributed to the resource owners as rent. At any state of technological knowledge, an opulent society might take steps to attain such a stationary state by suitably encouraging the

[36] Ibid. 738.

working classes to pursue higher moral and aesthetic purposes beyond their habitual standards of comfort. In particular, workers might be encouraged to practise birth control as a means of promoting their collective interest in having a real wage well above the subsistence level. And they might also be educated to assign more value to things other than the indefinite increase of population and wealth, including solitude and privacy, an unspoiled natural environment, and life-forms other than human beings. Moreover, as technology advances, this stationary state would tend to become even happier:

It is scarcely necessary to remark that a stationary condition of capital and population implies no stationary state of human improvement. There would be as much scope as ever for all kinds of mental culture, and moral and social progress . . . Even the industrial arts might be as earnestly and successfully cultivated, with this sole difference, that instead of serving no purpose but the increase of wealth, industrial improvements would produce their legitimate effect, that of abridging labour.[37]

Thus, the ultimate end-state towards which Mill's analysis points is not the gloomy spectacle traditionally associated with Ricardian theory. Of course, Ricardo and James Mill also *prescribed* voluntary birth control. But continued growth rather than any stationary state of population and capital was the goal of these 'old' radicals.

Perhaps what is most remarkable about Mill's defence of an ideal stationary state is his novel redirection of the three forces formerly associated with the progress of *wealth and population* towards a broader sort of progress, as he puts it, the promotion of 'utility in the largest sense, grounded on the permanent interests of man as a progressive being'.[38] Once society has attained a certain population and level of 'opulence', he thinks, political economy has done its main work and must now be subservient to other arts within an enlarged utilitarian 'Art of Living'. Technological improvements, increased security of person and property, and enhanced capacities for co-operative enterprise are hitherto to

---

[37] Ibid. 756.   [38] *OL, CW* xviii. 226.

be seen as features of a civilizing process with social goals more valuable than the mere increase of national wealth and population. In particular, once an opulent society has converged on Mill's stationary state, 'what is economically needed is a better distribution' of wealth for the given population.[39] Neither Ricardo nor James Mill showed a similar concern for this normative issue.

Capitalism Versus Socialism

Given that society's rules of property and distribution are entirely a matter of political choice (although the respective consequences of alternative systems of rules are not themselves choosable and are, indeed, the data on which any informed choice must rest), Mill considers whether 'persons who have no other interest in the matter than abstract justice and the general good of the community' would choose some form of capitalism or of socialism.[40] By capitalism he means an economy based on social rules that confer rights on individuals to own productive inputs and to compete with each other over the distribution of the product (for example, by negotiating suitable contracts which society then enforces by law). Many forms of capitalism are feasible because different systems of rules set different terms and conditions under which individuals may own inputs and compete over the division of the product. In contrast: 'What is characteristic of socialism is the joint ownership by all the members of the community of the instruments and the means of production; which carries with it the consequence that the division of the produce among the body of the owners must be a public act, performed according to rules laid down by the community.'[41] Socialism is based on rules which make inputs the common property of the community, from which it follows that the members of the community (or their political representatives) have authority to manage production and divide the output as they see fit. Many schemes of socialism are possible because

[39] *POPE, CW* iii. 755.   [40] *COS, CW* v. 711.   [41] Ibid. 738.

communities may choose different degrees of decentraliza-
tion in their organization of production and different for-
mulas for distributing the output. Communism as Mill uses
the term is a form of socialism whose scheme of production
may be highly decentralized (involving many separate 'self-
acting' communities of producers) and whose distribution
formula is 'absolute equality in the distribution of the
physical means of life and enjoyment'.[42] Any actual society's arrangements might involve a mixture of capitalism
and socialism thus understood, of course, but that would
not affect the normative question under consideration.

Mill's views are conveniently summarized in terms of two
claims. First, he indicates that both capitalism and socialism
in their best forms may be compatible with his ideal stationary state. At present, however: 'We are too ignorant either
of what individual agency in its best form, or socialism in
its best form, can accomplish, to be qualified to decide
which of the two will be the ultimate form of human
society.' He hazards a guess that 'the decision will probably
depend mainly on one consideration, viz. which of the two
systems is consistent with the greatest amount of human
liberty and spontaneity'.[43] Second, he also emphasizes that,
for the foreseeable future, the only option for those seeking
distributive justice is gradual reform of the existing private
property arrangements to establish capitalism 'as it might
be made': 'The laws of property [in any actual society] have
never yet conformed to the principles on which the justification of private property rests ... [T]he object to be principally aimed at in the present stage of human
improvement, is not the subversion of the system of individual property, but the improvement of it, and the full
participation of every member of the community in its
benefits.'[44] As existing rules of private property are re-

---

[42] POPE, CW ii. 203, 210; COS, CW v. 739. Note that the famous Marxist
formula 'that all should work according to their capacity, and receive according
to their wants' is attributed to Louis Blanc and said to be 'a still higher standard
of justice' than simple communism. Mill also suggests that central planning would
be a highly impractical way to go about organizing production (ibid. 738).

[43] POPE, CW ii. 208.   [44] Ibid. 207, 214.

formed and appropriate steps (i.e., universal education and birth control) are taken to bring about the ideal stationary state, capitalism may perhaps 'by a kind of spontaneous process' evolve into some form of socialism.[45] But there is no guarantee of this. A co-operative form of capitalism, in which all persons have certain equal property rights as well as other rights, may embody the highest standard of justice of which human beings prove capable.

To appreciate his position, it is crucial to keep in mind that Mill is ultimately concerned with the nature of fair rules of property and distribution under conditions of his happier stationary state. To compare capitalism and social-ism in their best forms, in other words, we must assume that a prudent policy of population control is in place so that real wages are well above subsistence. But we cannot expect workers to desire such a policy before they are suitably educated to recognize that birth control is indispensable to their collective interest. *A fortiori*, in a democracy where workers have the right to vote, we cannot expect such a policy to be legislated before the working-class majority demands it of their elected representatives. The fact is that Mill's ideal stationary state is not feasible in a democratic society until the working classes undergo an education process that promises to be slow and gradual. Yet, unless the stationary state becomes feasible, perfectly egalitarian rules of distribution will not prevent general unhappiness in the long run. Without 'universal education' and 'a due limitation of the numbers of the community', that is, neither socialism or capitalism can prevent the majority from fall-ing eventually into degradation and misery: '[I]f the supply of labourers is excessive, not even socialism can prevent their remuneration from being low.'[46] If the conditions of the ideal stationary state are realized, however, 'there could be no poverty, even under the present social institutions: and these [conditions] being supposed, the question of socialism is not, as generally stated by socialists, a question of flying to the sole refuge against the evils which now bear

---

[45] Ibid. iii. 793–4.   [46] Ibid. ii. 208, iii. 794–5.

down humanity; but a mere question of comparative advantages, which futurity must determine'.[47]

To compare socialism and capitalism in their best forms, however, not only must we assume an improved popular morality requisite to the ideal stationary state, we must also avoid conflating capitalism in its best form with institutions of private property as they now exist. 'The principle of private property has never yet had a fair trial in any country,' Mill insists, and, when properly understood, it would be 'found to have no necessary connexion with the physical and social evils which almost all socialist writers assume to be inseparable from it'.[48] Properly understood, it is an 'equitable principle' stipulating that the fruits of production ought to be distributed among individuals in proportion to their own productive efforts:

> Private property, in every defence made of it, is supposed to mean, the guarantee to individuals of the fruits of their own labour and abstinence . . . [W]hen limited to its essential elements, [it] consists in the recognition, in each person, of a right to the exclusive disposal of what he or she have produced by their own exertions, or received either by gift or by fair agreement, without force or fraud, from those who produced it. The foundation of the whole is, the right of producers to what they themselves have produced.[49]

Capitalism in its best form is grounded on this 'equitable principle of proportion between remuneration and exertion'. Carried to its logical conclusion, the principle would authorize division of the product entirely between workers and savers in proportion to the productive contributions made by their own labour and capital at the margin, with no provision made for the mere possession of natural resources because their long-run supplies are not dependent on any person's exertions. Existing rules of property deviate from the principle in important respects and, to that extent, are illegitimate from the perspective of capitalism itself. More on this in a moment.

Given that existing institutions are not equivalent to capitalism in its best form, Mill agrees with socialist critics

---

[47] Ibid. ii. 208. [48] Ibid. 207–8. [49] Ibid. 208, 215.

that the contemporary rules of property and distribution must be condemned because their evil consequences are contingent and could be remedied by institutional reform.[50] Nevertheless, he also argues that the critique of the existing system actually pressed by socialists is seriously flawed by 'exaggeration' and 'errors in political economy', where by 'errors' he means not mere policy disagreements but 'ignorance of economic facts, and of the causes by which the economic phenomena of society as it is, are actually determined'.[51] Even when they make valid criticisms, he goes on to emphasize, socialists fail to recognize that the existing capitalist regime might be suitably reformed without abandoning the 'equitable principle' of private property.

Mill concedes that socialists have a point, for example, when they claim that ordinary workers would have more incentive to be productive under socialism than under the existing system of hired labour. But socialists fail to see that this deficiency of the existing system can be repaired simply by introducing suitable profit-sharing arrangements between capitalists and workers.[52] Again, socialists are convincing, he thinks, when they argue that competition 'on the great scale of modern transactions' encourages the proliferation of unnecessary layers of dealers together with the spread of 'fraudulent practices', including 'adulteration', 'giving short measure', 'culpable insolvency', and so on.[53] But these problems too can largely be overcome without introducing socialism. Consumer co-operative associations can be established to deal directly with wholesalers or producers. Such consumer associations, 'though suggested by and partly grounded on socialistic principles, [are] consistent with the existing constitution of property'.[54] Moreover, 'culpable insolvency' can be minimized by investigating and punish-

---

[50] Ibid. 208–9; *COS, CW* v. 714–5. Note Mill's implicit appeal here to what he elsewhere calls 'ethology', the science of character formation, for a 'minuter analysis' of 'the filiation which connects' character faults and bad conduct 'with a defective organization of society'.

[51] Ibid. 727. For the 'errors' and 'exaggerations', see ibid. 727–31, 734–6; and *POPE, CW* iii. 794–6.

[52] *COS, CW* v. 742–3.   [53] Ibid. 731–3.   [54] Ibid. 732–3.

ing bankrupts for any commercial dishonesty (including fraudulent breaches of contract and negligent speculations with borrowed funds), rather than treating them lightly as 'objects of compassion' and focusing legal attention entirely on repayment of the creditors.[55]

Mill also agrees that socialists have valid objections against the high concentration of wealth in the hands of those who did not earn it by their own work and saving but instead received it as an inheritance or as rent from the mere possession of superior types of natural resources. But even these objections can be answered by reforming the existing arrangements in ways prescribed by the equitable principle of private property itself. That equitable principle justifies 'a system of legislation favoring equality of fortunes, so far as is consistent with the just claim of the individual to the fruits, whether great or small, of his or her own industry [labour and abstinence]'.[56] Capitalism based on the principle would not recognize individual rights to own natural resources *per se*, for example, so that any rents associated with mere possession of resources would in principle be taken by the community through the tax system.[57] Nor would capitalism thus understood recognize a right to acquire unlimited wealth by gift or inheritance. Instead, any surplus which a person acquired above some limited 'amount sufficient to constitute a moderate independence' would properly be confiscated, in which case givers would have a strong incentive to spread the wealth among various recipients.[58] These and other reforms of the existing idea of property would tend to promote a far more egalitarian distribution of wealth without subverting capitalism itself.

In fact, such property reforms, together with the education and birth control policies required to bring about the happier stationary state, would usher in an ideal capitalist society with 'these leading features: a well-paid and affluent body of labourers; no enormous fortunes, except what were earned and accumulated during a single lifetime; but a

---

[55] See ibid. 733; and *POPE*, *CW* iii. 906–12. [56] Ibid. 755.
[57] Ibid. ii. 227–32. [58] Ibid. iii. 755. See also ibid. ii. 218–26.

much larger body of persons than at present, not only exempt from the coarser toils, but with sufficient leisure, both physical and mental, from mechanical details, to cultivate freely the graces of life'. This is capitalism in its best form, and it is a worthy target of reform for 'a long period to come': 'This condition of society, so greatly preferable to the present, is not only perfectly compatible with the stationary state, but, it would seem, more naturally allied with that state than with any other.'[59]

Despite his defence of capitalism in its best form and his focus on gradual reform of existing institutions in that direction, however, Mill does take seriously the possibility that society will evolve beyond capitalism altogether. Some decentralized form of socialism, in which 'both sexes participate equally in the rights and in the government' of small-scale producer co-operatives, represents for him 'the nearest approach to social justice, and the most beneficial ordering of industrial affairs for the universal good, which it is possible at present to foresee'.[60] Whether most will in fact develop the moral and intellectual capacities required to implement something close to a perfectly egalitarian distribution must remain an open question for now. But socialist experiments along Fourier's lines, involving small-scale self-managed communes or villages, ought to be tried by enlightened workers in the meantime.[61]

To appreciate how a decentralized form of socialism might eventually emerge from capitalism in its best form, it is important to note that progress towards Mill's happier stationary state implies enhanced capacities of co-operation among workers. As the working classes become more enlightened and learn to co-operate to mutual advantage, the hierarchical wage relations between distinct classes of capitalists and workers will tend to wither away in favour of

[59] Ibid. iii. 755. See also COS, CW v. 749–53.   [60] POPE, CW iii. 794.
[61] For discussion of Fourier's scheme of decentralized socialism, see J. Beecher, *Charles Fourier: The Visionary and His World* (Berkeley, Calif., 1986); J. Beecher and R. Bienvenu, *The Utopian Vision of Charles Fourier* (Boston, 1971); C. J. Guarneri, *The Utopian Alternative: Fourierism in Nineteenth-Century America* (Ithaca, NJ, 1991); and N. V. Riasanovsky, *The Teaching of Charles Fourier* (Berkeley, Calif., 1969).

some classless society between equals: '[T]he relation of masters and workpeople will be gradually superseded by partnership, in one of two forms: in some cases, association of the labourers with the capitalist; in others, and perhaps finally in all, association of labourers among themselves.'[62] In this regard, increased capacities for co-operation lower the minimum rate of profit by strengthening the general desire of workers to make reasonable provision for the future wants of other members of their community. These more capable workers are more provident and more concerned about the interests of their fellows. Moreover, to the extent that such individuals are more worthy of trust from their fellows, investments of all kinds are less risky in their society. For both reasons, a stronger effective desire to save for others and an increased security of property and person, the minimum profit rate falls as workers develop their intellectual and moral abilities.[63] But as the minimum profit rate falls, less profit is necessary as an inducement for the average person to invest. As a result, even those with relatively small pools of capital will be increasingly willing to co-operate with others in joint investments. Capitalistic profit-sharing arrangements, where the enterprise is supervised by great capitalists who remain apart from the main body of workers but each individual is rewarded in proportion to the productive contribution made by his own labour and capital, are likely to be the preferred modes of co-operation for a long while. But, as popular morality advances further and wealth is diffused among the masses by property reforms, it is not impossible that this sort of co-operative capitalism will be replaced entirely by a competitive system of egalitarian partnerships among workers.

Nevertheless, despite his view that a competitive socialist economy might eventually emerge spontaneously from capitalism in its best form, Mill is careful to emphasize that even decentralized forms of socialism face serious, perhaps insurmountable, difficulties. Until 'motives of a higher character' are stronger than the desire for personal gain, for example,

---

[62] POPE, CW iii. 769.   [63] Ibid. ii. 163-4, iii. 737-8.

socialist managers are likely (to the extent they receive a fixed if not equal share decided by the collectivity) to be less hard-working and less innovative than private managers 'who own (or are personally responsible for) the capital'.[64] This disadvantage may never be overcome because the requisite strengthening of higher motives may never actually take place. Among other difficulties, Mill lays particular stress on the problem of majority despotism within any socialist or communist association. Popular intimidation of eccentric ideas and personal lifestyles is 'already one of the glaring evils' of the existing capitalist society, he thinks.[65] By inhibiting liberty of discussion and debate, such majority tyranny already tends, for example, to frustrate the process of intellectual and moral development which most must go through before an approach can be made to the happier stationary state. But the problem would be even worse in a socialist association where 'private life would be brought in a most unexampled degree within the dominion of public authority, and there would be less scope for the development of individual character and individual preferences than has hitherto existed among the full citizens of any state belonging to the progressive branches of the human family'.[66] Thus, although he recommends that more or less isolated socialist experiments ought to be tried even now among enlightened workers, Mill implies that institutions of private property remain essential 'for the development of individual character'. This is crucial because most persons must learn to become more tolerant of the moral rights of others to choose as they like in their private concerns before *either* capitalism or socialism is able 'to secure to all persons complete independence and freedom of action, subject to no restriction but that of not doing injury to others'.[67] Which of the two systems, socialism or capitalism in its best form, ultimately proves hospitable to 'the greatest amount of human liberty and spontaneity' must in the meantime be left an open question.

[64] COS, CW v. 739–45, 748–9. See also POPE, CW ii. 203–5, 210–14.
[65] Ibid. 209.   [66] COS, CW v. 746.   [67] POPE, CW ii. 208–9.

These difficulties would be compounded by others, Mill thinks, in the context of any revolutionary programme of the Marxist-Leninist variety that tried to impose socialism immediately on 'unprepared populations'. A socialist economy has no chance of success before existing populations have attained 'a high standard of both moral and intellectual education'. The required standard 'is very difficult' to attain, however, and 'the passage to it from our present condition can only be slow'.[68]

On Government: Principles of Taxation and of Laissez-Faire

Apart from whether the happier stationary state will involve a more egalitarian form of capitalism or a decentralized form of socialism, Mill implies that its enlightened citizens will continue to find government to be a generally expedient institution for performing various 'necessary' functions of one sort or another. Given that any government (however little it does) must have revenues if it is to exist, an important issue relates to fair principles of taxation. With the caveat that all persons should be legally guaranteed a subsistence income exempt from taxation, he generally argues for proportional taxation of any surplus income earned from one's own labour and saving under competitive conditions, and for sharply progressive taxation of all unearned surplus income including gifts, inheritances, resource rents, extraordinary capital gains, and the like. Whatever its other merits, his argument seems to be compatible with the equitable principle of private property because he is calling for proportional sacrifices by all able-bodied taxpayers from their (generally unequal) *earned* incomes above a subsistence wage. The equitable principle does not constrain taxation of unearned surplus incomes because the personal motive to accumulate such income is *not* sanctioned by the principle. A capitalist society seeking to foster efficient production and growth of national wealth might curtail personal desires to amass unearned wealth, for example, and simultaneously provide incentives to produce wealth from one's own labour and saving.[69]

Mill's proposed tax scheme is also generally compatible with the more egalitarian standards of socialism and communism. If all able persons are assigned equal income shares, for example, then all would pay equal taxes on their earned incomes above subsistence. As for taxation of the more or less disabled, it is usefully considered in conjunction with the assignment of their fair income shares.

Another important issue in this context is the generally expedient scope of government activity. If government ought to be limited to functions which are generally admitted to be expedient for it to perform, what can be said about where to draw the line between government and other social institutions, including competitive markets? It is worth emphasizing that Mill's answer to this question does not depend on the existing ideas of property: the answer remains the same whether capitalism or socialism or some mixture of the two exists. Even under pure socialism, a society may consider which functions are expediently performed by government agents and which are expediently left to free competition between plural small-scale voluntary associations of workers.

Without pretending to lay down any simple universal principle, Mill defends a general policy of *laissez-faire* with respect to economic activities: 'Laissez-faire . . . should be the general practice: every departure from it, unless required by some great good, is a certain evil'.[70] But significant 'departures' from the general policy *are* also said to be expedient. Recognizing that unregulated competitive markets will sometimes fail to promote society's goals (even its economic goals, including efficiency and growth), he prescribes government intervention in several types of cases. These include cases in which the consumer is an incompetent

[69] In the case of an overlapping generations model, e.g., government might use the tax system to redistribute wealth from resource owners to young workers and savers in order to facilitate sustained growth.

[70] *POPE, CW* iii. 945.

judge of the goods he wants to buy, for example, and cases in which the agent is an incompetent judge of his own interests for any of several reasons, including idiocy, childhood, or a blind disposition to form irrevocable judgements 'antecedently to experience' (as in contracting to become a slave or a spouse without any possibility of altering that status in the future).[71] Also mentioned are cases of 'natural monopoly': he suggests that government should generally confine itself to regulating private agency here even though private management may be less efficient than government management.[72] Then there are other cases in which government intervention is expedient to resolve collective action problems, as when suitable legal penalties are useful to give force to a group's unanimous wish for some outcome (say, a maximum working day) that may otherwise fail to occur because every person has an incentive to take a free ride on the co-operative efforts of his fellows.[73] A redistributive role for government is also held to be expedient to guarantee to each person her moral right to subsistence, with the caveat that any help beyond subsistence must come from voluntary charity.[74] Even problems caused by the absence of futures markets are noticed, as when he defends government intervention to facilitate colonization 'as a vent for surplus population'.[75] Also said to be expedient is government financing of such classic public goods as lighthouses, universities, and research institutes whose nature precludes adequate private financing because their benefits cannot easily be excluded from persons who refuse to pay a price for them.[76] Finally, apart from the foregoing list of 'large exceptions' to the principle of *laissez-faire* (all of which continue to be generally accepted by modern economists), Mill adds that, in any particular social context, government agency may be expedient in yet other cases not 'intrinsically suitable for it'. Many valuable things (including roads, railways, airlines, hospitals, publishing houses, and so on) that are not intrinsically public goods may nevertheless have to be provided

[71] Ibid. 947–54.   [72] Ibid. 954–6.   [73] Ibid. 956–60.
[74] Ibid. 960–2.   [75] Ibid. 962–7.   [76] Ibid. 968–70.

by government because private individuals, 'being either too poor to command the necessary resources, or too little advanced in intelligence to appreciate the ends, or not sufficiently practised in joint action to be capable of the means', will not provide them.[77]

As already emphasized, Mill's general policy of *laissez-faire*, marked by various 'large exceptions', applies under either capitalism or socialism. Another point worth emphasizing is that this policy is entirely distinct from his famous principle of individual liberty, which he says is intended to secure the 'absolute' sovereignty of the individual with respect to certain purely private actions that do not directly cause any 'perceptible damage' to other persons against their wishes. As he stresses:

[T]rade is a social act. Whoever undertakes to sell any description of goods to the public, does what affects the interests of other persons, and of society in general; and thus his conduct, in principle, comes within the jurisdiction of society . . . [T]he so-called doctrine of free trade [or *laissez-faire*] . . . rests on grounds different from . . . the principle of individual liberty.[78]

His rather complicated *laissez-faire* policy is driven by considerations of general expediency: its delicate balance between private competition and government intervention is defended as expedient for attaining any civil society's economic goals, including allocative efficiency. But the 'one very simple principle' of liberty is grounded on considerations of justice: its assignment of universal equal rights to make whatever purely private choices one likes is said to be part of what justice should mean in any civilized society. These two distinct doctrines are often conflated by a failure to recognize that the meaning of the term 'private' alters as we move between Mill's idea of a private choice and the

---

[77] Ibid. 970–1. Mill also makes clear that: 'Government aid, when given in default of private enterprise, should be so given as to be as far as possible a course of education for the people in the art of accomplishing great objects by individual energy and voluntary co-operation.' Note the relevance of these remarks to such topics as Keynesian fiscal policy and foreign aid to societies formerly enslaved under totalitarian despotisms.

[78] OL, *CW* xviii. 293.

common idea of a private market activity. 'Private' means 'causing no perceptible damage to others against their wishes' in the one case whereas it means 'not performed by government' in the other. Those who are accustomed to individual ownership often go on to further conflate 'not performed by government' with 'performed by individual *owners* in competitive markets'.

A proper distinction between these respective doctrines of *laissez-faire* and of liberty is crucial for understanding Mill's perspective on socialism. He expresses no doubts about the feasibility of implementing his general policy of *laissez-faire* under socialism, for example. A decentralized socialist economy, in which many small-scale producer co-operatives compete with each other in product and factor markets, is evidently the only form of socialism he takes seriously. What he fears, however, is that equal rights to liberty of purely self-regarding actions will never be adequately protected under any form of socialism. Given the present state of moral and intellectual imperfection, socialism is likely to make worse what is 'already one of the glaring evils' of competitive capitalist society. Even under a decentralized socialism, intolerant majorities *within* producer associations would be likely to suppress unconventional ideas and impose a uniform private lifestyle on all of the members. Moreover, *laissez-faire* might actually exacerbate this injustice: competition *between* the associations might tend to eliminate remaining inter-group differences with respect to ideas, opinions, and lifestyle. Indeed, this sort of commercial competition already encourages undue social conformity under capitalism.[79] Still, it remains an open question whether competitive capitalism will always afford relatively

---

[79] In *On Liberty*, Mill discusses this problem of mass conformity at length and proposes to remedy it through a package of various measures. These include: legal enforcement of the individual's right to choose as he likes with respect to purely private matters such as his ideas on all subjects, his intimate lifestyle, and so on; a programme of national education designed to promote tolerance of what others choose in such private matters; and active government support for social pluralism. The last policy might include special subsidies for intellectual and agricultural classes within a predominantly commercial society, e.g., as well as suitable immigration measures.

more protection for individual liberty and spontaneity than would decentralized socialism. Perhaps moral and intellectual improvement will one day make socialism hospitable to the greatest amount of individuality.

Mill's Relevance Today

Mill's Ricardian principles and, even more, his imaginative applications of them to the grand issues we have been discussing, remain highly relevant today. Some might contest this broad assertion on the grounds that a sharp break with the Ricardo–Mill tradition, referred to as the 'marginalist revolution' and associated with W. S. Jevons, Carl Menger, Leon Walras, F. Y. Edgeworth, and Alfred Marshall, was already under way when Mill died in 1873. This great discontinuity in the development of economics, so a familiar story goes, ushered in modern neo-classical theories of value, distribution, and growth that have little in common with their classical Ricardian predecessors. But, with due caveats, I think that modern economists such as Samuel Hollander and Paul Samuelson (as well as Marshall himself) are correct to stress continuity between classical and neo-classical analyses. This 'continuity thesis' does not deny that significant corrections and shifts of emphasis have occurred in the history of economic analysis, as when Ricardo remedied Smith's imperfect understanding of the basic distribution theorem according to which the general level of money wages varies inversely with the ordinary rate of profits, or when the marginalists shifted attention to the static conditions of general competitive equilibrium and emphasized the ramifications of variable factor proportions for values and prices. But it does insist that the classical doctrines of Smith, Ricardo, and Mill overlap in important respects not only with each other but with modern neo-classical doctrine as it has emerged through the writings of John Hicks, Paul Samuelson, Kenneth Arrow, Robert Solow, Frank Hahn, and others. From such a perspective, Mill is a pivotal figure within a well-defined scientific tradition and his work is of enduring importance as a rich and vibrant statement of the main ideas which, in more technically refined form, still constitute the pure theory of economics.

One important difference between the neo-classical and Ricardian frameworks is that neo-classical analysis generally makes no attempt to explain population dynamics. The Malthusian population doctrine (whereby population changes are related to the gap between market wages and a subsistence wage) is now usually ignored and population growth is treated as an exogenous variable. Nevertheless, until fairly recently, something of the Ricardo–Mill perspective was retained in neo-classical growth theory. The standard neo-classical models conceived growth in per capita wealth as a bounded process that terminates eventually in a 'steady state', in the absence of exogenous technological advances.[80] But now various explanatory models are proposed in which per capita growth is seen as an indefinitely sustained phenomenon driven by an endogenous process of technological improvement. In effect, by preventing the marginal productivity of capital from ever falling so low that investors can expect at most a minimum profit rate, continuous technological advance makes possible a rather remarkable dynamic equilibrium: population growth can coexist indefinitely with an even higher rate of growth in aggregate output.[81] Even if some such model is thought to explain best how Western economies have *actually* pro-

---

[80] See e.g. R. M. Solow, 'A Contribution to the Theory of Economic Growth', *Quarterly Journal of Economics*, 70 (1956), 65–94; Solow, 'Technical Change and the Aggregate Production Function', *Review of Economics and Statistics*, 39 (1957), 312–20; D. Cass, 'Optimum Growth in an Aggregative Model of Capital Accumulation', *Review of Economic Studies*, 32 (1965), 233–40; and J. A. Scheinkman, 'On Optimal Steady States of N-Sector Growth Models When Utility is Discounted', *Journal of Economic Theory*, 12 (1976), 11–30. Unlike the classical approach, however, the standard neo-classical models view population growth as an exogenous process. Thus, the steady state might not be stationary with respect to either population or capital stock but it is stationary with respect to capital per worker (i.e. the capital–labour ratio remains constant).

[81] See e.g. L. E. Jones and R. E. Manuelli, 'A Convex Model of Equilibrium Growth: Theory and Policy Implications', *Journal of Political Economy*, 98 (1990), 1008–38; Jones and Manuelli, 'Finite Lifetimes and Growth', *Journal of Economic Theory*, 58 (1992), 171–97; and E. O. Fisher, 'Sustained Growth in the Model of Overlapping Generations', *Journal of Economic Theory*, 58 (1992), 77–92. Other recent models of sustained growth depart from the neo-classical

gressed, however, Mill's distinctive *normative* perspective
retains its relevance. For he defends a particular stationary
state as more desirable than sustained growth of material
prosperity. In his view, increased technological knowledge
should be used for ends other than the indefinite increase of
wealth and population.[82]

Mill's discussions of capitalism and socialism and of the
expedient scope of government intervention in the market
also deserve careful attention. With the recent collapse of
the Soviet Union and its Marxist-Leninist programme of
'revolutionary socialism' (involving centralized government
planning of production and exchange), for example, modern
socialists are taking more seriously schemes of 'market socialism' in which a greater role is allowed for decentralized
decisions by self-managed worker co-operatives through
markets.[83] But 'market socialism' of this sort faces at least

paradigm by assuming that the endogenous process of technological change
brings either increasing returns in aggregate production or an absence of fixed
factors of production. See e.g. Paul Romer, 'Increasing Returns and Long-Run
Growth', *Journal of Political Economy*, 94 (1986), 1002–37; and M. Boldrin,
'Dynamic Externalities, Multiple Equilibria, and Growth', *Journal of Economic
Theory*, 58 (1992), 198–218. For more general discussion of technological advance
and economic growth, see also N. Rosenberg, *Inside the Black Box: Technology
and Economics* (Cambridge, 1982); and Rosenberg, *Technology and the Wealth of
Nations* (Stanford, Calif., 1992).

[82] Rostow rejects as 'premature' Mill's advocacy of population control 'in the
mid-nineteenth century'. In his view: 'All classes in the "most advanced" as well
as "backward" countries still had a great deal more to ask of the economic system
as the flow of new technologies expanded its potentialities for goods and
services, including a remarkable lengthening of life' (*Theorists of Growth*, 117).
Perhaps Mill's view is sufficiently ripe to be taken seriously now, however,
given our increasingly alarming proximity to 'a world from which solitude is
extirpated' and virtually all natural beauty is eradicated as an impediment to
man's uses.

[83] Various schemes of market socialism are discussed by, among others, David
Schweickart, *Capitalism or Worker Control?* (New York, 1980); Alex Nove, *The
Economics of Feasible Socialism* (London, 1983); Robert Dahl, *A Preface to
Economic Democracy* (Berkeley, Calif., 1985); Julian Le Grand and Saul Estrin
(eds.), *Market Socialism* (Oxford, 1989); and David Miller, *Market, State, and
Community* (Oxford, 1990). The modern example of former Yugoslavia is dis-
cussed by Saul Estrin, *Self-Management: Economic Theory and Yugoslav Practice*
(Cambridge, 1983), and by H. Lydall, *Yugoslav Socialism* (Oxford, 1984). The
ongoing experiment with self-managed worker co-operatives near the town of
Mondragon in northern Spain is discussed by H. Thomas and C. Logan,
Mondragon: An Economic Analysis (London, 1982).

two serious problems from a Millian perspective.[84] First, any such scheme is unlikely to succeed on a grand scale until most workers go through what promises to be a slow and arduous education process to develop the requisite moral and intellectual capacities. If capitalist firms are permitted to compete with the self-managed worker co-operatives, however, then the co-operatives are at a disadvantage given the prevailing predominantly self-interested type of character that competitive capitalism itself fosters (though hardly creates *de novo*). Second, to facilitate immediate establishment of market socialism, government must still be given broad powers to organize and control production. Market socialists usually suggest that all or most capital should be appropriated by a democratic government that represents society at large, with worker co-operatives paying a user fee proportional to the share of capital under their respective management. Such a tax could finance government direction of new investment as well as replacement of capital goods as they wear out. Such a major role for government is far removed from Mill's perspective in which highly co-operative workers voluntarily pool their own capitals and then self-manage their various enterprises in the context of a competitive economy. For Mill, the expedient scope of government is no different under socialism than it is under capitalism.

Finally, the continuing relevance of his practical policy judgements hints at what is, in my view, the greatest strength of Mill's political economy, namely, its grounding in a novel philosophical radicalism with powerful normative appeal for anyone concerned to promote liberal democracy. His imaginative applications of Ricardian principles are guided by his 'enlarged' utilitarian philosophy in ways that are still not generally appreciated in the literature. In this regard, it is important to see that the 'marginalist revolution' involved a normative reaffirmation of the 'old' philosophical radicalism associated with Bentham and Ricardo.

[84] For a more detailed critique of market socialism along similar lines, see Scott Arnold, *Market Socialism: A Critical Study* (forthcoming).

Jevons, Edgeworth, and even Marshall, unlike Stuart Mill, proposed more or less to operationalize the old programme by precisely measuring and comparing units of happiness across persons.[85] This normative programme was later refined (if not rendered vacuous) by the 'ordinalist revolution' of the 1930s and beyond, associated with Lord Lionel Robbins, Hicks, Samuelson, and Arrow. As a result, interpersonally comparable units of utility have been abandoned in favour of non-comparable preference orderings and Pareto efficiency is the main (perhaps sole) surviving criterion of the economic art.[86] But, even in its latest guise, the old programme still has a conservative feel from the vantage point of Mill's brand of radicalism.

A detailed discussion of Mill's novel utilitarian framework is beyond the scope of this introduction. Suffice it to say that, in my view, such a framework can accommodate considerations of justice (universal equal rights) that trump narrow considerations of economic policy (including efficiency and growth) whenever conflicts arise, and it can do so without introducing a false precision of the sort against which Mill himself complained and the ordinalists later rebelled.[87]

---

[85] Not only did Mill want to go beyond the old radicalism, he also made clear his aversion to what he considered the false precision of the marginalist gloss on it. In a letter to John Elliot Cairnes dated Dec. 5 1871, e.g., he complains that Jevons has 'a mania for encumbering questions with useless complications, and with a notation implying the existence of greater precision in the data than the questions admit of'. In his view, this 'vice . . . is one preeminently at variance with the wants of the time, which demand that scientific deductions should be made as simple and as easily intelligible as they can be without ceasing to be scientific' (*CW*, xvii. 1862–3). He seems to be alluding in this passage to the contemporary need to make political economy as accessible as possible to the working classes, to forestall their acceptance of revolutionary socialist doctrines which he argued involved serious errors of political economy.

[86] According to the standard of Pareto efficiency, one outcome cannot be judged better than another unless everyone prefers the one to the other. If individuals are wealth-seekers who always prefer more to less, however, then one outcome might be said to be better than another if (1) the first involves a greater national wealth than the second; and (2) steps could be taken to compensate every person who would lose wealth because of the move from the second to the first.

[87] For amplification of the argument see Riley, 'Mill's Classical Political Economy'; and Riley, *A Liberal Utilitarian Theory of Justice*.

NOTE ON THE TEXT

The present text of a major portion of the *Principles* is taken from the seventh and final library edition published by Longmans in 1871 (the first edition was published by Parker in 1848). A complete text of the seventh edition, including 'all substantive variants amongst the various editions', appears in *The Collected Works of John Stuart Mill*, vols. ii–iii, gen. ed. J. M. Robson (Toronto and London, 1965). As Professor Robson remarks in his textual introduction: '[T]he 7th edition best represents Mill's considered judgment, and is, because of the constant re-readings, more reliable than any previous edition. For him, and for the student of political economy from 1871 to the present, this is the best text' (p. lxxx). The present text contains no significant alterations except for the omission of: (1) certain passages and lengthy footnotes in Book IV, Ch. 7, in which Mill is illustrating the competitive success of some contemporary co-operative associations; and (2) certain lengthy footnotes in Book III, Chs. 2 and 3, and Book V, Ch. 6.

The text of the 'Chapters on Socialism' is taken from the *Fortnightly Review*, vol. xxv, NS (1879), where it was originally published posthumously in three instalments, the first appearing in the February issue (pp. 217–37), the second in the March issue (pp. 373–82), and the third in the April issue (pp. 513–30). As noted by Helen Taylor (Mill's stepdaughter) when she submitted them for publication, these chapters are 'rough drafts' which arguably 'possess great intrinsic value' as indications of Mill's views on the subject of socialism. The text of the 'Chapters' also appears in *The Collected Works*, vol. v (1967), 703–53. Mill's original manuscript has apparently been lost, a mishap 'deeply to be regretted', as Professor Robson says in his textual introduction, 'for the published version is edited to an unknown extent by Helen Taylor' (*Collected Works*, iv, p. xlvii).

The editor's explanatory notes at the end of the book are keyed to passages marked by an asterisk in the text. The

editor's footnotes, as opposed to Mill's, are placed within
square brackets [].

SELECT BIBLIOGRAPHY

Primary Works

The Collected Works of John Stuart Mill [*CW*], 33 vols., gen. ed. J. M. Robson (Toronto and London, 1965–91). This edition is now complete and is the standard reference for all Mill's writings. Vols. ii and iii contain the *Principles* (1848); and vol. iv and v contain Mill's essays which are of primary interest to economists, including *Essays on Some Unsettled Questions of Political Economy* (1844), 'Thornton on Labour and Its Claims' (1869), and 'Chapters on Socialism' (1879).

For an understanding of Mill's distinctive liberal utilitarian philosophy, including the place of his political economy within that philosophy, the following primary works are also indispensable:

A System of Logic Ratiocinative and Inductive (1843), in *CW* (1974), vii and viii.

On Liberty (1859), in *CW* (1977), xviii. 213–310.

Utilitarianism (1861), in *CW* (1969), x. 203–59.

Considerations on Representative Government (1861), in *CW* (1977), xix. 371–577.

An Examination of Sir William Hamilton's Philosophy (1865), in *CW* (1979), ix.

Auguste Comte and Positivism (1865), in *CW* (1969), x. 261–368.

The Subjection of Women (1869), in *CW* (1984), xxi. 259–340.

James Mill's Analysis of the Phenomena of the Human Mind (1869), in *CW* (1989), xxxi. 93–253.

Three Essays on Religion, ed. Helen Taylor (1874), in *CW* (1969), x. 369–489.

Secondary Works

W. Baumol and G. Becker, 'The Classical Monetary Theory: The Outcome of the Discussion', *Economica*, 19 (1952), 355–76.

C. Casarosa, 'The "New View" of the Ricardian Theory of Distribution and Economic Growth', in G. A. Caravale (ed.), *The Legacy of Ricardo* (Oxford, 1985), 45–58.

John S. Chipman, 'A Survey of the Theory of International Trade: I. The Classical Theory', *Econometrica*, 33 (1965), 477–519.

—— 'Mill's "Superstructure": How Well Does it Stand Up?' *History of Political Economy*, 11 (1979), 477–500.

F. Y. Edgeworth, 'John Stuart Mill', in R. H. I. Palgrave (ed.), *Dictionary of Political Economy* (London, 1910), ii. 756–63.

Evelyn L. Forget, 'J. S. Mill and J. E. Cairnes on Natural Value: The Role of Expectations in Late-Classical Thought', *History of Political Economy*, 21 (1989), 103–21.

—— 'John Stuart Mill's Business Cycle', *History of Political Economy*, 22 (1990), 629–42.

—— 'J. S. Mill and the Tory School: The Rhetorical Value of the Recantation', *History of Political Economy*, 24 (1992), 31–59.

John Hicks, 'From Classical to Post-Classical: The Work of J. S. Mill', in his *Classics and Moderns* (Cambridge, Mass., 1983), 60–70.

—— and Samuel Hollander, 'Mr. Ricardo and the Moderns', *Quarterly Journal of Economics*, 91 (1977), 351–69.

Samuel Hollander, 'The Reception of Ricardian Economics', *Oxford Economic Papers*, 29 (1977), 221–57.

—— 'On Professor Samuelson's Canonical Classical Model of Political Economy', *Journal of Economic Literature*, 18 (1980), 559–74.

—— 'On the Substantive Identity of the Ricardian and Neo-Classical Conceptions of Economic Organization', *Canadian Journal of Economics*, 15 (1982), 586–612.

—— 'The Wage Path in Classical Growth Models: Ricardo, Malthus and Mill', *Oxford Economic Papers*, 36 (1984), 200–12.

—— *The Economics of John Stuart Mill* (Toronto, 1985), i–ii.

—— *Classical Economics* (Oxford, 1987).

—— 'John Stuart Mill, as Economic Theorist', in J. Eatwell *et al.* (eds.), *The New Palgrave Dictionary of Economics* (London, 1987), iii. 471–6.

—— 'Ricardian Growth Theory: A Resolution of Some Problems in Textual Interpretation', *Oxford Economic Papers*, 42 (1990), 730–50. See also the separate critiques of Hollander's view presented by T. Peach and G. Stigler, with Hollander's reply, at, respectively, 751–64, 765–8, and 769–71.

L. C. Hunter, 'Mill and Cairnes on the Rate of Interest', *Oxford Economic Papers*, 11 (1959), 63–87.

Neil de Marchi, 'John Stuart Mill Interpretation Since Schumpeter', in W. O. Thweatt (ed.), *Classical Political Economy* (Boston, 1988), 137–62. See also the commentary by Samuel Hollander at pp. 163–77.

Alfred Marshall, 'Mr. Mill's Theory of Value', *Fortnightly Review*, NS 19 (1876), 591–602.

—— *Principles of Economics*, 8th edn. (London, 1920; first published 1890).

Takashi Negishi, *History of Economic Theory* (Amsterdam, 1989), 155–90.

Jonathan Riley, *Liberal Utilitarianism* (Cambridge, 1988).

—— 'Justice Under Capitalism', in J. Chapman and J. R. Pennock (eds.) *Markets and Justice: NOMOS XXXI* (New York, 1989), 122–62.

—— ' "One Very Simple Principle" ', *Utilitas*, 3 (1991), 1–35.

—— 'Individuality, Custom and Progress', *Utilitas*, 3 (1991), 223–50.

—— 'Philanthropy Under Capitalism', in D. Burlingame (ed.), *The Responsibilities of Wealth* (Indianapolis, 1992), 66–93.

—— 'Mill's Liberty Principle Applied', *Utilitas*, (forthcoming).

—— *A Liberal Utilitarian Theory of Justice*, (forthcoming).

—— 'Mill's Classical Political Economy', in J. Skorupski (ed.), *The Cambridge Companion to John Stuart Mill* (Cambridge, forthcoming).

W. W. Rostow, *Theorists of Economic Growth from David Hume to the Present* (Oxford, 1990).

Paul A. Samuelson, 'The Canonical Classical Model of Political Economy', *Journal of Economic Literature*, 16 (1978), 1415–34.

—— 'Noise and Signal in Debates Among Classical Economists: A Reply', *Journal of Economic Literature*, 18 (1980), 575–8.

—— 'Mathematical Vindication of Ricardo on Machinery', *Journal of Political Economy*, 96 (1988), 274–82.

—— 'Ricardo was Right!' *Scandinavian Journal of Economics*, 91 (1989), 47–62.

Joseph A. Schumpeter, *Capitalism, Socialism and Democracy* (New York, 1942).

—— *History of Economic Analysis* (Oxford, 1954).

V. R. Smith, 'John Stuart Mill's Famous Distinction Between Production and Distribution', *Economics and Philosophy*, 1 (1985), 267–84.

George J. Stigler, 'Mill on Economics and Society', in his *The Economist as Preacher and Other Essays* (Chicago, 1982), 75–85.

CHRONOLOGY

1806   Born in London, 20 May, eldest son of James Mill.

1809–20   Educated at home by his father, he begins Greek at age 3, Latin at age 8, and Logic at 'about' age 12; visits Jeremy Bentham on frequent occasions; goes through 'a complete course of political economy' in 1819, with particular attention to David Ricardo's 'great work' (*On the Principles of Political Economy and Taxation*, 1817); also in 1819, James Mill is appointed an Assistant Examiner of the East India Company, about a year after publication of his *History of British India*.

1820–1   Spends a year in France visiting Sir Samuel Bentham, brother of Jeremy Bentham; also passes 'some time' in the house of the eminent economist Jean Baptiste Say; shortly after his return, his father publishes *Elements of Political Economy*, 1821.

1821–2   Reads law with John Austin; becomes a fervent Benthamite upon reading Bentham's principal legal ideas as interpreted by Pierre Dumont in *Traites de legislation*, 1802; begins study of analytic psychology under his father's direction.

1822–4   Forms Utilitarian Society which meets once a fortnight in Bentham's house before breaking up in 1826; begins to write for newspapers and for the radical *Westminster Review*, founded by Bentham in 1823; becomes (in May 1823) a clerk in the East India Company, immediately under his father; at about the same time, brought before a magistrate for distributing literature advocating birth control, but is treated lightly by the authorities.

1825–9   Edits Bentham's *Rationale of Judicial Evidence*, published in 1827; learns German; meets regularly with several companions at Grote's house to discuss political economy, logic, and psychology, the exercises ending after discussion of James Mill's *Analysis of the Phenomena of the Human Mind*, published in 1829; also plays an active role in various public debates involving philosophical radicals and their various opponents, including Owenites, Tories, and followers of Coleridge; in the midst of this activity, suffers so-called 'mental crisis' during 1826–7 and subsequently turns away from narrow Benthamism in the direction of a more enlightened utilitarian philosophy.

1830   Meets Mrs Harriet Taylor, his future wife.

1830–1 Writes the five essays eventually published in slightly revised form as *Essays on Some Unsettled Questions of Political Economy*, 1844.

1834–40 Edits and (as of 1837) owns the *London and Westminster Review*, founded in 1834 by Sir William Molesworth who bought the old *Westminster* and merged it with his own *London Review*; as of 1840, ceases editing and sells the *Review* to William Hickson; James Mill dies in 1836 (23 June).

1843   Publishes *A System of Logic*.

1845–8 Rapidly writes the *Political Economy* in about 18 months and publishes it in 1848.

1849   John Taylor, Harriet's husband, dies (July).

1851   Marries Mrs Taylor (April).

1854–5 Suffering from consumption, he travels for more than six months without Harriet through France, Italy, Sicily, and Greece, taking many walks that restore his health.

1856   Promoted to Chief Examiner of India Correspondence, also the highest position held by his father in the East India Company.

1858   Retires on 'liberal compensation' after Parliament eliminates the East India Company as a Crown agency in the government of India; Harriet dies at Avignon (November).

1859   Publishes *On Liberty*, dedicated to his wife; spends a good part of each year in Avignon for the rest of his life, usually accompanied by his stepdaughter, Helen Taylor.

1861   Publishes *Considerations on Representative Government* and *Utilitarianism* (the latter in *Fraser's Magazine*).

1865   Publishes *An Examination of Sir William Hamilton's Philosophy* and *Auguste Comte and Positivism* (the latter a reprint of two essays published that same year in the *Westminster Review*); elected independent Liberal Member of Parliament for Westminster despite giving public notice to his constituents that he would not run a campaign, or bear any of the costs of his election, or be instructed by them.

1866–8   Serves as Chairman of the Jamaica Committee that for two years sought to prosecute Governor Eyre and his principal subordinates for unjustified military violence against Jamaican blacks, only to have a grand jury prevent the case from coming to trial after the Lord Chief Justice had charged that the colonial functionaries had exceeded their authority; delivers 1867 Inaugural Address as elected Rector of the University of St Andrews; promotes advanced liberal opinions in his parliamentary speeches with no hope of immediate practical success, for example, promotes both Thomas Hare's scheme of proportional representation and extension of the franchise to include women, neither measure finding its way into the Reform Act of 1867; at the 1868 general election, loses seat in House of Commons but refuses invitations to run again as a candidate for other constituencies.

1869   Publishes *The Subjection of Women* (written during 1860–1 at the suggestion of Helen Taylor) and edits (with Alexander Bain, George Grote, and Andrew Findlater) a second edition of his father's *Analysis of the Phenomena of the Human Mind*.

1873   Dies at Avignon (7 May) and is buried with his wife; Helen Taylor publishes posthumously several of his draft papers, including the *Autobiography* (written in 1869–70, published in 1873) and *Chapters on Socialism* (probably written in 1870, published in 1879 in the *Fortnightly Review*).

public notice to his constituents that he would not run a campaign, or bear any of the costs of his election, or be nominated by them.

1865–8   Sits as Chairman of the Jamaica Committee that for two years sought to prosecute Governor Eyre and his principal subordinates for unpunished military violence against Jamaican blacks, only to have a grand jury prevent the case from coming to trial after the Lord Chief Justice had charged that the colonial functionaries had exceeded their authority, delivers 1867 inaugural Address as elected Rector of the University of St An-drews, promotes advanced liberal opinions in his parlia-mentary speeches with no hope of immediate practical success, for example, promotes both Thomas Hare's scheme of proportional representation and extension of the franchise to include women, neither measure finding its way into the Reform Act of 1867; at the 1868 general election, loses seat in House of Commons but refuses invitations to run again as a candidate for other constit-uencies.

1869   Publishes The Subjection of Women (written during 1860–1 at the suggestion of Helen Taylor) and edits (with Alexander Bain, George Grote, and Andrew Find-later) a second edition of his father's Analysis of the Phenomena of the Human Mind.

1873   Dies at Avignon (7 May) and is buried with his wife, Helen Taylor publishes posthumously several of his great papers, including the Autobiography (written in 1869–70, published in 1873) and Chapters on Socialism (probably written in 1879, published in 1879 in the Fortnightly Review).

PRINCIPLES OF
POLITICAL ECONOMY

PRINCIPLES OF
POLITICAL ECONOMY
with Some of Their Applications to Social Philosophy
(7th edn., 1871)

by

JOHN STUART MILL

Book II, Chapters I–IV. 1;
Book III, Chapters I. 1–2 and XXVI;
Book IV; and
Book V.

BOOK II

DISTRIBUTION

I

OF PROPERTY

1. The principles which have been set forth in the first part of this Treatise, are, in certain respects, strongly distinguished from those, on the consideration of which we are now about to enter. The laws and conditions of the production of wealth partake of the character of physical truths. There is nothing optional or arbitrary in them. Whatever mankind produce, must be produced in the modes, and under the conditions, imposed by the constitution of external things, and by the inherent properties of their own bodily and mental structure. Whether they like it or not, their productions will be limited by the amount of their previous accumulation, and, that being given, it will be proportional to their energy, their skill, the perfection of their machinery, and their judicious use of the advantages of combined labour. Whether they like it or not, a double quantity of labour will not raise on the same land, a double quantity of food, unless some improvement takes place in the processes of cultivation. Whether they like it or not, the unproductive expenditure of individuals will *pro tanto** tend to impoverish the community, and only their productive expenditure will enrich it. The opinions, or the wishes, which may exist on these different matters, do not control the things themselves. We cannot, indeed, foresee to what extent the modes of production may be altered, or the productiveness of labour increased, by future extensions of our knowledge of the laws of nature, suggesting new processes of industry of which we have at present no conception. But howsoever we may succeed in making for ourselves more space within the limits set by the constitution of things, we know that

there must be limits. We cannot alter the ultimate properties either of matter or mind, but can only employ those properties more or less successfully, to bring about the events in which we are interested.

It is not so with the Distribution of Wealth. That is a matter of human institution solely. The things once there, mankind, individually or collectively, can do with them as they like. They can place them at the disposal of whomsoever they please, and on whatever terms. Further, in the social state, in every state except total solitude, any disposal whatever of them can only take place by the consent of society, or rather of those who dispose of its active force. Even what a person has produced by his individual toil, unaided by any one, he cannot keep, unless by the permission of society. Not only can society take it from him, but individuals could and would take it from him, if society only remained passive; if it did not either interfere *en masse*, or employ and pay people for the purpose of preventing him from being disturbed in the possession. The distribution of wealth, therefore, depends on the laws and customs of society. The rules by which it is determined, are what the opinions and feelings of the ruling portion of the community make them, and are very different in different ages and countries; and might be still more different, if mankind so chose.

The opinions and feelings of mankind, doubtless, are not a matter of chance. They are consequences of the fundamental laws of human nature, combined with the existing state of knowledge and experience, and the existing condition of social institutions and intellectual and moral culture. But the laws of the generation of human opinions are not within our present subject. They are part of the general theory of human progress, a far larger and more difficult subject of inquiry than political economy. We have here to consider, not the causes, but the consequences, of the rules according to which wealth may be distributed. Those, at least, are as little arbitrary, and have as much the character of physical laws, as the laws of production. Human beings can control their own acts, but not the consequences of their acts either to themselves or to others. Society can subject the distribution of wealth to whatever rules it thinks best: but what practical results will flow from the operation of those rules, must be discovered, like any other physical or mental truths, by observation and reasoning.

We proceed, then, to the consideration of the different modes of distributing the produce of land and labour, which have been adopted in practice, or may be conceived in theory. Among these, our attention is first claimed by that primary and fundamental institution, on which, unless in some exceptional and very limited cases, the economical arrangements of society have always rested, though in its secondary features it has varied, and is liable to vary. I mean, of course, the institution of individual property.

2. Private property, as an institution, did not owe its origin to any of those considerations of utility, which plead for the maintenance of it when established. Enough is known of rude ages, both from history and from analogous states of society in our own time, to show, that tribunals (which always precede laws) were originally established, not to determine rights, but to repress violence and terminate quarrels. With this object chiefly in view, they naturally enough gave legal effect to first occupancy, by treating as the aggressor the person who first commenced violence, by turning, or attempting to turn, another out of possession. The preservation of the peace, which was the original object of civil government, was thus attained; while by confirming, to those who already possessed it, even what was not the fruit of personal exertion, a guarantee was incidentally given to them and others that they would be protected in what was so.

In considering the institution of property as a question in social philosophy, we must leave out of consideration its actual origin in any of the existing nations of Europe. We may suppose a community unhampered by any previous possession; a body of colonists, occupying for the first time an uninhabited country; bringing nothing with them but what belonged to them in common, and having a clear field for the adoption of the institutions and polity which they judged most expedient; required, therefore, to choose whether they would conduct the work of production on the principle of individual property, or on some system of common ownership and collective agency.

If private property were adopted, we must presume that it would be accompanied by none of the initial inequalities and injustices which obstruct the beneficial operation of the principle in old societies. Every full grown man or woman, we must suppose, would be secured in the unfettered use and disposal of his or her bodily and mental faculties; and the instruments of production, the land and tools, would be divided fairly among them, so that all might start, in respect to outward appliances, on equal terms. It is possible also to conceive that in this original apportionment, compensation might be made for the injuries of nature, and the balance redressed by assigning to the less robust members of the community advantages in the distribution, sufficient to put them on a par with the rest. But the division, once made, would not again be interfered with; individuals would be left to their own exertions and to the ordinary chances, for making an advantageous use of what was assigned to them. If individual property, on the contrary, were excluded, the plan which must be adopted would be to hold the land and all instruments of production as the joint property of the community, and to carry on the operations of industry on the common account. The direction of the labour of the community would devolve upon a magistrate or magistrates, whom we may suppose elected by the suffrages of the community, and whom we must assume to be voluntarily obeyed by them. The division of the produce would in like manner be a public act. The principle might either be that of complete equality, or of apportionment to the necessities or deserts of individuals, in whatever manner might be conformable to the ideas of justice or policy prevailing in the community.

Examples of such associations, on a small scale, are the monastic orders, the Moravians,* the followers of Rapp,* and others: and from the hopes which they hold out of relief from the miseries and iniquities of a state of much inequality of wealth, schemes for a larger application of the same idea have reappeared and become popular at all periods of active speculation on the first principles of society. In an age like the present, when a general reconsideration of all first principles is felt to be inevitable, and when more than at any former period of history the suffering portions of the community have a voice in the discussion, it was impossible but that ideas of this nature should spread far and wide. The late revolutions in Europe* have thrown up a great amount of speculation of this character, and an unusual share of attention has consequently been drawn to the various forms which these ideas have assumed: nor is this attention likely to diminish, but on the contrary, to increase more and more.

The assailants of the principle of individual property may be divided into two classes: those whose scheme implies absolute equality in the distribution of the physical means of life and enjoyment, and those who admit inequality, but grounded on some principle, or supposed principle, of justice or general expediency, and not, like so many of the existing social inequalities, dependent on accident alone. At the head of the first class, as the earliest of those belonging to the present generation, must be placed Mr Owen and his followers.* M. Louis Blanc* and M. Cabet* have more recently become conspicuous as apostles of similar doctrines (though the former advocates equality of distribution only as a transition to a still higher standard of justice, that all should work according to their capacity, and receive according to their wants). The characteristic name for this economical system is Communism, a word of continental origin, only of late introduced into this country. The word Socialism, which originated among the English Communists, and was assumed by them as a name to designate their own doctrine, is now, on the Continent, employed in a larger sense; not necessarily implying Communism, or the entire abolition of private property, but applied to any system which requires that the land and the instruments of production should be the property, not of individuals, but of communities or associations, or of the government. Among such systems, the two of highest intellectual pretension are those which, from the names of their real or reputed authors, have been called St Simonism* and Fourierism,* the former defunct as a system, but which during the few years of its public promulgation, sowed the seeds of nearly all the Socialist tendencies which have since spread so widely in France: the second, still flourishing in the number, talent, and zeal of its adherents.

3. Whatever may be the merits or defects of these various schemes, they cannot be truly said to be impracticable. No reasonable person can doubt that a village community, composed of a few thousand inhabitants cultivating in joint ownership the same extent of land which at present feeds that number of people, and producing by combined labour and the most improved processes the manufactured articles which they required, could raise an amount of productions sufficient to maintain them in comfort; and would find the means of obtaining, and if need be, exacting, the quantity of labour necessary for this purpose, from every member of the association who was capable of work.

The objection ordinarily made to a system of community of property and equal distribution of the produce, that each person would be incessantly occupied in evading his fair share of the work, points, undoubtedly, to a real difficulty. But those who urge this objection, forget to how great an extent the same difficulty exists under the system on which nine-tenths of the business of society is now conducted. The objection supposes, that honest and efficient labour is only to be had from those who are themselves individually to reap the benefit of their own exertions. But how small a part of all the labour performed in England, from the lowest-paid to the highest, is done by persons working for their own benefit. From the Irish reaper or hodman to the chief justice or the minister of state, nearly all the work of society is remunerated by day wages or fixed salaries. A factory operative has less personal interest in his work than a member of a Communist association, since he is not, like him, working for a partnership of which he is himself a member. It will no doubt be said, that though the labourers themselves have not, in most cases, a personal interest in their work, they are watched and superintended, and their labour directed, and the mental part of the labour performed, by persons who have. Even this, however, is far from being universally the fact. In all public, and many of the largest and most successful private undertakings, not only the labours of detail but the control and superintendence are entrusted to salaried officers. And though the "master's eye," when the master is vigilant and intelligent, is of proverbial value, it must be remembered that in a Socialist farm or manufactory, each labourer would be under the eye not of one master, but of the whole community. In the extreme case of obstinate perseverance in not performing the due share of work, the community would have the same resources which society now has for compelling conformity to the necessary conditions of the association. Dismissal, the only remedy at present, is no remedy when any other labourer who may be engaged does no better than his predecessor: the power of dismissal only enables an employer to obtain from his workmen the customary amount of labour, but that customary labour may be of any degree of inefficiency. Even the labourer who loses his employment by idleness or negligence, has nothing worse to suffer, in the most unfavourable case, than the discipline of a workhouse, and if the desire to avoid this be a sufficient motive in the one system, it would be sufficient in the other. I am not undervaluing the strength of the incitement given to labour when the whole or a large share of the benefit of extra exertion belongs to the labourer. But under the present system of industry this incitement, in the great majority of cases, does not exist. If Communistic labour might be less vigorous than that of a peasant proprietor, or a workman labouring on his own account, it would probably be more energetic than that of a labourer for hire, who has no personal interest in the matter at all. The neglect by the uneducated classes of labourers for hire, of the duties which they engage to perform, is in the present state of society most flagrant. Now it is an admitted condition of the Communist scheme that all shall be educated: and this being supposed, the duties of the members of the association would doubtless be as diligently performed as those of the generality of salaried officers in the middle or higher classes; who are not supposed to be necessarily unfaithful to their trust, because so long as they are not dismissed, their pay is the same in however lax a manner their duty is fulfilled. Undoubtedly, as a general rule, remuneration by fixed salaries does not in any class of functionaries produce the maximum of zeal: and this is as much as can be reasonably alleged against Communistic labour.

That even this inferiority would necessarily exist, is by no means so certain as is assumed by those who are little used to carry their minds beyond the state of things with which they are familiar. Mankind are capable of a far greater amount of public spirit than the present age is accustomed to suppose possible. History bears witness to the success with which large bodies of human beings may be trained to feel the public interest their own. And no soil could be more favourable to the growth of such a feeling, than a Communist association, since all the ambition, and the bodily and mental activity, which are now exerted in the pursuit of separate and self-regarding interests, would require another sphere of employment, and would naturally find it in the pursuit of the general benefit of the community. The same cause, so often assigned in explanation of the devotion of the Catholic priest or monk to the interest of his order—that he has no interest apart from it—would, under Communism, attach the citizen to the community. And independently of the public motive, every member of the association would be amenable to the most universal, and one of the strongest, of personal motives, that of public opinion. The force of this motive in deterring from any act or omission positively reproved by the community, no one is likely to deny; but the power also of emulation, in exciting to the most strenuous exertions for the sake of the approbation and admiration of others, is borne witness to by experience in every situation in which human beings publicly compete with one another, even if it be in things frivolous, or from which the public derive no benefit. A contest, who can do most for the common good, is not the kind of competition which Socialists repudiate. To what extent, therefore, the energy of labour would be diminished by Communism, or whether in the long run it would be diminished at all, must be considered for the present an undecided question.

Another of the objections to Communism is similar to that, so often urged against poor-laws: that if every member of the community were assured of subsistence for himself and any number of children, on the sole condition of willingness to work, prudential restraint on the multiplication of mankind would be at an end, and population would start forward at a rate which would reduce the community, through successive stages of increasing discomfort, to actual starvation. There would certainly be much ground for this apprehension if Communism provided no motives to restraint, equivalent to those which it would take away. But Communism is precisely the state of things in which opinion might be expected to declare itself with greatest intensity against this kind of selfish intemperance. Any augmentation of numbers which diminished the comfort or increased the toil of the mass, would then cause (which now it does not) immediate and unmistakeable inconvenience to every individual in the association; inconvenience which could not then be imputed to the avarice of employers, or the unjust privileges of the rich. In such altered circumstances opinion could not fail to reprobate, and if reprobation did not suffice, to repress by penalties of some description, this or any other culpable self-indulgence at the expense of the community. The Communistic scheme, instead of being peculiarly open to the objection drawn from danger of over-population, has the recommendation of tending in an especial degree to the prevention of that evil.

A more real difficulty is that of fairly apportioning the labour of the community among its members. There are many kinds of work, and by what standard are they to be measured one against another? Who is to judge how much cotton spinning, or distributing goods from the stores, or bricklaying, or chimney sweeping, is equivalent to so much ploughing? The difficulty of making the adjustment between different qualities of labour is so strongly felt by Communist writers, that they have usually thought it necessary to provide that all should work by turns at every description of useful labour: an arrangement which, by putting an end to the division of employments, would sacrifice so much of the advantage of co-operative production as greatly to diminish the productiveness of labour. Besides, even in the same kind of work, nominal equality of labour would be so great a real inequality, that the feeling of justice would revolt against its being enforced. All persons are not equally fit for all labour; and the same quantity of labour is an unequal burthen on the weak and the strong, the hardy and the delicate, the quick and the slow, the dull and the intelligent.

But these difficulties, though real, are not necessarily insuperable. The apportionment of work to the strength and capacities of individuals, the mitigation of a general rule to provide for cases in which it would operate harshly, are not problems to which human intelligence, guided by a sense of justice, would be inadequate. And the worst and most unjust arrangement which could be made of these points, under a system aiming at equality, would be so far short of the inequality and injustice with which labour (not to speak of remuneration) is now apportioned, as to be scarcely worth counting in the comparison. We must remember too, that Communism, as a system of society, exists only in idea; that its difficulties, at present, are much better understood than its resources; and that the intellect of mankind is only beginning to contrive the means of organizing it in detail, so as to overcome the one and derive the greatest advantage from the other.

If, therefore, the choice were to be made between Communism with all its chances, and the present state of society with all its sufferings and injustices; if the institution of private property necessarily carried with it as a consequence, that the produce of labour should be apportioned as we now see it, almost in an inverse ratio to the labour—the largest portions to those who have never worked at all, the next largest to those whose work is almost nominal, and so in a descending scale, the remuneration dwindling as the work grows harder and more disagreeable, until the most fatiguing and exhausting bodily labour cannot count with certainty on being able to earn even the necessaries of life; if this or Communism were the alternative, all the difficulties, great or small, of Communism would be but as dust in the balance. But to make the comparison applicable, we must compare Communism at its best, with the régime of individual property, not as it is, but as it might be made. The principle of private property has never yet had a fair trial in any country; and less so, perhaps, in this country than in some others. The social arrangements of modern Europe commenced from a distribution of property which was the result, not of just partition, or acquisition by industry, but of conquest and violence: and notwithstanding what industry has been doing for many centuries to modify the work of force, the system still retains many and large traces of its origin. The laws of property have never yet conformed to the principles on which the justification of private property rests. They have made property of things which never ought to be property, and absolute property where only a qualified property ought to exist. They have not held the balance fairly between human beings, but have heaped impediments upon some, to give advantage to others; they have purposely fostered inequalities, and prevented all from starting fair in the race. That all should indeed start on perfectly equal terms, is inconsistent with any law of private property: but if as much pains as has been taken to aggravate the inequality of chances arising from the natural working of the principle, had been taken to temper that inequality by every means not subversive of the principle itself; if the tendency of legislation had been to favour the diffusion, instead of the concentration of wealth—to encourage the subdivision of the large masses, instead of striving to keep them together; the principle of individual property would have been found to have no necessary connexion with the physical and social evils which almost all Socialist writers assume to be inseparable from it.

Private property, in every defence made of it, is supposed to mean, the guarantee to individuals of the fruits of their own labour and abstinence. The guarantee to them of the fruits of the labour and abstinence of others, transmitted to them without any merit or exertion of their own, is not of the essence of the institution, but a mere incidental consequence, which, when it reaches a certain height, does not promote, but conflicts with, the ends which render private property legitimate. To judge of the final destination of the institution of property, we must suppose everything rectified, which causes the institution to work in a manner opposed to that equitable principle, of proportion between remuneration and exertion, on which in every vindication of it that will bear the light, it is assumed to be grounded. We must also suppose two conditions realized, without which neither Communism nor any other laws or institutions could make the condition of the mass of mankind other than degraded and miserable. One of these conditions is, universal education; the other, a due limitation of the numbers of the community. With these, there could be no poverty, even under the present social institutions: and these being supposed, the question of Socialism is not, as generally stated by Socialists, a question of flying to the sole refuge against the evils which now bear down humanity; but a mere question of comparative advantages, which futurity must determine. We are too ignorant either of what individual agency in its best form, or Socialism in its best form, can accomplish, to be qualified to decide which of the two will be the ultimate form of human society.

If a conjecture may be hazarded, the decision will probably depend mainly on one consideration, viz. which of the two systems is consistent with the greatest amount of human liberty and spontaneity. After the means of subsistence are assured, the next in strength of the personal wants of human beings is liberty; and (unlike the physical wants, which as civilization advances become more moderate and more amenable to control) it increases instead of diminishing in intensity, as the intelligence and the moral faculties are more developed. The perfection both of social arrangements and of practical morality would be, to secure to all persons complete independence and freedom of action, subject to no restriction but that of not doing injury to others: and the education which taught or the social institutions which required them to exchange the control of their own actions for any amount of comfort or affluence, or to renounce liberty for the sake of equality, would deprive them of one of the most elevated characteristics of human nature. It remains to be discovered how far the preservation of this characteristic would be found compatible with the Communistic organization of society. No doubt, this, like all the other objections to the Socialist schemes, is vastly exaggerated. The members of the association need not be required to live together more than they do now, nor need they be controlled in the disposal of their individual share of the produce, and of the probably large amount of leisure which, if they limited their production to things really worth producing, they would possess. Individuals need not be chained to an occupation, or to a particular locality. The restraints of Communism would be freedom in comparison with the present condition of the majority of the human race. The generality of labourers in this and most other countries, have as little choice of occupation or freedom of locomotion, are practically as dependent on fixed rules and on the will of others, as they could be on any system short of actual slavery; to say nothing of the entire domestic subjection of one half the species, to which it is the signal honour of Owenism and most other forms of Socialism that they assign equal rights, in all respects, with those of the hitherto dominant sex. But it is not by comparison with the present bad state of society that the claims of Communism can be estimated; nor is it sufficient that it should promise greater personal and mental freedom than is now enjoyed by those who have not enough of either to deserve the name. The question is, whether there would be any asylum left for individuality of character; whether public opinion would not be a tyrannical yoke; whether the absolute dependence of each on all, and surveillance of each by all, would not grind all down into a tame uniformity of thoughts, feelings, and actions. This is already one of the glaring evils of the existing state of society, notwithstanding a much greater diversity of education and pursuits, and a much less absolute dependence of the individual on the mass, than would exist in the Communistic régime. No society in which eccentricity is a matter of reproach, can be in a wholesome state. It is yet to be ascertained whether the Communistic scheme would be consistent with that multiform development of human nature, those manifold unlikenesses, that diversity of tastes and talents, and variety of intellectual points of view, which not only form a great part of the interest of human life, but by bringing intellects into stimulating collision, and by presenting to each innumerable notions that he would not have conceived of himself, are the mainspring of mental and moral progression.

4. I have thus far confined my observations to the Communistic doctrine, which forms the extreme limit of Socialism; according to which not only the instruments of production, the land and capital, are the joint property of the community, but the produce is divided and the labour apportioned, as far as possible, equally. The objections, whether well or ill grounded, to which Socialism is liable, apply to this form of it in their greatest force. The other varieties of Socialism mainly differ from Communism, in not relying solely on what M. Louis Blanc calls the point of honour of industry, but retaining more or less of the incentives to labour derived from private pecuniary interest. Thus it is already a modification of the strict theory of Communism, when the principle is professed of proportioning remuneration to labour. The attempts which have been made in France to carry Socialism into practical effect, by associations of workmen manufacturing on their own account, mostly began by sharing the remuneration equally, without regard to the quantity of work done by the individual: but in almost every case this plan was after a short time abandoned, and recourse was had to working by the piece. The original principle appeals to a higher standard of

justice, and is adapted to a much higher moral condition of human nature. The proportioning of remuneration to work done, is really just, only in so far as the more or less of the work is a matter of choice: when it depends on natural difference of strength or capacity, this principle of remuneration is in itself an injustice: it is giving to those who have; assigning most to those who are already most favoured by nature.* Considered, however, as a compromise with the selfish type of character formed by the present standard of morality, and fostered by the existing social institutions, it is highly expedient; and until education shall have been entirely regenerated, is far more likely to prove immediately successful, than an attempt at a higher ideal.

The two elaborate forms of non-communistic Socialism known as St Simonism and Fourierism, are totally free from the objections usually urged against Communism; and though they are open to others of their own, yet by the great intellectual power which in many respects distinguishes them, and by their large and philosophic treatment of some of the fundamental problems of society and morality, they may justly be counted among the most remarkable productions of the past and present age.

The St Simonian scheme does not contemplate an equal, but an unequal division of the produce; it does not propose that all should be occupied alike, but differently, according to their vocation or capacity; the function of each being assigned, like grades in a regiment, by the choice of the directing authority, and the remuneration being by salary, proportioned to the importance, in the eyes of that authority, of the function itself, and the merits of the person who fulfils it. For the constitution of the ruling body, different plans might be adopted, consistently with the essentials of the system. It might be appointed by popular suffrage. In the idea of the original authors, the rulers were supposed to be persons of genius and virtue, who obtained the voluntary adhesion of the rest by the force of mental superiority. That the scheme might in some peculiar states of society work with advantage, is not improbable. There is indeed a successful experiment, of a somewhat similar kind on record, to which

I have once alluded; that of the Jesuits in Paraguay.* A race of savages, belonging to a portion of mankind more averse to consecutive exertion for a distant object than any other authentically known to us, was brought under the mental dominion of civilized and instructed men who were united among themselves by a system of community of goods. To the absolute authority of these men they reverentially submitted themselves, and were induced by them to learn the arts of civilized life, and to practise labours for the community, which no inducement that could have been offered would have prevailed on them to practise for themselves. This social system was of short duration, being prematurely destroyed by diplomatic arrangements and foreign force. That it could be brought into action at all was probably owing to the immense distance in point of knowledge and intellect which separated the few rulers from the whole body of the ruled, without any intermediate orders, either social or intellectual. In any other circumstances it would probably have been a complete failure. It supposes an absolute despotism in the heads of the association; which would probably not be much improved if the depositaries of the despotism (contrary to the views of the authors of the system) were varied from time to time according to the result of a popular canvass. But to suppose that one or a few human beings, howsoever selected, could, by whatever machinery of subordinate agency, be qualified to adapt each person's work to his capacity, and proportion each person's remuneration to his merits—to be, in fact, the dispensers of distributive justice to every member of a community; or that any use which they could make of this power would give general satisfaction, or would be submitted to without the aid of force—is a supposition almost too chimerical to be reasoned against. A fixed rule, like that of equality, might be acquiesced in, and so might chance, or an external necessity; but that a handful of human beings should weigh everybody in the balance, and give more to one and less to another at their sole pleasure and judgment would not be borne, unless from persons believed to be more than men, and backed by supernatural terrors.

The most skilfully combined, and with the greatest fore-sight of objections, of all the forms of Socialism, is that commonly known as Fourierism. This system does not contemplate the abolition of private property, nor even of inheritance; on the contrary, it avowedly takes into consideration, as an element in the distribution of the produce, capital as well as labour. It proposes that the operations of industry should be carried on by associations of about two thousand members, combining their labour on a district of about a square league in extent, under the guidance of chiefs selected by themselves. In the distribution, a certain minimum is first assigned for the subsistence of every member of the community, whether capable or not of labour. The remainder of the produce is shared in certain proportions, to be determined beforehand, among the three elements, Labour, Capital, and Talent. The capital of the community may be owned in unequal shares by different members, who would in that case receive, as in any other joint-stock company, proportional dividends. The claim of each person on the share of the produce apportioned to talent, is estimated by the grade or rank which the individual occupies in the several groups of labourers to which he or she belongs; these grades being in all cases conferred by the choice of his or her companions. The remuneration, when received, would not of necessity be expended or enjoyed in common; there would be separate *ménages** for all who preferred them, and no other community of living is contemplated, than that all the members of the association should reside in the same pile of buildings; for saving of labour and expense, not only in building, but in every branch of domestic economy; and in order that, the whole of the buying and selling operations of the community being performed by a single agent, the enormous portion of the produce of industry now carried off by the profits of mere distributors might be reduced to the smallest amount possible.

This system, unlike Communism, does not, in theory at least, withdraw any of the motives to exertion which exist in the present state of society. On the contrary, if the arrangement worked according to the intentions of its contrivers, it would even strengthen those motives; since each person would have much more certainty of reaping individually the fruits of increased skill or energy, bodily or mental, than under the present social arrangements can be felt by any but those who are in the most advantageous positions, or to whom the chapter of accidents is more than ordinarily favourable. The Fourierists, however, have still another resource. They believe that they have solved the great and fundamental problem of rendering labour attractive. That this is not impracticable, they contend by very strong arguments; in particular by one which they have in common with the Owenites, viz., that scarcely any labour, however severe, undergone by human beings for the sake of subsistence, exceeds in intensity that which other human beings, whose subsistence is already provided for, are found ready and even eager to undergo for pleasure. This certainly is a most significant fact, and one from which the student in social philosophy may draw important instruction. But the argument founded on it may easily be stretched too far. If occupations full of discomfort and fatigue are freely pursued by many persons as amusements, who does not see that they are amusements exactly because they are pursued freely, and may be discontinued at pleasure? The liberty of quitting a position often makes the whole difference between its being painful and pleasurable. Many a person remains in the same town, street, or house from January to December, without a wish or a thought tending towards removal, who, if confined to that same place by the mandate of authority, would find the imprisonment absolutely intolerable.

According to the Fourierists, scarcely any kind of useful labour is naturally and necessarily disagreeable, unless it is either regarded as dishonourable, or is immoderate in degree, or destitute of the stimulus of sympathy and emulation. Excessive toil needs not, they contend, be undergone by any one, in a society in which there would be no idle class, and no labour wasted, as so enormous an amount of labour is now wasted, in useless things; and where full advantage would be taken of the power of association, both in increasing the efficiency of production, and in economizing consumption. The other requisites for rendering labour attractive would, they think, be found in the execution of all labour by social groups, to any number of which the same individual might simultaneously belong, at his or her own choice: their grade in each being determined by the degree of service which they were found capable of rendering, as appreciated by the suffrages of their comrades. It is inferred from the diversity of tastes and talents, that every member of the community would be attached to several groups, employing themselves in various kinds of occupation, some bodily, others mental, and would be capable of occupying a high place in some one or more; so that a real equality, or something more nearly approaching to it than might at first be supposed, would practically result: not, from the compression, but, on the contrary, from the largest possible development, of the various natural superiorities residing in each individual.

Even from so brief an outline, it must be evident that this system does no violence to any of the general laws by which human action, even in the present imperfect state of moral and intellectual cultivation, is influenced; and that it would be extremely rash to pronounce it incapable of success, or unfitted to realize a great part of the hopes founded on it by its partisans. With regard to this, as to all other varieties of Socialism, the thing to be desired, and to which they have a just claim, is opportunity of trial. They are all capable of being tried on a moderate scale, and at no risk, either personal or pecuniary, to any except those who try them. It is for experience to determine how far or how soon any one or more of the possible systems of community of property will be fitted to substitute itself for the 'organization of industry' based on private ownership of land and capital. In the meantime we may, without attempting to limit the ultimate capabilities of human nature, affirm, that the political economist, for a considerable time to come, will be chiefly concerned with the conditions of existence and progress belonging to a society founded on private property and individual competition; and that the object to be principally aimed at in the present stage of human improvement, is not the subversion of the system of individual property, but the improvement of it, and the full participation of every member of the community in its benefits.

THE SAME SUBJECT CONTINUED

1. It is next to be considered, what is included in the idea of private property, and by what considerations the application of the principle should be bounded.

The institution of property, when limited to its essential elements, consists in the recognition, in each person, of a right to the exclusive disposal of what he or she have produced by their own exertions, or received either by gift or by fair agreement, without force or fraud, from those who produced it. The foundation of the whole is, the right of producers to what they themselves have produced. It may be objected, therefore, to the institution as it now exists, that it recognises rights of property in individuals over things which they have not produced. For example (it may be said) the operatives in a manufactory create, by their labour and skill, the whole produce; yet, instead of its belonging to them, the law gives them only their stipulated hire, and transfers the produce to some one who has merely supplied the funds, without perhaps contributing anything to the work itself, even in the form of superintendence. The answer to this is, that the labour of manufacture is only one of the conditions which must combine for the production of the commodity. The labour cannot be carried on without materials and machinery, nor without a stock of necessaries provided in advance, to maintain the labourers during the production. All these things are the fruits of previous labour. If the labourers were possessed of them, they would not need to divide the produce with any one; but while they have them not, an equivalent must be given to those who have, both for the antecedent labour, and for the abstinence by which the produce of that labour, instead of being expended on indulgences, has been reserved for this use. The capital may not have been, and in most cases was not, created by the labour and abstinence of the present possessor; but it was created by the labour and abstinence of some former person, who may indeed have been wrongfully dispossessed of it, but who, in the present age of the world, much more probably transferred his claims to the present capitalist by gift or voluntary contract: and the abstinence at least must have been continued by each successive owner, down to the present. If it be said, as it may with truth, that those who have inherited the savings of others have an advantage which they may have in no way deserved, over the industrious whose predecessors have not left them anything; I not only admit, but strenuously contend, that this unearned advantage should be curtailed, as much as is consistent with justice to those who thought fit to dispose of their savings by giving them to their descendants. But while it is true that the labourers are at a disadvantage compared with those whose predecessors have saved, it is also true that the labourers are far better off than if those predecessors had not saved. They share in the advantage, though not to an equal extent with the inheritors. The terms of co-operation between present labour and the fruits of past labour and saving, are a subject for adjustment between the two parties. Each is necessary to the other. The capitalists can do nothing without labourers, nor the labourers without capital. If the labourers compete for employment, the capitalists on their part compete for labour, to the full extent of the circulating capital of the country. Competition is often spoken of as if it were necessarily a cause of misery and degradation to the labouring class; as if high wages were not precisely as much a product of competition as low wages. The remuneration of labour is as much the result of the law of competition in the United States, as it is in Ireland, and much more completely so than in England.

The right of property includes then, the freedom of acquiring by contract. The right of each to what he has produced, implies a right to what has been produced by others, if obtained by their free consent; since the producers must either have given it from good will, or exchanged it for what they esteemed an equivalent, and to prevent them from doing so would be to infringe their right of property in the product of their own industry.

2. Before proceeding to consider the things which the principle of individual property does not include, we must specify one more thing which it does include: and this is that a title, after a certain period, should be given by prescription. According to the fundamental idea of property, indeed, nothing ought to be treated as such, which has been acquired by force or fraud, or appropriated in ignorance of a prior title vested in some other person; but it is necessary to the security of rightful possessors, that they should not be molested by charges of wrongful acquisition, when by the lapse of time witnesses must have perished or been lost sight of, and the real character of the transaction can no longer be cleared up. Possession which has not been legally questioned within a moderate number of years, ought to be, as by the laws of all nations it is, a complete title. Even when the acquisition was wrongful, the dispossession, after a generation has elapsed, of the probably bona fide possessors, by the revival of a claim which had been long dormant, would generally be a greater injustice, and almost always a greater private and public mischief, than leaving the original wrong without atonement. It may seem hard that a claim, originally just, should be defeated by mere lapse of time; but there is a time after which (even looking at the individual case, and without regard to the general effect on the security of possessors), the balance of hardship turns the other way. With the injustices of men, as with the convulsions and disasters of nature, the longer they remain unrepaired, the greater become the obstacles to repairing them, arising from the aftergrowths which would have to be torn up or broken through. In no human transactions, not even in the simplest and clearest, does it follow that a thing is fit to be done now, because it was fit to be done sixty years ago. It is scarcely needful to remark, that these reasons for not disturbing acts of injustice of old date, cannot apply to unjust systems or institutions; since a bad law or usage is not one bad act, in the remote past, but a perpetual repetition of bad acts, as long as the law or usage lasts.

Such, then, being the essentials of private property, it is now to be considered, to what extent the forms in which the institution has existed in different states of society, or still exists, are necessary consequences of its principle, or are recommended by the reasons on which it is grounded.

3. Nothing is implied in property but the right of each to his (or her) own faculties, to what he can produce by them, and to whatever he can get for them in a fair market; together with his right to give this to any other person if he chooses, and the right of that other to receive and enjoy it. It follows, therefore, that although the right of bequest, or gift after death, forms part of the idea of private property, the right of inheritance, as distinguished from bequest, does not. That the property of persons who have made no disposition of it during their lifetime, should pass first to their children, and failing them, to the nearest relations, may be a proper arrangement or not, but is no consequence of the principle of private property. Although there belong to the decision of such questions many considerations besides those of political economy, it is not foreign to the plan of this work to suggest, for the judgment of thinkers, the view of them which most recommends itself to the writer's mind.

No presumption in favour of existing ideas on this subject is to be derived from their antiquity. In early ages, the property of a deceased person passed to his children and nearest relatives by so natural and obvious an arrangement, that no other was likely to be even thought of in competition with it. In the first place, they were usually present on the spot: they were in possession, and if they had no other title, had that, so important in an early state of society, of first occupancy. Secondly, they were already, in a manner, joint owners of his property during his life. If the property was in land, it had generally been conferred by the State on a family rather than on an individual: if it consisted of cattle or moveable goods, it had probably been acquired, and was certainly protected and defended, by the united efforts of all members of the family who were of an age to work or fight. Exclusive individual property in the modern sense, scarcely entered into the ideas of the time; and when the first magistrate of the association died, he really left nothing vacant but his own share in the division, which devolved on the member of the family who succeeded to his authority. To have disposed of the property otherwise, would have been to break up a little commonwealth, united by ideas, interest, and habits, and to cast them adrift on the world. These considerations, though rather felt than reasoned about, had so great an influence on the minds of mankind, as to create the idea of an inherent right in the children to the possessions of their ancestor; a right which it was not competent to himself to defeat. Bequest, in a primitive state of society, was seldom recognised; a clear proof, were there no other, that property was conceived in a manner totally different from the conception of it in the present time.[1]

But the feudal family, the last historical form of patriarchal life, has long perished, and the unit of society is not now the family or clan, composed of all the reputed descendants of a common ancestor, but the individual; or at most a pair of individuals, with their unemancipated children. Property is now inherent in individuals, not in families: the children when grown up do not follow the occupations or fortunes of the parent: if they participate in the parent's pecuniary means it is at his or her pleasure, and not by a voice in the ownership and government of the whole, but generally by the exclusive enjoyment of a part; and in this country at least (except as far as entails or settlements are an obstacle) it is in the power of parents to disinherit even their children, and leave their fortune to strangers. More distant relatives are in general almost as completely detached from the family and its interests as if they were in no way connected with it. The only claim they are supposed to have on their richer relations, is to a preference, *ceteris paribus*, in good offices, and some aid in case of actual necessity.

So great a change in the constitution of society must make a considerable difference in the grounds on which the

[1] See, for admirable illustrations of this and many kindred points, Mr Maine's profound work on Ancient Law and its relation to Modern Ideas [Henry J. S. Maine, *Ancient Law: Its Connection with the Early History of Society, and its Relation to Modern Ideas* (London, 1861)].

disposal of property by inheritance should rest. The reasons usually assigned by modern writers for giving the property of a person who dies intestate, to the children, or nearest relatives, are, first, the supposition that in so disposing of it, the law is more likely than in any other mode to do what the proprietor would have done, if he had done anything; and secondly, the hardship, to those who lived with their parents and partook in their opulence, of being cast down from the enjoyments of wealth into poverty and privation.

There is some force in both these arguments. The law ought, no doubt, to do for the children or dependents of an intestate, whatever it was the duty of the parent or protector to have done, so far as this can be known by any one besides himself. Since, however, the law cannot decide on individual claims, but must proceed by general rules, it is next to be considered what these rules should be.

We may first remark, that in regard to collateral relatives, it is not, unless on grounds personal to the particular individual, the duty of any one to make a pecuniary provision for them. No one now expects it, unless there happen to be no direct heirs; nor would it be expected even then, if the expectation were not created by the provisions of the law in case of intestacy. I see, therefore, no reason why collateral inheritance should exist at all. Mr. Bentham long ago proposed, and other high authorities have agreed in the opinion, that if there are no heirs either in the descending or in the ascending line, the property, in case of intestacy, should escheat to the State. With respect to the more remote degrees of collateral relationship, the point is not very likely to be disputed. Few will maintain that there is any good reason why the accumulations of some childless miser should on his death (as every now and then happens) go to enrich a distant relative who never saw him, who perhaps never knew himself to be related to him until there was something to be gained by it, and who had no moral claim upon him of any kind, more than the most entire stranger. But the reason of the case applies alike to all collaterals, even in the nearest degree. Collaterals have no real claims, but such as may be equally strong in the case of non-relatives; and in the one case as in the other, where valid claims exist, the proper mode of paying regard to them is by bequest.

The claims of children are of a different nature: they are real, and indefeasible. But even of these, I venture to think that the measure usually taken is an erroneous one: what is due to children is in some respects underrated, in others, as it appears to me, exaggerated. One of the most binding of all obligations, that of not bringing children into the world unless they can be maintained in comfort during childhood, and brought up with a likelihood of supporting themselves when of full age, is both disregarded in practice and made light of in theory in a manner disgraceful to human intelligence. On the other hand, when the parent possesses property, the claims of the children upon it seem to me to be the subject of an opposite error. Whatever fortune a parent may have inherited, or still more, may have acquired, I cannot admit that he owes to his children, merely because they are his children, to leave them rich, without the necessity of any exertion. I could not admit it, even if to be so left were always, and certainly, for the good of the children themselves. But this is in the highest degree uncertain. It depends on individual character. Without supposing extreme cases, it may be affirmed that in a majority of instances the good not only of society but of the individuals would be better consulted by bequeathing to them a moderate, than a large provision. This, which is a commonplace of moralists ancient and modern, is felt to be true by many intelligent parents, and would be acted upon much more frequently, if they did not allow themselves to consider less what really is, than what will be thought by others to be, advantageous to the children.

The duties of parents to their children are those which are indissolubly attached to the fact of causing the existence of a human being. The parent owes to society to endeavour to make the child a good and valuable member of it, and owes to the children to provide, so far as depends on him, such education, and such appliances and means, as will enable them to start with a fair chance of achieving by their own exertions a successful life. To this every child has a claim;

and I cannot admit, that as a child he has a claim to more. There is a case in which these obligations present themselves in their true light, without any extrinsic circumstances to disguise or confuse them: it is that of an illegitimate child. To such a child it is generally felt that there is due from the parent, the amount of provision for his welfare which will enable him to make his life on the whole a desirable one. I hold that to no child, merely as such, anything more is due, than what is admitted to be due to an illegitimate child: and that no child for whom thus much has been done, has, unless on the score of previously raised expectations, any grievance, if the remainder of the parent's fortune is devoted to public uses, or to the benefit of individuals on whom in the parent's opinion it is better bestowed.

In order to give the children that fair chance of a desirable existence, to which they are entitled, it is generally necessary that they should not be brought up from childhood in habits of luxury which they will not have the means of indulging in after-life. This, again, is a duty often flagrantly violated by possessors of terminable incomes, who have little property to leave. When the children of rich parents have lived, as it is natural they should do, in habits corresponding to the scale of expenditure in which the parents indulge, it is generally the duty of the parents to make a greater provision for them, than would suffice for children otherwise brought up. I say generally, because even here there is another side to the question. It is a proposition quite capable of being maintained, that to a strong nature which has to make its way against narrow circumstances, to have known early some of the feelings and experiences of wealth, is an advantage both in the formation of character and in the happiness of life. But allowing that children have a just ground of complaint, who have been brought up to require luxuries which they are not afterwards likely to obtain, and that their claim, therefore, is good to a provision bearing some relation to the mode of their bringing up; this, too, is a claim which is particularly liable to be stretched further than its reasons warrant. The case is exactly that of the younger children of the nobility and landed gentry, the bulk of whose fortune passes to the eldest son. The other sons, who are usually numerous, are brought up in the same habits of luxury as the future heir, and they receive as a younger brother's portion, generally what the reason of the case dictates, namely, enough to support, in the habits of life to which they are accustomed, themselves, but not a wife or children. It really is no grievance to any man, that for the means of marrying and of supporting a family, he has to depend on his own exertions.

A provision, then, such as is admitted to be reasonable in the case of illegitimate children, for younger children, wherever in short the justice of the case, and the real interests of the individuals and of society, are the only things considered, is, I conceive, all that parents owe to their children, and all, therefore, which the State owes to the children of those who die intestate. The surplus, if any, I hold that it may rightfully appropriate to the general purposes of the community. I would not, however, be supposed to recommend that parents should never do more for their children than what, merely as children, they have a moral right to. In some cases it is imperative, in many laudable, and in all allowable, to do much more. For this, however, the means are afforded by the liberty of bequest. It is due, not to the children but to the parents, that they should have the power of showing marks of affection, of requiting services and sacrifices, and of bestowing their wealth according to their own preferences, or their own judgment of fitness.

4. Whether the power of bequest should itself be subject to limitation, is an ulterior question of great importance. Unlike inheritance *ab intestato*,* bequest is one of the attributes of property: the ownership of a thing cannot be looked upon as complete without the power of bestowing it, at death or during life, at the owner's pleasure: and all the reasons, which recommend that private property should exist, recommend *pro tanto* this extension of it. But property is only a means to an end, not itself the end. Like all other proprietary rights, and even in a greater degree than most, the power of bequest may be so exercised as to conflict with

the permanent interests of the human race. It does so, when, not content with bequeathing an estate to A, the testator prescribes that on A's death it shall pass to his eldest son, and to that son's son, and so on for ever. No doubt, persons have occasionally exerted themselves more strenuously to acquire a fortune from the hope of founding a family in perpetuity; but the mischiefs to society of such perpetuities outweigh the value of this incentive to exertion, and the incentives in the case of those who have the opportunity of making large fortunes are strong enough without it. A similar abuse of the power of bequest is committed when a person who does the meritorious act of leaving property for public uses, attempts to prescribe the details of its application in perpetuity; when in founding a place of education (for instance) he dictates, for ever, what doctrines shall be taught. It being impossible that any one should know what doctrines will be fit to be taught after he has been dead for centuries, the law ought not to give effect to such dispositions of property, unless subject to the perpetual revision (after a certain interval has elapsed) of a fitting authority.

These are obvious limitations. But even the simplest exercise of the right of bequest, that of determining the person to whom property shall pass immediately on the death of the testator, has always been reckoned among the privileges which might be limited or varied, according to views of expediency. The limitations, hitherto, have been almost solely in favour of children. In England the right is in principle unlimited, almost the only impediment being that arising from a settlement by a former proprietor, in which case the holder for the time being cannot indeed bequeath his possessions, but only because there is nothing to bequeath, he having merely a life interest. By the Roman law, on which the civil legislation of the Continent of Europe is principally founded, bequest originally was not permitted at all, and even after it was introduced, a *legitima portio** was compulsorily reserved for each child; and such is still the law in some of the Continental nations. By the French law since the Revolution, the parent can only dispose by will, of a portion equal to the share of one child, each of the children taking an equal portion. This entail, as it may be called, of the bulk of every one's property upon the children collectively, seems to me as little defensible in principle as an entail in favour of one child, though it does not shock so directly the idea of justice. I cannot admit that parents should be compelled to leave to their children even that provision which, as children, I have contended that they have a moral claim to. Children may forfeit that claim by general unworthiness, or particular ill-conduct to the parents: they may have other resources or prospects: what has been previously done for them, in the way of education and advancement in life, may fully satisfy their moral claim; or others may have claims superior to theirs.

The extreme restriction of the power of bequest in French law, was adopted as a democratic expedient, to break down the custom of primogeniture, and counteract the tendency of inherited property to collect in large masses. I agree in thinking these objects eminently desirable; but the means used are not, I think, the most judicious. Were I framing a code of laws according to what seems to me best in itself, without regard to existing opinions and sentiments, I should prefer to restrict, not what any one might bequeath, but what any one should be permitted to acquire, by bequest or inheritance. Each person should have power to dispose by will of his or her whole property; but not to lavish it in enriching some one individual, beyond a certain maximum, which should be fixed sufficiently high to afford the means of comfortable independence. The inequalities of property which arise from unequal industry, frugality, perseverance, talents, and to a certain extent even opportunities, are inseparable from the principle of private property, and if we accept the principle, we must bear with these consequences of it: but I see nothing objectionable in fixing a limit to what any one may acquire by the mere favour of others, without any exercise of his faculties, and in requiring that if he desires any further accession of fortune, he shall work for it.[1]

---

[1] In the case of capital employed, in the hands of the owner himself, in carrying on any of the operations of industry, there are strong grounds for leaving to him the power of bequeathing to one person the whole of the funds actually engaged

I do not conceive that the degree of limitation which this would impose on the right of bequest, would be felt as a burthensome restraint by any testator who estimated a large fortune at its true value, that of the pleasures and advantages that can be purchased with it: on even the most extravagant estimate of which, it must be apparent to every one, that the difference to the happiness of the possessor between a moderate independence and five times as much, is insignificant when weighed against the enjoyment that might be given, and the permanent benefits diffused, by some other disposal of the four-fifths. So long indeed as the opinion practically prevails, that the best thing which can be done for objects of affection is to heap on them to satiety those intrinsically worthless things on which large fortunes are mostly expended, there might be little use in enacting such a law, even if it were possible to get it passed, since if there were the inclination, there would generally be the power of evading it. The law would be unavailing unless the popular sentiment went energetically along with it; which (judging from the tenacious adherence of public opinion in France to the law of compulsory division) it would in some states of society and government be very likely to do, however much the contrary may be the fact in England and at the present time. If the restriction could be made practically effectual, the benefit would be great. Wealth which could no longer be employed in over-enriching a few, would either be devoted to objects of public usefulness, or if bestowed on individuals, would be distributed among a large number. While those enormous fortunes which no one needs for any personal purpose but ostentation or improper power, would become much less numerous, there would be a great multiplication of persons in easy circumstances, with the advant-

in a single enterprise. It is well that he should be enabled to leave the enterprise under the control of whichever of his heirs he regards as best fitted to conduct it virtuously and efficiently: and the necessity (very frequent and inconvenient under the French law) would be thus obviated, of breaking up a manufacturing or commerical establishment at the death of its chief. In like manner, it should be allowed to a proprietor who leaves to one of his successors the moral burthen of keeping up an ancestral mansion and park or pleasure-ground, to bestow along with them as much other property as is required for their sufficient maintenance.

ages of leisure, and all the real enjoyments which wealth can give, except those of vanity; a class by whom the services which a nation having leisured classes is entitled to expect from them, either by their direct exertions or by the tone they give to the feelings and tastes of the public, would be rendered in a much more beneficial manner than at present. A large portion also of the accumulations of successful industry would probably be devoted to public uses, either by direct bequests to the State, or by the endowment of institutions; as is already done very largely in the United States, where the ideas and practice in the matter of inheritance seem to be unusually rational and beneficial.[1]

5. The next point to be considered is, whether the reasons on which the institution of property rests, are applicable to all things in which a right of exclusive ownership is at present recognised; and if not, on what other grounds the recognition is defensible.

The essential principle of property being to assure to all persons what they have produced by their labour and accumulated by their abstinence, this principle cannot apply to what is not the produce of labour, the raw material of the earth. If the land derived its productive power wholly from nature, and not at all from industry, or if there were any means of discriminating what is derived from each source, it not only would not be necessary, but it would be

[1] 'Munificent bequests and donations for public purposes, whether charitable or educational, form a striking feature in the modern history of the United States, and especially of New England. Not only is it common for rich capitalists to leave by will a portion of their fortune towards the endowment of national institutions, but individuals during their lifetime make magnificent grants of money for the same objects. There is here no compulsory law for the equal partition of property among children, as in France, and on the other hand, no custom of entail or primogeniture, as in England, so that the affluent feel themselves at liberty to share their wealth between their kindred and the public; it being impossible to found a family, and parents having frequently the happiness of seeing all their children well provided for and independent long before their death. I have seen a list of bequests and donations made during the last thirty years for the benefit of religious, charitable, and literary institutions in the state of Massachusetts alone, and they amounted to no less a sum than six millions of dollars, or more than a million sterling.'—Lyell's *Travels in America*, i. 263 [-4].

the height of injustice, to let the gift of nature be engrossed by individuals. The use of the land in agriculture must indeed, for the time being, be of necessity exclusive; the same person who has ploughed and sown must be permitted to reap: but the land might be occupied for one season only, as among the ancient Germans; or might be periodically redivided as population increased: or the State might be the universal landlord, and the cultivators tenants under it, either on lease or at will.

But though land is not the produce of industry, most of its valuable qualities are so. Labour is not only requisite for using, but almost equally so for fashioning, the instrument. Considerable labour is often required at the commencement, to clear the land for cultivation. In many cases, even when cleared, its productiveness is wholly the effect of labour and art. The Bedford Level produced little or nothing until artificially drained. The bogs of Ireland, until the same thing is done to them, can produce little besides fuel. One of the barrenest soils in the world, composed of the material of the Goodwin Sands, the Pays de Waes in Flanders, has been so fertilized by industry, as to have become one of the most productive in Europe. Cultivation also requires buildings and fences, which are wholly the produce of labour. The fruits of this industry cannot be reaped in a short period. The labour and outlay are immediate, the benefit is spread over many years, perhaps over all future time. A holder will not incur this labour and outlay when strangers and not himself will be benefited by it. If he undertakes such improvements, he must have a sufficient period before him in which to profit by them: and he is in no way so sure of having always a sufficient period as when his tenure is perpetual.[1]

6. These are the reasons which form the justification in an economical point of view, of property in land. It is seen, that they are only valid, in so far as the proprietor of land is its improver. Whenever, in any country, the proprietor,

[Note omitted.]

generally speaking, ceases to be the improver, political economy has nothing to say in defence of landed property, as there established. In no sound theory of private property was it ever contemplated that the proprietor of land should be merely a sinecurist quartered on it.

In Great Britain, the landed proprietor is not unfrequently an improver. But it cannot be said that he is generally so. And in the majority of cases he grants the liberty of cultivation on such terms, as to prevent improvements from being made by any one else. In the southern parts of the island, as there are usually no leases, permanent improvements can scarcely be made except by the landlord's capital; accordingly the South, compared with the North of England, and with the Lowlands of Scotland, is still extremely backward in agricultural improvement. The truth is, that any very general improvement of land by the landlords, is hardly compatible with a law or custom of primogeniture. When the land goes wholly to the heir, it generally goes to him severed from the pecuniary resources which would enable him to improve it, the personal property being absorbed by the provision for younger children, and the land itself often heavily burthened for the same purpose. There is therefore but a small proportion of landlords who have the means of making expensive improvements, unless they do it with borrowed money, and by adding to the mortgages with which in most cases the land was already burthened when they received it. But the position of the owner of a deeply mortgaged estate is so precarious; economy is so unwelcome to one whose apparent fortune greatly exceeds his real means, and the vicissitudes of rent and price which only trench upon the margin of his income, are so formidable to one who can call little more than the margin his own, that it is no wonder if few landlords find themselves in a condition to make immediate sacrifices for the sake of future profit. Were they ever so much inclined, those alone can prudently do it, who have seriously studied the principles of scientific agriculture: and great landlords have seldom seriously studied anything. They might at least hold out inducements to the farmers to do what they will not or cannot do themselves; but even in granting leases, it is in England a general complaint that they tie up their tenants by covenants grounded on the practices of an obsolete and exploded agriculture; while most of them, by withholding leases altogether, and giving the farmer no guarantee of possession beyond a single harvest, keep the land on a footing little more favourable to improvement than in the time of our barbarous ancestors,

> ——immetata quibus jugera liberas
> Fruges et Cererem ferunt,
> Nec cultura placet longior annuā.*

Landed property in England is thus very far from completely fulfilling the conditions which render its existence economically justifiable. But if insufficiently realized even in England, in Ireland those conditions are not complied with at all. With individual exceptions (some of them very honourable ones), the owners of Irish estates do nothing for the land but drain it of its produce. What has been epigrammatically said in the discussions on 'peculiar burthens' is literally true when applied to them; that the greatest 'burthen on land' is the landlords. Returning nothing to the soil, they consume its whole produce, minus the potatoes strictly necessary to keep the inhabitants from dying of famine; and when they have any purpose of improvement, the preparatory step usually consists in not leaving even this pittance, but turning out the people to beggary if not to starvation.[1] When landed property has placed itself upon this footing it ceases to be defensible, and the time has come for making some new arrangement of the matter.

When the 'sacredness of property' is talked of, it should always be remembered, that any such sacredness does not belong in the same degree to landed property. No man made the land. It is the original inheritance of the whole

---

[1] I must beg the reader to bear in mind that this paragraph was written more than twenty years ago. So wonderful are the changes, both moral and economical, taking place in our age, that, without perpetually re-writing a work like the present, it is impossible to keep up with them.

species.* Its appropriation is wholly a question of general expediency. When private property in land is not expedient, it is unjust. It is no hardship to any one, to be excluded from what others have produced: they were not bound to produce it for his use, and he loses nothing by not sharing in what otherwise would not have existed at all. But it is some hardship to be born into the world and to find all nature's gifts previously engrossed, and no place left for the new-comer. To reconcile people to this, after they have once admitted into their minds the idea that any moral rights belong to them as human beings, it will always be necessary to convince them that the exclusive appropriation is good for mankind on the whole, themselves included. But this is what no sane human being could be persuaded of, if the relation between the landowner and the cultivator were the same everywhere as it has been in Ireland.

Landed property is felt, even by those most tenacious of its rights, to be a different thing from other property; and where the bulk of the community have been disinherited of their share of it, and it has become the exclusive attribute of a small minority, men have generally tried to reconcile it, at least in theory, to their sense of justice, by endeavouring to attach duties to it, and erecting it into a sort of magistracy, either moral or legal. But if the state is at liberty to treat the possessors of land as public functionaries, it is only going one step further to say, that it is at liberty to discard them. The claim of the landowners to the land is altogether subordinate to the general policy of the state. The principle of property gives them no right to the land, but only a right to compensation for whatever portion of their interest in the land it may be the policy of the state to deprive them of. To that, their claim is indefeasible. It is due to landowners, and to owners of any property whatever, recognized as such by the state, that they should not be dispossessed of it without receiving its pecuniary value, or an annual income equal to what they derived from it. This is due on the general principles on which property rests. If the land was bought with the produce of the labour and abstinence of themselves or their ancestors, compensation is due to them on that ground; even if otherwise, it is still due on the ground of prescription. Nor can it ever be necessary for accomplishing an object by which the community altogether will gain, that a particular portion of the community should be immolated. When the property is of a kind to which peculiar affections attach themselves, the compensation ought to exceed a bare pecuniary equivalent. But, subject to this proviso, the state is at liberty to deal with landed property as the general interests of the community may require, even to the extent, if it so happen, of doing with the whole, what is done with a part whenever a bill is passed for a railroad or a new street. The community has too much at stake in the proper cultivation of the land, and in the conditions annexed to the occupancy of it, to leave these things to the discretion of a class of persons called landlords, when they have shown themselves unfit for the trust. The legislature, which if it pleased might convert the whole body of landlords into fundholders or pensioners, might *a fortiori*, commute the average receipts of Irish landowners into a fixed rent charge, and raise the tenants into proprietors; supposing always that the full market value of the land was tendered to the landlords, in case they preferred that to accepting the conditions proposed.

There will be another place for discussing the various modes of landed property and tenure, and the advantages and inconveniences of each; in this chapter our concern is with the right itself, the grounds which justify it, and (as a corollary from these) the conditions by which it should be limited. To me it seems almost an axiom that property in land should be interpreted strictly, and that the balance in all cases of doubt should incline against the proprietor. The reverse is the case with property in moveables, and in all things the product of labour: over these, the owner's power both of use and of exclusion should be absolute, except where positive evil to others would result from it: but in the case of land, no exclusive right should be permitted in any individual, which cannot be shown to be productive of positive good. To be allowed any exclusive right at all, over a portion of the common inheritance, while there are others who have no portion, is already a privilege. No quantity of moveable goods which a person can acquire by his labour, prevents others from acquiring the like by the same means; but from the very nature of the case, whoever owns land, keeps others out of the enjoyment of it. The privilege, or monopoly, is only defensible as a necessary evil; it becomes an injustice when carried to any point to which the compensating good does not follow it.

For instance, the exclusive right to the land for purposes of cultivation does not imply an exclusive right to it for purposes of access; and no such right ought to be recognized, except to the extent necessary to protect the produce against damage, and the owner's privacy against invasion. The pretension of two Dukes to shut up a part of the Highlands, and exclude the rest of mankind from many square miles of mountain scenery to prevent disturbance to wild animals, is an abuse; it exceeds the legitimate bounds of the right of landed property. When land is not intended to be cultivated, no good reason can in general be given for its being private property at all; and if any one is permitted to call it his, he ought to know that he holds it by sufferance of the community, and on an implied condition that his ownership, since it cannot possibly do them any good, at least shall not deprive them of any, which could have derived from the land if it had been unappropriated. Even in the case of cultivated land, a man whom, though only one among millions, the law permits to hold thousands of acres as his single share, is not entitled to think that all this is given to him to use and abuse, and deal with as if it concerned nobody but himself. The rents or profits which he can obtain from it are at his sole disposal; but with regard to the land, in everything which he does with it, and in everything which he abstains from doing, he is morally bound, and should whenever the case admits be legally compelled, to make his interest and pleasure consistent with the public good. The species at large still retains, of its original claim to the soil of the planet which it inhabits, as much as is compatible with the purposes for which it has parted with the remainder.

7. Besides property in the produce of labour, and property in land, there are other things which are or have been subjects of property, in which no proprietary rights ought to exist at all. But as the civilized world has in general made up its mind on most of these, there is no necessity for dwelling on them in this place. At the head of them, is property in human beings. It is almost superfluous to observe, that this institution can have no place in any society even pretending to be founded on justice, or on fellowship between human creatures. But, iniquitous as it is, yet when the state has expressly legalized it, and human beings, for generations, have been bought, sold, and inherited under sanction of law, it is another wrong, in abolishing the property, not to make full compensation. This wrong was avoided by the great measure of justice in 1833,* one of the most virtuous acts, as well as the most practically beneficent, ever done collectively by a nation. Other examples of property which ought not to have been created, are properties in public trusts; such as judicial offices under the old French régime, and the heritable jurisdictions which, in countries not wholly emerged from feudality, pass with the land. Our own country affords, as cases in point, that of a commission in the army, and of an advowson, or right of nomination to an ecclesiastical benefice. A property is also sometimes created in a right of taxing the public; in a monopoly, for instance, or other exclusive privilege. These abuses prevail most in semi-barbarous countries but are not without example in the most civilized. In France there are several important trades and professions, including notaries, attorneys, brokers, appraisers, printers, and (until lately) bakers and butchers, of which the numbers are limited by law. The *brevet** or privilege of one of the permitted number consequently brings a high price in the market. When such is the case, compensation probably could not with justice be refused, on the abolition of the privilege. There are other cases in which this would be more doubtful. The question would turn upon what, in the peculiar circumstances, was sufficient to constitute prescription; and whether the legal recognition which the abuse had obtained, was sufficient to

constitute it an institution, or amounted only to an occasional licence. It would be absurd to claim compensation for losses caused by changes in a tariff, a thing confessedly variable from year to year; or for monopolies like those granted to individuals by the Tudors, favours of a despotic authority, which the power that gave was competent at any time to recall.

So much on the institution of property, a subject of which, for the purposes of political economy, it was indispensable to treat, but on which we could not usefully confine ourselves to economical considerations. We have now to inquire on what principles and with what results the distribution of the produce of land and labour is effected, under the relations which this institution creates among the different members of the community.

III

OF THE CLASSES AMONG WHOM
THE PRODUCE IS DISTRIBUTED

1. Private property being assumed as a fact, we have next to enumerate the different classes of persons to whom it gives rise; whose concurrence, or at least whose permission, is necessary to production, and who are therefore able to stipulate for a share of the produce. We have to inquire, according to what laws the produce distributes itself among these classes, by the spontaneous action of the interests of those concerned: after which, a further question will be, what effects are or might be produced by laws, institutions, and measures of government, in superseding or modifying that spontaneous distribution.

The three requisites of production, as has been so often repeated, are labour, capital, and land: understanding by capital, the means and appliances which are the accumulated results of previous labour, and by land, the materials and instruments supplied by nature, whether contained in the interior of the earth, or constituting its surface. Since each of these elements of production may be separately appropriated, the industrial community may be considered as divided into landowners, capitalists, and productive labourers. Each of these classes, as such, obtains a share of the produce: no other person or class obtains anything, except by concession from them. The remainder of the community is, in fact, supported at their expense, giving, if any equivalent, one consisting of unproductive services. These three classes, therefore, are considered in political economy as making up the whole community.

2. But although these three sometimes exist as separate classes, dividing the produce among them, they do not necessarily or always so exist. The fact is so much otherwise, that there are only one or two communities in which the complete separation of these classes is the general rule.

England and Scotland, with parts of Belgium and Holland, are almost the only countries in the world, where the land, capital, and labour employed in agriculture, are generally the property of separate owners. The ordinary case is, that the same person owns either two of these requisites, or all three.

The case in which the same person owns all three, embraces the two extremes of existing society, in respect to the independence and dignity of the labouring class. First, when the labourer himself is the proprietor. This is the commonest case in the Northern States of the American Union; one of the commonest in France, Switzerland, the three Scandinavian kingdoms, and parts of Germany;[1] and a common case in parts of Italy and in Belgium. In all these countries there are, no doubt, large landed properties, and a still greater number which, without being large, require the occasional or constant aid of hired labourers. Much, however, of the land is owned in portions too small to require any other labour than that of the peasant and his family, or fully to occupy even that. The capital employed is not always that of the peasant proprietor, many of these small properties being mortgaged to obtain the means of cultivating; but the capital is invested at the peasant's risk, and though he pays interest for it, it gives to no one any right of interference, except, perhaps, eventually to take possession of the land, if the interest ceases to be paid.

The other case in which the land, labour, and capital, belong to the same person, is the case of slave countries, in which the labourers themselves are owned by the landowner. Our West India colonies before emancipation, and the sugar colonies of the nations by whom a similar act of justice is still unperformed, are examples of large establishments for agricultural and manufacturing labour (the production of sugar and rum is a combination of both) in which the land, the factories (if they may be so called), the machinery, and the degraded labourers, are all the property of a capitalist. In this case, as well as in its extreme

[1] [Note omitted.]

opposite, the case of the peasant proprietor, there is no division of the produce.

3. When the three requisites are not all owned by the same person, it often happens that two of them are so. Sometimes the same person owns the capital and the land, but not the labour. The landlord makes his engagement directly with the labourer, and supplies the whole or part of the stock necessary for cultivation. This system is the usual one in those parts of Continental Europe, in which the labourers are neither serfs on the one hand, nor proprietors on the other. It was very common in France before the Revolution, and is still much practised in some parts of that country, when the land is not the property of the cultivator. It prevails generally in the level districts of Italy, except those principally pastoral, such as the Maremma of Tuscany and the Campagna of Rome. On this system the division of the produce is between two classes, the landowner and the labourer.

In other cases again the labourer does not own the land, but owns the little stock employed on it, the landlord not being in the habit of supplying any. This system generally prevails in Ireland. It is nearly universal in India, and in most countries of the East; whether the government retains, as it generally does, the ownership of the soil, or allows portions to become, either absolutely or in a qualified sense, the property of individuals. In India, however, things are so far better than in Ireland, that the owner of land is in the habit of making advances to the cultivators, if they cannot cultivate without them. For these advances the native landed proprietor usually demands high interest; but the principal landowner, the government, makes them gratuitously, recovering the advance after the harvest, together with the rent. The produce is here divided as before, between the same two classes, the landowner and the labourer.

These are the principal variations in the classification of those among whom the produce of agricultural labour is distributed. In the case of manufacturing industry there never are more than two classes, the labourers and the capitalists. The original artisans in all countries were either slaves, or the women of the family. In the manufacturing establishments of the ancients, whether on a large or on a small scale, the labourers were usually the property of the capitalist. In general, if any manual labour was thought compatible with the dignity of a freeman, it was only agricultural labour. The converse system, in which the capital was owned by the labourer, was coeval with free labour, and under it the first great advances of manufacturing industry were achieved. The artisan owned the loom or the few tools he used, and worked on his own account; or at least ended by doing so, though he usually worked for another, first as apprentice and next as journeyman, for a certain number of years before he could be admitted a master. But the status of a permanent journeyman, all his life a hired labourer and nothing more, had no place in the crafts and guilds of the middle ages. In country villages, where a carpenter or a blacksmith cannot live and support hired labourers on the returns of his business, he is even now his own workman; and shopkeepers in similar circumstances are their own shopmen, or shopwomen. But wherever the extent of the market admits of it, the distinction is now fully established between the class of capitalists, or employers of labour, and the class of labourers; the capitalists, in general, contributing no other labour than that of direction and superintendence.

IV

OF COMPETITION, AND CUSTOM

1. Under the rule of individual property, the division of the produce is the result of two determining agencies: Competition, and Custom. It is important to ascertain the amount of influence which belongs to each of these causes, and in what manner the operation of one is modified by the other.

Political economists generally, and English political economists above others, have been accustomed to lay almost exclusive stress upon the first of these agencies; to exaggerate the effect of competition, and to take into little account the other and conflicting principle. They are apt to express themselves as if they thought that competition actually does, in all cases, whatever it can be shown to be the tendency of competition to do. This is partly intelligible, if we consider that only through the principle of competition has political economy any pretension to the character of a science. So far as rents, profits, wages, prices, are determined by competition, laws may be assigned for them. Assume competition to be their exclusive regulator, and principles of broad generality and scientific precision may be laid down, according to which they will be regulated. The political economist justly deems this his proper business: and as an abstract or hypothetical science, political economy cannot be required to do, and indeed cannot do, anything more. But it would be a great misconception of the actual course of human affairs, to suppose that competition exercises in fact this unlimited sway. I am not speaking of monopolies, either natural or artificial, or of any interferences of authority with the liberty of production or exchange. Such disturbing causes have always been allowed for by political economists. I speak of cases in which there is nothing to restrain competition; no hindrance to it either in the nature of the case or in artificial obstacles; yet in which the result is not determined by competition, but by custom or usage; competition either not taking place at all, or producing its effect in quite a different manner from that which is ordinarily assumed to be natural to it.

custom or usage, competition either not taking place at all, or producing its effect in quite a different manner from that which is ordinarily assumed to be natural to it.

BOOK III

EXCHANGE

I

OF VALUE

1. The subject on which we are now about to enter fills so important and conspicuous a position in political economy, that in the apprehension of some thinkers its boundaries confound themselves with those of the science itself. One eminent writer has proposed as a name for Political Economy, 'Catallactics', or the science of exchanges:* by others it has been called the Science of Values. If these denominations had appeared to me logically correct, I must have placed the discussion of the elementary laws of value at the commencement of our inquiry, instead of postponing it to the Third Part; and the possibility of so long deferring it is alone a sufficient proof that this view of the nature of Political Economy is too confined. It is true that in the preceding Books we have not escaped the necessity of anticipating some small portion of the theory of Value, especially as to the value of labour and of land. It is nevertheless evident, that of the two great departments of Political Economy, the production of wealth and its distribution, the consideration of Value has to do with the latter alone; and with that, only so far as competition, and not usage or custom, is the distributing agency. The conditions and laws of Production would be the same as they are, if the arrangements of society did not depend on Exchange, or did not admit of it. Even in the present system of industrial life, in which employments are minutely subdivided, and all concerned in production depend for their remuneration on the price of a particular commodity, exchange is not the fundamental law of the distribution of the produce, no more than roads and carriages are the essential laws of motion, but merely a part of the machinery for

effecting it. To confound these ideas, seems to me, not only a logical, but a practical blunder. It is a case of the error too common in political economy, of not distinguishing between necessities arising from the nature of things, and those created by social arrangements: an error, which appears to me to be at all times producing two opposite mischiefs; on the one hand, causing political economists to class the merely temporary truths of their subject among its permanent and universal laws; and on the other, leading many persons to mistake the permanent laws of Production (such as those on which the necessity is grounded of restraining population) for temporary accidents arising from the existing constitution of society—which those who would frame a new system of social arrangements, are at liberty to disregard.

In a state of society, however, in which the industrial system is entirely founded on purchase and sale, each individual, for the most part, living not on things in the production of which he himself bears a part, but on things obtained by a double exchange, a sale followed by a purchase—the question of Value is fundamental. Almost every speculation respecting the economical interests of a society thus constituted, implies some theory of Value: the smallest error on that subject infects with corresponding error all our other conclusions; and anything vague or misty in our conception of it, creates confusion and uncertainty in everything else. Happily, there is nothing in the laws of Value which remains for the present or any future writer to clear up; the theory of the subject is complete: the only difficulty to be overcome is that of so stating it as to solve by anticipation the chief perplexities which occur in applying it: and to do this, some minuteness of exposition, and considerable demands on the patience of the reader, are unavoidable. He will be amply repaid, however (if a stranger to these inquiries), by the ease and rapidity with which a thorough understanding of this subject will enable him to fathom most of the remaining questions of political economy.

2. We must begin by settling our phraseology. Adam Smith, in a passage often quoted, has touched upon the most

obvious ambiguity of the word value; which, in one of its senses, signifies usefulness, in another, power of purchasing; in his own language, value in use and value in exchange. But (as Mr De Quincey* has remarked) in illustrating this double meaning, Adam Smith has himself fallen into another ambiguity. Things (he says) which have the greatest value in use have often little or no value in exchange; which is true, since that which can be obtained without labour or sacrifice will command no price, however useful or needful it may be. But he proceeds to add, that things which have the greatest value in exchange, as a diamond for example, may have little or no value in use. This is employing the word use, not in the sense in which political economy is concerned with it, but in that other sense in which use is opposed to pleasure. Political economy has nothing to do with the comparative estimation of different uses in the judgement of a philosopher or a moralist. The use of a thing, in political economy, means its capacity to satisfy a desire, or serve a purpose. Diamonds have this capacity in a high degree, and unless they had it, would not bear any price. Value in use, or as Mr De Quincey calls it, *teleologic* value, is the extreme limit of value in exchange. The exchange value of a thing may fall short, to any amount, of its value in use; but that it can ever exceed the value in use, implies a contradiction; it supposes that persons will give, to possess a thing, more than the utmost value which they themselves put upon it as a means of gratifying their inclinations.

The word Value, when used without adjunct, always means, in political economy, value in exchange; or as it has been called by Adam Smith and his successors, exchangeable value, a phrase which no amount of authority that can be quoted for it can make other than bad English. Mr De Quincey substitutes the term Exchange Value, which is unexceptionable.

Exchange value requires to be distinguished from Price. The words Value and Price were used as synonymous by the early political economists, and are not always discriminated even by Ricardo. But the most accurate modern writers, to

avoid the wasteful expenditure of two good scientific terms
on a single idea, have employed Price to express the value
of a thing in relation to money; the quantity of money for
which it will exchange. By the price of a thing, therefore, we
shall henceforth understand its value in money; by the
value, or exchange value of a thing, its general power
of purchasing; the command which its possession gives over
purchaseable commodities in general.

XXVI

OF DISTRIBUTION, AS AFFECTED BY EXCHANGE

1. We have now completed, as far as is compatible with our purposes and limits, the exposition of the machinery through which the produce of a country is apportioned among the different classes of its inhabitants; which is no other than the machinery of Exchange, and has for the exponents of its operation, the laws of Value and of Price. We shall now avail ourselves of the light thus acquired, to cast a retrospective glance at the subject of Distribution. The division of the produce among the three classes, Labourers, Capitalists, and Landlords, when considered without any reference to Exchange, appeared to depend on certain general laws. It is fit that we should now consider whether these same laws still operate, when the distribution takes place through the complex mechanism of exchange and money; or whether the properties of the mechanism interfere with and modify the presiding principles.

The primary division of the produce of human exertion and frugality is, as we have seen, into three shares, wages, profits, and rent; and these shares are portioned out to the persons entitled to them, in the form of money, and by a process of exchange; or rather, the capitalist, with whom in the usual arrangements of society the produce remains, pays in money, to the other two sharers, the market value of their labour and land. If we examine, on what the pecuniary value of labour, and the pecuniary value of the use of land, depend, we shall find that it is on the very same causes by which we found that wages and rent would be regulated if there were no money and no exchange of commodities.

It is evident, in the first place, that the law of Wages is not affected by the existence or non-existence of Exchange or Money. Wages depend on the ratio between population and capital; and would do so if all the capital in the world were the property of one association, or if the capitalists among whom it is shared maintained each an establishment for the production of every article consumed in the community, exchange of commodities having no existence. As the ratio between capital and population, in all old countries, depends on the strength of the checks by which the too rapid increase of population is restrained, it may be said, popularly speaking, that wages depend on the checks to population; that when the check is not death, by starvation or disease, wages depend on the prudence of the labouring people; and that wages in any country are habitually at the lowest rate, to which in that country the labourer will suffer them to be depressed rather than put a restraint upon multiplication.

What is here meant, however, by wages, is the labourer's real scale of comfort; the quantity he obtains of the things which nature or habit has made necessary or agreeable to him: wages in the sense in which they are of importance to the receiver. In the sense in which they are of importance to the payer, they do not depend exclusively on such simple principles. Wages in the first sense, the wages on which the labourer's comfort depends, we will call real wages, or wages in kind. Wages in the second sense, we may be permitted to call, for the present, money wages; assuming, as it is allowable to do, that money remains for the time an invariable standard, no alteration taking place in the conditions under which the circulating medium itself is produced or obtained. If money itself undergoes no variation in cost, the money price of labour is an exact measure of the Cost of Labour, and may be made use of as a convenient symbol to express it.

The money wages of labour are a compound result of two elements: first, real wages, or wages in kind, or in other words, the quantity which the labourer obtains of the ordinary articles of consumption; and secondly, the money prices of those articles. In all old countries—all countries in which the increase of population is in any degree checked by the difficulty of obtaining subsistence—the habitual money price of labour is that which will just enable the labourers, one with another, to purchase the commodities without which they either cannot or will not keep up the population at its customary rate of increase. Their standard of comfort being given, (and by the standard of comfort in a labouring class, is meant that, rather than forego which, they will abstain from multiplication,) money wages depend on the money price, and therefore on the cost of production, of the various articles which the labourers habitually consume: because if their wages cannot procure them a given quantity of these, their increase will slacken, and their wages rise. Of these articles, food and other agricultural produce are so much the principal, as to leave little influence to anything else.

It is at this point that we are enabled to invoke the aid of the principles which have been laid down in this Third Part. The cost of production of food and agricultural produce has been analyzed in a preceding chapter.* It depends on the productiveness of the least fertile land, or of the least productively employed portion of capital, which the necessities of society have as yet put in requisition for agricultural purposes. The cost of production of the food grown in these least advantageous circumstances, determines, as we have seen, the exchange value and money price of the whole. In any given state, therefore, of the labourers' habits, their money wages depend on the productiveness of the least fertile land, or least productive agricultural capital; on the point which cultivation has reached in its downward progress—in its encroachments on the barren lands, and its gradually increased strain upon the powers of the more fertile. Now, the force which urges cultivation in this downward course, is the increase of people; while the counterforce which checks the descent, is the improvement of agricultural science and practice, enabling the same soil to yield to the same labour more ample returns. The costliness of the most costly part of the produce of cultivation, is an exact expression of the state, at any given moment, of the race which population and agricultural skill are always running against each other.

2. It is well said by Dr Chalmers,* that many of the most important lessons in political economy are to be learnt at

the extreme margin of cultivation, the last point which the culture of the soil has reached in its contest with the spontaneous agencies of nature. The degree of productiveness of this extreme margin, is an index to the existing state of the distribution of the produce among the three classes, of labourers, capitalists, and landlords.

When the demand of an increasing population for more food cannot be satisfied without extending cultivation to less fertile land or incurring additional outlay, with a less proportional return, on land already in cultivation, it is a necessary condition of this increase of agricultural produce, that the value and price of that produce must first rise. But as soon as the price has risen sufficiently to give to the additional outlay of capital the ordinary profit, the rise will not go on still further for the purpose of enabling the new land, or the new expenditure on old land, to yield rent as well as profit. The land or capital last put in requisition, and occupying what Dr Chalmers calls the margin of cultivation, will yield, and continue to yield, no rent. But if this yields no rent, the rent afforded by all other land or agricultural capital will be exactly so much as it produces more than this. The price of food will always on the average be such, that the worst land, and the least productive instalment of the capital employed on the better lands, shall just replace the expenses with the ordinary profit. If the least favoured land and capital just do thus much, all other land and capital will yield an extra profit, equal to the proceeds of the extra produce due to their superior productiveness; and this extra profit becomes, by competition, the prize of the landlords. Exchange, and money, therefore, make no difference in the law of rent: it is the same as we originally found it. Rent is the extra return made to agricultural capital when employed with peculiar advantages; the exact equivalent of what those advantages enable the producers to economize in the cost of production: the value and price of the produce being regulated by the cost of production to those producers who have no advantages; by the return to that portion of agricultural capital, the circumstances of which are the least favourable.

3. Wages and Rent being thus regulated by the same principles when paid in money, as they would be if apportioned in kind, it follows that Profits are so likewise. For the surplus, after replacing wages and paying rent, constitutes Profits.

We found in the last chapter of the Second Book, that the advances of the capitalist, when analysed to their ultimate elements, consist either in the purchase or maintenance of labour, or in the profits of former capitalists; and that therefore profits, in the last resort, depend upon the Cost of Labour, falling as that rises, and rising as it falls. Let us endeavour to trace more minutely the operation of this law.

There are two modes in which the Cost of Labour, which is correctly represented (money being supposed invariable) by the money wages of the labourer, may be increased. The labourer may obtain greater comforts; wages in kind—real wages—may rise. Or the progress of population may force down cultivation to inferior soils, and more costly processes; thus raising the cost of production, the value, and the price, of the chief articles of the labourer's consumption. On either of these suppositions, the rate of profit will fall.

If the labourer obtains more abundant commodities, only by reason of their greater cheapness; if he obtains a greater quantity, but not on the whole a greater cost; real wages will be increased, but not money wages, and there will be nothing to affect the rate of profit. But if he obtains a greater quantity of commodities of which the cost of production is not lowered, he obtains a greater cost; his money wages are higher. The expense of these increased money wages falls wholly on the capitalist. There are no conceivable means by which he can shake it off. It may be said—it is, not unfrequently, said—that he will get rid of it by raising his price. But this opinion we have already, and more than once, fully refuted.[1]

The doctrine, indeed, that a rise of wages causes an equivalent rise of prices, is, as we formerly observed, self-contradictory: for if it did so, it would not be a rise of

---

[1] [Bk. III, Ch. IV. 2, and Ch. XXV. 4. Not included in this edn.]

wages; the labourer would get no more of any commodity than he had before, let his money wages rise ever so much; a rise of real wages would be an impossibility. This being equally contrary to reason and to fact, it is evident that a rise of money wages does not raise prices; that high wages are not a cause of high prices. A rise of general wages falls on profits. There is no possible alternative.

Having disposed of the case in which the increase of money wages, and of the Cost of Labour, arises from the labourer's obtaining more ample wages in kind, let us now suppose it to arise from the increased cost of production of the things which he consumes; owing to an increase of population, unaccompanied by an equivalent increase of agricultural skill. The augmented supply required by the population would not be obtained, unless the price of food rose sufficiently to remunerate the farmer for the increased cost of production. The farmer, however, in this case sustains a twofold disadvantage. He has to carry on his cultivation under less favourable conditions of productiveness than before. For this, as it is a disadvantage belonging to him only as a farmer, and not shared by other employers, he will, on the general principles of value, be compensated by a rise of the price of his commodity: indeed, until this rise has taken place, he will not bring to market the required increase of produce. But this very rise of price involves him in another necessity, for which he is not compensated. As the real wages of labour are by supposition unaltered, he must pay higher money wages to his labourers. This necessity, being common to him with all other capitalists, forms no ground for a rise of price. The price will rise, until it has placed him in as good a situation in respect of profits, as other employers of labour: it will rise so as to indemnify him for the increased labour which he must now employ in order to produce a given quantity of food: but the increased wages of that labour are a burthen common to all, and for which no one can be indemnified. It will be paid wholly from profits.

Thus we see that increased wages, when common to all descriptions of productive labourers, and when really representing a greater Cost of Labour, are always and necessarily at the expense of profits. And by reversing the cases, we should find in like manner that diminished wages, when representing a really diminished Cost of Labour, are equivalent to a rise of profits. But the opposition of pecuniary interest thus indicated between the class of capitalists and that of labourers, is to a great extent only apparent. Real wages are a very different thing from the Cost of Labour, and are generally highest at the times and places where, from the easy terms on which the land yields all the produce as yet required from it, the value and price of food being low, the cost of labour to the employer, notwithstanding its ample remuneration, is comparatively cheap, and the rate of profit consequently high. We thus obtain a full confirmation of our original theorem that Profits depend on the Cost of Labour: or, to express the meaning with still greater accuracy, the rate of profit and the cost of labour vary inversely as one another, and are joint effects of the same agencies or causes.

But does not this proposition require to be slightly modified, by making allowance for that portion (though comparatively small) of the expenses of the capitalist, which does not consist in wages paid by himself or reimbursed to previous capitalists, but in the profits of those previous capitalists? Suppose, for example, an invention in the manufacture of leather, the advantage of which should consist in rendering it unnecessary that the hides should remain for so great a length of time in the tan-pit. Shoemakers, saddlers, and other workers in leather, would save a part of that portion of the cost of their material which consists of the tanner's profits during the time his capital is locked up; and this saving, it may be said, is a source from which they might derive an increase of profit, though wages and the Cost of Labour remained exactly the same. In the case here supposed, however, the consumer alone would benefit, since the prices of shoes, harness, and all other articles into which leather enters, would fall, until the profits of the producers were reduced to the general level. To obviate this objection, let us suppose that a similar saving of expense takes place in all departments of production at once. In that case, since values and prices would not be affected, profits would probably be raised; but if we look more closely into the case we shall find, that it is because the cost of labour would be lowered. In this as in any other case of increase in the general productiveness of labour, if the labourer obtained only the same real wages, profits would be raised: but the same real wages would imply a smaller Cost of Labour; the cost of production of all things having been, by the supposition, diminished. If, on the other hand, the real wages of labour rose proportionally, and the Cost of Labour to the employer remained the same, the advances of the capitalist would bear the same ratio to his returns as before, and the rate of profit would be unaltered. The reader who may wish for a more minute examination of this point, will find it in the volume of separate Essays* to which reference has before been made.[1] The question is too intricate in comparison with its importance, to be further entered into in a work like the present; and I will merely say, that it seems to result from the considerations adduced in the Essay, that there is nothing in the case in question to affect the integrity of the theory which affirms an exact correspondence, in an inverse direction, between the rate of profit and the Cost of Labour.

[1] Essay IV on *Profits and Interest*.

BOOK IV

INFLUENCE OF THE PROGRESS OF SOCIETY ON PRODUCTION AND DISTRIBUTION

I

GENERAL CHARACTERISTICS OF A PROGRESSIVE STATE OF WEALTH

1. The three preceding Parts include as detailed a view as our limits permit, of what, by a happy generalization of a mathematical phrase, has been called the Statics of the subject. We have surveyed the field of economical facts, and have examined how they stand related to one another as causes and effects; what circumstances determine the amount of production, of employment for labour, of capital and population; what laws regulate rent, profits, and wages; under what conditions and in what proportions commodities are interchanged between individuals and between countries. We have thus obtained a collective view of the economical phenomena of society, considered as existing simultaneously. We have ascertained, to a certain extent, the principles of their interdependence; and when the state of some of the elements is known, we should now be able to infer, in a general way, the contemporaneous state of most of the others. All this, however, has only put us in possession of the economical laws of a stationary and unchanging society. We have still to consider the economical condition of mankind as liable to change, and indeed (in the more advanced portions of the race, and in all regions to which their influence reaches) as at all times undergoing progressive changes. We have to consider what these changes are, what are their laws, and what their ultimate tendencies; thereby adding a theory of motion to our theory of equilibrium—the Dynamics of political economy to the Statics.

In this inquiry, it is natural to commence by tracing the operation of known and acknowledged agencies. Whatever may be the other changes which the economy of society is destined to undergo, there is one actually in progress, concerning which there can be no dispute. In the leading countries of the world, and in all others as they come within the influence of those leading countries, there is at least one progressive movement which continues with little interruption from year to year and from generation to generation; a progress in wealth; an advancement of what is called material prosperity. All the nations which we are accustomed to call civilized, increase gradually in production and in population: and there is no reason to doubt, that not only these nations will for some time continue so to increase, but that most of the other nations of the world, including some not yet founded, will successively enter upon the same career. It will, therefore, be our first object to examine the nature and consequences of this progressive change; the elements which constitute it, and the effects it produces on the various economical facts of which we have been tracing the laws, and especially on wages, profits, rents, values, and prices.

2. Of the features which characterize this progressive economical movement of civilized nations, that which first excites attention, through its intimate connexion with the phenomena of Production, is the perpetual, and so far as human foresight can extend, the unlimited, growth of man's power over nature. Our knowledge of the properties and laws of physical objects shows no sign of approaching its ultimate boundaries: it is advancing more rapidly, and in a greater number of directions at once, than in any previous age or generation, and affording such frequent glimpses of unexplored fields beyond, as to justify the belief that our acquaintance with nature is still almost in its infancy. This increasing physical knowledge is now, too, more rapidly than at any former period, converted, by practical ingenuity, into physical power. The most marvellous of modern inventions, one which realizes the imaginary feats of the magician,

not metaphorically but literally—the electro-magnetic tele-graph—sprang into existence but a few years after the establishment of the scientific theory which it realizes and exemplifies. Lastly, the manual part of these great scientific operations is now never wanting to the intellectual: there is no difficulty in finding or forming, in a sufficient number of the working hands of the community, the skill requisite for executing the most delicate processes of the application of science to practical uses. From this union of conditions, it is impossible not to look forward to a vast multiplication and long succession of contrivances for economizing labour and increasing its produce; and to an ever wider diffusion of the use and benefit of those contrivances.

Another change, which has always hitherto characterized, and will assuredly continue to characterize, the progress of civilized society, is a continual increase of the security of person and property. The people of every country in Europe, the most backward as well as the most advanced, are, in each generation, better protected against the violence and rapa-city of one another, both by a more efficient judicature and police for the suppression of private crime, and by the decay and destruction of those mischievous privileges which en-abled certain classes of the community to prey with impunity upon the rest. They are also, in every generation, better protected, either by institutions or by manners and opinion, against arbitrary exercise of the power of government. Even in semi-barbarous Russia, acts of spoliation directed against individuals, who have not made themselves politically obnoxious, are not supposed to be now so frequent as much to affect any person's feelings of security. Taxation, in all European countries, grows less arbitrary and oppressive, both in itself and in the manner of levying it. Wars, and the destruction they cause, are now usually confined, in almost every country, to those distant and outlying possessions at which it comes into contact with savages. Even the vicissi-tudes of fortune which arise from inevitable natural cala-mities, are more and more softened to those on whom they fall, by the continual extension of the salutary practice of insurance.

Of this increased security, one of the most unfailing effects is a great increase both of production and of accumulation. Industry and frugality cannot exist, where there is not a preponderant probability that those who labour and spare will be permitted to enjoy. And the nearer this probability approaches to certainty, the more do industry and frugality become pervading qualities in a people. Experience has shown that a large proportion of the results of labour and abstinence may be taken away by fixed taxation, without impairing, and sometimes even with the effect of stimulating, the qualities from which a great production and an abundant capital take their rise. But those qualities are not proof against a high degree of uncertainty. The Government may carry off a part; but there must be assurance that it will not interfere, nor suffer any one to interfere, with the remainder.

One of the changes which most infallibly attend the progress of modern society, is an improvement in the business capacities of the general mass of mankind. I do not mean that the practical sagacity of an individual human being is greater than formerly. I am inclined to believe that economical progress has hitherto had even a contrary effect. A person of good natural endowments, in a rude state of society, can do a great number of things tolerably well, has a greater power of adapting means to ends, is more capable of extricating himself and others from an unforeseen embarrassment, than ninety-nine in a hundred of those who have known only what is called the civilized form of life. How far these points of inferiority of faculties are compensated, and by what means they might be compensated still more completely, to the civilized man as an individual being, is a question belonging to a different inquiry from the present. But to civilized human beings collectively considered, the compensation is ample. What is lost in the separate efficiency of each, is far more than made up by the greater capacity of united action. In proportion as they put off the qualities of the savage, they become amenable to discipline; capable of adhering to plans concerted beforehand, and about which they may not have been consulted; of subordinating their individual caprice to a preconceived determination, and performing severally the parts allotted to them in a combined undertaking. Works of all sorts, impracticable to the savage or the half-civilized, are daily accomplished by civilized nations, not by any greatness of faculties in the actual agents, but through the fact that each is able to rely with certainty on the others for the portion of the work which they respectively undertake. The peculiar characteristic, in short, of civilized beings, is the capacity of co-operation; and this, like other faculties, tends to improve by practice, and becomes capable of assuming a constantly wider sphere of action.

Accordingly there is no more certain incident of the progressive change taking place in society, than the continual growth of the principle and practice of co-operation. Associations of individuals voluntarily combining their small contributions, now perform works, both of an industrial and of many other characters, which no one person or small number of persons are rich enough to accomplish, or for the performance of which the few persons capable of accomplishing them were formerly enabled to exact the most inordinate remuneration. As wealth increases and business capacity improves, we may look forward to a great extension of establishments, both for industrial and other purposes, formed by the collective contributions of large numbers; establishments like those called by the technical name of joint-stock companies, or the associations less formally constituted, which are so numerous in England, to raise funds for public or philanthropic objects, or, lastly, those associations of workpeople either for production, or to buy goods for their common consumption, which are now specially known by the name of co-operative societies.

The progress which is to be expected in the physical sciences and arts, combined with the greater security of property, and greater freedom in disposing of it, which are obvious features in the civilization of modern nations, and with the more extensive and more skilful employment of the joint-stock principle, afford space and scope for an indefinite increase of capital and production, and for the increase

of population which is its ordinary accompaniment. That
the growth of population will overpass the increase of
production, there is not much reason to apprehend; and
that it should even keep pace with it, is inconsistent with the
supposition of any real improvement in the poorest classes
of the people. It is, however, quite possible that there might
be a great progress in industrial improvement, and in the
signs of what is commonly called national prosperity; a
great increase of aggregate wealth, and even, in some
respects, a better distribution of it; that not only the rich
might grow richer, but many of the poor might grow rich,
that the intermediate classes might become more numerous
and powerful, and the means of enjoyable existence be more
and more largely diffused, while yet the great class at the
base of the whole might increase in numbers only, and not
in comfort nor in cultivation. We must, therefore, in considering the effects of the progress of industry, admit as a
supposition, however greatly we deprecate as a fact, an increase of population as long-continued, as indefinite, and
possibly even as rapid, as the increase of production and
accumulation.

With these preliminary observations on the causes of
change at work in a society which is in a state of economical
progress, I proceed to a more detailed examination of the
changes themselves.

II

INFLUENCE OF THE PROGRESS
OF INDUSTRY AND POPULATION
ON VALUES AND PRICES

1. The changes which the progress of industry causes or presupposes in the circumstances of production, are necessarily attended with changes in the values of commodities.

The permanent values of all things which are neither under a natural nor under an artificial monopoly, depend, as we have seen, on their cost of production. But the increasing power which mankind are constantly acquiring over nature, increases more and more the efficiency of human exertion, or in other words, diminishes cost of production. All inventions by which a greater quantity of any commodity can be produced with the same labour, or the same quantity with less labour, or which abridge the process, so that the capital employed needs not be advanced for so long a time, lessen the cost of production of the commodity. As, however, value is relative; if inventions and improvements in production were made in all commodities, and all in the same degree, there would be no alteration in values. Things would continue to exchange for each other at the same rates as before; and mankind would obtain a greater quantity of all things in return for their labour and abstinence, without having that greater abundance measured and declared (as it is when it affects only one thing) by the diminished exchange value of the commodity.

As for prices, in these circumstances they would be affected or not, according as the improvements in production did or did not extend to the precious metals. If the materials of money were an exception to the general diminution of cost of production, the values of all other things would fall in relation to money, that is there would be a fall of general prices throughout the world. But if money, like other things, and in the same degree as other things, were obtained in greater abundance and cheapness, prices would be no more affected than values would: and there would be no visible sign in the state of the markets, of any of the changes which had taken place; except that there would be (if people continued to labour as much as before) a greater quantity of all sorts of commodities, circulated at the same prices by a greater quantity of money.

Improvements in production are not the only circumstance accompanying the progress of industry, which tends to diminish the cost of producing, or at least of obtaining, commodities. Another circumstance is the increase of intercourse between different parts of the world. As commerce extends, and the ignorant attempts to restrain it by tariffs become obsolete, commodities tend more and more to be produced in the places in which their production can be carried on at the least expense of labour and capital to mankind. As civilization spreads, and security of person and property becomes established, in parts of the world which have not hitherto had that advantage, the productive capabilities of those places are called into fuller activity, for the benefit both of their own inhabitants and of foreigners. The ignorance and misgovernment in which many of the regions most favoured by nature are still grovelling, afford work, probably, for many generations before those countries will be raised even to the present level of the most civilized parts of Europe. Much will also depend on the increasing migration of labour and capital to unoccupied parts of the earth, of which the soil, climate, and situation are found, by the ample means of exploration now possessed, to promise not only a large return to industry, but great facilities of producing commodities suited to the markets of old countries. Much as the collective industry of the earth is likely to be increased in efficiency by the extension of science and of the industrial arts, a still more active source of increased cheapness of production will be found, probably, for some time to come, in the gradually unfolding consequences of Free Trade, and in the increasing scale on which Emigration and Colonization will be carried on.

From the causes now enumerated, unless counteracted by others, the progress of things enables a country to obtain at less and less of real cost, not only its own productions but those of foreign countries. Indeed, whatever diminishes the cost of its own productions, when of an exportable character, enables it, as we have already seen, to obtain its imports at less real cost.

2. But is it the fact, that these tendencies are not counteracted? Has the progress of wealth and industry no effect in regard to cost of production, but to diminish it? Are no causes of an opposite character brought into operation by the same progress, sufficient in some cases not only to neutralize, but to overcome the former, and convert the descending movement of cost of production into an ascending movement? We are already aware that there are such causes, and that, in the case of the most important classes of commodities, food and materials, there is a tendency diametrically opposite to that of which we have been speaking. The cost of production of these commodities tends to increase.

This is not a property inherent in the commodities themselves. If population were stationary, and the produce of the earth never needed to be augmented in quantity, there would be no cause for greater cost of production. Mankind would, on the contrary, have the full benefit of all improvements in agriculture, or in the arts subsidiary to it, and there would be no difference, in this respect, between the products of agriculture and those of manufactures. The only products of industry, which, if population did not increase, would be liable to a real increase of cost of production, are those which, depending on a material which is not renewed, are either wholly or partially exhaustible; such as coal, and most if not all metals; for even iron, the most abundant as well as most useful of metallic products, which forms an ingredient of most minerals and of almost all rocks, is susceptible of exhaustion so far as regards its richest and most tractable ores.

When, however, population increases, as it has never yet failed to do when the increase of industry and of the means of subsistence made room for it, the demand for most of the productions of the earth, and particularly for food, increases in a corresponding proportion. And then comes into effect that fundamental law of production from the soil, on which we have so frequently had occasion to expatiate; the law, that increased labour, in any given state of agricultural skill, is attended with a less than proportional increase of produce. The cost of production of the fruits of the earth increases, *ceteris paribus*, with every increase of the demand.

No tendency of a like kind exists with respect to manufactured articles. The tendency is in the contrary direction. The larger the scale on which manufacturing operations are carried on, the more cheaply they can in general be performed. Mr Senior* has gone the length of enunciating as an inherent law of manufacturing industry, that in it increased production takes place at a smaller cost, while in agricultural industry increased production takes place at a greater cost. I cannot think, however, that even in manufactures, increased cheapness follows increased production by anything amounting to a law. It is a probable and usual, but not a necessary, consequence.

As manufactures, however, depend for their materials either upon agriculture, or mining, or the spontaneous produce of the earth, manufacturing industry is subject, in respect of one of its essentials, to the same law as agriculture. But the crude material generally forms so small a portion of the total cost, that any tendency which may exist to a progressive increase in that single item, is much overbalanced by the diminution continually taking place in all the other elements; to which diminution it is impossible at present to assign any limit.

The tendency, then, being to a perpetual increase of the productive power of labour in manufactures, while in agriculture and mining there is a conflict between two tendencies, the one towards an increase of productive power, the other towards a diminution of it, the cost of production being lessened by every improvement in the processes, and augmented by every addition to population; it follows that the exchange values of manufactured articles, compared with the products of agriculture and of mines, have, as population and industry advance, a certain and decided tendency to fall. Money being a product of mines, it may also be laid down as a rule, that manufactured articles tend, as society advances, to fall in money price. The industrial history of modern nations, especially during the last hundred years, fully bears out this assertion.

3. Whether agricultural produce increases in absolute as well as comparative cost of production, depends on the conflict of the two antagonist agencies, increase of population, and improvement in agricultural skill. In some, perhaps in most, states of society, (looking at the whole surface of the earth,) both agricultural skill and population are either stationary, or increase very slowly, and the cost of production of food, therefore, is nearly stationary. In a society which is advancing in wealth, population generally increases faster than agricultural skill, and food consequently tends to become more costly; but there are times when a strong impulse sets in towards agricultural improvement. Such an impulse has shown itself in Great Britain during the last twenty or thirty years. In England and Scotland agricultural skill has of late increased considerably faster than population, insomuch that food and other agricultural produce, notwithstanding the increase of people, can be grown at less cost than they were thirty years ago: and the abolition of the Corn Laws has given an additional stimulus to the spirit of improvement. In some other countries, and particularly in France, the improvement of agriculture gains ground still more decidedly upon population, because though agriculture, except in a few provinces, advances slowly, population advances still more slowly, and even with increasing slowness; its growth being kept down, not by poverty, which is diminishing, but by prudence.

Which of the two conflicting agencies is gaining upon the other at any particular time, might be conjectured with tolerable accuracy from the money price of agricultural produce (supposing bullion not to vary materially in value), provided a sufficient number of years could be taken, to form an average independent of the fluctuations of seasons.

This, however, is hardly practicable, since Mr Tooke* has shown that even so long a period as half a century may include a much greater proportion of abundant and a smaller of deficient seasons than is properly due to it. A mere average, therefore, might lead to conclusions only the more misleading, for their deceptive semblance of accuracy. There would be less danger of error in taking the average of only a small number of years, and correcting it by a conjectural allowance for the character of the seasons, than in trusting to a longer average without any such correction. It is hardly necessary to add, that in founding conclusions on quoted prices, allowance must also be made as far as possible for any changes in the general exchange value of the precious metals.[1]

4. Thus far, of the effect of the progress of society on the permanent or average values and prices of commodities. It remains to be considered, in what manner the same progress affects their fluctuations. Concerning the answer to this question there can be no doubt. It tends in a very high degree to diminish them.

In poor and backward societies, as in the East, and in Europe during the Middle Ages, extraordinary differences in the price of the same commodity might exist in places not very distant from each other, because the want of roads and canals, the imperfection of marine navigation, and the insecurity of communications generally, prevented things from being transported from the places where they were cheap to those where they were dear. The things most liable to fluctuations in value, those directly influenced by the seasons, and especially food, were seldom carried to any great distances. Each locality depended, as a general rule, on its own produce and that of its immediate neighbourhood. In most years, accordingly, there was, in some part or other of any large country, a real dearth. Almost every

[1] A still better criterion, perhaps, than that suggested in the text, would be the increase or diminution of the amount of the labourer's wages estimated in agricultural produce.

season must be unpropitious to some among the many soils and climates to be found in an extensive tract of country; but as the same season is also in general more than ordinarily favourable to others, it is only occasionally that the aggregate produce of the whole country is deficient, and even then in a less degree than that of many separate portions; while a deficiency at all considerable, extending to the whole world, is a thing almost unknown. In modern times, therefore, there is only dearth, where there formerly would have been famine, and sufficiency everywhere when anciently there would have been scarcity in some places and superfluity in others.

The same change has taken place with respect to all other articles of commerce. The safety and cheapness of communications, which enable a deficiency in one place to be supplied from the surplus of another, at a moderate or even a small advance on the ordinary price, render the fluctuations of prices much less extreme than formerly. This effect is much promoted by the existence of large capitals, belonging to what are called speculative merchants, whose business it is to buy goods in order to resell them at a profit. These dealers naturally buying things when they are cheapest, and storing them up to be brought again into the market when the price has become unusually high; the tendency of their operations is to equalize price, or at least to moderate its inequalities. The prices of things are neither so much depressed at one time, nor so much raised at another, as they would be if speculative dealers did not exist.

Speculators, therefore, have a highly useful office in the economy of society; and (contrary to common opinion) the most useful portion of the class are those who speculate in commodities affected by the vicissitudes of seasons. If there were no corn-dealers, not only would the price of corn be liable to variations much more extreme than at present, but in a deficient season the necessary supplies might not be forthcoming at all. Unless there were speculators in corn, or unless, in default of dealers, the farmers became speculators, the price in a season of abundance would fall without any limit or check, except the wasteful consumption that would invariably follow. That any part of the surplus of one year remains to supply the deficiency of another, is owing either to farmers who withhold corn from the market, or to dealers who buy it when at the cheapest and lay it up in store.

5. Among persons who have not much considered the subject, there is a notion that the gains of speculators are often made by causing an artificial scarcity; that they create a high price by their own purchases, and then profit by it. This may easily be shown to be fallacious. If a corn-dealer makes purchases on speculation, and produces a rise, when there is neither at the time nor afterwards any cause for a rise of price except his own proceedings; he no doubt appears to grow richer as long as his purchases continue, because he is a holder of an article which is quoted at a higher and higher price: but this apparent gain only seems within his reach so long as he does not attempt to realize it. If he has bought, for instance, a million of quarters, and by withholding them from the market, has raised the price ten shillings a quarter; just so much as the price has been raised by withdrawing a million quarters, will it be lowered by bringing them back, and the best that he can hope is that he will lose nothing except interest and his expenses. If by a gradual and cautious sale he is able to realize, on some portion of his stores, a part of the increased price, so also he will undoubtedly have had to pay a part of that price on some portion of his purchases. He runs considerable risk of incurring a still greater loss; for the temporary high price is very likely to have tempted others, who had no share in causing it, and who might otherwise not have found their way to his market at all, to bring their corn there, and intercept a part of the advantage. So that instead of profiting by a scarcity caused by himself, he is by no means unlikely, after buying in an average market, to be forced to sell in a superabundant one.

As an individual speculator cannot gain by a rise of price solely of his own creating, so neither can a number of speculators gain collectively by a rise which their operations have artificially produced. Some among a number of speculators may gain, by superior judgement or good fortune in selecting the time for realizing, but they make this gain at the expense, not of the consumer, but of the other speculators who are less judicious. They, in fact, convert to their own benefit the high price produced by the speculations of the others, leaving to these the loss resulting from the recoil. It is not to be denied, therefore, that speculators may enrich themselves by other people's loss. But it is by the losses of other speculators. As much must have been lost by one set of dealers as is gained by another set.

When a speculation in a commodity proves profitable to the speculators as a body, it is because, in the interval between their buying and reselling, the price rises from some cause independent of them, their only connexion with it consisting in having foreseen it. In this case, their purchases make the price begin to rise sooner than it otherwise would do, thus spreading the privation of the consumers over a longer period, but mitigating it at the time of its greatest height: evidently to the general advantage. In this, however, it is assumed that they have not overrated the rise which they looked forward to. For it often happens that speculative purchases are made in the expectation of some increase of demand, or deficiency of supply, which after all does not occur, or not to the extent which the speculator expected. In that case the speculation, instead of moderating fluctuation, has caused a fluctuation of price which otherwise would not have happened, or aggravated one which would. But in that case, the speculation is a losing one, to the speculators collectively, however much some individuals may gain by it. All that part of the rise of price by which it exceeds what there are independent grounds for, cannot give to the speculators as a body any benefit, since the price is as much depressed by their sales as it was raised by their purchases; and while they gain nothing by it, they lose, not only their trouble and expenses, but almost always much more, through the effects incident to the artificial rise of price, in checking consumption, and bringing forward

supplies from unforeseen quarters. The operations, therefore, of speculative dealers, are useful to the public whenever
profitable to themselves; and though they are sometimes
injurious to the public, by heightening the fluctuations
which their more usual office is to alleviate, yet whenever
this happens the speculators are the greatest losers. The
interest, in short, of the speculators as a body, coincides
with the interest of the public; and as they can only fail to
serve the public interest in proportion as they miss their
own, the best way to promote the one is to leave them to
pursue the other in perfect freedom.

I do not deny that speculators may aggravate a *local*
scarcity. In collecting corn from the villages to supply the
towns, they make the dearth penetrate into nooks and
corners which might otherwise have escaped from bearing
their share of it. To buy and resell in the same place, tends
to alleviate scarcity; to buy in one place and resell in
another, may increase it in the former of the two places, but
relieves it in the latter, where the price is higher, and which,
therefore, by the very supposition, is likely to be suffering
more. And these sufferings always fall hardest on the
poorest consumers, since the rich, by outbidding, can obtain
their accustomed supply undiminished if they choose. To no
persons, therefore, are the operations of corn-dealers on the
whole so beneficial as to the poor. Accidentally and exceptionally, the poor may suffer from them: it might sometimes
be more advantageous to the rural poor to have corn cheap
in winter, when they are entirely dependent on it, even if the
consequence were a dearth in spring, when they can perhaps
obtain partial substitutes. But there are no substitutes,
procurable at that season, which serve in any great degree
to replace bread-corn as the chief article of food: if there
were, its price would fall in the spring, instead of continuing, as it always does, to rise till the approach of harvest.

There is an opposition of immediate interest, at the
moment of sale, between the dealer in corn and the consumer, as there always is between the seller and the buyer:
and a time of dearth being that in which the speculator
makes his largest profits, he is an object of dislike and

jealousy at that time, to those who are suffering while he is gaining. It is an error, however, to suppose that the corn-dealer's business affords him any extraordinary profit: he makes his gains not constantly, but at particular times, and they must therefore occasionally be great, but the chances of profit in a business in which there is so much competition, cannot on the whole be greater than in other employments. A year of scarcity, in which great gains are made by corn-dealers, rarely comes to an end without a recoil which places many of them in the list of bankrupts. There have been few more promising seasons for corn-dealers than the year 1847, and seldom was there a greater break-up among the speculators than in the autumn of that year. The chances of failure, in this most precarious trade, are a set off against great occasional profits. If the corn-dealer were to sell his stores, during a dearth, at a lower price than that which the competition of the consumers assigns to him, he would make a sacrifice, to charity or philanthropy, of the fair profits of his employment, which may be quite as reasonably required from any other person of equal means. His business being a useful one, it is the interest of the public that the ordinary motives should exist for carrying it on, and that neither law nor opinion should prevent an operation beneficial to the public from being attended with as much private advantage as is compatible with full and free competition.

It appears, then, that the fluctuations of values and prices arising from variations of supply, or from alterations in real (as distinguished from speculative) demand, may be expected to become more moderate as society advances. With regard to those which arise from miscalculation, and especially from the alternations of undue expansion and excessive contraction of credit, which occupy so conspicuous a place among commercial phenomena, the same thing cannot be affirmed with equal confidence. Such vicissitudes, beginning with irrational speculation and ending with a commercial crisis, have not hitherto become either less frequent or less violent with the growth of capital and extension of industry. Rather they may be said to have become more so: in consequence, as is often said, of increased competition; but, as I prefer to say, of a low rate of profits and interest, which makes capitalists dissatisfied with the ordinary course of safe mercantile gains. The connexion of this low rate of profit with the advance of population and accumulation, is one of the points to be illustrated in the ensuing chapters.

III

INFLUENCE OF THE PROGRESS
OF INDUSTRY AND POPULATION,
ON RENTS, PROFITS, AND WAGES

1. Continuing the inquiry into the nature of the economical changes taking place in a society which is in a state of
industrial progress, we shall next consider what is the effect
of that progress on the distribution of the produce among
the various classes who share in it. We may confine our
attention to the system of distribution which is the most
complex, and which virtually includes all others—that in
which the produce of manufactures is shared between two
classes, labourers and capitalists, and the produce of agriculture among three, labourers, capitalists, and landlords.

The characteristic features of what is commonly meant by
industrial progress, resolve themselves mainly into three, increase of capital, increase of population, and improvements
in production; understanding the last expression in its widest
sense, to include the process of procuring commodities from
a distance, as well as that of producing them. The other
changes which take place are chiefly consequences of these;
as, for example, the tendency to a progressive increase of
the cost of production of food; arising from an increased
demand, which may be occasioned either by increased population, or by an increase of capital and wages, enabling the
poorer classes to increase their consumption. It will be
convenient to set out by considering each of the three
causes, as operating separately; after which we can suppose
them combined in any manner we think fit.

Let us first suppose that population increases, capital and
the arts of production remaining stationary. One of the
effects of this change of circumstances is sufficiently obvious: wages will fall; the labouring class will be reduced to
an inferior condition. The state of the capitalist, on the
contrary, will be improved. With the same capital, he can
purchase more labour, and obtain more produce. His rate

of profit is increased. The dependence of the rate of profits on the cost of labour is here verified; for the labourer obtaining a diminished quantity of commodities, and no alteration being supposed in the circumstances of their production, the diminished quantity represents a diminished cost. The labourer obtains not only a smaller real reward, but the product of a smaller quantity of labour. The first circumstance is the important one to himself, the last to his employer.

Nothing has occurred, thus far, to affect in any way the value of any commodity; and no reason, therefore, has yet shown itself, why rent should be either raised or lowered. But if we look forward another stage in the series of effects, we may see our way to such a consequence. The labourers have increased in numbers: their condition is reduced in the same proportion; the increased numbers divide among them only the produce of the same amount of labour as before. But they may economize in their other comforts, and not in their food: each may consume as much food, and of as costly a quality as previously; or they may submit to a reduction, but not in proportion to the increase of numbers. On this supposition, notwithstanding the diminution of real wages, the increased population will require an increased quantity of food. But since industrial skill and knowledge are supposed to be stationary, more food can only be obtained by resorting to worse land, or to methods of cultivation which are less productive in proportion to the outlay. Capital for this extension of agriculture will not be wanting; for though, by hypothesis, no addition takes place to the capital in existence, a sufficient amount can be spared from the industry which previously supplied the other and less pressing wants which the labourers have been obliged to curtail. The additional supply of food, therefore, will be produced, but produced at a greater cost; and the exchange value of agricultural produce must rise. It may be objected, that profits having risen, the extra cost of producing food can be defrayed from profits, without any increase of price. It could, undoubtedly, but it will not; because if it did, the agriculturist would be placed in an inferior position to other capitalists. The increase of profits, being the effect of diminished wages, is common to all employers of labour. The increased expenses arising from the necessity of a more costly cultivation, affect the agriculturist alone. For this peculiar burthen he must be peculiarly compensated, whether the general rate of profit be high or low. He will not submit indefinitely to a deduction from his profits, to which other capitalists are not subject. He will not extend his cultivation by laying out fresh capital, unless for a return sufficient to yield him as high a profit as could be obtained by the same capital in other investments. The value, therefore, of his commodity will rise, and rise in proportion to the increased cost. The farmer will thus be indemnified for the burthen which is peculiar to himself, and will also enjoy the augmented rate of profit which is common to all capitalists.

It follows, from principles with which we are already familiar, that in these circumstances rent will rise. Any land can afford to pay, and under free competition will pay, a rent equal to the excess of its produce above the return to an equal capital on the worst land, or under the least favourable conditions. Whenever, therefore, agriculture is driven to descend to worse land, or more onerous processes, rent rises. Its rise will be twofold, for, in the first place, rent in kind, or corn rent, will rise; and in the second, since the value of agricultural produce has also risen, rent, estimated in manufactured or foreign commodities (which is represented, *ceteris paribus*, by money rent) will rise still more.

The steps of the process (if, after what has been formerly said, it is necessary to retrace them) are as follows. Corn rises in price, to repay with the ordinary profit the capital required for producing additional corn on worse land or by more costly processes. So far as regards this additional corn, the increased price is but an equivalent for the additional expense; but the rise, extending to all corn, affords on all, except the last produced, an extra profit. If the farmer was accustomed to produce 100 quarters of wheat at 40s., and 120 quarters are now required, of which the last twenty cannot be produced under 45s., he obtains the extra five shillings on the entire 120 quarters, and not on the last twenty alone. He has thus an extra £25 beyond the ordinary profits, and this, in a state of free competition, he will not be able to retain. He cannot however be compelled to give it up to the consumer, since a less price than 45s. would be inconsistent with the production of the last twenty quarters. The price, then, will remain at 45s., and the £25 will be transferred by competition not to the consumer but to the landlord. A rise of rents is therefore inevitably consequent on an increased demand for agricultural produce, when unaccompanied by increased facilities for its production. A truth which, after this final illustration, we may henceforth take for granted.

The new element now introduced—an increased demand for food—besides occasioning an increase of rent, still further disturbs the distribution of the produce between capitalists and labourers. The increase of population will have diminished the reward of labour: and if its cost is diminished as greatly as its real remuneration, profits will be increased by the full amount. If, however, the increase of population leads to an increased production of food, which cannot be supplied but at an enhanced cost of production, the cost of labour will not be so much diminished as the real reward of it, and profits, therefore, will not be so much raised. It is even possible that they might not be raised at all. The labourers may previously have been so well provided for, that the whole of what they now lose may be struck off from their other indulgences, and they may not, either by necessity or choice, undergo any reduction in the quantity or quality of their food. To produce the food for the increased number may be attended with such an increase of expense, that wages, though reduced in quantity, may represent as great a cost, may be the product of as much labour, as before, and the capitalist may not be at all benefited. On this supposition the loss to the labourer is partly absorbed in the additional labour required for producing the last instalment of agricultural produce; and the remainder is gained by the landlord, the only sharer who always benefits by an increase of population.

2. Let us now reverse our hypothesis, and instead of supposing capital stationary and population advancing, let us suppose capital advancing and population stationary; the facilities of production, both natural and acquired, being, as before, unaltered. The real wages of labour, instead of falling, will now rise; and since the cost of production of the things consumed by the labourer is not diminished, this rise of wages implies an equivalent increase of the cost of labour, and diminution of profits. To state the same deduction in other terms; the labourers not being more numerous, and the productive power of their labour being only the same as before, there is no increase of the produce; the increase of wages, therefore, must be at the charge of the capitalist. It is not impossible that the cost of labour might be increased in even a greater ratio than its real remuneration. The improved condition of the labourers may increase the demand for food. The labourers may have been so ill off before, as not to have food enough; and may now consume more: or they may choose to expend their increased means partly or wholly in a more costly quality of food, requiring more labour and more land; wheat, for example, instead of oats, or potatoes. This extension of agriculture implies, as usual, a greater cost of production and a higher price, so that besides the increase of the cost of labour arising from the increase of its reward, there will be a further increase (and an additional fall of profits) from the increased costliness of the commodities of which that reward consists. The same causes will produce a rise of rent. What the capitalists lose, above what the labourers gain, is partly transferred to the landlord, and partly swallowed up in the cost of growing food on worse land or by a less productive process.

3. Having disposed of the two simple cases, an increasing population and stationary capital, and an increasing capital and stationary population, we are prepared to take into consideration the mixed case, in which the two elements of expansion are combined, both population and capital increasing. If either element increases faster than the other, the case is so far assimilated with one or other of the two

preceding: we shall suppose them, therefore, to increase with equal rapidity; the test of equality being, that each labourer obtains the same commodities as before, and the same quantity of those commodities. Let us examine what will be the effect, on rent and profits, of this double progress.

Population having increased, without any falling off in the labourer's condition, there is of course a demand for more food. The arts of production being supposed stationary, this food must be produced at an increased cost. To compensate for this greater cost of the additional food, the price of agricultural produce must rise. The rise extending over the whole amount of food produced, though the increased expenses only apply to a part, there is a greatly increased extra profit, which, by competition, is transferred to the landlord. Rent will rise both in quantity of produce and in cost; while wages, being supposed to be the same in quantity, will be greater in cost. The labourer obtaining the same amount of necessaries, money wages have risen; and as the rise is common to all branches of production, the capitalist cannot indemnify himself by changing his employment, and the loss must be borne by profits.

It appears, then, that the tendency of an increase of capital and population is to add to rent at the expense of profits: though rent does not gain all that profits lose, a part being absorbed in increased expenses of production, that is, in hiring or feeding a greater number of labourers to obtain a given amount of agricultural produce. By profits, must of course be understood the *rate* of profit; for a lower rate of profit on a larger capital may yield a larger gross profit, considered absolutely, though a smaller in proportion to the entire produce.

This tendency of profits to fall, is from time to time counteracted by improvements in production: whether arising from increase of knowledge, or from an increased use of the knowledge already possessed. This is the third of the three elements, the effects of which on the distribution of the produce we undertook to investigate; and the investigation will be facilitated by supposing, as in the case of the other two elements, that it operates, in the first instance, alone.

4. Let us then suppose capital and population stationary, and a sudden improvement made in the arts of production; by the invention of more efficient machines, or less costly processes, or by obtaining access to cheaper commodities through foreign trade.

The improvement may either be in some of the necessaries or indulgences which enter into the habitual consumption of the labouring class; or it may be applicable only to luxuries consumed exclusively by richer people. Very few, however, of the great industrial improvements are altogether of this last description. Agricultural improvements, except such as specially relate to some of the rarer and more peculiar products, act directly upon the principal objects of the labourer's expenditure. The steam-engine, and every other invention which affords a manageable power, are applicable to all things, and of course to those consumed by the labourer. Even the power-loom and the spinning-jenny, though applied to the most delicate fabrics, are available no less for the coarse cottons and woollens worn by the labouring class. All improvements in locomotion cheapen the transport of necessaries as well as of luxuries. Seldom is a new branch of trade opened, without, either directly or in some indirect way, causing some of the articles which the mass of the people consume to be either produced or imported at smaller cost. It may safely be affirmed, therefore, that improvements in production generally tend to cheapen the commodities on which the wages of the labouring class are expended.

In so far as the commodities affected by an improvement are those which the labourers generally do not consume, the improvement has no effect in altering the distribution of the produce. Those particular commodities, indeed, are cheapened; being produced at less cost, they fall in value and in price, and all who consume them, whether landlords, capitalists, or skilled and privileged labourers, obtain increased means of enjoyment. The rate of profits, however, is not raised. There is a larger gross profit, reckoned in quantity of commodities. But the capital also, if estimated in those commodities, has risen in value. The profit is the same percentage on the capital that it was before. The capitalists are not benefited as capitalists, but as consumers. The landlords and the privileged classes of labourers, if they are consumers of the same commodities, share the same benefit.

The case is different with improvements which diminish the cost of production of the necessaries of life, or of commodities which enter habitually into the consumption of the great mass of labourers. The play of the different forces being here rather complex, it is necessary to analyse it with some minuteness.

As formerly observed,[1] there are two kinds of agricultural improvements. Some consist in a mere saving of labour, and enable a given quantity of food to be produced at less cost, but not on a smaller surface of land than before. Others enable a given extent of land to yield not only the same produce with less labour, but a greater produce; so that if no greater produce is required, a part of the land already under culture may be dispensed with. As the part rejected will be the least productive portion, the market will thenceforth be regulated by a better description of land than what was previously the worst under cultivation.

To place the effect of the improvement in a clear light, we must suppose it to take place suddenly, so as to leave no time during its introduction, for any increase of capital or of population. Its first effect will be a fall of the value and price of agricultural produce. This is a necessary consequence of either kind of improvement, but especially of the last.

An improvement of the first kind, not increasing the produce, does not dispense with any portion of the land; the margin of cultivation (as Dr Chalmers terms it) remains where it was; agriculture does not recede, either in extent of cultivated land, or in elaborateness of method: and the price continues to be regulated by the same land, and by the same

[1] [Bk. I, Ch. XII. Not included in present edn.]

capital, as before. But since that land or capital, and all other land or capital which produces food, now yields its produce at smaller cost, the price of food will fall proportionally. If one-tenth of the expense of production has been saved, the price of produce will fall one-tenth.

But suppose the improvement to be of the second kind; enabling the land to produce, not only the same corn with one-tenth less labour, but a tenth more corn with the same labour. Here the effect is still more decided. Cultivation can now be contracted, and the market supplied from a smaller quantity of land. Even if this smaller surface of land were of the same average quality as the larger surface, the price would fall one-tenth, because the same produce would be obtained with a tenth less labour. But since the portion of land abandoned will be the least fertile portion, the price of produce will thenceforth be regulated by a better quality of land than before. In addition, therefore, to the original diminution of one-tenth in the cost of production, there will be a further diminution, corresponding with the recession of the 'margin' of agriculture to land of greater fertility. There will thus be a twofold fall of price.

Let us now examine the effect of the improvements, thus suddenly made, on the division of the produce; and in the first place, on rent. By the former of the two kinds of improvement, rent would be diminished. By the second, it would be diminished still more.

Suppose that the demand for food requires the cultivation of three qualities of land, yielding, on an equal surface, and at an equal expense, 100, 80, and 60 bushels of wheat. The price of wheat will, on the average, be just sufficient to enable the third quality to be cultivated with the ordinary profit. The first quality therefore will yield forty and the second twenty bushels of extra profit, constituting the rent of the landlord. And first, let an improvement be made, which, without enabling more corn to be grown, enables the same corn to be grown with one-fourth less labour. The price of wheat will fall one-fourth, and 80 bushels will be sold for the price for which 60 were sold before. But the produce of the land which produces 60 bushels is still required, and the expenses being as much reduced as the price, that land can still be cultivated with the ordinary profit. The first and second qualities will therefore continue to yield a surplus of 40 and 20 bushels, and corn rent will remain the same as before. But corn having fallen in price one-fourth, the same corn rent is equivalent to a fourth less of money and of all other commodities. So far, therefore, as the landlord expends his income in manufactured or foreign products, he is one-fourth worse off than before. His income as landlord is reduced to three-quarters of its amount: it is only as a consumer of corn that he is as well off.

If the improvement is of the other kind, rent will fall in a still greater ratio. Suppose that the amount of produce which the market requires, can be grown not only with a fourth less labour, but on a fourth less land. If all the land already in cultivation continued to be cultivated, it would yield a produce much larger than necessary. Land, equivalent to a fourth of the produce, must now be abandoned: and as the third quality yielded exactly one-fourth, (being 60 out of 240,) that quality will go out of cultivation. The 240 bushels can now be grown on land of the first and second qualities only; being, on the first, 100 bushels plus one-third, or $133\frac{1}{3}$ bushels; on the second, 80 bushels plus one-third, or $106\frac{2}{3}$ bushels; together 240. The second quality of land, instead of the third, is now the lowest, and regulates the price. Instead of 60, it is sufficient if $106\frac{2}{3}$ bushels repay the capital with the ordinary profit. The price of wheat will consequently fall, not in the ratio of 60 to 80, as in the other case, but in the ratio of 60 to $106\frac{2}{3}$. Even this gives an insufficient idea of the degree in which rent will be affected. The whole produce of the second quality of land will now be required to repay the expenses of production. That land, being the worst in cultivation, will pay no rent. And the first quality will only yield the difference between $133\frac{1}{3}$ bushels and $106\frac{2}{3}$, being $26\frac{2}{3}$ bushels instead of 40. The landlords collectively will have lost $33\frac{1}{3}$ out of 60 bushels in corn rent alone, while the value and price of what is left will have been diminished in the ratio of 60 to $106\frac{2}{3}$.

It thus appears, that the interest of the landlord is decidedly hostile to the sudden and general introduction of agricultural improvements. This assertion has been called a paradox, and made a ground for accusing its first promulgator, Ricardo, of great intellectual perverseness, to say nothing worse. I cannot discern in what the paradox consists; and the obliquity of vision seems to me to be on the side of his assailants. The opinion is only made to appear absurd by stating it unfairly. If the assertion were that a landlord is injured by the improvement of his estate, it would certainly be indefensible; but what is asserted is, that he is injured by the improvement of the estates of other people, although his own is included. Nobody doubts that he would gain greatly by the improvement if he could keep it to himself, and unite the two benefits, an increased produce from his land, and a price as high as before. But if the increase of produce took place simultaneously on all lands, the price would not be as high as before; and there is nothing unreasonable in supposing that the landlords would be, not benefited, but injured. It is admitted that whatever permanently reduces the price of produce diminishes rent: and it is quite in accordance with common notions to suppose that if, by the increased productiveness of land, less land were required for cultivation, its value, like that of other articles for which the demand had diminished, would fall.

I am quite willing to admit that rents have not really been lowered by the progress of agricultural improvement; but why? Because improvement has never in reality been sudden, but always slow; at no time much outstripping, and often falling far short of, the growth of capital and population, which tends as much to raise rent, as the other to lower it, and which is enabled, as we shall presently see, to raise it much higher, by means of the additional margin afforded by improvements in agriculture. First, however, we must examine in what manner the sudden cheapening of agricultural produce would affect profits and wages.

In the beginning, money wages would probably remain the same as before, and the labourers would have the full benefit of the cheapness. They would be enabled to increase their consumption either of food or of other articles, and would receive the same cost, and a greater quantity. So far, profits would be unaffected. But the permanent remuneration of the labourers essentially depends on what we have called their habitual standard; the extent of the requirements which, as a class, they insist on satisfying before they choose to have children. If their tastes and requirements receive a durable impress from the sudden improvement in their condition, the benefit to the class will be permanent. But the same cause which enables them to purchase greater comforts and indulgences with the same wages, would enable them to purchase the same amount of comforts and indulgences with lower wages; and a greater population may now exist, without reducing the labourers below the condition to which they are accustomed. Hitherto this and no other has been the use which the labourers have commonly made of any increase of their means of living; they have treated it simply as convertible into food for a greater number of children. It is probable, therefore, that population would be stimulated, and that after the lapse of a generation the real wages of labour would be no higher than before the improvement: the reduction being partly brought about by a fall of money wages, and partly through the price of food, the cost of which, from the demand occasioned by the increase of population, would be increased. To the extent to which money wages fell, profits would rise; the capitalist obtaining a greater quantity of equally efficient labour by the same outlay of capital. We thus see that a diminution of the cost of living, whether arising from agricultural improvements or from the importation of foreign produce, if the habits and requirements of the labourers are not raised, usually lowers money wages and rent, and raises the general rate of profit.

What is true of improvements which cheapen the production of food, is true also of the substitution of a cheaper for a more costly variety of it. The same land yields to the same labour a much greater quantity of human nutriment in the form of maize or potatoes, than in the form of wheat. If the labourers were to give up bread, and feed only on those cheaper products, taking as their compensation not a greater quantity of other consumable commodities, but earlier marriages and larger families, the cost of labour would be much diminished, and if labour continued equally efficient, profits would rise; while rent would be much lowered, since food for the whole population could be raised on half or a third part of the land now sown with corn. At the same time, it being evident that land too barren to be cultivated for wheat might be made in case of necessity to yield potatoes sufficient to support the little labour necessary for producing them, cultivation might ultimately descend lower, and rent eventually rise higher, on a potato or maize system, than on a corn system; because the land would be capable of feeding a much larger population before reaching the limit of its powers.

If the improvement, which we suppose to take place, is not in the production of food, but of some manufactured article consumed by the labouring class, the effect on wages and profits will at first be the same; but the effect on rent very different. It will not be lowered; it will even, if the ultimate effect of the improvement is an increase of population, be raised: in which last case profits will be lowered. The reasons are too evident to require statement.

5. We have considered, on the one hand, the manner in which the distribution of the produce into rent, profits, and wages, is affected by the ordinary increase of population and capital, and on the other, how it is affected by improvements in production, and more especially in agriculture. We have found that the former cause lowers profits, and raises rent and the cost of labour: while the tendency of agricultural improvements is to diminish rent; and all improvements which cheapen any article of the labourer's consumption, tend to diminish the cost of labour and to raise profits. The tendency of each cause in its separate state being thus ascertained, it is easy to determine the tendency of the actual course of things, in which the two movements are going on simultaneously, capital and population increasing with tolerable steadiness, while improvements in agriculture

are made from time to time, and the knowledge and practice of improved methods become diffused gradually through the community.

The habits and requirements of the labouring classes being given (which determine their real wages), rents, profits, and money wages at any given time, are the result of the composition of these rival forces. If during any period agricultural improvement advances faster than population, rent and money wages during that period will tend downward, and profits upward. If population advances more rapidly than agricultural improvement, either the labourers will submit to a reduction in the quantity or quality of their food, or if not, rent and money wages will progressively rise, and profits will fall.

Agricultural skill and knowledge are of slow growth, and still slower diffusion. Inventions and discoveries, too, occur only occasionally, while the increase of population and capital are continuous agencies. It therefore seldom happens that improvement, even during a short time, has so much the start of population and capital as actually to lower rent, or raise the rate of profits. There are many countries in which the growth of population and capital is not rapid, but in these agricultural improvement is less active still. Population almost everywhere treads close on the heels of agricultural improvement, and effaces its effects as fast as they are produced.

The reason why agricultural improvement seldom lowers rent, is that it seldom cheapens food, but only prevents it from growing dearer; and seldom, if ever, throws land out of cultivation, but only enables worse and worse land to be taken in for the supply of an increasing demand. What is sometimes called the natural state of a country which is but half cultivated, namely, that the land is highly productive, and food obtained in great abundance by little labour, is only true of unoccupied countries colonized by a civilized people. In the United States the worst land in cultivation is of a high quality (except sometimes in the immediate vicinity of markets or means of conveyance, where a bad quality is compensated by a good situation); and even if no further improvements were made in agriculture or locomotion, cultivation would have many steps yet to descend, before the increase of population and capital would be brought to a stand; but in Europe five hundred years ago, though so thinly peopled in comparison to the present population, it is probable that the worst land under the plough was, from the rude state of agriculture, quite as unproductive as the worst land now cultivated; and that cultivation had approached as near to the ultimate limit of profitable tillage, in those times as in the present. What the agricultural improvements since made have really done is, by increasing the capacity of production of land in general, to enable tillage to extend downwards to a much worse natural quality of land than the worst which at that time would have admitted of cultivation by a capitalist for profit; thus rendering a much greater increase of capital and population possible, and removing always a little and a little further off, the barrier which restrains them; population meanwhile always pressing so hard against the barrier, that there is never any visible margin left for it to seize, every inch of ground made vacant for it by improvement being at once filled up by its advancing columns. Agricultural improvement may thus be considered to be not so much a counter-force conflicting with increase of population, as a partial relaxation of the bonds which confine that increase.

The effects produced on the division of the produce by an increase of production, under the joint influence of increase of population and capital and improvements of agriculture, are very different from those deduced from the hypothetical cases previously discussed. In particular, the effect on rent is most materially different. We remarked that—while a great agricultural improvement made suddenly and universally would in the first instance inevitably lower rent—such improvements enable rent, in the progress of society, to rise gradually to a much higher limit than it could otherwise attain, since they enable a much lower quality of land to be ultimately cultivated. But in the case we are now supposing, which nearly corresponds to the usual course of things, this ultimate effect becomes the immediate effect. Suppose

cultivation to have reached, or almost reached, the utmost
limit permitted by the state of the industrial arts, and rent,
therefore, to have attained nearly the highest point to which
it can be carried by the progress of population and capital,
with the existing amount of skill and knowledge. If a great
agricultural improvement were suddenly introduced, it might
throw back rent for a considerable space, leaving it to regain
its lost ground by the progress of population and capital,
and afterwards to go on further. But, taking place, as such
improvement always does, very gradually, it causes no
retrograde movement of either rent or cultivation; it merely
enables the one to go on rising, and the other extending,
long after they must otherwise have stopped. It would do
this even without the necessity of resorting to a worse
quality of land; simply by enabling the lands already in
cultivation to yield a greater produce, with no increase of
the proportional cost. If by improvements of agriculture all
the lands in cultivation could be made, even with double
labour and capital, to yield a double produce, (supposing
that in the meantime population increased so as to require
this double quantity) all rents would be doubled.

To illustrate the point, let us revert to the numerical
example in a former page. Three qualities of land yield
respectively 100, 80, and 60 bushels to the same outlay on
the same extent of surface. If No. 1 could be made to yield
200, No. 2, 160, and No. 3, 120 bushels, at only double the
expense, and therefore without any increase of the cost of
production, and if the population, having doubled, required
all this increased quantity, the rent of No. 1 would be 80
bushels instead of 40, and of No. 2, 40 instead of 20, while
the price and value per bushel would be the same as before:
so that corn rent and money rent would both be doubled. I
need not point out the difference between this result, and
what we have shown would take place if there were an
improvement in production without the accompaniment of
an increased demand for food.

Agricultural improvement, then, is always ultimately, and
in the manner in which it generally takes place also immediately, beneficial to the landlord. We may add, that when

it takes place in that manner, it is beneficial to no one else. When the demand for produce fully keeps pace with the increased capacity of production, food is not cheapened; the labourers are not, even temporarily, benefited; the cost of labour is not diminished, nor profits raised. There is a greater aggregate production, a greater produce divided among the labourers, and a larger gross profit; but the wages being shared among a larger population, and the profits spread over a larger capital, no labourer is better off, nor does any capitalist derive from the same amount of capital a larger income.

The result of this long investigation may be summed up as follows. The economical progress of a society constituted of landlords, capitalists, and labourers, tends to the progressive enrichment of the landlord class; while the cost of the labourer's subsistence tends on the whole to increase, and profits to fall. Agricultural improvements are a counteracting force to the two last effects; but the first, though a case is conceivable in which it would be temporarily checked, is ultimately in a high degree promoted by those improvements; and the increase of population tends to transfer all the benefits derived from agricultural improvement to the landlords alone. What other consequences, in addition to these, or in modification of them, arise from the industrial progress of a society thus constituted, I shall endeavour to show in the succeeding chapter.

IV

OF THE TENDENCY OF PROFITS TO A MINIMUM

1. The tendency of profits to fall as society advances, which has been brought to notice in the preceding chapter, was early recognised by writers on industry and commerce; but the laws which govern profits not being then understood, the phenomenon was ascribed to a wrong cause. Adam Smith considered profits to be determined by what he called the competition of capital; and concluded that when capital increased, this competition must likewise increase, and profits must fall. It is not quite certain what sort of competition Adam Smith had here in view. His words in the chapter on Profits of Stock[1] are, "When the stocks of many rich merchants are turned into the same trade, their mutual competition naturally tends to lower its profits; and when there is a like increase of stock in all the different trades carried on in the same society, the same competition must produce the same effect in them all." This passage would lead us to infer that, in Adam Smith's opinion, the manner in which the competition of capital lowers profits is by lowering prices; that being usually the mode in which an increased investment of capital in any particular trade, lowers the profits of that trade. But if this was his meaning, he overlooked the circumstance, that the fall of price, which if confined to one commodity really does lower the profits of the producer, ceases to have that effect as soon as it extends to all commodities; because, when all things have fallen, nothing has really fallen, except nominally; and even computed in money, the expenses of every producer have diminished as much as his returns. Unless indeed labour be the one commodity which has not fallen in money price, when all other things have: if so, what has really taken place is a rise of wages; and it is that, and not the fall of prices, which has lowered the profits of capital. There is another

[1] *Wealth of Nations*, bk. i, ch. 9.

thing which escaped the notice of Adam Smith; that the supposed universal fall of prices, through increased competition of capitals, is a thing which cannot take place. Prices are not determined by the competition of the sellers only, but also by that of the buyers; by demand as well as supply. The demand which affects money prices consists of all the money in the hands of the community, destined to be laid out in commodities; and as long as the proportion of this to the commodities is not diminished, there is no fall of general prices. Now, howsoever capital may increase, and give rise to an increased production of commodities, a full share of the capital will be drawn to the business of producing or importing money, and the quantity of money will be augmented in an equal ratio with the quantity of commodities. For if this were not the case, and if money, therefore, were, as the theory supposes, perpetually acquiring increased purchasing power, those who produced or imported it would obtain constantly increasing profits; and this could not happen without attracting labour and capital to that occupation from other employments. If a general fall of prices, and increased value of money, were really to occur, it could only be as a consequence of increased cost of production, from the gradual exhaustion of the mines.

It is not tenable, therefore, in theory, that the increase of capital produces, or tends to produce, a general decline of money prices. Neither is it true, that any general decline of prices, as capital increased, has manifested itself in fact. The only things observed to fall in price with the progress of society, are those in which there have been improvements in production, greater than have taken place in the production of the precious metals; as for example, all spun and woven fabrics. Other things, again, instead of falling, have risen in price, because their cost of production, compared with that of gold and silver, has increased. Among these are all kinds of food, comparison being made with a much earlier period of history. The doctrine, therefore, that competition of capital lowers profits by lowering prices, is incorrect in fact, as well as unsound in principle.

But it is not certain that Adam Smith really held that doctrine; for his language on the subject is wavering and unsteady, denoting the absence of a definite and well-digested opinion. Occasionally he seems to think that the mode in which the competition of capital lowers profits, is by raising wages. And when speaking of the rate of profit in new colonies, he seems on the very verge of grasping the complete theory of the subject. 'As the colony increases, the profits of stock gradually diminish. When the most fertile and best situated lands have been all occupied, less profit can be made by the cultivators of what is inferior both in soil and situation.' Had Adam Smith meditated longer on the subject, and systematized his view of it by harmonizing with each other the various glimpses which he caught of it from different points, he would have perceived that this last is the true cause of the fall of profits usually consequent upon increase of capital.

2. Mr Wakefield,* in his Commentary on Adam Smith, and his important writings on Colonization, takes a much clearer view of the subject, and arrives, through a substantially correct series of deductions, at practical conclusions which appear to me just and important; but he is not equally happy in incorporating his valuable speculations with the results of previous thought, and reconciling them with other truths. Some of the theories of Dr Chalmers, in his chapter 'On the Increase and Limits of Capital', and the two chapters which follow it, coincide in their tendency and spirit with those of Mr Wakefield; but Dr Chalmers' ideas, though delivered, as is his custom, with a most attractive semblance of clearness, are really on this subject much more confused than even those of Adam Smith, and more decidedly infected with the often refuted notion that the competition of capital lowers general prices; the subject of Money apparently not having been included among the parts of Political Economy which this acute and vigorous writer had carefully studied.

Mr Wakefield's explanation of the fall of profits is briefly this. Production is limited not solely by the quantity of capital and of labour, but also by the extent of the 'field of employment'. The field of employment for capital is two-fold; the land of the country, and the capacity of foreign markets to take its manufactured commodities. On a limited extent of land, only a limited quantity of capital can find employment at a profit. As the quantity of capital approaches this limit, profit falls; when the limit is attained, profit is annihilated; and can only be restored through an extension of the field of employment, either by the acquisition of fertile land, or by opening new markets in foreign countries, from which food and materials can be purchased with the products of domestic capital. These propositions are, in my opinion, substantially true; and, even to the phraseology in which they are expressed, considered as adapted to popular and practical rather than scientific uses, I have nothing to object. The error which seems to me imputable to Mr Wakefield is that of supposing his doctrines to be in contradiction to the principles of the best school of preceding political economists, instead of being, as they really are, corollaries from those principles; though corollaries which, perhaps, would not always have been admitted by those political economists themselves.

The most scientific treatment of the subject which I have met with, is in an essay on the effects of Machinery, published in the *Westminster Review* for January 1826, by Mr William Ellis;[1] which was doubtless unknown to Mr Wakefield, but which had preceded him, though by a different path, in several of his leading conclusions. This essay excited little notice, partly from being published anonymously in a periodical, and partly because it was much in advance of the state of political economy at the time. In Mr Ellis's view of the subject, the questions and difficulties raised by Mr Wakefield's speculations and by those of Dr Chalmers, find a solution consistent with the principles of political economy laid down in the present treatise.

[1] Now so much better known through his apostolic exertions, by pen, purse, and person, for the improvement of popular education, and especially for the introduction into it of the elements of practical Political Economy. [*JSM refers to* 'Employment of Machinery,' *Westminster Review*, 5 (1826), 101–30.]

3. There is at every time and place some particular rate of profit, which is the lowest that will induce the people of that country and time to accumulate savings, and to employ those savings productively. This minimum rate of profit varies according to circumstances. It depends on two elements. One is, the strength of the effective desire of accumulation; the comparative estimate made by the people of that place and era, of future interests when weighed against present. This element chiefly affects the inclination to save. The other element, which affects not so much the willingness to save as the disposition to employ savings productively, is the degree of security of capital engaged in industrial operations. A state of general insecurity, no doubt affects also the disposition to save. A hoard may be a source of additional danger to its reputed possessor. But as it may also be a powerful means of averting dangers, the effects in this respect may perhaps be looked upon as balanced. But in employing any funds which a person may possess as capital on his own account, or in lending it to others to be so employed, there is always some additional risk, over and above that incurred by keeping it idle in his own custody. This extra risk is great in proportion as the general state of society is insecure: it may be equivalent to twenty, thirty, or fifty per cent, or to no more than one or two; something, however, it must always be: and for this, the expectation of profit must be sufficient to compensate.

There would be adequate motives for a certain amount of saving, even if capital yielded no profit. There would be an inducement to lay by in good times a provision for bad; to reserve something for sickness and infirmity, or as a means of leisure and independence in the latter part of life, or a help to children in the outset of it. Savings, however, which have only these ends in view, have not much tendency to increase the amount of capital permanently in existence. These motives only prompt persons to save at one period of life what they purpose to consume at another, or what will be consumed by their children before they can completely provide for themselves. The savings by which an addition is made to the national capital, usually emanate from the desire of persons to improve what is termed their condition in life, or to make a provision for children or others, independent of their exertions. Now, to the strength of these inclinations it makes a very material difference how much of the desired object can be effected by a given amount and duration of self-denial; which again depends on the rate of profit. And there is in every country some rate of profit, below which persons in general will not find sufficient motive to save for the mere purpose of growing richer, or of leaving others better off than themselves. Any accumulation, therefore, by which the general capital is increased, requires as its necessary condition a certain rate of profit; a rate which an average person will deem to be an equivalent for abstinence, with the addition of a sufficient insurance against risk. There are always some persons in whom the effective desire of accumulation is above the average, and to whom less than this rate of profit is a sufficient inducement to save; but these merely step into the place of others whose taste for expense and indulgence is beyond the average, and who, instead of saving, perhaps even dissipate what they have received.

I have already observed that this minimum rate of profit, less than which is not consistent with the further increase of capital, is lower in some states of society than in others; and I may add, that the kind of social progress characteristic of our present civilization tends to diminish it. In the first place, one of the acknowledged effects of that progress is an increase of general security. Destruction by wars, and spoliation by private or public violence, are less and less to be apprehended: and the improvements which may be looked for in education and in the administration of justice, or, in their default, increased regard for opinion, afford a growing protection against fraud and reckless mismanagement. The risks attending the investment of savings in productive employment require, therefore, a smaller rate of profit to compensate for them than was required a century ago, and will hereafter require less than at present. In the second place, it is also one of the consequences of civilization that mankind become less the slaves of the moment, and more habituated to carry their desires and purposes forward into a distant future. This increase of providence is a natural result of the increased assurance with which futurity can be looked forward to; and is, besides, favoured by most of the influences which an industrial life exercises over the passions and inclinations of human nature. In proportion as life has fewer vicissitudes, as habits become more fixed, and great prizes are less and less to be hoped for by any other means than long perseverance, mankind become more willing to sacrifice present indulgence for future objects. This increased capacity of forethought and self-control may assuredly find other things to exercise itself upon than increase of riches, and some considerations connected with this topic will shortly be touched upon. The present kind of social progress, however, decidedly tends, though not perhaps to increase the desire of accumulation, yet to weaken the obstacles to it, and to diminish the amount of profit which people absolutely require as an inducement to save and accumulate. For these two reasons, diminution of risk and increase of providence, a profit or interest of three or four per cent is as sufficient a motive to the increase of capital in England at the present day, as thirty or forty per cent in the Burmese Empire, or in England at the time of King John. In Holland during the last century a return of two per cent, on government security, was consistent with an undiminished, if not with an increasing capital. But though the minimum rate of profit is thus liable to vary, and though to specify exactly what it is would at any given time be impossible, such a minimum always exists; and whether it be high or low, when once it is reached, no further increase of capital can for the present take place. The country has then attained what is known to political economists under the name of the stationary state.

4. We now arrive at the fundamental proposition which this chapter is intended to inculcate. When a country has long possessed a large production, and a large net income to make savings from, and when, therefore, the means have long existed of making a great annual addition to capital;

(the country not having, like America, a large reserve of fertile land still unused;) it is one of the characteristics of such a country, that the rate of profit is habitually within, as it were, a hand's breadth of the minimum, and the country therefore on the very verge of the stationary state. By this I do not mean that this state is likely, in any of the great countries of Europe, to be soon actually reached, or that capital does not still yield a profit considerably greater than what is barely sufficient to induce the people of those countries to save and accumulate. My meaning is, that it would require but a short time to reduce profits to the minimum, if capital continued to increase at its present rate, and no circumstances having a tendency to raise the rate of profit occurred in the meantime. The expansion of capital would soon reach its ultimate boundary, if the boundary itself did not continually open and leave more space.

In England, the ordinary rate of interest on government securities, in which the risk is next to nothing, may be estimated at a little more than three per cent: in all other investments, therefore, the interest or profit calculated upon (exclusively of what is properly a remuneration for talent or exertion) must be as much more than this amount, as is equivalent to the degree of risk to which the capital is thought to be exposed. Let us suppose that in England even so small a net profit as one per cent, exclusive of insurance against risk, would constitute a sufficient inducement to save, but that less than this would not be a sufficient inducement. I now say, that the mere continuance of the present annual increase of capital, if no circumstance occurred to counteract its effect, would suffice in a small number of years to reduce the rate of net profit to one per cent.

To fulfil the conditions of the hypothesis, we must suppose an entire cessation of the exportation of capital for foreign investment. No more capital sent abroad for railways or loans; no more emigrants taking capital with them, to the colonies, or to other countries; no fresh advances made, or credits given, by bankers or merchants to their foreign correspondents. We must also assume that there are no fresh loans for unproductive expenditure, by the government, or on mortgage, or otherwise; and none of the waste of capital which now takes place by the failure of undertakings which people are tempted to engage in by the hope of a better income than can be obtained in safe paths at the present habitually low rate of profit. We must suppose the entire savings of the community to be annually invested in really productive employment within the country itself; and no new channels opened by industrial inventions, or by a more extensive substitution of the best known processes for inferior ones.

Few persons would hesitate to say, that there would be great difficulty in finding remunerative employment every year for so much new capital, and most would conclude that there would be what used to be termed a general glut; that commodities would be produced, and remain unsold, or be sold only at a loss. But the full examination which we have already given to this question,[1] has shown that this is not the mode in which the inconvenience would be experienced. The difficulty would not consist in any want of a market. If the new capital were duly shared among many varieties of employment, it would raise up a demand for its own produce, and there would be no cause why any part of that produce should remain longer on hand than formerly. What would really be, not merely difficult, but impossible, would be to employ this capital without submitting to a rapid reduction of the rate of profit.

As capital increased, population either would also increase, or it would not. If it did not, wages would rise, and a greater capital would be distributed in wages among the same number of labourers. There being no more labour than before, and no improvements to render the labour more efficient, there would not be any increase of the produce; and as the capital, however largely increased, would only obtain the same gross return, the whole savings of each year would be exactly so much subtracted from the profits of the next and of every following year. It is hardly necessary to say that in such circumstances profits would

---

[1] [Bk. III, Ch. XIV. Not included in present edn.]

very soon fall to the point at which further increase of capital would cease. An augmentation of capital, much more rapid than that of population, must soon reach its extreme limit, unless accompanied by increased efficiency of labour (through inventions and discoveries, or improved mental and physical education), or unless some of the idle people, or of the unproductive labourers, became productive.

If population did increase with the increase of capital, and in proportion to it, the fall of profits would still be inevitable. Increased population implies increased demand for agricultural produce. In the absence of industrial improvements, this demand can only be supplied at an increased cost of production, either by cultivating worse land, or by a more elaborate and costly cultivation of the land already under tillage. The cost of the labourer's subsistence is therefore increased; and unless the labourer submits to a deterioration of his condition, profits must fall. In an old country like England, if, in addition to supposing all improvement in domestic agriculture suspended, we suppose that there is no increased production in foreign countries for the English market, the fall of profits would be very rapid. If both these avenues to an increased supply of food were closed, and population continued to increase, as it is said to do, at the rate of a thousand a day, all waste land which admits of cultivation in the existing state of knowledge would soon be cultivated, and the cost of production and price of food would be so increased, that, if the labourers received the increased money wages necessary to compensate for their increased expenses, profits would very soon reach the minimum. The fall of profits would be retarded if money wages did not rise, or rose in a less degree; but the margin which can be gained by a deterioration of the labourers condition is a very narrow one: in general they cannot bear much reduction; when they can, they have also a higher standard of necessary requirements, and *will* not. On the whole, therefore, we may assume that in such a country as England, if the present annual amount of savings were to continue, without any of the counteracting circumstances which now keep in check the natural influence of those savings in reducing profit, the rate of profit would speedily attain the minimum, and all further accumulation of capital would for the present cease.

5. What, then, are these counteracting circumstances, which, in the existing state of things, maintain a tolerably equal struggle against the downward tendency of profits, and prevent the great annual savings which take place in this country, from depressing the rate of profit much nearer to that lowest point to which it is always tending, and which, left to itself, it would so promptly attain? The resisting agencies are of several kinds.

First among them, we may notice one which is so simple and so conspicuous, that some political economists, especially M. de Sismondi* and Dr Chalmers, have attended to it almost to the exclusion of all others. This is, the waste of capital in periods of over-trading and rash speculation, and in the commercial revulsions by which such times are always followed. It is true that a great part of what is lost at such periods is not destroyed, but merely transferred, like a gambler's losses, to more successful speculators. But even of these mere transfers, a large portion is always to foreigners, by the hasty purchase of unusual quantities of foreign goods at advanced prices. And much also is absolutely wasted. Mines are opened, railways or bridges made, and many other works of uncertain profit commenced, and in these enterprises much capital is sunk which yields either no return, or none adequate to the outlay. Factories are built and machinery erected beyond what the market requires, or can keep in employment. Even if they are kept in employment, the capital is no less sunk; it has been converted from circulating into fixed capital, and has ceased to have any influence on wages or profits. Besides this, there is a great unproductive consumption of capital, during the stagnation which follows a period of general over-trading. Establishments are shut up, or kept working without any profit, hands are discharged, and numbers of persons in all ranks, being deprived of their income, and thrown for support on their savings, find themselves, after the crisis has passed away, in a condition of more or less impoverishment. Such are the effects of a commercial revulsion: and that such revulsions are almost periodical, is a consequence of the very tendency of profits which we are considering. By the time a few years have passed over without a crisis, so much additional capital has been accumulated, that it is no longer possible to invest it at the accustomed profit: all public securities rise to a high price, the rate of interest on the best mercantile security falls very low, and the complaint is general among persons in business that no money is to be made. Does not this demonstrate how speedily profit would be at the minimum, and the stationary condition of capital would be attained, if these accumulations went on without any counteracting principle? But the diminished scale of all safe gains, inclines persons to give a ready ear to any projects which hold out, though at the risk of loss, the hope of a higher rate of profit; and speculations ensue, which, with the subsequent revulsions, destroy, or transfer to foreigners, a considerable amount of capital, produce a temporary rise of interest and profit, make room for fresh accumulations, and the same round is recommenced.

This, doubtless, is one considerable cause which arrests profits in their descent to the minimum, by sweeping away from time to time a part of the accumulated mass by which they are forced down. But this is not, as might be inferred from the language of some writers, the principal cause. If it were, the capital of the country would not increase; but in England it does increase greatly and rapidly. This is shown by the increasing productiveness of almost all taxes, by the continual growth of all the signs of national wealth, and by the rapid increase of population, while the condition of the labourers is certainly not declining, but on the whole improving. These things prove that each commercial revulsion, however disastrous, is very far from destroying all the capital which has been added to the accumulations of the country since the last revulsion preceding it, and that, invariably, room is either found or made for the profitable employment of a perpetually increasing capital, consistently with not forcing down profits to a lower rate.

6. This brings us to the second of the counter-agencies, namely, improvements in production. These evidently have the effect of extending what Mr Wakefield terms the field of employment, that is, they enable a greater amount of capital to be accumulated and employed without depressing the rate of profit: provided always that they do not raise, to a proportional extent, the habits and requirements of the labourer. If the labouring class gain the full advantage of the increased cheapness, in other words, if money wages do not fall, profits are not raised, nor their fall retarded. But if the labourers people up to the improvement in their condition, and so relapse to their previous state, profits will rise. All inventions which cheapen any of the things consumed by the labourers, unless their requirements are raised in an equivalent degree, in time lower money wages: and by doing so, enable a greater capital to be accumulated and employed, before profits fall back to what they were previously.

Improvements which only affect things consumed exclusively by the richer classes, do not operate precisely in the same manner. The cheapening of lace or velvet has no effect in diminishing the cost of labour; and no mode can be pointed out in which it can raise the rate of profit, so as to make room for a larger capital before the minimum is attained. It, however, produces an effect which is virtually equivalent; it lowers, or tends to lower, the minimum itself. In the first place, increased cheapness of articles of consumption promotes the inclination to save, by affording to all consumers a surplus which they may lay by, consistently with their accustomed manner of living; and unless they were previously suffering actual hardships, it will require little self-denial to save some part at least of this surplus. In the next place, whatever enables people to live equally well on a smaller income, inclines them to lay by capital for a lower rate of profit. If people can live on an independence of £500 a year in the same manner as they formerly could on one of £1,000, some persons will be induced to save in hopes of the one, who would have been deterred by the more remote prospect of the other. All improvements, therefore, in the production of almost any commodity, tend in some degree to widen the interval which has to be passed before arriving at the stationary state: but this effect belongs in a much greater degree to the improvements which affect the articles consumed by the labourer, since these conduce to it in two ways; they induce people to accumulate for a lower profit, and they also raise the rate of profit itself.

7. Equivalent in effect to improvements in production, is the acquisition of any new power of obtaining cheap commodities from foreign countries. If necessaries are cheapened, whether they are so by improvements at home or importation from abroad, is exactly the same thing to wages and profits. Unless the labourer obtains, and by an improvement of his habitual standard, keeps, the whole benefit, the cost of labour is lowered, and the rate of profit raised. As long as food can continue to be imported for an increasing population without any diminution of cheapness, so long the declension of profits through the increase of population and capital is arrested, and accumulation may go on without making the rate of profit draw nearer to the minimum. And on this ground it is believed by some, that the repeal of the corn laws has opened to this country a long era of rapid increase of capital with an undiminished rate of profit.

Before inquiring whether this expectation is reasonable, one remark must be made, which is much at variance with commonly received notions. Foreign trade does not necessarily increase the field of employment for capital. It is not the mere opening of a market for a country's productions, that tends to raise the rate of profits. If nothing were obtained in exchange for those productions but the luxuries of the rich, the expenses of no capitalist would be diminished; profits would not be at all raised, nor room made for the accumulation of more capital without submitting to a reduction of profits: and if the attainment of the stationary state were at all retarded, it would only be because the diminished cost at which a certain degree of luxury could be enjoyed, might induce people, in that prospect, to make fresh savings for a lower profit than they formerly were willing to do. When foreign trade makes room for more capital at the same profit, it is by enabling the necessaries of life, or the habitual articles of the labourer's consumption, to be obtained at smaller cost. It may do this in two ways; by the importation either of those commodities themselves, or of the means and appliances for producing them. Cheap iron has, in a certain measure, the same effect on profits and the cost of labour as cheap corn, because cheap iron makes cheap tools for agriculture and cheap machinery for clothing. But a foreign trade which neither directly, nor by any indirect consequence, increases the cheapness of anything consumed by the labourers, does not, any more than an invention or discovery in the like case, tend to raise profits or retard their fall; it merely substitutes the production of goods for foreign markets, in the room of the home production of luxuries, leaving the employment for capital neither greater nor less than before. It is true, that there is scarcely any export trade which, in a country that already imports necessaries or materials, comes within these conditions: for every increase of exports enables the country to obtain all its imports on cheaper terms than before.

A country which, as is now the case with England, admits food of all kinds, and all necessaries and the materials of necessaries, to be freely imported from all parts of the world, no longer depends on the fertility of her own soil to keep up her rate of profits, but on the soil of the whole world. It remains to consider how far this resource can be counted upon, for making head during a very long period against the tendency of profits to decline as capital increases.

It must, of course, be supposed that with the increase of capital, population also increases; for if it did not, the consequent rise of wages would bring down profits, in spite of any cheapness of food. Suppose then that the population of Great Britain goes on increasing at its present rate, and demands every year a supply of imported food considerably beyond that of the year preceding. This annual increase in the food demanded from the exporting countries, can only be obtained either by great improvements in their agriculture, or by the application of a great additional capital to the growth of food. The former is likely to be a very slow process, from the rudeness and ignorance of the agricultural classes in the food-exporting countries of Europe, while the British colonies and the United States are already in possession of most of the improvements yet made, so far as suitable to their circumstances. There remains as a resource, the extension of cultivation. And on this it is to be remarked, that the capital by which any such extension can take place, is mostly still to be created. In Poland, Russia, Hungary, Spain, the increase of capital is extremely slow. In America it is rapid, but not more rapid than the population. The principal fund at present available for supplying this country with a yearly increasing importation of food, is that portion of the annual savings of America which has heretofore been applied to increasing the manufacturing establishments of the United States, and which free trade in corn may possibly divert from that purpose to growing food for our market. This limited source of supply, unless great improvements take place in agriculture, cannot be expected to keep pace with the growing demand of so rapidly increasing a population as that of Great Britain; and if our population and capital continue to increase with their present rapidity, the only mode in which food can continue to be supplied cheaply to the one, is by sending the other abroad to produce it.

8. This brings us to the last of the counter-forces which check the downward tendency of profits, in a country whose capital increases faster than that of its neighbours, and whose profits are therefore nearer to the minimum. This is, the perpetual overflow of capital into colonies or foreign countries, to seek higher profits than can be obtained at home. I believe this to have been for many years one of the principal causes by which the decline of profits in England has been arrested. It has a twofold operation. In the first place, it does what a fire, or an inundation, or a commercial crisis would have done: it carries off a part of the increase of capital from which the reduction of profits proceeds.

Secondly, the capital so carried off is not lost, but is chiefly employed either in founding colonies, which become large exporters of cheap agricultural produce, or in extending and perhaps improving the agriculture of older communities. It is to the emigration of English capital, that we have chiefly to look for keeping up a supply of cheap food and cheap materials of clothing, proportional to the increase of our population; thus enabling an increasing capital to find employment in the country, without reduction of profit, in producing manufactured articles with which to pay for this supply of raw produce. Thus, the exportation of capital is an agent of great efficacy in extending the field of employment for that which remains: and it may be said truly that, up to a certain point, the more capital we send away, the more we shall possess and be able to retain at home.

In countries which are further advanced in industry and population, and have therefore a lower rate of profit, than others, there is always, long before the actual minimum is reached, a practical minimum, viz. when profits have fallen so much below what they are elsewhere, that, were they to fall lower, all further accumulations would go abroad. In the present state of the industry of the world, when there is occasion, in any rich and improving country, to take the minimum of profits at all into consideration for practical purposes, it is only this practical minimum that needs be considered. As long as there are old countries where capital increases very rapidly, and new countries where profit is still high, profits in the old countries will not sink to the rate which would put a stop to accumulation; the fall is stopped at the point which sends capital abroad. It is only, however, by improvements in production, and even in the production of things consumed by labourers, that the capital of a country like England is prevented from speedily reaching that degree of lowness of profit, which would cause all further savings to be sent to find employment in the colonies, or in foreign countries.

CONSEQUENCES OF THE TENDENCY
OF PROFITS TO A MINIMUM

1. The theory of the effect of accumulation on profits, laid down in the preceding chapter, materially alters many of the practical conclusions which might otherwise be supposed to follow from the general principles of Political Economy, and which were, indeed, long admitted as true by the highest authorities on the subject.

It must greatly abate, or rather, altogether destroy, in countries where profits are low, the immense importance which used to be attached by political economists to the effects which an event or a measure of government might have in adding to or subtracting from the capital of the country. We have now seen that the lowness of profits is a proof that the spirit of accumulation is so active, and that the increase of capital has proceeded at so rapid a rate, as to outstrip the two counter-agencies, improvements in production, and increased supply of cheap necessaries from abroad: and that unless a considerable portion of the annual increase of capital were either periodically destroyed, or exported for foreign investment, the country would speedily attain the point at which further accumulation would cease, or at least spontaneously slacken, so as no longer to overpass the march of invention in the arts which produce the necessaries of life. In such a state of things as this, a sudden addition to the capital of the country, unaccompanied by any increase of productive power, would be but of transitory duration; since by depressing profits and interest, it would either diminish by a corresponding amount the savings which would be made from income in the year or two following, or it would cause an equivalent amount to be sent abroad, or to be wasted in rash speculations. Neither, on the other hand, would a sudden abstraction of capital, unless of inordinate amount, have any real effect in impoverishing the country. After a few months or years, there would exist in the country just as much capital as if none had been taken away. The abstraction, by raising profits and interest, would give a fresh stimulus to the accumulative principle, which would speedily fill up the vacuum. Probably, indeed, the only effect that would ensue, would be that for some time afterwards less capital would be exported, and less thrown away in hazardous speculation.

In the first place, then, this view of things greatly weakens, in a wealthy and industrious country, the force of the economical argument against the expenditure of public money for really valuable, even though industriously unproductive, purposes. If for any great object of justice or philanthropic policy, such as the industrial regeneration of Ireland, or a comprehensive measure of colonization or of public education, it were proposed to raise a large sum by way of loan, politicians need not demur to the abstraction of so much capital, as tending to dry up the permanent sources of the country's wealth, and diminish the fund which supplies the subsistence of the labouring population. The utmost expense which could be requisite for any of these purposes, would not in all probability deprive one labourer of employment, or diminish the next year's production by one ell of cloth or one bushel of grain. In poor countries, the capital of the country requires the legislator's sedulous care; he is bound to be most cautious of encroaching upon it, and should favour to the utmost its accumulation at home, and its introduction from abroad. But in rich, populous, and highly cultivated countries, it is not capital which is the deficient element, but fertile land; and what the legislator should desire and promote, is not a greater aggregate saving, but a greater return to savings, either by improved cultivation, or by access to the produce of more fertile lands in other parts of the globe. In such countries, the government may take any moderate portion of the capital of the country and expend it as revenue, without affecting the national wealth: the whole being either drawn from that portion of the annual savings which would otherwise be sent abroad, or being subtracted from the unproductive expenditure of individuals for the next year or two, since every million spent makes room for another million to be saved before reaching the overflowing point. When the object in view is worth the sacrifice of such an amount of the expenditure that furnishes the daily enjoyments of the people, the only well-grounded economical objection against taking the necessary funds directly from capital, consists of the inconveniences attending the process of raising a revenue by taxation, to pay the interest of a debt.

The same considerations enable us to throw aside as unworthy of regard, one of the common arguments against emigration as a means of relief for the labouring class. Emigration, it is said, can do no good to the labourers, if, in order to defray the cost, as much must be taken away from the capital of the country as from its population. That anything like this proportion could require to be abstracted from capital for the purpose even of the most extensive colonization, few, I should think, would now assert: but even on that untenable supposition, it is an error to suppose that no benefit would be conferred on the labouring class. If one-tenth of the labouring people of England were transferred to the colonies, and along with them one-tenth of the circulating capital of the country, either wages, or profits, or both, would be greatly benefited, by the diminished pressure of capital and population upon the fertility of the land. There would be a reduced demand for food: the inferior arable lands would be thrown out of cultivation, and would become pasture; the superior would be cultivated less highly, but with a greater proportional return; food would be lowered in price, and though money wages would not rise, every labourer would be considerably improved in circumstances, an improvement which, if no increased stimulus to population and fall of wages ensued, would be permanent; while if there did, profits would rise, and accumulation start forward so as to repair the loss of capital. The landlords alone would sustain some loss of income; and even they, only if colonization went to the length of actually diminishing capital and population, but not if it merely carried off the annual increase.

2. From the same principles we are now able to arrive at a final conclusion respecting the effects which machinery, and generally the sinking of capital for a productive purpose, produce upon the immediate and ultimate interests of the labouring class. The characteristic property of this class of industrial improvements is the conversion of circulating capital into fixed: and it was shown in the first Book,[1] that in a country where capital accumulates slowly, the introduction of machinery, permanent improvements of land, and the like, might be, for the time, extremely injurious; since the capital so employed might be directly taken from the wages fund, the subsistence of the people and the employment for labour curtailed, and the gross annual produce of the country actually diminished. But in a country of great annual savings and low profits, no such effects need be apprehended. Since even the emigration of capital, or its unproductive expenditure, or its absolute waste, do not in such a country, if confined within any moderate bounds, at all diminish the aggregate amount of the wages fund—still less can the mere conversion of a like sum into fixed capital, which continues to be productive, have that effect. It merely draws off at one orifice what was already flowing out at another; or if not, the greater vacant space left in the reservoir does but cause a greater quantity to flow in. Accordingly, in spite of the mischievous derangements of the money-market which were at one time occasioned by the sinking of great sums in railways, I was never able to agree with those who apprehended mischief, from this source, to the productive resources of the country. Not on the absurd ground (which to any one acquainted with the elements of the subject needs no confutation) that railway expenditure is a mere transfer of capital from hand to hand, by which nothing is lost or destroyed. This is true of what is spent in the purchase of the land; a portion too of what is paid to parliamentary agents, counsel, engineers, and surveyors, is saved by those who receive it, and becomes capital again: but what is laid out in the bona fide construction of the

---

[1] [Bk. I, Ch. VI. 2. Not included in present edn.]

railway itself, is lost and gone; when once expended, it is incapable of ever being paid in wages or applied to the maintenance of labourers again; as a matter of account, the result is that so much food and clothing and tools have been consumed, and the country has got a railway instead. But what I would urge is, that sums so applied are mostly a mere appropriation of the annual overflowing which would otherwise have gone abroad, or been thrown away unprofitably, leaving neither a railway nor any other tangible result. The railway gambling of 1844 and 1845 probably saved the country from a depression of profits and interest, and a rise of all public and private securities, which would have engendered still wilder speculations, and when the effects came afterwards to be complicated by the scarcity of food, would have ended in a still more formidable crisis than was experienced in the years immediately following. In the poorer countries of Europe, the rage for railway construction might have had worse consequences than in England, were it not that in those countries such enterprises are in a great measure carried on by foreign capital. The railway operations of the various nations of the world may be looked upon as a sort of competition for the overflowing capital of the countries where profit is low and capital abundant, as England and Holland. The English railway speculations are a struggle to keep our annual increase of capital at home; those of foreign countries are an effort to obtain it.[1]

It already appears from these considerations, that the conversion of circulating capital into fixed, whether by railways, or manufactories, or ships, or machinery, or canals, or mines, or works of drainage and irrigation, is not likely, in any rich country, to diminish the gross produce or the amount of employment for labour. How much then is the case strengthened, when we consider that these transformations of capital are of the nature of improvements in

[1] It is hardly needful to point out how fully the remarks in the text have been verified by subsequent facts. The capital of the country, far from having been in any degree impaired by the large amount sunk in railway construction, was soon again overflowing.

production, which, instead of ultimately diminishing circulating capital, are the necessary conditions of its increase, since they alone enable a country to possess a constantly augmenting capital without reducing profits to the rate which would cause accumulation to stop. There is hardly any increase of fixed capital which does not enable the country to contain eventually a larger circulating capital, than it otherwise could possess and employ within its own limits; for there is hardly any creation of fixed capital which, when it proves successful, does not cheapen the articles on which wages are habitually expended. All capital sunk in the permanent improvement of land, lessens the cost of food and materials; almost all improvements in machinery cheapen the labourer's clothing or lodging, or the tools with which these are made; improvements in locomotion, such as railways, cheapen to the consumer all things which are brought from a distance. All these improvements make the labourers better off with the same money wages, better off if they do not increase their rate of multiplication. But if they do, and wages consequently fall, at least profits rise, and, while accumulation receives an immediate stimulus, room is made for a greater amount of capital before a sufficient motive arises for sending it abroad. Even the improvements which do not cheapen the things consumed by the labourer, and which, therefore, do not raise profits nor retain capital in the country, nevertheless, as we have seen, by lowering the minimum of profit for which people will ultimately consent to save, leave an ampler margin than previously for eventual accumulation, before arriving at the stationary state.

We may conclude, then, that improvements in production, and emigration of capital to the more fertile soils and unworked mines of the uninhabited or thinly peopled parts of the globe, do not, as appears to a superficial view, diminish the gross produce and the demand for labour at home; but, on the contrary, are what we have chiefly to depend on for increasing both, and are even the necessary conditions of any great or prolonged augmentation of either. Nor is it any exaggeration to say, that within certain, and not very narrow, limits, the more capital a country like England expends in these two ways, the more she will have left.

BOOK IV. INFLUENCE OF PROGRESS   123

and not very narrow, limits; the more capital a country like
England expends in these two days, the more she will have
left.

VI

OF THE STATIONARY STATE

1. The preceding chapters comprise the general theory of
the economical progress of society, in the sense in which
those terms are commonly understood; the progress of
capital, of population, and of the productive arts. But in
contemplating any progressive movement, not in its nature
unlimited, the mind is not satisfied with merely tracing the
laws of the movement; it cannot but ask the further question, to what goal? Towards what ultimate point is society
tending by its industrial progress? When the progress ceases,
in what condition are we to expect that it will leave
mankind?

It must always have been seen, more or less distinctly, by
political economists, that the increase of wealth is not
boundless: that at the end of what they term the progressive
state lies the stationary state, that all progress in wealth is
but a postponement of this, and that each step in advance
is an approach to it. We have now been led to recognise that
this ultimate goal is at all times near enough to be fully in
view; that we are always on the verge of it, and that if we
have not reached it long ago, it is because the goal itself
flies before us. The richest and most prosperous countries
would very soon attain the stationary state, if no further
improvements were made in the productive arts, and if there
were a suspension of the overflow of capital from those
countries into the uncultivated or ill-cultivated regions of
the earth.

This impossibility of ultimately avoiding the stationary
state—this irresistible necessity that the stream of human
industry should finally spread itself out into an apparently
stagnant sea—must have been, to the political economists
of the last two generations, an unpleasing and discouraging
prospect; for the tone and tendency of their speculations
goes completely to identify all that is economically desirable with the progressive state, and with that alone. With

Mr M'Culloch,* for example, prosperity does not mean a large production and a good distribution of wealth, but a rapid increase of it; his test of prosperity is high profits; and as the tendency of that very increase of wealth, which he calls prosperity, is towards low profits, economical progress, according to him, must tend to the extinction of prosperity. Adam Smith always assumes that the condition of the mass of the people, though it may not be positively distressed, must be pinched and stinted in a stationary condition of wealth, and can only be satisfactory in a progressive state. The doctrine that, to however distant a time incessant struggling may put off our doom, the progress of society must "end in shallows and in miseries", far from being, as many people still believe, a wicked invention of Mr Malthus, was either expressly or tacitly affirmed by his most distinguished predecessors, and can only be successfully combated on his principles. Before attention had been directed to the principle of population as the active force in determining the remuneration of labour, the increase of mankind was virtually treated as a constant quantity; it was, at all events, assumed that in the natural and normal state of human affairs population must constantly increase, from which it followed that a constant increase of the means of support was essential to the physical comfort of the mass of mankind. The publication of Mr Malthus' Essay* is the era from which better views of this subject must be dated; and notwithstanding the acknowledged errors of his first edition, few writers have done more than himself, in the subsequent editions, to promote these juster and more hopeful anticipations.

Even in a progressive state of capital, in old countries, a conscientious or prudential restraint on population is indispensable, to prevent the increase of numbers from outstripping the increase of capital, and the condition of the classes who are at the bottom of society from being deteriorated. Where there is not, in the people, or in some very large proportion of them, a resolute resistance to this deterioration—a determination to preserve an established standard of comfort—the condition of the poorest class sinks, even in a progressive state, to the lowest point which they will consent to endure. The same determination would be equally effectual to keep up their condition in the stationary state, and would be quite as likely to exist. Indeed, even now, the countries in which the greatest prudence is manifested in the regulating of population, are often those in which capital increases least rapidly. Where there is an indefinite prospect of employment for increased numbers, there is apt to appear less necessity for prudential restraint. If it were evident that a new hand could not obtain employment but by displacing, or succeeding to, one already employed, the combined influences of prudence and public opinion might in some measure be relied on for restricting the coming generation within the numbers necessary for replacing the present.

2. I cannot, therefore, regard the stationary state of capital and wealth with the unaffected aversion so generally manifested towards it by political economists of the old school. I am inclined to believe that it would be, on the whole, a very considerable improvement on our present condition. I confess I am not charmed with the ideal of life held out by those who think that the normal state of human beings is that of struggling to get on; that the trampling, crushing, elbowing, and treading on each other's heels, which form the existing type of social life, are the most desirable lot of human kind, or anything but the disagreeable symptoms of one of the phases of industrial progress. It may be a necessary stage in the progress of civilization, and those European nations which have hitherto been so fortunate as to be preserved from it, may have it yet to undergo. It is an incident of growth, not a mark of decline, for it is not necessarily destructive of the higher aspirations and the heroic virtues; as America, in her great civil war,* has proved to the world, both by her conduct as a people and by numerous splendid individual examples, and as England, it is to be hoped, would also prove, on an equally trying and exciting occasion. But it is not a kind of social perfection which philanthropists to come will feel any very eager desire to assist in realizing. Most fitting, indeed, is it,

that while riches are power, and to grow as rich as possible the universal object of ambition, the path to its attainment should be open to all, without favour or partiality. But the best state for human nature is that in which, while no one is poor, no one desires to be richer, nor has any reason to fear being thrust back, by the efforts of others to push themselves forward.

That the energies of mankind should be kept in employment by the struggle for riches, as they were formerly by the struggle of war, until the better minds succeed in educating the others into better things, is undoubtedly more desirable than that they should rust and stagnate. While minds are coarse they require coarse stimuli, and let them have them. In the meantime, those who do not accept the present very early stage of human improvement as its ultimate type, may be excused for being comparatively indifferent to the kind of economical progress which excites the congratulations of ordinary politicians; the mere increase of production and accumulation. For the safety of national independence it is essential that a country should not fall much behind its neighbours in these things. But in themselves they are of little importance, so long as either the increase of population or anything else prevents the mass of the people from reaping any part of the benefit of them. I know not why it should be matter of congratulation that persons who are already richer than any one needs to be, should have doubled their means of consuming things which give little or no pleasure except as representative of wealth; or that numbers of individuals should pass over, every year, from the middle classes into a richer class, or from the class of the occupied rich to that of the unoccupied. It is only in the backward countries of the world that increased production is still an important object: in those most advanced, what is economically needed is a better distribution, of which one indispensable means is a stricter restraint on population. Levelling institutions, either of a just or of an unjust kind, cannot alone accomplish it; they may lower the heights of society, but they cannot, of themselves, permanently raise the depths.

On the other hand, we may suppose this better distribution of property attained, by the joint effect of the prudence and frugality of individuals, and of a system of legislation favouring equality of fortunes, so far as is consistent with the just claim of the individual to the fruits, whether great or small, of his or her own industry. We may suppose, for instance (according to the suggestion thrown out in a former chapter[1]), a limitation of the sum which any one person may acquire by gift or inheritance, to the amount sufficient to constitute a moderate independence. Under this twofold influence, society would exhibit these leading features: a well-paid and affluent body of labourers; no enormous fortunes, except what were earned and accumulated during a single lifetime; but a much larger body of persons than at present, not only exempt from the coarser toils, but with sufficient leisure, both physical and mental, from mechanical details, to cultivate freely the graces of life, and afford examples of them to the classes less favourably circumstanced for their growth. This condition of society, so greatly preferable to the present, is not only perfectly compatible with the stationary state, but, it would seem, more naturally allied with that state than with any other.

There is room in the world, no doubt, and even in old countries, for a great increase of population, supposing the arts of life to go on improving, and capital to increase. But even if innocuous, I confess I see very little reason for desiring it. The density of population necessary to enable mankind to obtain, in the greatest degree, all the advantages both of co-operation and of social intercourse, has, in all the most populous countries, been attained. A population may be too crowded, though all be amply supplied with food and raiment. It is not good for man to be kept perforce at all times in the presence of his species. A world from which solitude is extirpated, is a very poor ideal. Solitude, in the sense of being often alone, is essential to any depth of meditation or of character; and solitude in the presence of natural beauty and grandeur, is the cradle of thoughts

[1] [Bk. II, Ch. II. 4.]

and aspirations which are not only good for the individual, but which society could ill do without. Nor is there much satisfaction in contemplating the world with nothing left to the spontaneous activity of nature; with every rood of land brought into cultivation, which is capable of growing food for human beings; every flowery waste or natural pasture ploughed up, all quadrupeds or birds which are not domesticated for man's use exterminated as his rivals for food, every hedgerow or superfluous tree rooted out, and scarcely a place left where a wild shrub or flower could grow without being eradicated as a weed in the name of improved agriculture. If the earth must lose that great portion of its pleasantness which it owes to things that the unlimited increase of wealth and population would extirpate from it, for the mere purpose of enabling it to support a larger, but not a better or a happier population, I sincerely hope, for the sake of posterity, that they will be content to be stationary, long before necessity compels them to it.

It is scarcely necessary to remark that a stationary condition of capital and population implies no stationary state of human improvement. There would be as much scope as ever for all kinds of mental culture, and moral and social progress; as much room for improving the Art of Living* and much more likelihood of its being improved, when minds ceased to be engrossed by the art of getting on. Even the industrial arts might be as earnestly and as successfully cultivated, with this sole difference, that instead of serving no purpose but the increase of wealth, industrial improvements would produce their legitimate effect, that of abridging labour. Hitherto it is questionable if all the mechanical inventions yet made have lightened the day's toil of any human being. They have enabled a greater population to live the same life of drudgery and imprisonment, and an increased number of manufacturers and others to make fortunes. They have increased the comforts of the middle classes. But they have not yet begun to effect those great changes in human destiny, which it is in their nature and in their futurity to accomplish. Only when, in addition to just institutions, the increase of mankind shall be under the

deliberate guidance of judicious foresight, can the conquests
made from the powers of nature by the intellect and energy
of scientific discoverers, become the common property of
the species, and the means of improving and elevating the
universal lot.

VII

ON THE PROBABLE FUTURITY OF THE LABOURING CLASSES

1 The observations in the preceding chapter had for their principal object to deprecate a false ideal of human society. Their applicability to the practical purposes of present times, consists in moderating the inordinate importance attached to the mere increase of production, and fixing attention upon improved distribution, and a large remuneration of labour, as the two desiderata. Whether the aggregate produce increases absolutely or not, is a thing in which, after a certain amount has been obtained, neither the legislator nor the philanthropist need feel any strong interest: but, that it should increase relatively to the number of those who share in it, is of the utmost possible importance; and this, (whether the wealth of mankind be stationary, or increasing at the most rapid rate ever known in an old country,) must depend on the opinions and habits of the most numerous class, the class of manual labourers.

When I speak, either in this place or elsewhere, of 'the labouring classes', or of labourers as a 'class', I use those phrases in compliance with custom, and as descriptive of an existing, but by no means a necessary or permanent, state of social relations. I do not recognise as either just or salutary, a state of society in which there is any 'class' which is not labouring; any human beings, exempt from bearing their share of the necessary labours of human life, except those unable to labour, or who have fairly earned rest by previous toil. So long, however, as the great social evil exists of a non-labouring class, labourers also constitute a class, and may be spoken of, though only provisionally, in that character.

Considered in its moral and social aspect, the state of the labouring people has latterly been a subject of much more speculation and discussion than formerly; and the opinion that it is not now what it ought to be, has become very general. The suggestions which have been promulgated, and the controversies which have been excited, on detached points rather than on the foundations of the subject, have put in evidence the existence of two conflicting theories, respecting the social position desirable for manual labourers. The one may be called the theory of dependence and protection, the other that of self-dependence.

According to the former theory, the lot of the poor, in all things which affect them collectively, should be regulated *for* them, not *by* them. They should not be required or encouraged to think for themselves, or give to their own reflection or forecast an influential voice in the determination of their destiny. It is supposed to be the duty of the higher classes to think for them, and to take the responsibility of their lot, as the commander and officers of an army take that of the soldiers composing it. This function, it is contended, the higher classes should prepare themselves to perform conscientiously, and their whole demeanour should impress the poor with a reliance on it, in order that, while yielding passive and active obedience to the rules prescribed for them they may resign themselves in all other respects to a trustful *insouciance*,* and repose under the shadow of their protectors. The relation between rich and poor, according to this theory (a theory also applied to the relation between men and women) should be only partly authoritative; it should be amiable, moral, and sentimental: affectionate tutelage on the one side, respectful and grateful deference on the other. The rich should be *in loco parentis*ary to the poor, guiding and restraining them like children. Of spontaneous action on their part there should be no need. They should be called on for nothing but to do their day's work, and to be moral and religious. Their morality and religion should be provided for them by their superiors, who should see them properly taught it, and should do all that is necessary to ensure their being, in return for labour and attachment, properly fed, clothed, housed, spiritually edified, and innocently amused.

This is the ideal of the future, in the minds of those whose dissatisfaction with the present assumes the form of affection and regret towards the past. Like other ideals, it exercises an unconscious influence on the opinions and sentiments of numbers who never consciously guide themselves by any ideal. It has also this in common with other ideals, that it has never been historically realized. It makes its appeal to our imaginative sympathies in the character of a restoration of the good times of our forefathers. But no times can be pointed out in which the higher classes of this or any other country performed a part even distantly resembling the one assigned to them in this theory. It is an idealization, grounded on the conduct and character of here and there an individual. All privileged and powerful classes, as such, have used their power in the interest of their own selfishness, and have indulged their self-importance in despising, and not in lovingly caring for, those who were, in their estimation, degraded, by being under the necessity of working for their benefit. I do not affirm that what has always been must always be, or that human improvement has no tendency to correct the intensely selfish feelings engendered by power; but though the evil may be lessened, it cannot be eradicated, until the power itself is withdrawn. This, at least, seems to me undeniable, that long before the superior classes could be sufficiently improved to govern in the tutelary manner supposed, the inferior classes would be too much improved to be so governed.

I am quite sensible of all that is seductive in the picture of society which this theory presents. Though the facts of it have no prototype in the past, the feelings have. In them lies all that there is of reality in the conception. As the idea is essentially repulsive of a society only held together by the relations and feelings arising out of pecuniary interests, so there is something naturally attractive in a form of society abounding in strong personal attachments and disinterested self-devotion. Of such feelings it must be admitted that the relation of protector and protected has hitherto been the richest source. The strongest attachments of human beings in general, are towards the things or the persons that stand between them and some dreaded evil. Hence, in an age of lawless violence and insecurity, and general hardness and roughness of manners, in which life is beset with dangers and sufferings at every step, to those who have neither a commanding position of their own, nor a claim on the protection of some one who has—a generous giving of protection, and a grateful receiving of it, are the strongest ties which connect human beings; the feelings arising from that relation are their warmest feelings; all the enthusiasm and tenderness of the most sensitive natures gather round it; loyalty on the one part and chivalry on the other are principles exalted into passions. I do not desire to depreciate these qualities. The error lies in not perceiving, that these virtues and sentiments, like the clanship and the hospitality of the wandering Arab, belong emphatically to a rude and imperfect state of the social union; and that the feelings between protector and protected, whether between kings and subjects, rich and poor, or men and women, can no longer have this beautiful and endearing character, where there are no longer any serious dangers from which to protect. What is there in the present state of society to make it natural that human beings, of ordinary strength and courage, should glow with the warmest gratitude and devotion in return for protection? The laws protect them, wherever the laws do not criminally fail in their duty. To be under the power of some one, instead of being as formerly the sole condition of safety, is now, speaking generally, the only situation which exposes to grievous wrong. The so-called protectors are now the only persons against whom, in any ordinary circumstances, protection is needed. The brutality and tyranny with which every police report is filled, are those of husbands to wives, of parents to children. That the law does not prevent these atrocities, that it is only now making a first timid attempt to repress and punish them, is no matter of necessity, but the deep disgrace of those by whom the laws are made and administered. No man or woman who either possesses or is able to earn an independent livelihood, requires any other protection than that which the law could and ought to give. This being the case, it argues great ignorance of human nature to continue taking for granted that relations founded on protection must always subsist, and not to see that the assumption of the part of protector, and of the power which belongs to it, without any of the necessities which justify it, must engender feelings opposite to loyalty.

Of the working men, at least in the more advanced countries of Europe, it may be pronounced certain, that the patriarchal or paternal system of government is one to which they will not again be subject. That question was decided, when they were taught to read, and allowed access to newspapers and political tracts; when dissenting preachers were suffered to go among them, and appeal to their faculties and feelings in opposition to the creeds professed and countenanced by their superiors; when they were brought together in numbers, to work socially under the same roof; when railways enabled them to shift from place to place, and change their patrons and employers as easily as their coats; when they were encouraged to seek a share in the government, by means of the electoral franchise. The working classes have taken their interests into their own hands, and are perpetually showing that they think the interests of their employers not identical with their own, but opposite to them. Some among the higher classes flatter themselves that these tendencies may be counteracted by moral and religious education: but they have let the time go by for giving an education which can serve their purpose. The principles of the Reformation have reached as low down in society as reading and writing, and the poor will not much longer accept morals and religion of other people's prescribing. I speak more particularly of this country, especially the town population, and the districts of the most scientific agriculture or the highest wages, Scotland and the north of England. Among the more inert and less modernized agricultural population of the southern counties, it might be possible for the gentry to retain, for some time longer, something of the ancient deference and submission of the poor, by bribing them with high wages and constant employment; by insuring them support, and never requiring them to do anything which they do not like. But these are two conditions which never have been combined, and never can be, for long together. A guarantee of subsistence can only be practically kept up, when work is enforced and superfluous multiplication restrained by at least a moral compulsion. It is then, that the would-be revivers of old times which they do not understand, would feel practically in how hopeless a task they were engaged. The whole fabric of patriarchal or seignorial influence, attempted to be raised on the foundation of caressing the poor, would be shattered against the necessity of enforcing a stringent Poor-law.

2. It is on a far other basis that the well-being and well-doing of the labouring people must henceforth rest. The poor have come out of leading-strings, and cannot any longer be governed or treated like children. To their own qualities must now be commended the care of their destiny. Modern nations will have to learn the lesson, that the well-being of a people must exist by means of the justice and self-government, the δικαιούνη and σωφροσύνη, of the individual citizens. The theory of dependence attempts to dispense with the necessity of these qualities in the dependent classes. But now, when even in position they are becoming less and less dependent, and their minds less and less acquiescent in the degree of dependence which remains, the virtues of independence are those which they stand in need of. Whatever advice, exhortation, or guidance is held out to the labouring classes, must henceforth be tendered to them as equals, and accepted by them with their eyes open. The prospect of the future depends on the degree in which they can be made rational beings.

There is no reason to believe that prospect other than hopeful. The progress indeed has hitherto been, and still is, slow. But there is a spontaneous education going on in the minds of the multitude, which may be greatly accelerated and improved by artificial aids. The instruction obtained from newspapers and political tracts may not be the most solid kind of instruction, but it is an immense improvement upon none at all. What it does for a people, has been admirably exemplified during the cotton crisis, in the case of the Lancashire spinners and weavers,* who have acted with the consistent good sense and forbearance so justly applauded, simply because, being readers of newspapers, they understood the causes of the calamity which had befallen them, and knew that it was in no way imputable either to their employers or to the Government. It is not certain that their conduct would have been as rational and exemplary, if the distress had preceded the salutary measure of fiscal emancipation which gave existence to the penny press. The institutions for lectures and discussion, the collective deliberations on questions of common interest, the trades unions, the political agitation, all serve to awaken public spirit, to diffuse variety of ideas among the mass, and to excite thought and reflection in the more intelligent. Although the too early attainment of political franchises by the least educated class might retard, instead of promoting, their improvement, there can be little doubt that it has been greatly stimulated by the attempt to acquire them. In the meantime, the working classes are now part of the public; in all discussions on matters of general interest they, or a portion of them, are now partakers; all who use the press as an instrument may, if it so happens, have them for an audience; the avenues of instruction through which the middle classes acquire such ideas as they have, are accessible to, at least, the operatives in the towns. With these resources, it cannot be doubted that they will increase in intelligence, even by their own unaided efforts; while there is reason to hope that great improvements both in the quality and quantity of school education will be effected by the exertions either of government or of individuals, and that the progress of the mass of the people in mental cultivation, and in the virtues which are dependent on it, will take place more rapidly, and with fewer intermittences and aberrations, than if left to itself.

From this increase of intelligence, several effects may be confidently anticipated. First: that they will become even less willing than at present to be led and governed, and directed into the way they should go, by the mere authority and prestige of superiors. If they have not now, still less will they have hereafter, any deferential awe, or religious principle of obedience, holding them in mental subjection to a class above them. The theory of dependence and protection will be more and more intolerable to them, and they will require that their conduct and condition shall be essentially self-governed. It is, at the same time, quite possible that they may demand, in many cases, the intervention of the legislature in their affairs, and the regulation by law of various things which concern them, often under very mistaken ideas of their interest. Still, it is their own will, their own ideas and suggestions, to which they will demand that effect should be given, and not rules laid down for them by other people. It is quite consistent with this, that they should feel respect for superiority of intellect and knowledge, and defer much to the opinions, on any subject, of those whom they think well acquainted with it. Such deference is deeply grounded in human nature; but they will judge for themselves of the persons who are and are not entitled to it.

3. It appears to me impossible but that the increase of intelligence, of education, and of the love of independence among the working classes, must be attended with a corresponding growth of the good sense which manifests itself in provident habits of conduct, and that population, therefore, will bear a gradually diminishing ratio to capital and employment. This most desirable result would be much accelerated by another change, which lies in the direct line of the best tendencies of the time; the opening of industrial occupations freely to both sexes. The same reasons which make it no longer necessary that the poor should depend on the rich, make it equally unnecessary that women should depend on men; and the least which justice requires is that law and custom should not enforce dependence (when the correlative protection has become superfluous) by ordaining that a woman, who does not happen to have a provision by inheritance, shall have scarcely any means open to her of gaining a livelihood, except as a wife and mother. Let women who prefer that occupation, adopt it; but that there should be no option, no other *carrière** possible for the great majority of women, except in the humbler depart-

ments of life, is a flagrant social injustice. The ideas and institutions by which the accident of sex is made the groundwork of an inequality of legal rights, and a forced dissimilarity of social functions, must ere long be recognized as the greatest hindrance to moral, social, and even intellectual improvement. On the present occasion I shall only indicate, among the probable consequences of the industrial and social independence of women, a great diminution of the evil of over-population. It is by devoting one-half of the human species to that exclusive function, by making it fill the entire life of one sex, and interweave itself with almost all the objects of the other, that the animal instinct in question is nursed into the disproportionate preponderance which it has hitherto exercised in human life.

4. The political consequences of the increasing power and importance of the operative classes, and of the growing ascendancy of numbers, which, even in England and under the present institutions, is rapidly giving to the will of the majority at least a negative voice in the acts of government, are too wide a subject to be discussed in this place. But, confining ourselves to economical considerations, and notwithstanding the effect which improved intelligence in the working classes, together with just laws, may have in altering the distribution of the produce to their advantage, I cannot think that they will be permanently contented with the condition of labouring for wages as their ultimate state. They may be willing to pass through the class of servants in their way to that of employers; but not to remain in it all their lives. To begin as hired labourers, then after a few years to work on their own account, and finally employ others, is the normal condition of labourers in a new country, rapidly increasing in wealth and population, like America or Australia. But in an old and fully peopled country, those who begin life as labourers for hire, as a general rule, continue such to the end, unless they sink into the still lower grade of recipients of public charity. In the present stage of human progress, when ideas of equality are daily spreading more widely among the poorer classes, and can no longer

be checked by anything short of the entire suppression of printed discussion and even of freedom of speech, it is not to be expected that the division of the human race into two hereditary classes, employers and employed, can be permanently maintained. The relation is nearly as unsatisfactory to the payer of wages as to the receiver. If the rich regard the poor as, by a kind of natural law, their servants and dependents, the rich in their turn are regarded as a mere prey and pasture for the poor; the subject of demands and expectations wholly indefinite, increasing in extent with every concession made to them. The total absence of regard for justice or fairness in the relations between the two, is as marked on the side of the employed as on that of the employers. We look in vain among the working classes in general for the just pride which will choose to give good work for good wages; for the most part, their sole endeavour is to receive as much, and return as little in the shape of service, as possible. It will sooner or later become insupportable to the employing classes, to live in close and hourly contact with persons whose interests and feelings are in hostility to them. Capitalists are almost as much interested as labourers in placing the operations of industry on such a footing, that those who labour for them may feel the same interest in the work, which is felt by those who labour on their own account.

The opinion expressed in a former part of this treatise respecting small landed properties and peasant proprietors, may have made the reader anticipate that a wide diffusion of property in land is the resource on which I rely for exempting at least the agricultural labourers from exclusive dependence on labour for hire. Such, however, is not my opinion. I indeed deem that form of agricultural economy to be most groundlessly cried down, and to be greatly preferable, in its aggregate effects on human happiness, to hired labour in any form in which it exists at present; because the prudential check to population acts more directly, and is shown by experience to be more efficacious; and because, in point of security, of independence, of exercise of any other than the animal faculties, the state of a peasant proprietor is far superior to that of an agricultural labourer in this or any other old country. Where the former system already exists, and works on the whole satisfactorily, I should regret, in the present state of human intelligence, to see it abolished in order to make way for the other, under a pedantic notion of agricultural improvement as a thing necessarily the same in every diversity of circumstances. In a backward state of industrial improvement, as in Ireland, I should urge its introduction, in preference to an exclusive system of hired labour; as a more powerful instrument for raising a population from semi-savage listlessness and recklessness, to persevering industry and prudent calculation.

But a people who have once adopted the large system of production, either in manufactures or in agriculture, are not likely to recede from it; and when population is kept in due proportion to the means of support, it is not desirable that they should. Labour is unquestionably more productive on the system of large industrial enterprises; the produce, if not greater absolutely, is greater in proportion to the labour employed: the same number of persons can be supported equally well with less toil and greater leisure; which will be wholly an advantage, as soon as civilization and improvement have so far advanced, that what is a benefit to the whole shall be a benefit to each individual composing it. And in the moral aspect of the question, which is still more important than the economical, something better should be aimed at as the goal of industrial improvement, than to disperse mankind over the earth in single families, each ruled internally, as families now are, by a patriarchal despot, and having scarcely any community of interest, or necessary mental communion, with other human beings. The domination of the head of the family over the other members, in this state of things, is absolute; while the effect on his own mind tends towards concentration of all interests in the family, considered as an expansion of self, and absorption of all passions in that of exclusive possession, of all cares in those of preservation and acquisition. As a step out of the merely animal state into the human, out of reckless abandonment to brute instincts into prudential foresight and self-government, this moral condition may be seen without displeasure. But if public spirit, generous sentiments, or true justice and equality are desired, association, not isolation, of interests, is the school in which these excellences are nurtured. The aim of improvement should be not solely to place human beings in a condition in which they will be able to do without one another, but to enable them to work with or for one another in relations not involving dependence. Hitherto there has been no alternative for those who lived by their labour, but that of labouring either each for himself alone, or for a master. But the civilizing and improving influences of association, and the efficiency and economy of production on a large scale, may be obtained without dividing the producers into two parties with hostile interests and feelings, the many who do the work being mere servants under the command of the one who supplies the funds, and having no interest of their own in the enterprise except to earn their wages with as little labour as possible. The speculations and discussions of the last fifty years, and the events of the last thirty, are abundantly conclusive on this point. If the improvement which even triumphant military despotism has only retarded, not stopped, shall continue its course, there can be little doubt that the status of hired labourers will gradually tend to confine itself to the description of workpeople whose low moral qualities render them unfit for anything more independent: and that the relation of masters and workpeople will be gradually superseded by partnership, in one of two forms: in some cases, association of the labourers with the capitalist; in others, and perhaps finally in all, association of labourers among themselves.

5. The first of these forms of association has long been practised, not indeed as a rule, but as an exception. In several departments of industry there are already cases in which every one who contributes to the work, either by labour or by pecuniary resources, has a partner's interest in it, proportional to the value of his contribution. It is already

a common practice to remunerate those in whom peculiar trust is reposed, by means of a percentage on the profits: and cases exist in which the principle is, with excellent success, carried down to the class of mere manual labourers.

In the American ships trading to China, it has long been the custom for every sailor to have an interest in the profits of the voyage; and to this has been ascribed the general good conduct of those seamen, and the extreme rarity of any collision between them and the government or people of the country. An instance in England, not so well known as it deserves to be, is that of the Cornish miners. 'In Cornwall the mines are worked strictly on the system of joint adventure; gangs of miners contracting with the agent, who represents the owner of the mine, to execute a certain portion of a vein and fit the ore for market, at the price of so much in the pound of the sum for which the ore is sold. These contracts are put up at certain regular periods, generally every two months, and taken by a voluntary partnership of men accustomed to the mine. This system has its disadvantages, in consequence of the uncertainty and irregularity of the earnings, and consequent necessity of living for long periods on credit; but it has advantages which more than counterbalance these drawbacks. It pro-duces a degree of intelligence, independence, and moral elevation, which raise the condition and character of the Cornish miner far above that of the generality of the labouring class. We are told by Dr Barham, that "they are not only, as a class, intelligent for labourers, but men of considerable knowledge". Also, that "they have a character of independence, something American, the system by which the contracts are let giving the takers entire freedom to make arrangements among themselves; so that each man feels, as a partner in his little firm, that he meets his employers on nearly equal terms".... With this basis of intelligence and independence in their character, we are not surprised when we hear that "a very great number of miners are now located on possessions of their own, leased for three lives or ninety-nine years, on which they have built houses"; or that "£281,541 are deposited in saving banks in

Cornwall, of which two-thirds are estimated to belong to miners".[1]

Mr Babbage,* who also gives an account of this system, observes that the payment to the crews of whaling ships is governed by a similar principle; and that 'the profits arising from fishing with nets on the south coast of England are thus divided: one-half the produce belongs to the owner of the boat and net; the other half is divided in equal portions between the persons using it, who are also bound to assist in repairing the net when required.' Mr Babbage has the great merit of having pointed out the practicability, and the advantage, of extending the principle to manufacturing industry generally.[2]

Some attention has been excited by an experiment of this nature, commenced above thirty years ago by a Paris tradesman, a house-painter, M. Leclaire,[3] and described by him in a pamphlet published in the year 1842. M. Leclaire, according to his statement, employs on an average two hundred workmen, whom he pays in the usual manner, by fixed wages or salaries. He assigns to himself, besides interest for his capital, a fixed allowance for his labour and responsibility as manager. At the end of the year, the surplus profits are divided among the body, himself included, in the proportion of their salaries.[4] The reasons by which M. Leclaire was led to adopt this system are highly instructive. Finding the conduct of his workmen unsatisfactory, he first tried the effect of giving higher wages, and by this he managed to obtain a body of excellent workmen,

[1] This passage is from the Prize Essay on the Causes and Remedies of National Distress, by Mr Samuel Laing [*Atlas Prize Essay. National Distress: its Causes and Remedies* (London, 1844), 40-1]. The extracts which it includes are from the Appendix to the Report of the Children's Employment Commission.

[2] *Economy of Machinery and Manufactures*, 3rd edition, ch. 26.

[3] His establishment is 11, Rue Saint Georges.

[4] It appears, however, that the workmen whom M. Leclaire had admitted to this participation of profits, were only a portion (rather less than half) of the whole number whom he employed. This is explained by another part of his system. M. Leclaire pays the full market rate of wages to all his workmen. The share of profit assigned to them is, therefore, a clear addition to the ordinary gains of their class, which he very laudably uses as an instrument of improvement, by making it the reward of desert, or the recompense for peculiar trust.

who would not quit his service for any other. 'Having thus succeeded' (I quote from an abstract of the pamphlet in Chambers' Journal[1]), 'in producing some sort of stability in the arrangement of his establishment, M. Leclaire expected, he says, to enjoy greater peace of mind. In this, however, he was disappointed. So long as he was able to superintend everything himself, from the general concerns of his business down to its minutest details, he did enjoy a certain satisfaction; but from the moment that, owing to the increase of his business, he found that he could be nothing more than the centre from which orders were issued, and to which reports were brought in, his former anxiety and discomfort returned upon him.' He speaks lightly of the other sources of anxiety to which a tradesman is subject, but describes as an incessant cause of vexation the losses arising from the misconduct of workmen. An employer 'will find workmen whose indifference to his interests is such that they do not perform two-thirds of the amount of work which they are capable of; hence the continual fretting of masters, who, seeing their interests neglected, believe themselves entitled to suppose that workmen are constantly conspiring to ruin those from whom they derive their livelihood. If the journeyman were sure of constant employment, his position would in some respects be more enviable than that of the master, because he is assured of a certain amount of day's wages, which he will get whether he works much or little. He runs no risk, and has no other motive to stimulate him to do his best than his own sense of duty. The master, on the other hand, depends greatly on chance for his returns: his position is one of continual irritation and anxiety. This would no longer be the case to the same extent, if the interests of the master and those of the workmen were bound up with each other, connected by some bond of mutual security, such as that which would be obtained by the plan of a yearly division of profits.'

Even in the first year during which M. Leclaire's experiment was in complete operation, the success was remarkable. Not

[1] For September 27, 1845.

one of his journeymen who worked as many as three hundred days, earned in that year less than 1,500 francs, and some considerably more. His highest rate of daily wages being four francs, or 1,200 francs for 300 days, the remaining 300 francs, or £12, must have been the smallest amount which any journeyman, who worked that number of days, obtained as his proportion of the surplus profit. M. Leclaire describes in strong terms the improvement which was already manifest in the habits and demeanour of his workmen, not merely when at work, and in their relations with their employer, but at other times and in other relations, showing increased respect both for others and for themselves. M. Chevalier, in a work published in 1848,[1] stated on M. Leclaire's authority, that the increased zeal of the workpeople continued to be a full compensation to him, even in a pecuniary sense, for the share of profit which he renounced in their favour [...][2]

The beneficent example set by M. Leclaire has been followed, with brilliant success, by other employers of labour on a large scale at Paris; [...]

Until the passing of the Limited Liability Act,* it was held that an arrangement similar to M. Leclaire's would

---

[1] Lettres sur l'Organisation du Travail [Paris, 1848], par Michel Chevalier, lettre xiv.

[2] At the present time M. Leclaire's establishment is conducted on a somewhat altered system though the principle of dividing the profits is maintained. There are now three partners in the concern: M. Leclaire himself, one other person (M. Defournaux), and a Provident Society (Société de Secours Mutuels), of which all persons in his employment are the members. (this Society owns an excellent library, and has scientific, technical, and other lectures regularly delivered to it.) Each of the three partners has 100,000 francs invested in the concern; M. Leclaire having advanced to the Provident Society as much as was necessary to supply the orginal insufficiency of their own funds. The partnership, on the part of the Society, is limited; on that of M. Leclaire and M. Defournaux, unlimited. These two receive 6000 francs (240l.) per annum each as wages of superintendence. Of the annual profits they receive half, though owning two-thirds of the capital. The remaining half belongs to the employés and workpeople; two-fifths of it being paid to the Provident Society, and the other three-fifts divided among the body. M. Leclaire, however, now reserves to himself the right of deciding who shall share in the distribution, and to what amount; only binding himself never to retain any part, but to bestow whatever has not been awarded to individuals, on the Provident Society. It is further provided that in case of the retirement of both the private partners, the goodwill and plant shall become, without payment, the property of the Society.

have been impossible in England, as the workmen could not, in the previous state of the law, have been associated in the profits, without being liable for losses. One of the many benefits of that great legislative improvement has been to render partnerships of this description possible, and we may now expect to see them carried into practice. Messrs. Briggs, of the Whitwood and Methley collieries, near Normanton in Yorkshire, have taken the first step. They now work these mines by a company, two-thirds of the capital of which they themselves continue to hold, but undertake, in the allotment of the remaining third, to give the preference to the 'officials and operatives employed in the concern'; and, what is of still greater importance, whenever the annual profit exceeds 10 per cent, one-half the excess is divided among the workpeople and employés, whether shareholders or not, in proportion to their earnings during the year. It is highly honourable to these important employers of labour to have initiated a system so full of benefit both to the operatives employed and to the general interest of social improvement: and they express no more than a just confidence in the principle when they say, that 'the adoption of the mode of appropriation thus recommended would, it is believed, add so great an element of success to the undertaking as to increase rather than diminish the dividend to the shareholders'.

6. The form of association, however, which if mankind continue to improve, must be expected in the end to predominate, is not that which can exist between a capitalist as chief, and workpeople without a voice in the management, but the association of the labourers themselves on terms of equality, collectively owning the capital with which they carry on their operations, and working under managers elected and removable by themselves. So long as this idea remained in a state of theory, in the writings of Owen or of Louis Blanc, it may have appeared, to the common modes of judgment, incapable of being realized, and not likely to be tried unless by seizing on the existing capital, and confiscating it for the benefit of the labourers; which is even

now imagined by many persons, and pretended by more, both in England and on the Continent, to be the meaning and purpose of Socialism. But there is a capacity of exertion and self-denial in the masses of mankind, which is never known but on the rare occasions on which it is appealed to in the name of some great idea or elevated sentiment. Such an appeal was made by the French Revolution of 1848. For the first time it then seemed to the intelligent and generous of the working classes of a great nation, that they had obtained a government who sincerely desired the freedom and dignity of the many, and who did not look upon it as their natural and legitimate state to be instruments of production, worked for the benefit of the possessors of capital. Under this encouragement, the ideas sown by Socialist writers, of an emancipation of labour to be effected by means of association, throve and fructified; and many working people came to the resolution, not only that they would work for one another, instead of working for a master tradesman or manufacturer, but that they would also free themselves, at whatever cost of labour or privation, from the necessity of paying, out of the produce of their industry, a heavy tribute for the use of capital; that they would extinguish this tax, not by robbing the capitalists of what they or their predecessors had acquired by labour and preserved by economy, but by honestly acquiring capital for themselves. If only a few operatives had attempted this arduous task, or if, while many attempted it, a few only had succeeded, their success might have been deemed to furnish no argument for their system as a permanent mode of industrial organization. But, excluding all the instances of failure, there exist, or existed a short time ago, upwards of a hundred successful, and many eminently prosperous, associations of operatives in Paris alone, besides a considerable number in the departments. [...]

The capital of most of the associations was originally confined to the few tools belonging to the founders, and the small sums which could be collected from their savings, or which were lent to them by other workpeople as poor as themselves. In some cases, however, loans of capital were

made to them by the republican government: but the associations which obtained these advances, or at least which
obtained them before they had already achieved success,
are, it appears, in general by no means the most prosperous.
The most striking instances of prosperity are in the case of
those who have had nothing to rely on but their own slender
means and the small loans of fellow-workmen, and who
lived on bread and water while they devoted the whole
surplus of their gains to the formation of a capital. [...]

The same admirable qualities by which the associations
were carried through their early struggles, maintained them
in their increasing prosperity. Their rules of discipline,
instead of being more lax, are stricter than those of ordinary
workshops; but being rules self-imposed, for the manifest
good of the community, and not for the convenience of an
employer regarded as having an opposite interest, they are
far more scrupulously obeyed, and the voluntary obedience
carries with it a sense of personal worth and dignity. With
wonderful rapidity the associated work-people have learnt
to correct those of the ideas they set out with, which are in
opposition to the teaching of reason and experience. Almost
all the associations, at first, excluded piece-work, and gave
equal wages whether the work done was more or less.
Almost all have abandoned this system, and after allowing
to every one a fixed minimum, sufficient for subsistence,
they apportion all further remuneration according to the
work done: most of them even dividing the profits at the
end of the year, in the same proportion as the earnings.[1]

---

[1] Even the association founded by M. Louis Blanc, that of the tailors of Clichy,
after eighteen months' trial of this system, adopted piece-work. [...] One of the
most discreditable indications of a low moral condition given of late by part of
the English working classes, is the opposition to piece-work. When the payment
per piece is not sufficiently high, that is a just ground of objection. But dislike to
piece-work in itself, except under mistaken notions, must be dislike to justness
and fairness; a desire to cheat, by not giving work in proportion to pay.
Piece-work is the perfection of contract; and contract, in all work, and in the most
minute detail—the principle of so much pay for so much service, carried out to
the utmost extremity—is the system, of all others, in the present state of society
and degree of civilization, most favourable to the worker; though most unfavourable to the non-worker who wishes to be paid for being idle.

It is the declared principle of most of these associations, that they do not exist for the mere private benefit of the individual members, but for the promotion of the co-operative cause. With every extension, therefore, of their business, they take in additional members, not (when they remain faithful to their original plan) to receive wages from them as hired labourers, but to enter at once into the full benefits of the association, without being required to bring anything in, except their labour: the only condition imposed is that of receiving during a few years a smaller share in the annual division of profits, as some equivalent for the sacrifices of the founders. When members quit the association, which they are always at liberty to do, they carry none of the capital with them: it remains an indivisible property, of which the members for the time being have the use, but not the arbitrary disposal: by the stipulations of most of the contracts, even if the association breaks up, the capital cannot be divided, but must be devoted entire to some work of beneficence or of public utility. A fixed, and generally a considerable, proportion of the annual profits is not shared among the members, but added to the capital of the association, or devoted to the repayment of advances previously made to it: another portion is set aside to provide for the sick and disabled, and another to form a fund for extending the practice of association, or aiding other associations in their need. The managers are paid, like other members, for the time which is occupied in management, usually at the rate of the highest paid labour: but the rule is adhered to, that the exercise of power shall never be an occasion of profit. [...]

The vitality of these associations must indeed be great, to have enabled about twenty of them to survive not only the anti-socialist reaction, which for the time discredited all attempts to enable workpeople to be their own employers—not only the *tracasseries** of the police, and the hostile policy of the government since the usurpation—but in addition to these obstacles, all the difficulties arising from the trying condition of financial and commercial affairs from 1854 to 1858. Of the prosperity attained by some of them even while passing through this difficult period, I have given examples which must be conclusive to all minds as to the brilliant future reserved for the principle of co-operation.[1]

It is not in France alone that these associations have commenced a career of prosperity. To say nothing at present of Germany, Piedmont, and Switzerland (where the Konsum-Verein of Zürich is one of the most prosperous co-operative associations in Europe), England can produce cases of success rivalling even those which I have cited from France. Under the impulse commenced by Mr Owen, and more recently propagated by the writings and personal efforts of a band of friends, chiefly clergymen and barristers, to whose noble exertions too much praise can scarcely be given, the good seed was widely sown; the necessary alterations in the English law of partnership were obtained from Parliament, on the benevolent and public-spirited initiative of Mr Slaney; many industrial associations, and a still greater number of co-operative stores for retail purchases, were founded. Among these are already many instances of remarkable prosperity, the most signal of which are the Leeds Flour Mill, and the Rochdale Society of Equitable Pioneers. Of this last association, the most successful of all, the history has been written in a very interesting manner by Mr Holyoake;[2] and the notoriety which by this and other

---

[1] In the last few years the co-operative movement among the French working-classes has taken a fresh start. An interesting account of the Provision Association (Association Alimentaire) of Grenoble has been given in a pamphlet by M. Casimir Périer (Les Sociétés de Co-opération); and in the *Times* of November 24, 1864, we read the following passage:—'While a certain number of operatives stand out for more wages, or fewer hours of labour, others who have also seceded, have associated for the purpose of carrying on their respective trades on their own account, and have collected funds for the purchase of instruments of labour. They have founded a society, "Société Générale d'Approvisionnement et de Consommation". It numbers between 300 and 400 members, who have already opened a "co-operative store" at Passy, which is now within the limits of Paris. They calculate that by May next, fifteen new self-supporting associations of the same kind will be ready to commence operations; so that the number will be for Paris alone from 50 to 60.'

[2] 'Self-help by the People—History of Co-operation in Rochdale' [London, 1858]. An instructive account of this and other co-operative associations has also been written in the 'Companion to the Almanack' for 1862, by Mr John Plummer, of Kettering; himself one of the most inspiring examples of mental cultivation and high principle in a self-instructed working man.

means has been given to facts so encouraging, is causing a rapid extension of associations with similar objects in Lancashire, Yorkshire, London, and elsewhere. [...]

It is not necessary to enter into any details respecting the subsequent history of English Co-operation; the less so, as it is now one of the recognized elements in the progressive movement of the age, and, as such, has latterly been the subject of elaborate articles in most of our leading periodicals, one of the most recent and best of which was in the Edinburgh Review for October 1864: and the progress of Co-operation from month to month is regularly chronicled in the 'Co-operator'.* I must not, however, omit to mention the last great step in advance in reference to the Co-operative Stores, the formation in the North of England (and another is in course of formation in London) of a Wholesale Society, to dispense with the services of the wholesale merchant as well as of the retail dealer, and extend to the Societies the advantage which each society gives to its own members, by an agency for co-operative purchases, of foreign as well as domestic commodities, direct from the producers.

It is hardly possible to take any but a hopeful view of the prospects of mankind, when, in two leading countries of the world, the obscure depths of society contain simple working men whose integrity, good sense, self-command, and honourable confidence in one another, have enabled them to carry these noble experiments to the triumphant issue which the facts recorded in the preceding pages attest.[1]

From the progressive advance of the co-operative movement, a great increase may be looked for even in the aggregate productiveness of industry. The sources of the increase are twofold. In the first place, the class of mere distributors, who are not producers but auxiliaries of production, and whose inordinate numbers, far more than the gains of capitalists, are the cause why so great a portion of the wealth produced does not reach the producers—will be reduced to more modest dimensions. Distributors differ

---

[1] [Not included in present edn.]

from producers in this, that when producers increase, even though in any given department of industry they may be too numerous, they actually produce more: but the multiplication of distributors does not make more distribution to be done, more wealth to be distributed; it does but divide the same work among a greater number of persons, seldom even cheapening the process. By limiting the distributors to the number really required for making the commodities accessible to the consumers—which is the direct effect of the co-operative system—a vast number of hands will be set free for production, and the capital which feeds and the gains which remunerate them will be applied to feed and remunerate producers. This great economy of the world's resources would be realized even if co-operation stopped at associations for purchase and consumption, without extending to production.

The other mode in which co-operation tends, still more efficaciously, to increase the productiveness of labour, consists in the vast stimulus given to productive energies, by placing the labourers, as a mass, in a relation to their work which would make it their principle and their interest—at present it is neither—to do the utmost, instead of the least possible, in exchange for their remuneration. It is scarcely possible to rate too highly this material benefit, which yet is as nothing compared with the moral revolution in society that would accompany it: the healing of the standing feud between capital and labour; the transformation of human life, from a conflict of classes struggling for opposite interests, to a friendly rivalry in the pursuit of a good common to all; the elevation of the dignity of labour; a new sense of security and independence in the labouring class; and the conversion of each human being's daily occupation into a school of the social sympathies and the practical intelligence.

Such is the noble idea which the promoters of Co-operation should have before them. But to attain, in any degree, these objects, it is indispensable that all, and not some only, of those who do the work should be identified in interest with the prosperity of the undertaking. Associations which, when they have been successful, renounce the essential principle of the system, and become joint-stock companies of a limited number of shareholders, who differ from those of other companies only in being working men; associations which employ hired labourers without any interest in the profits (and I grieve to say that the Manufacturing Society even of Rochdale has thus degenerated) are, no doubt, exercising a lawful right in honestly employing the existing system of society to improve their position as individuals, but it is not from them that anything need be expected towards replacing that system by a better. Neither will such societies, in the long run, succeed in keeping their ground against individual competition. Individual management, by the one person principally interested, has great advantages over every description of collective management. Co-operation has but one thing to oppose to those advantages—the common interest of all the workers in the work. When individual capitalists, as they will certainly do, add this to their other points of advantage; when, even if only to increase their gains, they take up the practice which these co-operative societies have dropped, and connect the pecuniary interest of every person in their employment with the most efficient and most economical management of the concern; they are likely to gain an easy victory over societies which retain the defects, while they cannot possess the full advantages, of the old system.

Under the most favourable supposition, it will be desirable, and perhaps for a considerable length of time, that individual capitalists, associating their work-people in the profits, should coexist with even those co-operative societies which are faithful to the co-operative principle. Unity of authority makes many things possible, which could not or would not be undertaken subject to the chance of divided councils or changes in the management. A private capitalist, exempt from the control of a body, if he is a person of capacity, is considerably more likely than almost any association to run judicious risks, and originate costly improvements. Co-operative societies may be depended on for adopting improvements after they have been tested by success, but individuals are more likely to commence things previously untried. Even in ordinary business, the competition of capable persons who in the event of failure are to have all the loss, and in case of success the greater part of the gain, will be very useful in keeping the managers of co-operative societies up to the due pitch of activity and vigilance.

When, however, co-operative societies shall have sufficiently multiplied, it is not probable that any but the least valuable work-people will any longer consent to work all their lives for wages merely; both private capitalists and associations will gradually find it necessary to make the entire body of labourers participants in profits. Eventually, and in perhaps a less remote future than may be supposed, we may, through the co-operative principle, see our way to a change in society, which would combine the freedom and independence of the individual, with the moral, intellectual, and economical advantages of aggregate production; and which, without violence or spoliation, or even any sudden disturbance of existing habits and expectations, would realize, at least in the industrial department, the best aspirations of the democratic spirit, by putting an end to the division of society into the industrious and the idle, and effacing all social distinctions but those fairly earned by personal services and exertions. Associations like those which we have described, by the very process of their success, are a course of education in those moral and active qualities by which alone success can be either deserved or attained. As associations multiplied, they would tend more and more to absorb all work-people, except those who have too little understanding, or too little virtue, to be capable of learning to act on any other system than that of narrow selfishness. As this change proceeded, owners of capital would gradually find it to their advantage, instead of maintaining the struggle of the old system with work-people of only the worst description, to lend their capital to the associations; to do this at a diminishing rate of interest, and at last, perhaps, even to exchange their capital for terminable annuities. In this or some such mode, the existing accumulations of capital might honestly, and by a kind of spontaneous process, become in the end the joint property of all who participate in their productive employment: a transformation which, thus effected, (and assuming of course that both sexes participate equally in the rights and in the government of the association)[1] would be the nearest approach to social justice, and the most beneficial ordering of industrial affairs for the universal good, which it is possible at present to foresee.

7. I agree, then, with the Socialist writers in their conception of the form which industrial operations tend to assume in the advance of improvement; and I entirely share their opinion that the time is ripe for commencing this transformation, and that it should by all just and effectual means be aided and encouraged. But while I agree and sympathize with Socialists in this practical portion of their aims, I utterly dissent from the most conspicuous and vehement part of their teaching, their declamations against competition. With moral conceptions in many respects far ahead of the existing arrangements of society, they have in general very confused and erroneous notions of its actual working; and one of their greatest errors, as I conceive, is to charge upon competition all the economical evils which at present exist. They forget that wherever competition is not, monopoly is; and that monopoly, in all its forms, is the taxation of the industrious for the support of indolence, if not of plunder. They forget, too, that with the exception of competition among labourers, all other competition is for the benefit of the labourers, by cheapening the articles they consume; that competition even in the labour market is a source not of low but of high wages, wherever the competi-

---

[1] In this respect also the Rochdale Society has given an example of reason and justice, worthy of the good sense and good feeling manifested in their general proceedings. 'The Rochdale Store', says Mr. Holyoake, 'renders incidental but valuable aid towards realizing the civil independence of women. Women may be members of this Store, and vote in its proceedings. Single and married women join. Many married women become members because their husbands will not take the trouble, and others join in it in self-defence, to prevent the husband from spending their money in drink. The husband cannot withdraw the savings at the Store standing in the wife's name, unless she signs the order.'

tion *for* labour exceeds the competition *of* labour, as in America, in the colonies, and in the skilled trades; and never could be a cause of low wages, save by the overstocking of the labour market through the too great numbers of the labourers' families; while, if the supply of labourers is excessive, not even Socialism can prevent their remuneration from being low. Besides, if association were universal, there would be no competition between labourer and labourer; and that between association and association would be for the benefit of the consumers, that is, of the associations; of the industrious classes generally.

I do not pretend that there are no inconveniences in competition, or that the moral objections urged against it by Socialist writers, as a source of jealousy and hostility among those engaged in the same occupation, are altogether groundless. [...] But if competition has its evils, it prevents greater evils. It is the common error of Socialists to overlook the natural indolence of mankind; their tendency to be passive, to be the slaves of habit, to persist indefinitely in a course once chosen. Let them once attain any state of existence which they consider tolerable, and the danger to be apprehended is that they will thenceforth stagnate; will not exert themselves to improve, and by letting their faculties rust, will lose even the energy required to preserve them from deterioration. Competition may not be the best conceivable stimulus, but it is at present a necessary one, and no one can foresee the time when it will not be indispensable to progress. Even confining ourselves to the industrial department, in which, more than in any other, the majority may be supposed to be competent judges of improvements; it would be difficult to induce the general assembly of an association to submit to the trouble and inconvenience of altering their habits by adopting some new and promising invention, unless their knowledge of the existence of rival associations made them apprehend that what they would not consent to do, others would, and that they would be left behind in the race.

Instead of looking upon competition as the baneful and anti-social principle which it is held to be by the generality

of Socialists, I conceive that, even in the present state of
society and industry, every restriction of it is an evil, and
every extension of it, even if for the time injuriously affecting some class of labourers, is always an ultimate good. To
be protected against competition is to be protected in
idleness, in mental dulness; to be saved the necessity of
being as active and as intelligent as other people; and if it
is also to be protected against being underbid for employment by a less highly paid class of labourers, this is only
where old custom, or local and partial monopoly, has
placed some particular class of artizans in a privileged
position as compared with the rest; and the time has come
when the interest of universal improvement is no longer
promoted by prolonging the privileges of a few. If the
slopsellers and others of their class have lowered the wages
of tailors, and some other artizans, by making them an
affair of competition instead of custom, so much the better
in the end. What is now required is not to bolster up old
customs, whereby limited classes of labouring people obtain
partial gains which interest them in keeping up the present
organization of society, but to introduce new general practices beneficial to all; and there is reason to rejoice at
whatever makes the privileged classes of skilled artizans feel
that they have the same interests, and depend for their
remuneration on the same general causes, and must resort
for the improvement of their condition to the same remedies,
as the less fortunately circumstanced and comparatively
helpless multitude.

BOOK V

ON THE INFLUENCE OF GOVERNMENT

I

OF THE FUNCTIONS OF GOVERNMENT
IN GENERAL

1. One of the most disputed questions both in political science and in practical statesmanship at this particular period, relates to the proper limits of the functions and agency of governments. At other times it has been a subject of controversy how governments should be constituted, and according to what principles and rules they should exercise their authority; but it is now almost equally a question, to what departments of human affairs that authority should extend. And when the tide sets so strongly towards changes in government and legislation, as a means of improving the condition of mankind, this discussion is more likely to increase than to diminish in interest. On the one hand, impatient reformers, thinking it easier and shorter to get possession of the government than of the intellects and disposition of the public, are under a constant temptation to stretch the province of government beyond due bounds: while, on the other, mankind have been so much accustomed by their rulers to interference for purposes other than the public good, or under an erroneous conception of what that good requires, and so many rash proposals are made by sincere lovers of improvement, for attempting, by compulsory regulation, the attainment of objects which can only be effectually or only usefully compassed by opinion and discussion, that there has grown up a spirit of resistance *in limine** to the interference of government, merely as such, and a disposition to restrict its sphere of action within the narrowest bounds. From differences in the historical development of different nations, not necessary to be here dwelt upon,

the former excess, that of exaggerating the province of government, prevails most, both in theory and in practice, among the Continental nations, while in England the contrary spirit has hitherto been predominant.

The general principles of the question, in so far as it is a question of principle, I shall make an attempt to determine in a later chapter of this Book: after first considering the effects produced by the conduct of government in the exercise of the functions universally acknowledged to belong to it. For this purpose, there must be a specification of the functions which are either inseparable from the idea of a government, or are exercised habitually and without objection by all governments; as distinguished from those respecting which it has been considered questionable whether governments should exercise them or not. The former may be termed the *necessary*, the latter the *optional*, functions of government. By the term optional it is not meant to imply, that it can ever be a matter of indifference, or of arbitrary choice, whether the government should or should not take upon itself the functions in question; but only that the expediency of its exercising them does not amount to necessity, and is a subject on which diversity of opinion does or may exist.

2. In attempting to enumerate the necessary functions of government, we find them to be considerably more multifarious than most people are at first aware of, and not capable of being circumscribed by those very definite lines of demarcation, which, in the inconsiderateness of popular discussion, it is often attempted to draw round them. We sometimes, for example, hear it said that governments ought to confine themselves to affording protection against force and fraud: that, these two things apart, people should be free agents, able to take care of themselves, and that so long as a person practises no violence or deception, to the injury of others in person or property, legislators and governments are in no way called on to concern themselves about him. But why should people be protected by their government, that is, by their own collective strength, against

violence and fraud, and not against other evils, except that the expediency is more obvious? If nothing, but what people cannot possibly do for themselves, can be fit to be done for them by government, people might be required to protect themselves by their skill and courage even against force, or to beg or buy protection against it, as they actually do where the government is not capable of protecting them: and against fraud every one has the protection of his own wits. But without further anticipating the discussion of principles, it is sufficient on the present occasion to consider facts.

Under which of these heads, the repression of force or of fraud, are we to place the operation, for example, of the laws of inheritance? Some such laws must exist in all societies. It may be said, perhaps, that in this matter government has merely to give effect to the disposition which an individual makes of his own property by will. This, however, is at least extremely disputable; there is probably no country by whose laws the power of testamentary disposition is perfectly absolute. And suppose the very common case of there being no will: does not the law, that is, the government, decide on principles of general expediency, who shall take the succession? and in case the successor is in any manner incompetent, does it not appoint persons, frequently officers of its own, to collect the property and apply it to his benefit? There are many other cases in which the government undertakes the administration of property, because the public interest, or perhaps only that of the particular persons concerned, is thought to require it. This is often done in case of litigated property; and in cases of judicially declared insolvency. It has never been contended that in doing these things, a government exceeds its province.

Nor is the function of the law in defining property itself, so simple a thing as may be supposed. It may be imagined, perhaps, that the law has only to declare and protect the right of every one to what he has himself produced, or acquired by the voluntary consent, fairly obtained, of those who produced it. But is there nothing recognized as property except what has been produced? Is there not the earth itself, its forests and waters, and all other natural riches, above and below the surface? These are the inheritance of the human race, and there must be regulations for the common enjoyment of it. What rights, and under what conditions, a person shall be allowed to exercise over any portion of this common inheritance, cannot be left undecided. No function of government is less optional than the regulation of these things, or more completely involved in the idea of civilized society.

Again, the legitimacy is conceded of repressing violence or treachery; but under which of these heads are we to place the obligation imposed on people to perform their contracts? Non-performance does not necessarily imply fraud; the person who entered into the contract may have sincerely intended to fulfil it: and the term fraud, which can scarcely admit of being extended even to the case of voluntary breach of contract when no deception was practised, is certainly not applicable when the omission to perform is a case of negligence. Is it no part of the duty of governments to enforce contracts? Here the doctrine of non-interference would no doubt be stretched a little, and it would be said, that enforcing contracts is not regulating the affairs of individuals at the pleasure of government, but giving effect to their own expressed desire. Let us acquiesce in this enlargement of the restrictive theory, and take it for what it is worth. But governments do not limit their concern with contracts to a simple enforcement. They take upon themselves to determine what contracts are fit to be enforced. It is not enough that one person, not being either cheated or compelled, makes a promise to another. There are promises by which it is not for the public good that persons should have the power of binding themselves. To say nothing of engagements to do something contrary to law, there are engagements which the law refuses to enforce, for reasons connected with the interest of the promiser, or with the general policy of the state. A contract by which a person sells himself to another as a slave, would be declared void by the tribunals of this and of most other European countries. There are few nations whose laws enforce a contract for what is looked upon as prostitution, or any matrimonial engagement of which the conditions vary in any respect from those which the law has thought fit to prescribe. But when once it is admitted that there are any engagements which for reasons of expediency the law ought not to enforce, the same question is necessarily opened with respect to all engagements. Whether, for example, the law should enforce a contract to labour, when the wages are too low or the hours of work too severe: whether it should enforce a contract by which a person binds himself to remain, for more than a very limited period, in the service of a given individual: whether a contract of marriage, entered into for life, should continue to be enforced against the deliberate will of the persons, or of either of the persons, who entered into it. Every question which can possibly arise as to the policy of contracts, and of the relations which they establish among human beings, is a question for the legislator; and one which he cannot escape from considering, and in some way or other deciding.

Again, the prevention and suppression of force and fraud afford appropriate employment for soldiers, policemen, and criminal judges; but there are also civil tribunals. The punishment of wrong is one business of an administration of justice, but the decision of disputes is another. Innumerable disputes arise between persons, without *mala fides** on either side, through misconception of their legal rights, or from not being agreed about the facts, on the proof of which those rights are legally dependent. It is not for the general interest that the State should appoint persons to clear up these uncertainties and terminate these disputes? It cannot be said to be a case of absolute necessity. People might appoint an arbitrator, and engage to submit to his decision; and they do so where there are no courts of justice, or where the courts are not trusted, or where their delays and expenses, or the irrationality of their rules of evidence, deter people from resorting to them. Still, it is universally thought right that the State should establish civil tribunals; and if their defects often drive people to have recourse to substitutes, even then the power held in reserve of carrying the case before a legally constituted court, gives to the substitutes their principal efficacy.

Not only does the State undertake to decide disputes, it takes precautions beforehand that disputes may not arise. The laws of most countries lay down rules for determining many things, not because it is of much consequence in what way they are determined, but in order that they may be determined somehow, and there may be no question on the subject. The law prescribes forms of words for many kinds of contract, in order that no dispute or misunderstanding may arise about their meaning: it makes provision that if a dispute does arise, evidence shall be procurable for deciding it, by requiring that the document be attested by witnesses and executed with certain formalities. The law preserves authentic evidence of facts to which legal consequences are attached, by keeping a registry of such facts; as of births, deaths, and marriages, of wills and contracts, and of judicial proceedings. In doing these things, it has never been alleged that government oversteps the proper limits of its functions.

Again, however wide a scope we may allow to the doctrine that individuals are the proper guardians of their own interests, and that government owes nothing to them but to save them from being interfered with by other people, the doctrine can never be applicable to any persons but those who are capable of acting in their own behalf. The individual may be an infant, or a lunatic, or fallen into imbecility. The law surely must look after the interests of such persons. It does not necessarily do this through officers of its own. It often devolves the trust upon some relative or connexion. But in doing so is its duty ended? Can it make over the interests of one person to the control of another, and be excused from supervision, or from holding the person thus trusted, responsible for the discharge of the trust?

There is a multitude of cases in which governments, with general approbation, assume powers and execute functions for which no reason can be assigned except the simple one, that they conduce to general convenience. We may take as an example, the function (which is a monopoly too) of

coining money. This is assumed for no more recondite purpose than that of saving to individuals the trouble, delay,
and expense of weighing and assaying. No one, however,
even of those most jealous of state interference, has objected
to this as an improper exercise of the powers of government.
Prescribing a set of standard weights and measures is
another instance. Paving, lighting, and cleansing the streets
and thoroughfares, is another; whether done by the general
government, or as is more usual, and generally more advisable, by a municipal authority. Making or improving harbours, building lighthouses, making surveys in order to have
accurate maps and charts, raising dykes to keep the sea out,
and embankments to keep rivers in, are cases in point.

Examples might be indefinitely multiplied without intrud-
ing on any disputed ground. But enough has been said to
show that the admitted functions of government embrace a
much wider field than can easily be included within the
ring-fence of any restrictive definition, and that it is hardly
possible to find any ground of justification common to
them all, except the comprehensive one of general expediency; nor to limit the interference of government by any
universal rule, save the simple and vague one, that it should
never be admitted but when the case of expediency is
strong.

3. Some observations, however, may be usefully bestowed
on the nature of the considerations on which the question
of government interference is most likely to turn, and on the
mode of estimating the comparative magnitude of the ex-
pediencies involved. This will form the last of the three
parts, into which our discussion of the principles and effects
of government interference may conveniently be divided.
The following will be our division of the subject.

We shall first consider the economical effects arising from
the manner in which governments perform their necessary
and acknowledged functions.

We shall then pass to certain governmental interferences
of what I have termed the optional kind (i.e. overstepping
the boundaries of the universally acknowledged functions)

which have heretofore taken place, and in some cases still take place, under the influence of false general theories.

It will lastly remain to inquire whether, independently of any false theory, and consistently with a correct view of the laws which regulate human affairs, there be any cases of the optional class in which governmental interference is really advisable, and what are those cases.

The first of these divisions is of an extremely miscellaneous character: since the necessary functions of government, and those which are so manifestly expedient that they have never or very rarely been objected to, are, as already pointed out, too various to be brought under any very simple classification. Those, however, which are of principal importance, which alone it is necessary here to consider, may be reduced to the following general heads.

First, the means adopted by governments to raise the revenue which is the condition of their existence.

Secondly, the nature of the laws which they prescribe on the two great subjects of Property and Contracts.

Thirdly, the excellences or defects of the system of means by which they enforce generally the execution of their laws, namely, their judicature and police.

We commence with the first head, that is, with the theory of Taxation.

II

ON THE GENERAL PRINCIPLES OF TAXATION

1. The qualities desirable, economically speaking, in a system of taxation, have been embodied by Adam Smith in four maxims or principles, which, having been generally concurred in by subsequent writers, may be said to have become classical, and this chapter cannot be better commenced than by quoting them.[1]

'1. The subjects of every state ought to contribute to the support of the government, as nearly as possible in proportion to their respective abilities: that is, in proportion to the revenue which they respectively enjoy under the protection of the state. In the observation or neglect of this maxim consists what is called the equality or inequality of taxation.

'2. The tax which each individual is bound to pay ought to be certain, and not arbitrary. The time of payment, the manner of payment, the quantity to be paid, ought all to be clear and plain to the contributor, and to every other person. Where it is otherwise, every person subject to the tax is put more or less in the power of the tax-gatherer, who can either aggravate the tax upon any obnoxious contributor, or extort by the terror of such aggravation, some present or perquisite to himself. The uncertainty of taxation encourages the insolence and favours the corruption of an order of men who are naturally unpopular, even when they are neither insolent nor corrupt. The certainty of what each individual ought to pay is, in taxation, a matter of so great importance, that a very considerable degree of inequality, it appears, I believe, from the experience of all nations, is not near so great an evil, as a very small degree of uncertainty.

'3. Every tax ought to be levied at the time, or in the manner, in which it is most likely to be convenient for

---

[1] *Wealth of Nations*, bk. v, ch. ii.

the contributor to pay it. A tax upon the rent of land or of houses, payable at the same term at which such rents are usually paid, is levied at a time when it is most likely to be convenient for the contributor to pay; or when he is most likely to have wherewithal to pay. Taxes upon such consumable goods as are articles of luxury, are all finally paid by the consumer, and generally in a manner that is very convenient to him. He pays them by little and little, as he has occasion to buy the goods. As he is at liberty, too, either to buy or not to buy, as he pleases, it must be his own fault if he ever suffers any considerable inconvenience from such taxes.

'4. Every tax ought to be so contrived as both to take out and to keep out of the pockets of the people as little as possible over and above what it brings into the public treasury of the state. A tax may either take out or keep out of the pockets of the people a great deal more than it brings into the public treasury, in the four following ways. First, the levying of it may require a great number of officers, whose salaries may eat up the greater part of the produce of the tax, and whose perquisites may impose another additional tax upon the people.' Secondly, it may divert a portion of the labour and capital of the community from a more to a less productive employment. 'Thirdly, by the forfeitures and other penalties which those unfortunate individuals incur who attempt unsuccessfully to evade the tax, it may frequently ruin them, and thereby put an end to the benefit which the community might have derived from the employment of their capitals. An injudicious tax offers a great temptation to smuggling. Fourthly, by subjecting the people to the frequent visits and the odious examination of the tax-gatherers, it may expose them to much unnecessary trouble, vexation, and oppression:' to which may be added, that the restrictive regulations to which trades and manufactures are often subjected to prevent evasion of a tax, are not only in themselves troublesome and expensive, but often oppose insuperable obstacles to making improvements in the processes.

The last three of these four maxims require little other explanation or illustration than is contained in the passage itself. How far any given tax conforms to, or conflicts with them, is a matter to be considered in the discussion of particular taxes. But the first of the four points, equality of taxation, requires to be more fully examined, being a thing often imperfectly understood, and on which many false notions have become to a certain degree accredited, through the absence of any definite principles of judgement in the popular mind.

2. For what reason ought equality to be the rule in matters of taxation? For the reason, that it ought to be so in all affairs of government. As a government ought to make no distinction of persons or classes in the strength of their claims on it, whatever sacrifices it requires from them should be made to bear as nearly as possible with the same pressure upon all, which, it must be observed, is the mode by which least sacrifice is occasioned on the whole. If any one bears less than his fair share of the burthen, some other person must suffer more than his share, and the alleviation to the one is not, *ceteris paribus*, so great a good to him, as the increased pressure upon the other is an evil. Equality of taxation, therefore, as a maxim of politics, means equality of sacrifice. It means apportioning the contribution of each person towards the expenses of government, so that he shall feel neither more nor less inconvenience from his share of the payment than every other person experiences from his. This standard, like other standards of perfection, cannot be completely realized; but the first object in every practical discussion should be to know what perfection is.

There are persons, however, who are not content with the general principles of justice as a basis to ground a rule of finance upon, but must have something, as they think, more specifically appropriate to the subject. What best pleases them is, to regard the taxes paid by each member of the community as an equivalent for value received, in the shape of service to himself; and they prefer to rest the justice of making each contribute in proportion to his means, upon

the ground, that he who has twice as much property to be
protected, receives, on an accurate calculation, twice as
much protection, and ought, on the principles of bargain
and sale, to pay twice as much for it. Since, however, the
assumption that government exists solely for the protection
of property, is not one to be deliberately adhered to; some
consistent adherents of the *quid pro quo* principle go on to
observe, that protection being required for person as well as
property, and everybody's person receiving the same amount
of protection, a poll-tax of a fixed sum per head is a proper
equivalent for this part of the benefits of government, while
the remaining part, protection to property, should be paid
for in proportion to property. There is in this adjustment a
false air of nice adaptation, very acceptable to some minds.
But in the first place, it is not admissible that the protection
of persons and that of property are the sole purposes of
government. The ends of government are as comprehensive
as those of the social union. They consist of all the good,
and all the immunity from evil, which the existence of
government can be made either directly or indirectly to
bestow. In the second place, the practice of setting definite
values on things essentially indefinite, and making them a
ground of practical conclusions, is peculiarly fertile in false
views of social questions. It cannot be admitted, that to be
protected in the ownership of ten times as much property,
is to be ten times as much protected. Neither can it be truly
said that the protection of £1,000 a year costs the state ten
times as much as that of £100 a year, rather than twice
as much, or exactly as much. The same judges, soldiers,
and sailors who protect the one protect the other, and the
larger income does not necessarily, though it may sometimes, require even more policemen. Whether the labour and
expense of the protection, or the feelings of the protected
person, or any other definite thing be made the standard,
there is no such proportion as the one supposed, nor any
other definable proportion. If we wanted to estimate the
degrees of benefit which different persons derive from the
protection of government, we should have to consider who
would suffer most if that protection were withdrawn: to

which question if any answer could be made, it must be, that those would suffer most who were weakest in mind or body, either by nature or by position. Indeed, such persons would almost infallibly be slaves. If there were any justice, therefore, in the theory of justice now under consideration, those who are least capable of helping or defending themselves, being those to whom the protection of government is the most indispensable, ought to pay the greatest share of its price: the reverse of the true idea of distributive justice, which consists not in imitating but in redressing the inequalities and wrongs of nature.

Government must be regarded as so pre-eminently a concern of all, that to determine who are most interested in it is of no real importance. If a person or class of persons receive so small a share of the benefit as makes it necessary to raise the question, there is something else than taxation which is amiss, and the thing to be done is to remedy the defect, instead of recognising it and making it a ground for demanding less taxes. As, in a case of voluntary subscription for a purpose in which all are interested, all are thought to have done their part fairly when each has contributed according to his means, that is, has made an equal sacrifice for the common object; in like manner should this be the principle of compulsory contributions: and it is superfluous to look for a more ingenious or recondite ground to rest the principle upon.

3. Setting out, then, from the maxim that equal sacrifices ought to be demanded from all, we have next to inquire whether this is in fact done, by making each contribute the same percentage on his pecuniary means. Many persons maintain the negative, saying that a tenth part taken from a small income is a heavier burthen than the same fraction deducted from one much larger: and on this is grounded the very popular scheme of what is called a graduated property tax, viz. an income tax in which the percentage rises with the amount of the income.

On the best consideration I am able to give to this question, it appears to me that the portion of truth which the doctrine contains, arises principally from the difference between a tax which can be saved from luxuries, and one which trenches, in ever so small a degree, upon the necessaries of life. To take a thousand a year from the possessor of ten thousand, would not deprive him of anything really conducive either to the support or to the comfort of existence; and if such *would* be the effect of taking five pounds from one whose income is fifty, the sacrifice required from the last is not only greater than, but entirely incommensurable with, that imposed upon the first. The mode of adjusting these inequalities of pressure, which seems to be the most equitable, is that recommended by Bentham, of leaving a certain minimum of income, sufficient to provide the necessaries of life, untaxed. Suppose £50 a year to be sufficient to provide the number of persons ordinarily supported from a single income, with the requisites of life and health, and with protection against habitual bodily suffering, but not with any indulgence. This then should be made the minimum, and incomes exceeding it should pay taxes not upon their whole amount, but upon the surplus. If the tax be ten per cent, an income of £60 should be considered as a net income of £10, and charged with £1 a year, while an income of £1,000 should be charged as one of £950. Each would then pay a fixed proportion, not of his whole means, but of his superfluities.[1] An income not exceeding £50 should not be taxed at all, either directly or by taxes on necessaries; for as by supposition this is the smallest income which labour ought to be able to command, the government ought not to be a party to making it smaller. This arrangement however would constitute a reason, in addition to others which might be stated, for maintaining taxes on articles of luxury consumed by the poor. The immunity extended to the income required for necessaries, should depend on its being actually expended for that purpose; and the poor who, not having more than enough for necessaries, divert any part of it to indulgences, should

---

[1] This principle of assessment has been partially adopted by Mr Gladstone in renewing the income-tax. From £100, at which the tax begins, up to £200, the income only pays tax on the excess above £60.

like other people contribute their quota out of those indulgences to the expenses of the state.

The exemption in favour of the smaller incomes should not, I think, be stretched further than to the amount of income needful for life, health, and immunity from bodily pain. If £50 a year is sufficient (which may be doubted) for these purposes, an income of £100 a year would, as it seems to me, obtain all the relief it is entitled to, compared with one of £1,000, by being taxed only on £50 of its amount. It may be said, indeed, that to take £100 from £1,000 (even giving back five pounds) is a heavier impost than £1,000 taken from £10,000 (giving back the same five pounds). But this doctrine seems to me too disputable altogether, and even if true at all, not true to a sufficient extent, to be made the foundation of any rule of taxation. Whether the person with £10,000 a year cares less for £1,000 than the person with only £1,000 a year cares for £100, and if so, how much less, does not appear to me capable of being decided with the degree of certainty on which a legislator or a financier ought to act.

Some indeed contend that the rule of proportional taxation bears harder upon the moderate than upon the large incomes, because the same proportional payment has more tendency in the former case than in the latter, to reduce the payer to a lower grade of social rank. The fact appears to me more than questionable. But even admitting it, I object to its being considered incumbent on government to shape its course by such considerations, or to recognize the notion that social importance is or can be determined by amount of expenditure. Government ought to set an example of rating all things at their true value, and riches, therefore, at the worth, for comfort or pleasure, of the things which they will buy: and ought not to sanction the vulgarity of prizing them for the pitiful vanity of being known to possess them, or the paltry shame of being suspected to be without them, the presiding motives of three-fourths of the expenditure of the middle classes. The sacrifices of real comfort or indulgence which government requires, it is bound to apportion among all persons with as much equality as possible; but their sacrifices of the imaginary dignity dependent on expense, it may spare itself the trouble of estimating.

Both in England and on the Continent a graduated property tax (*l'impôt progressif*) has been advocated, on the avowed ground that the state should use the instrument of taxation as a means of mitigating the inequalities of wealth. I am as desirous as any one, that means should be taken to diminish those inequalities, but not so as to relieve the prodigal at the expense of the prudent. To tax the larger incomes at a higher percentage than the smaller, is to lay a tax on industry and economy; to impose a penalty on people for having worked harder and saved more than their neighbours. It is not the fortunes which are earned, but those which are unearned, that it is for the public good to place under limitation. A just and wise legislation would abstain from holding out motives for dissipating rather than saving the earnings of honest exertion. Its impartiality between competitors would consist in endeavouring that they should all start fair, and not in hanging a weight upon the swift to diminish the distance between them and the slow. Many, indeed, fail with greater efforts than those with which others succeed, not from difference of merits, but difference of opportunities; but if all were done which it would be in the power of a good government to do, by instruction and by legislation, to diminish this inequality of opportunities, the differences of fortune arising from people's own earnings could not justly give umbrage. With respect to the large fortunes acquired by gift or inheritance, the power of bequeathing is one of those privileges of property which are fit subjects for regulation on grounds of general expediency; and I have already suggested,[1] as a possible mode of restraining the accumulation of large fortunes in the hands of those who have not earned them by exertion, a limitation of the amount which any one person should be permitted to acquire by gift, bequest, or inheritance. Apart from this, and from the proposal of Bentham (also discussed in a former chapter) that collateral inheritance *ab intestato* should

[1] *Supra*, Bk. II, Ch. II.

cease, and the property escheat to the state, I conceive that inheritances and legacies, exceeding a certain amount, are highly proper subjects for taxation: and that the revenue from them should be as great as it can be made without giving rise to evasions, by donation *inter vivos** concealment of property, such as it would be impossible adequately to check. The principle of graduation (as it is called,) that is, of levying a larger percentage on a larger sum, though its application to general taxation would be in my opinion objectionable, seems to me both just and expedient as applied to legacy and inheritance duties.

The objection to a graduated property tax applies in an aggravated degree to the proposition of an exclusive tax on what is called 'realized property,' that is, property not forming a part of any capital engaged in business, or rather in business under the superintendence of the owner: as land, the public funds, money lent on mortgage, and shares (I presume) in joint stock companies. Except the proposal of applying a sponge to the national debt, no such palpable violation of common honesty has found sufficient support in this country, during the present generation, to be regarded as within the domain of discussion. It has not the palliation of a graduated property tax, that of laying the burthen on those best able to bear it; for 'realized property' includes the far larger portion of the provision made for those who are unable to work, and consists, in great part, of extremely small fractions. I can hardly conceive a more shameless pretension, than that the major part of the property of the country, that of merchants, manufacturers, farmers, and shopkeepers, should be exempted from its share of taxation; that these classes should only begin to pay their proportion after retiring from business, and if they never retire should be excused from it altogether. But even this does not give an adequate idea of the injustice of the proposition. The burthen thus exclusively thrown on the owners of the smaller portion of the wealth of the community, would not even be a burthen on that *class* of persons in perpetual succession, but would fall exclusively on those who happened to compose it when the tax was laid on. As land and those particular securities would thence-forth yield a smaller net income, relatively to the general interest of capital and to the profits of trade; the balance would rectify itself by a permanent depreciation of those kinds of property. Future buyers would acquire land and securities at a reduction of price, equivalent to the peculiar tax, which tax they would, therefore, escape from paying; while the original possessors would remain burthened with it even after parting with the property, since they would have sold their land or securities at a loss of value equival-ent to the fee-simple of the tax. Its imposition would thus be tantamount to the confiscation for public uses of a per-centage of their property, equal to the percentage laid on their income by the tax. That such a proposition should find any favour, is a striking instance of the want of conscience in matters of taxation, resulting from the absence of any fixed principles in the public mind, and of any indication of a sense of justice on the subject in the general conduct of governments. Should the scheme ever enlist a large party in its support, the fact would indicate a laxity of pecuniary integrity in national affairs, scarcely inferior to American repudiation.

4. Whether the profits of trade may not rightfully be taxed at a lower rate than incomes derived from interest or rent, is part of the more comprehensive question, so often mooted on the occasion of the present income tax, whether life incomes should be subjected to the same rate of taxation as perpetual incomes: whether salaries, for example, or annuities, or the gains of professions, should pay the same percentage as the income from inheritable property.

The existing tax treats all kinds of incomes exactly alike, taking its sevenpence (now fourpence) in the pound, as well from the person whose income dies with him, as from the landholder, stockholder, or mortgagee, who can transmit his fortune undiminished to his descendants. This is a visible injustice: yet it does not arithmetically violate the rule that taxation ought to be in proportion to means. When it is said that a temporary income ought to be taxed less than a permanent one, the reply is irresistible, that it is taxed less; for the income which lasts only ten years pays the tax only ten years, while that which lasts for ever pays for ever. On this point some financial reformers are guilty of a great fallacy. They contend that incomes ought to be assessed to the income tax not in proportion to their annual amount, but to their capitalized value: that, for example, if the value of a perpetual annuity of £100 is £3,000, and a life annuity of the same amount, being worth only half the number of years' purchase, could only be sold for £1,500, the perpetual income should pay twice as much per cent income tax as the terminable income: if the one pays £10 a year the other should pay only £5. But in this argument there is the obvious oversight, that it values the incomes by one standard and the payments by another; it capitalizes the incomes, but forgets to capitalize the payments. An annuity worth £3,000 ought, it is alleged, to be taxed twice as highly as one which is only worth £1,500, and no assertion can be more unquestionable; but it is forgotten that the income worth £3,000 pays to the supposed income tax £10 a year in perpetuity, which is equivalent, by supposition, to £300, while the terminable income pays the same £10 only during the life of its owner, which on the same calculation is a value of £150, and could actually be bought for that sum. Already, therefore, the income which is only half as valuable, pays only half as much to the tax; and if in addition to this its annual quota were reduced from £10 to £5, it would pay, not half, but a fourth part only of the payment demanded from the perpetual income. To make it just that the one income should pay only half as much per annum as the other, it would be necessary that it should pay that half for the same period, that is, in perpetuity.

The rule of payment which this school of financial reformers contend for, would be very proper if the tax were only to be levied once, to meet some national emergency. On the principle of requiring from all payers an equal sacrifice, every person who had anything belonging to him, reversioners included, would be called on for a payment proportioned to the present value of his property. I wonder it does

not occur to the reformers in question, that precisely because this principle of assessment would be just in the case
of a payment made once for all, it cannot possibly be just
for a permanent tax. When each pays only once, one person
pays no oftener than another; and the proportion which
would be just in that case, cannot also be just if one person
has to make the payment only once, and the other several
times. This, however, is the type of the case which actually
occurs. The permanent incomes pay the tax as much oftener
than the temporary ones, as a perpetuity exceeds the certain
or uncertain length of time which forms the duration of the
income for life or years.

All attempts to establish a claim in favour of terminable
incomes on numerical grounds—to make out, in short, that
a proportional tax is not a proportional tax—are manifestly
absurd. The claim does not rest on grounds of arithmetic,
but of human wants and feelings. It is not because the
temporary annuitant has smaller means, but because he has
greater necessities, that he ought to be assessed at a lower
rate.

In spite of the nominal equality of income, A, an annuitant of £1,000 a year, cannot so well afford to pay £100 out
of it, as B who derives the same annual sum from heritable
property; A having usually a demand on his income which
B has not, namely, to provide by saving for children or
others; to which, in the case of salaries or professional
gains, must generally be added a provision for his own later
years; while B may expend his whole income without injury
to his old age, and still have it all to bestow on others after
his death. If A, in order to meet these exigencies, must lay
by £300 of his income, to take £100 from him as income
tax is to take £100 from £700, since it must be retrenched
from that part only of his means which he can afford to
spend on his own consumption. Were he to throw it rateably
on what he spends and on what he saves, abating £70 from
his consumption and £30 from his annual saving, then
indeed his immediate sacrifice would be proportionately the
same as B's: but then his children or his old age would be
worse provided for in consequence of the tax. The capital

sum which would be accumulated for them would be one-tenth less, and on the reduced income afforded by this reduced capital, they would be a second time charged with income tax; while B's heirs would only be charged once.

The principle, therefore, of equality of taxation, interpreted in its only just sense, equality of sacrifice, requires that a person who has no means of providing for old age, or for those in whom he is interested, except by saving from income, should have the tax remitted on all that part of his income which is really and bona fide applied to that purpose.

If, indeed, reliance could be placed on the conscience of the contributors, or sufficient security taken for the correctness of their statements by collateral precautions, the proper mode of assessing an income tax would be to tax only the part of income devoted to expenditure, exempting that which is saved. For when saved and invested (and all savings, speaking generally, are invested) it thenceforth pays income tax on the interest or profit which it brings, notwithstanding that it has already been taxed on the principal. Unless, therefore, savings are exempted from income tax, the contributors are twice taxed on what they save, and only once on what they spend. A person who spends all he receives, pays 7d. in the pound, or say three per cent, to the tax, and no more; but if he saves part of the year's income and buys stock, then in addition to the three per cent which he has paid on the principal, and which diminishes the interest in the same ratio, he pays three per cent annually on the interest itself, which is equivalent to an immediate payment of a second three per cent on the principal. So that while unproductive expenditure pays only three per cent, savings pay six per cent: or more correctly, three per cent on the whole, and another three per cent on the remaining ninety-seven. The difference thus created to the disadvantage of prudence and economy, is not only impolitic but unjust. To tax the sum invested, and afterwards tax also the proceeds of the investment, is to tax the same portion of the contributor's means twice over. The principal and the interest cannot both together form part of his resources;

they are the same portion twice counted: if he has the interest, it is because he abstains from using the principal; if he spends the principal, he does not receive the interest. Yet because he can do either of the two, he is taxed as if he could do both, and could have the benefit of the saving and that of the spending, concurrently with one another.

It has been urged as an objection to exempting savings from taxation, that the law ought not to disturb, by artificial interference, the natural competition between the motives for saving and those for spending. But we have seen that the law disturbs this natural competition when it taxes savings, not when it spares them; for as the savings pay at any rate the full tax as soon as they are invested, their exemption from payment in the earlier stage is necessary to prevent them from paying twice, while money spent in unproductive consumption pays only once. It has been further objected, that since the rich have the greatest means of saving, any privilege given to savings is an advantage bestowed on the rich at the expense of the poor. I answer, that it is bestowed on them only in proportion as they abdicate the personal use of their riches; in proportion as they divert their income from the supply of their own wants, to a productive investment, through which, instead of being consumed by themselves, it is distributed in wages among the poor. If this be favouring the rich, I should like to have it pointed out, what mode of assessing taxation can deserve the name of favouring the poor.

No income tax is really just, from which savings are not exempted; and no income tax ought to be voted without that provision, if the form of the returns, and the nature of the evidence required, could be so arranged as to prevent the exemption from being taken fraudulent advantage of, by saving with one hand and getting into debt with the other, or by spending in the following year what had been passed tax-free as saving in the year preceding. If this difficulty could be surmounted, the difficulties and complexities arising from the comparative claims of temporary and permanent incomes, would disappear; for, since temporary incomes have no just claim to lighter taxation than permanent incomes, except in so far as their possessors are more called upon to save, the exemption of what they do save would fully satisfy the claim. But if no plan can be devised for the exemption of actual savings, sufficiently free from liability to fraud, it is necessary, as the next thing in point of justice, to take into account in assessing the tax, what the different classes of contributors *ought* to save. And there would probably be no other mode of doing this than the rough expedient of two different rates of assessment. There would be great difficulty in taking into account differences of duration between one terminable income and another; and in the most frequent case, that of incomes dependent on life, differences of age and health would constitute such extreme diversity as it would be impossible to take proper cognizance of. It would probably be necessary to be content with one uniform rate for all incomes of inheritance, and another uniform rate for all those which necessarily terminate with the life of the individual. In fixing the proportion between the two rates, there must inevitably be something arbitrary; perhaps a deduction of one-fourth in favour of life-incomes would be as little objectionable as any which could be made, it being thus assumed that one-fourth of a life-income is, on the average of all ages and states of health, a suitable proportion to be laid by as a provision for successors and for old age.[1]

---

[1] Mr Hubbard, the first person who, as a practical legislator, has attempted the rectification of the income tax on principles of unimpeachable justice, and whose well-conceived plan wants little of being as near an approximation to a just assessment as it is likely that means could be found of carrying into practical effect, proposes a deduction not of a fourth but of a third, in favour of industrial and professional incomes. He fixes on this ratio, on the ground that, independently of all consideration as to what the industrial and professional classes ought to save, the attainable evidence goes to prove that a third of their incomes is what on an average they do save, over and above the proportion saved by other classes. 'The savings' (Mr Hubbard observes) 'effected out of incomes derived from invested property are estimated at one-tenth. The savings effected out of industrial incomes are estimated at four-tenths. The amounts which would be assessed under these two classes being nearly equal, the adjustment is simplified by striking off one-tenth on either side, and then reducing by three-tenths, or one-third, the assessable amount of industrial incomes.' Proposed Report (p. xiv of the Report and Evidence of the Committee of 1861). In such an estimate there must be a large element of conjecture; but in so far as it can be substantiated, it affords a valid ground for the practical conclusion which Mr Hubbard founds on it.

Of the net profits of persons in business, a part, as before observed, may be considered as interest on capital, and of a perpetual character, and the remaining part as remuneration for the skill and labour of superintendence. The surplus beyond interest depends on the life of the individual, and even on his continuance in business, and is entitled to the full amount of exemption allowed to terminable incomes. It has also, I conceive, a just claim to a further amount of exemption in consideration of its precariousness. An income which some not unusual vicissitude may reduce to nothing, or even convert into a loss, is not the same thing to the feelings of the possessor as a permanent income of £1,000 a year, even though on an average of years it may yield £1,000 a year. If life-incomes were assessed at three-fourths of their amount, the profits of business, after deducting interest on capital, should not only be assessed at three-fourths, but should pay, on that assessment, a lower rate. Or perhaps the claims of justice in this respect might be

Several writers on the subject, including Mr Mill in his Elements of Political Economy, and Mr M'Culloch in his work on Taxation, have contended that as much should be deducted as would be sufficient to insure the possessor's life for a sum which would give to his successors for ever an income equal to what he reserves for himself; since this is what the possessor of heritable property can do without saving at all: in other words, that temporary incomes should be converted into perpetual incomes of equal present value, and taxed as such. If the owners of life-incomes actually did save this large proportion of their income, or even a still larger, I would gladly grant them an exemption from taxation on the whole amount, since, if practical means could be found of doing it, I would exempt savings altogether. But I cannot admit that they have a claim to exemption on the general assumption of their being obliged to save this amount. Owners of life-incomes are not bound to forego the enjoyment of them for the sake of leaving to a perpetual line of successors an independent provision equal to their own temporary one; and no one ever dreams of doing so. Least of all is it to be required or expected from those whose incomes are the fruits of personal exertion, that they should leave to their posterity for ever, without any necessity for exertion, the same incomes which they allow to themselves. All they are bound to do, even for their children, is to place them in circumstances in which they will have favourable chances of earning their own living. To give, however, either to children or to others, by bequest, being a legitimate inclination, which these persons cannot indulge without laying by a part of their income, while the owners of heritable property can; this real inequality in cases where the incomes themselves are equal, should be considered, to a reasonable degree, in the adjustment of taxation, so as to require from both, as nearly as practicable, an equal sacrifice.

sufficiently met by allowing the deduction of a fourth on the entire income, interest included.

These are the chief cases, of ordinary occurrence, in which any difficulty arises in interpreting the maxim of equality of taxation. The proper sense to be put upon it, as we have seen in the preceding example, is, that people should be taxed, not in proportion to what they have, but to what they can afford to spend. It is no objection to this principle that we cannot apply it consistently to all cases. A person with a life-income and precarious health, or who has many persons depending on his exertions, must, if he wishes to provide for them after his death, be more rigidly economical than one who has a life-income of equal amount with a strong constitution, and few claims upon him; and if it be conceded that taxation cannot accommodate itself to these distinctions, it is argued that there is no use in attending to any distinctions, where the absolute amount of income is the same. But the difficulty of doing perfect justice is no reason against doing as much as we can. Though it may be a hardship to an annuitant whose life is only worth five years' purchase, to be allowed no greater abatement than is granted to one whose life is worth twenty, it is better for him even so, than if neither of them were allowed any abatement at all.

5. Before leaving the subject of Equality of Taxation, I must remark that there are cases in which exceptions may be made to it, consistently with that equal justice which is the groundwork of the rule. Suppose that there is a kind of income which constantly tends to increase, without any exertion or sacrifice on the part of the owners: those owners constituting a class in the community, whom the natural course of things progressively enriches, consistently with complete passiveness on their own part. In such a case it would be no violation of the principles on which private property is grounded, if the state should appropriate this increase of wealth, or part of it, as it arises. This would not properly be taking anything from anybody; it would merely be applying an accession of wealth, created by circumstances,

to the benefit of society, instead of allowing it to become an unearned appendage to the riches of a particular class.

Now this is actually the case with rent. The ordinary progress of a society which increases in wealth, is at all times tending to augment the incomes of landlords; to give them both a greater amount and a greater proportion of the wealth of the community, independently of any trouble or outlay incurred by themselves. They grow richer, as it were in their sleep, without working, risking, or economizing. What claim have they, on the general principle of social justice, to this accession of riches? In what would they have been wronged if society had, from the beginning, reserved the right of taxing the spontaneous increase of rent, to the highest amount required by financial exigencies? I admit that it would be unjust to come upon each individual estate, and lay hold of the increase which might be found to have taken place in its rental; because there would be no means of distinguishing in individual cases, between an increase owing solely to the general circumstances of society, and one which was the effect of skill and expenditure on the part of the proprietor. The only admissible mode of proceeding would be by a general measure. The first step should be a valuation of all the land in the country. The present value of all land should be exempt from the tax; but after an interval had elapsed, during which society had increased in population and capital, a rough estimate might be made of the spontaneous increase which had accrued to rent since the valuation was made. Of this the average price of produce would be some criterion: if that had risen, it would be certain that rent had increased, and (as already shown) even in a greater ratio than the rise of price. On this and other data, an approximate estimate might be made, how much value had been added to the land of the country by natural causes; and in laying on a general land-tax, which for fear of miscalculation should be considerably within the amount thus indicated, there would be an assurance of not touching any increase of income which might be the result of capital expended or industry exerted by the proprietor.

But though there could be no question as to the justice of taxing the increase of rent, if society had avowedly reserved the right, has not society waived that right by not exercising it? In England, for example, have not all who bought land for the last century or more, given value not only for the existing income, but for the prospects of increase, under an implied assurance of being only taxed in the same proportion with other incomes? This objection, in so far as valid, has a different degree of validity in different countries; depending on the degree of desuetude into which society has allowed a right to fall, which, as no one can doubt, it once fully possessed. In most countries of Europe, the right to take by taxation, as exigency might require, an indefinite portion of the rent of land, has never been allowed to slumber. In several parts of the Continent, the land-tax forms a large proportion of the public revenues, and has always been confessedly liable to be raised or lowered without reference to other taxes. In these countries no one can pretend to have become the owner of land on the faith of never being called upon to pay an increased land-tax. In England the land-tax has not varied since the early part of the last century. The last act of the legislature in relation to its amount, was to diminish it; and though the subsequent increase in the rental of the country has been immense, not only from agriculture, but from the growth of towns and the increase of buildings, the ascendency of landholders in the legislature has prevented any tax from being imposed, as it so justly might, upon the very large portion of this increase which was unearned, and, as it were, accidental. For the expectations thus raised, it appears to me that an amply sufficient allowance is made, if the whole increase of income which has accrued during this long period from a mere natural law, without exertion or sacrifice, is held sacred from any peculiar taxation. From the present date, or any subsequent time at which the legislature may think fit to assert the principle, I see no objection to declaring that the future increment of rent should be liable to special taxation; in doing which all injustice to the landlords would be obviated, if the present market-price of their land were secured to them; since that includes the present value of all future expectations. With reference to such a tax, perhaps a safer criterion than either a rise of rents or a rise of the price of corn, would be a general rise in the price of land. It would be easy to keep the tax within the amount which would reduce the market value of land below the original valuation: and up to that point, whatever the amount of the tax might be, no injustice would be done to the proprietors.

6. But whatever may be thought of the legitimacy of making the State a sharer in all future increase of rent from natural causes, the existing land-tax (which in this country unfortunately is very small) ought not to be regarded as a tax, but as a rent-charge in favour of the public; a portion of the rent, reserved from the beginning by the State, which has never belonged to or formed part of the income of the landlords, and should not therefore be counted to them as part of their taxation, so as to exempt them from their fair share of every other tax. As well might the tithe be regarded as a tax on the landlords: as well, in Bengal, where the State, though entitled to the whole rent of the land, gave away one-tenth of it to individuals, retaining the other nine-tenths, might those nine-tenths be considered as an unequal and unjust tax on the grantees of the tenth. That a person owns part of the rent, does not make the rest of it his just right, injuriously withheld from him. The landlords originally held their estates subject to feudal burthens, for which the present land-tax is an exceedingly small equivalent, and for their relief from which they should have been required to pay a much higher price. All who have bought land since the tax existed have bought it subject to the tax. There is not the smallest pretence for looking upon it as a payment exacted from the existing race of landlords.

These observations are applicable to a land-tax, only in so far as it is a peculiar tax, and not when it is merely a mode of levying from the landlords the equivalent of what is taken from other classes. In France, for example, there are peculiar taxes on other kinds of property and income (the *mobilier** and the *patente**), and supposing the land-tax to be not more than equivalent to these, there would be no ground for contending that the state had reserved to itself a rent-charge on the land. But wherever and in so far as income derived from land is prescriptively subject to a deduction for public purposes, beyond the rate of taxation levied on other incomes, the surplus is not properly taxation, but a share of the property in the soil, reserved by the state. In this country there are no peculiar taxes on other classes, corresponding to, or intended to countervail, the land-tax. The whole of it, therefore, is not taxation, but a rent-charge, and is as if the state had retained, not a portion of the rent, but a portion of the land. It is no more a burthen on the landlord, than the share of one joint tenant is a burthen on the other. The landlords are entitled to no compensation for it, nor have they any claim to its being allowed for, as part of their taxes. Its continuance on the existing footing is no infringement of the principle of Equal Taxation.[1]

We shall hereafter consider, in treating of Indirect Taxation, how far, and with what modifications, the rule of equality is applicable to that department.

7. In addition to the preceding rules, another general rule of taxation is sometimes laid down, namely, that it should fall on income, and not on capital. That taxation should not encroach upon the amount of the national capital, is indeed of the greatest importance; but this encroachment, when it occurs, is not so much a consequence of any particular mode of taxation, as of its excessive amount. Over-taxation, carried to a sufficient extent, is quite capable of ruining the most industrious community, especially when it is in any degree arbitrary, so that the payer is never certain how much or how little he shall be allowed to keep; or when it

---

[1] The same remarks obviously apply to those local taxes, of the peculiar pressure of which on landed property so much has been said by the remnant of the Protectionists. As much of these burthens as is of old standing, ought to be regarded as a prescriptive deduction or reservation, for public purposes, of a portion of the rent. And any recent additions have either been incurred for the benefit of the owners of landed property, or occasioned by their fault: in neither case giving them any just ground of complaint.

is so laid on as to render industry and economy a bad calculation. But if these errors be avoided, and the amount of taxation be not greater than it is at present even in the most heavily taxed country of Europe, there is no danger lest it should deprive the country of a portion of its capital.

To provide that taxation shall fall entirely on income, and not at all on capital, is beyond the power of any system of fiscal arrangements. There is no tax which is not partly paid from what would otherwise have been saved; no tax, the amount of which, if remitted, would be wholly employed in increased expenditure, and no part whatever laid by as an addition to capital. All taxes, therefore, are in some sense partly paid out of capital; and in a poor country it is impossible to impose any tax which will not impede the increase of the national wealth. But in a country where capital abounds, and the spirit of accumulation is strong, this effect of taxation is scarcely felt. Capital having reached the stage in which, were it not for a perpetual succession of improvements in production, any further increase would soon be stopped—and having so strong a tendency even to outrun those improvements, that profits are only kept above the minimum by emigration of capital, or by a periodical sweep called a commercial crisis; to take from capital by taxation what emigration would remove, or a commercial crisis destroy, is only to do what either of those causes would have done, namely, to make a clear space for further saving.

I cannot, therefore, attach any importance, in a wealthy country, to the objection made against taxes on legacies and inheritances, that they are taxes on capital. It is perfectly true that they are so. As Ricardo observes, if £100 are taken from any one in a tax on houses or on wine, he will probably save it, or a part of it, by living in a cheaper house, consuming less wine, or retrenching from some other of his expenses; but if the same sum be taken from him because he has received a legacy of £1,000, he considers the legacy as only £900, and feels no more inducement than at any other time (probably feels rather less inducement) to economize in his expenditure. The tax, therefore, is wholly paid out of capital: and there are countries in which this would be a serious objection. But in the first place, the argument cannot apply to any country which has a national debt, and devotes any portion of revenue to paying it off; since the produce of the tax, thus applied, still remains capital, and is merely transferred from the tax-payer to the fundholder. But the objection is never applicable in a country which increases rapidly in wealth. The amount which would be derived, even from a very high legacy duty, in each year, is but a small fraction of the annual increase of capital in such a country; and its abstraction would but make room for saving to an equivalent amount: while the effect of not taking it, is to prevent that amount of saving, or cause the savings, when made, to be sent abroad for investment. A country which, like England, accumulates capital not only for itself, but for half the world, may be said to defray the whole of its public expenses from its overflowings; and its wealth is probably at this moment as great as if it had no taxes at all. What its taxes really do is, to subtract from its means, not of production, but of enjoyment; since whatever any one pays in taxes, he could, if it were not taken for that purpose, employ in indulging his ease, or in gratifying some want or taste which at present remains unsatisfied.

III

OF DIRECT TAXES

1. Taxes are either direct or indirect. A direct tax is one which is demanded from the very persons who, it is intended or desired, should pay it. Indirect taxes are those which are demanded from one person in the expectation and intention that he shall indemnify himself at the expense of another: such as the excise or customs. The producer or importer of a commodity is called upon to pay a tax on it, not with the intention to levy a peculiar contribution upon him, but to tax through him the consumers of the commodity, from whom it is supposed that he will recover the amount by means of an advance in price.

Direct taxes are either on income, or on expenditure. Most taxes on expenditure are indirect, but some are direct, being imposed not on the producer or seller of an article, but immediately on the consumer. A house-tax, for example, is a direct tax on expenditure, if levied, as it usually is, on the occupier of the house. If levied on the builder or owner, it would be an indirect tax. A window-tax is a direct tax on expenditure; so are the taxes on horses and carriages, and the rest of what are called the assessed taxes.

The sources of income are rent, profits, and wages. This includes every sort of income, except gift or plunder. Taxes may be laid on any one of the three kinds of income, or an uniform tax on all of them. We will consider these in their order.

2. A tax on rent falls wholly on the landlord. There are no means by which he can shift the burthen upon any one else. It does not affect the value or price of agricultural produce, for this is determined by the cost of production in the most unfavourable circumstances, and in those circumstances, as we have so often demonstrated, no rent is paid. A tax on rent, therefore, has no effect, other than its

obvious one. It merely takes so much from the landlord, and transfers it to the state.

This, however, is, in strict exactness, only true of the rent which is the result either of natural causes, or of improvements made by tenants. When the landlord makes improvements which increase the productive power of his land, he is remunerated for them by an extra payment from the tenant; and this payment, which to the landlord is properly a profit on capital, is blended and confounded with rent; which indeed it really is, to the tenant, and in respect of the economical laws which determine its amount. A tax on rent, if extending to this portion of it, would discourage landlords from making improvements: but it does not follow that it would raise the price of agricultural produce. The same improvements might be made with the tenant's capital, or even with the landlord's if lent by him to the tenant; provided he is willing to give the tenant so long a lease as will enable him to indemnify himself before it expires. But whatever hinders improvements from being made in the manner in which people prefer to make them, will often prevent them from being made at all: and on this account a tax on rent would be inexpedient, unless some means could be devised of excluding from its operation that portion of the nominal rent which may be regarded as landlord's profit. This argument, however, is not ·needed for the condemnation of such a tax. A peculiar tax on the income of any class, not balanced by taxes on other classes, is a violation of justice, and amounts to a partial confiscation. I have already shown grounds for excepting from this censure a tax which, sparing existing rents, should content itself with appropriating a portion of any future increase arising from the mere action of natural causes. But even this could not be justly done, without offering as an alternative the market price of the land. In the case of a tax on rent which is not peculiar, but accompanied by an equivalent tax on other incomes, the objection grounded on its reaching the profit arising from improvements is less applicable: since, profits being taxed as well as rent, the profit which assumes the form of rent is liable to its share in common with other profits; but since profits altogether ought, for reasons formerly stated, to be taxed somewhat lower than rent properly so called, the objection is only diminished, not removed.

3. A tax on profits, like a tax on rent, must, at least in its immediate operation, fall wholly on the payer. All profits being alike affected, no relief can be obtained by a change of employment. If a tax were laid on the profits of any one branch of productive employment, the tax would be virtually an increase of the cost of production, and the value and price of the article would rise accordingly; by which the tax would be thrown upon the consumers of the commodity, and would not affect profits. But a general and equal tax on all profits would not affect general prices, and would fall, at least in the first instance, on capitalists alone.

There is, however, an ulterior effect, which, in a rich and prosperous country, requires to be taken into account. When the capital accumulated is so great and the rate of annual accumulation so rapid, that the country is only kept from attaining the stationary state by the emigration of capital, or by continual improvements in production; any circumstance which virtually lowers the rate of profit cannot be without a decided influence on these phenomena. It may operate in different ways. The curtailment of profit, and the consequent increased difficulty in making a fortune or obtaining a subsistence by the employment of capital, may act as a stimulus to inventions, and to the use of them when made. If improvements in production are much accelerated, and if these improvements cheapen, directly or indirectly, any of the things habitually consumed by the labourer, profits may rise, and rise sufficiently to make up for all that is taken from them by the tax. In that case the tax will have been realized without loss to any one, the produce of the country being increased by an equal, or what would in that case be a far greater amount. The tax, however, must even in this case be considered as paid from profits, because the receivers of profits are those who would be benefited if it were taken off.

But though the artificial abstraction of a portion of profits would have a real tendency to accelerate improvements in production, no considerable improvements might actually result, or only of such a kind as not to raise general profits at all, or not to raise them so much as the tax had diminished them. If so, the rate of profit would be brought closer to that practical minimum, to which it is constantly approaching: and this diminished return to capital would either give a decided check to further accumulation, or would cause a greater proportion than before of the annual increase to be sent abroad, or wasted in unprofitable speculations. At its first imposition the tax falls wholly on profits: but the amount of increase of capital, which the tax prevents, would, if it had been allowed to continue, have tended to reduce profits to the same level; and at every period of ten or twenty years there will be found less difference between profits as they are, and profits as they would in that case have been: until at last there is no difference, and the tax is thrown either upon the labourer or upon the landlord. The real effect of a tax on profits is to make the country possess at any given period, a smaller capital and a smaller aggregate production, and to make the stationary state be attained earlier, and with a smaller sum of national wealth. It is possible that a tax on profits might even diminish the existing capital of the country. If the rate of profit is already at the practical minimum, that is, at the point at which all that portion of the annual increment which would tend to reduce profits is carried off either by exportation or by speculation; then if a tax is imposed which reduces profits still lower, the same causes which previously carried off the increase would probably carry off a portion of the existing capital. A tax on profits is thus, in a state of capital and accumulation like that in England, extremely detrimental to the national wealth. And this effect is not confined to the case of a peculiar, and therefore intrinsically unjust, tax on profits. The mere fact that profits have to bear their share of a heavy general taxation, tends, in the same manner as a peculiar tax, to drive capital abroad, to stimulate imprudent speculations by diminishing safe gains, to discourage further accumulation, and to accelerate the attainment of the stationary state. This is thought to have been the principal cause of the decline of Holland, or rather of her having ceased to make progress.

Even in countries which do not accumulate so fast as to be always within a short interval of the stationary state, it seems impossible that, if capital is accumulating at all, its accumulation should not be in some degree retarded by the abstraction of a portion of its profit; and unless the effect in stimulating improvements be a full counter-balance, it is inevitable that a part of the burthen will be thrown off the capitalist, upon the labourer or the landlord. One or other of these is always the loser by a diminished rate of accumulation. If population continues to increase as before, the labourer suffers: if not, cultivation is checked in its advance, and the landlords lose the accession of rent which would have accrued to them. The only countries in which a tax on profits seems likely to be permanently a burthen on capitalists exclusively, are those in which capital is stationary, because there is no new accumulation. In such countries the tax might not prevent the old capital from being kept up through habit, or from unwillingness to submit to impoverishment, and so the capitalist might continue to bear the whole of the tax. It is seen from these considerations that the effects of a tax on profits are much more complex, more various, and in some points more uncertain, than writers on the subject have commonly supposed.

4. We now turn to Taxes on Wages. The incidence of these is very different, according as the wages taxed are those of ordinary unskilled labour, or are the remuneration of such skilled or privileged employments, whether manual or intellectual, as are taken out of the sphere of competition by a natural or conferred monopoly.

I have already remarked, that in the present low state of popular education, all the higher grades of mental or educated labour are at a monopoly price; exceeding the wages of common workmen in a degree very far beyond that which is due to the expense, trouble, and loss of time required in qualifying for the employment. Any tax levied on these gains, which still leaves them above (or not below) their just proportion, falls on those who pay it; they have no means of relieving themselves at the expense of any other class. The same thing is true of ordinary wages, in cases like that of the United States, or of a new colony, where, capital increasing as rapidly as population can increase, wages are kept up by the increase of capital, and not by the adherence of the labourers to a fixed standard of comforts. In such a case some deterioration of their condition, whether by a tax or otherwise, might possibly take place without checking the increase of population. The tax would in that case fall on the labourers themselves, and would reduce them prematurely to that lower state to which, on the same supposition with regard to their habits, they would in any case have been reduced ultimately, by the inevitable diminution in the rate of increase of capital, through the occupation of all the fertile land.

Some will object that, even in this case, a tax on wages cannot be detrimental to the labourers, since the money raised by it, being expended in the country, comes back to the labourers again through the demand for labour. The fallacy, however, of this doctrine has been so completely exhibited in the First Book,[1] that I need do little more than refer to that exposition. It was there shown that funds expended unproductively have no tendency to raise or keep up wages, unless when expended in the direct purchase of labour. If the government took a tax of a shilling a week from every labourer, and laid it all out in hiring labourers for military service, public works, or the like, it would, no doubt, indemnify the labourers as a class for all that the tax took from them. That would really be 'spending the money among the people'. But if it expended the whole in buying goods, or in adding to the salaries of employés who bought goods with it, this would not increase the demand for labour, or tend to raise wages. Without, however, reverting to general principles, we may rely on an obvious *reductio ad*

---

[1] [Bk. I, Ch. V. 9. Not included in present edn.]

*absurdum** If to take money from the labourers and spend
it in commodities is giving it back to the labourers, then, to
take money from other classes, and spend it in the same
manner, must be giving it to the labourers; consequently,
the more a government takes in taxes, the greater will be the
demand for labour, and the more opulent the condition of
the labourers. A proposition the absurdity of which no one
can fail to see.

In the condition of most communities, wages are regulated by the habitual standard of living to which the labourers adhere, and on less than which they will not multiply.
Where there exists such a standard, a tax on wages will
indeed for a time be borne by the labourers themselves; but
unless this temporary depression has the effect of lowering
the standard itself, the increase of population will receive a
check, which will raise wages, and restore the labourers to
their previous condition. On whom, in this case, will the tax
fall? According to Adam Smith, on the community generally, in their character of consumers; since the rise of wages,
he thought, would raise general prices. We have seen,
however, that general prices depend on other causes, and
are never raised by any circumstance which affects all kinds
of productive employment in the same manner and degree.
A rise of wages occasioned by a tax, must, like any other
increase of the cost of labour, be defrayed from profits. To
attempt to tax day-labourers, in an old country, is merely
to impose an extra tax upon all employers of common
labour; unless the tax has the much worse effect of permanently lowering the standard of comfortable subsistence in
the minds of the poorest class.

We find in the preceding considerations an additional
argument for the opinion already expressed, that direct
taxations should stop short of the class of incomes which do
not exceed what is necessary for healthful existence. These
very small incomes are mostly derived from manual labour;
and, as we now see, any tax imposed on these, either
permanently degrades the habits of the labouring class, or
falls on profits, and burthens capitalists with an indirect
tax, in addition to their share of the direct taxes; which is

doubly objectionable, both as a violation of the fundamental rule of equality, and for the reasons which, as already
shown, render a peculiar tax on profits detrimental to the
public wealth, and consequently to the means which society
possesses of paying any taxes whatever.

5. We now pass, from taxes on the separate kinds of
income, to a tax attempted to be assessed fairly upon all
kinds; in other words, an Income Tax. The discussion of the
conditions necessary for making this tax consistent with
justice, has been anticipated in the last chapter. We shall
suppose, therefore, that these conditions are complied with.
They are, first, that incomes below a certain amount should
be altogether untaxed. This minimum should not be higher
than the amount which suffices for the necessaries of the
existing population. The exemption from the present income tax, of all incomes under £100 a year, and the lower
percentage formerly levied on those between £100 and £150,
are only defensible on the ground that almost all the
indirect taxes press more heavily on incomes between £50
and £150 than on any others whatever. The second condition is, that incomes above the limit should be taxed only in
proportion to the surplus by which they exceed the limit.
Thirdly, that all sums saved from income and invested,
should be exempt from the tax: or if this be found impracticable, that life incomes, and incomes from business and
professions, should be less heavily taxed than inheritable
incomes, in a degree as nearly as possible equivalent to
the increased need of economy arising from their terminable
character: allowance being also made, in the case of variable incomes, for their precariousness.

An income-tax, fairly assessed on these principles, would
be, in point of justice, the least exceptionable of all taxes.
The objection to it, in the present low state of public
morality, is the impossibility of ascertaining the real incomes of the contributors. The supposed hardship of compelling people to disclose the amount of their incomes,
ought not, in my opinion, to count for much. One of the
social evils of this country is the practice, amounting to a

custom, of maintaining, or attempting to maintain, the appearance to the world of a larger income than is possessed; and it would be far better for the interest of those who yield to this weakness, if the extent of their means were universally and exactly known, and the temptation removed to expending more than they can afford, or stinting real wants in order to make a false show externally. At the same time, the reason of the case, even on this point, is not so exclusively on one side of the argument as is sometimes supposed. So long as the vulgar of any country are in the debased state of mind which this national habit presupposes—so long as their respect (if such a word can be applied to it) is proportioned to what they suppose to be each person's pecuniary means—it may be doubted whether anything which would remove all uncertainty as to that point, would not considerably increase the presumption and arrogance of the vulgar rich, and their insolence towards those above them in mind and character, but below them in fortune.

Notwithstanding, too, what is called the inquisitorial nature of the tax, no amount of inquisitorial power which would be tolerated by a people the most disposed to submit to it, could enable the revenue officers to assess the tax from actual knowledge of the circumstances of contributors. Rents, salaries, annuities, and all fixed incomes, can be exactly ascertained. But the variable gains of professions, and still more the profits of business, which the person interested cannot always himself exactly ascertain, can still less be estimated with any approach to fairness by a tax-collector. The main reliance must be placed, and always has been placed, on the returns made by the person himself. No production of accounts is of much avail, except against the more flagrant cases of falsehood; and even against these the check is very imperfect, for if fraud is intended, false accounts can generally be framed which it will baffle any means of inquiry possessed by the revenue officers to detect: the easy resource of omitting entries on the credit side being often sufficient without the aid of fictitious debts or disbursements. The tax, therefore, on whatever principles of equality it may be imposed, is in practice unequal in one of the worst ways, falling heaviest on the most conscientious. The unscrupulous succeed in evading a great proportion of what they should pay; even persons of integrity in their ordinary transactions are tempted to palter with their consciences, at least to the extent of deciding in their own favour all points on which the smallest doubt or discussion could arise: while the strictly veracious may be made to pay more than the state intended, by the powers of arbitrary assessment necessarily intrusted to the Commissioners, as the last defence against the tax-payer's power of concealment.

It is to be feared, therefore, that the fairness which belongs to the principle of an income tax, cannot be made to attach to it in practice: and that this tax, while apparently the most just of all modes of raising a revenue, is in effect more unjust than many others which are prima facie more objectionable. This consideration would lead us to concur in the opinion which, until of late, has usually prevailed— that direct taxes on income should be reserved as an extraordinary resource for great national emergencies, in which the necessity of a large additional revenue overrules all objections.

The difficulties of a fair income tax have elicited a proposition for a direct tax of so much per cent, not on income but on expenditure; the aggregate amount of each person's expenditure being ascertained, as the amount of income now is, from statements furnished by the contributors themselves. The author of this suggestion, Mr Revans, in a clever pamphlet on the subject,[1] contends that the returns which persons would furnish of their expenditure would be more trustworthy than those which they now make of their income, inasmuch as expenditure is in its own nature more public than income, and false representations of it more easily detected. He cannot, I think, have sufficiently considered, how few of the items in the annual expenditure of most families can be judged of with any

---

[1] [John Revans, 'A Percentage Tax on Domestic Expenditure to supply the whole of the Public Revenue' (London, 1847).]

approximation to correctness from the external signs. The only security would still be the veracity of individuals, and there is no reason for supposing that their statements would be more trustworthy on the subject of their expenses than that of their revenues; especially as, the expenditure of most persons being composed of many more items than their income, there would be more scope for concealment and suppression in the detail of expenses than even of receipts.

The taxes on expenditure at present in force, either in this or in other countries, fall only on particular kinds of expenditure, and differ no otherwise from taxes on commodities than in being paid directly by the person who consumes or uses the article, instead of being advanced by the producer or seller, and reimbursed in the price. The taxes on horses and carriages, on dogs, on servants, are all of this nature. They evidently fall on the persons from whom they are levied—those who use the commodity taxed. A tax of a similar description, and more important, is a house-tax; which must be considered at somewhat greater length.

6. The rent of a house consists of two parts, the ground-rent, and what Adam Smith calls the building-rent. The first is determined by the ordinary principles of rent. It is the remuneration given for the use of the portion of land occupied by the house and its appurtenances; and varies from a mere equivalent for the rent which the ground would afford in agriculture, to the monopoly rents paid for advantageous situations in populous thoroughfares. The rent of the house itself, as distinguished from the ground, is the equivalent given for the labour and capital expended on the building. The fact of its being received in quarterly or half-yearly payments, makes no difference in the principles by which it is regulated. It comprises the ordinary profit on the builder's capital, and an annuity, sufficient at the current rate of interest, after paying for all repairs chargeable on the proprietor, to replace the original capital by the time the house is worn out, or by the expiration of the usual term of a building lease.

A tax of so much per cent on the gross rent, falls on both those portions alike. The more highly a house is rented, the more it pays to the tax, whether the quality of the situation or that of the house itself is the cause. The incidence, however, of these two portions of the tax must be considered separately.

As much of it as is a tax on building-rent, must ultimately fall on the consumer, in other words the occupier. For as the profits of building are already not above the ordinary rate, they would, if the tax fell on the owner and not on the occupier, become lower than the profits of untaxed employments, and houses would not be built. It is probable however that for some time after the tax was first imposed, a great part of it would fall, not on the renter, but on the owner of the house. A large proportion of the consumers either could not afford, or would not choose, to pay their former rent with the tax in addition, but would content themselves with a lower scale of accommodation. Houses therefore would be for a time in excess of the demand. The consequence of such excess, in the case of most other articles, would be an almost immediate diminution of the supply: but so durable a commodity as houses does not rapidly diminish in amount. New buildings indeed, of the class for which the demand had decreased, would cease to be erected, except for special reasons; but in the meantime the temporary superfluity would lower rents, and the consumers would obtain perhaps nearly the same accommodation as formerly, for the same aggregate payment, rent and tax together. By degrees, however, as the existing houses wore out, or as increase of population demanded a greater supply, rents would again rise; until it became profitable to recommence building, which would not be until the tax was wholly transferred to the occupier. In the end, therefore, the occupier bears that portion of a tax on rent, which falls on the payment made for the house itself, exclusively of the ground it stands on.

The case is partly different with the portion which is a tax on ground-rent. As taxes on rent, properly so called, fall on the landlord, a tax on ground-rent, one would suppose, must fall on the ground-landlord, at least after the expiration of the building lease. It will not however fall wholly on the landlord, unless with the tax on ground-rent there is combined an equivalent tax on agricultural rent. The lowest rent of land let for building is very little above the rent which the same ground would yield in agriculture: since it is reasonable to suppose that land, unless in case of exceptional circumstances, is let or sold for building as soon as it is decidedly worth more for that purpose than for cultivation. If, therefore, a tax were laid on ground-rents without being also laid on agricultural rents, it would, unless of trifling amount, reduce the return from the lowest ground-rents below the ordinary return from land, and would check further building quite as effectually as if it were a tax on building-rents, until either the increased demand of a growing population, or a diminution of supply by the ordinary causes of destruction, had raised the rent by a full equivalent for the tax. But whatever raises the lowest ground-rents, raises all others, since each exceeds the lowest by the market value of its peculiar advantages. If, therefore, the tax on ground-rents were a fixed sum per square foot, the more valuable situations paying no more than those least in request, this fixed payment would ultimately fall on the occupier. Suppose the lowest ground-rent to be £10 per acre, and the highest £1000, a tax of £1 per acre on ground-rents would ultimately raise the former to £11, and the latter consequently to £1001, since the difference of value between the two situations would be exactly what it was before: the annual pound, therefore, would be paid by the occupier. But a tax on ground-rent is supposed to be a portion of a house-tax, which is not a fixed payment, but a percentage on the rent. The cheapest site, therefore, being supposed as before to pay £1, the dearest would pay £100, of which only the £1 could be thrown upon the occupier, since the rent would still be only raised to £1001. Consequently, £99 of the £100 levied from the expensive site, would fall on the ground-landlord. A house-tax thus requires to be considered in a double aspect, as a tax on all occupiers of houses, and a tax on ground-rents.

In the vast majority of houses, the ground-rent forms but a small proportion of the annual payment made for the house, and nearly all the tax falls on the occupier. It is only in exceptional cases, like that of the favourite situations in large towns, that the predominant element in the rent of the house is the ground-rent; and among the very few kinds of income which are fit subjects for peculiar taxation, these ground-rents hold the principal place, being the most gigantic example extant of enormous accessions of riches acquired rapidly, and in many cases unexpectedly, by a few families, from the mere accident of their possessing certain tracts of land, without their having themselves aided in the acquisition by the smallest exertion, outlay, or risk. So far therefore as a house-tax falls on the ground-landlord, it is liable to no valid objection.

In so far as it falls on the occupier, if justly proportioned to the value of the house, it is one of the fairest and most unobjectionable of all taxes. No part of a person's expenditure is a better criterion of his means, or bears, on the whole, more nearly the same proportion to them. A house-tax is a nearer approach to a fair income tax, than a direct assessment on income can easily be; having the great advantage, that it makes spontaneously all the allowances which it is so difficult to make, and so impracticable to make exactly, in assessing an income tax: for if what a person pays in house-rent is a test of anything, it is a test not of what he possesses, but of what he thinks he can afford to spend. The equality of this tax can only be seriously questioned on two grounds. The first is, that a miser may escape it. This objection applies to all taxes on expenditure: nothing but a direct tax on income can reach a miser. But as misers do not now hoard their treasure, but invest it in productive employments, it not only adds to the national wealth, and consequently to the general means of paying taxes, but the payment claimable from itself is only transferred from the principal sum to the income afterwards derived from it, which pays taxes as soon as it comes to be expended. The second objection is, that a person may require a larger and more expensive house, not from having greater means, but from having a larger family. Of this, however, he is not entitled to complain; since having a large family is at a person's own choice: and, so far as concerns the public interest, is a thing rather to be discouraged than promoted.[1]

A large portion of the taxation of this country is raised by a house-tax. The parochial taxation of the towns entirely, and of the rural districts partially, consists of an assessment on house-rent. The window-tax, which was also a house-tax, but of a bad kind, operating as a tax on light, and a cause of deformity in building, was exchanged in 1851 for a house-tax properly so called, but on a much lower scale than that which existed previously to 1834. It is to be lamented that the new tax retains the unjust principle on which the old house-tax was assessed, and which contributed quite as much as the selfishness of the middle classes to produce the outcry against the tax. The public were justly scandalized on learning that residences like Chatsworth or Belvoir were only rated on an imaginary rent of perhaps £200 a year, under the pretext that owing to the great expense of keeping them up, they could not be let for more. Probably, indeed, they could not be let even for that, and if the argument were a fair one, they ought not to have been taxed at all. But a house-tax is not intended as a tax

---

[1] Another common objection is that large and expensive accommodation is often required, not as a residence, but for business. But it is an admitted principle that buildings or portions of buildings occupied exclusively for business, such as shops, warehouses, or manufactories, ought to be exempted from house-tax. The plea that persons in business may be compelled to live in situations, such as the great thoroughfares of London, where house-rent is at a monopoly rate, seems to me unworthy of regard: since no one does so but because the extra profit which he expects to derive from the situation, is more than an equivalent to him for the extra cost. But in any case, the bulk of the tax on this extra rent will not fall on him, but on the ground-landlord.

It has been also objected that house-rent in the rural districts is much lower than in towns, and lower in some towns and in some rural districts than in others: so that a tax proportioned to it would have a corresponding inequality of pressure. To this, however, it may be answered, that in places where house-rent is low, persons of the same amount of income usually live in larger and better houses, and thus expend in house-rent more nearly the same proportion of their incomes than might at first sight appear. Or if not, the probability will be, that many of them live in those places precisely because they are too poor to live elsewhere, and have therefore the strongest claim to be taxed lightly. In some cases, it is precisely because the people are poor, that house-rent remains low.

on incomes derived from houses, but on expenditure incurred for them. The thing which it is wished to ascertain is what a house costs to the person who lives in it, not what it would bring in if let to someone else. When the occupier is not the owner, and does not hold on a repairing lease, the rent he pays is the measure of what the house costs him: but when he is the owner, some other measure must be sought. A valuation should be made of the house, not at what it would sell for, but at what would be the cost of rebuilding it, and this valuation might be periodically corrected by an allowance for what it had lost in value by time, or gained by repairs and improvements. The amount of the amended valuation would form a principal sum, the interest of which, at the current price of the public funds, would form the annual value at which the building should be assessed to the tax.

As incomes below a certain amount ought to be exempt from income tax, so ought houses below a certain value, from house-tax, on the universal principle of sparing from all taxation the absolute necessaries of healthful existence. In order that the occupiers of lodgings, as well as of houses, might benefit, as in justice they ought, by this exemption, it might be optional with the owners to have every portion of a house which is occupied by a separate tenant, valued and assessed separately, as is now usually the case with chambers.

IV

OF TAXES ON COMMODITIES

1. By taxes on commodities are commonly meant, those which are levied either on the producers, or on the carriers or dealers who intervene between them and the final purchasers for consumption. Taxes imposed directly on the consumers of particular commodities, such as a house-tax, or the tax in this country on horses and carriages, might be called taxes on commodities, but are not; the phrase being by custom, confined to indirect taxes—those which are advanced by one person, to be, as is expected and intended, reimbursed by another. Taxes on commodities are either on production within the country, or on importation into it, or on conveyance or sale within it; and are classed respectively as excise, customs, or tolls and transit duties. To whichever class they belong, and at whatever stage in the progress of the community they may be imposed, they are equivalent to an increase of the cost of production; using that term in its most enlarged sense, which includes the cost of transport and distribution, or, in common phrase, of bringing the commodity to market.

When the cost of production is increased artificially by a tax, the effect is the same as when it is increased by natural causes. If only one or a few commodities are affected, their value and price rise, so as to compensate the producer or dealer for the peculiar burthen; but if there were a tax on all commodities, exactly proportioned to their value, no such compensation would be obtained: there would neither be a general rise of values, which is an absurdity, nor of prices, which depend on causes entirely different. There would, however, as Mr M'Culloch has pointed out, be a disturbance of values, some falling, others rising, owing to a circumstance, the effect of which on values and prices we formerly discussed; the different durability of the capital employed in different occupations. The gross produce of industry consists of two parts; one portion serving to replace the capital consumed, while the other portion is profit. Now equal capitals in two branches of production must have equal expectations of profit; but if a greater portion of the one than of the other is fixed capital, or if that fixed capital is more durable, there will be a less consumption of capital in the year, and less will be required to replace it, so that the profit, if absolutely the same, will form a greater proportion of the annual returns. To derive from a capital of £1,000 a profit of £100, the one producer may have to sell produce to the value of £1,100, the other only to the value of £500. If on these two branches of industry a tax be imposed of five per cent *ad valorem*, the last will be charged only with £25, the first with £55; leaving to the one £75 profit, to the other only £45. To equalize, therefore, their expectation of profit, the one commodity must rise in price, or the other must fall, or both: commodities made chiefly by immediate labour must rise in value, as compared with those which are chiefly made by machinery. It is unnecessary to prosecute this branch of the inquiry any further.

2. A tax on any one commodity, whether laid on its production, its importation, its carriage from place to place, or its sale, and whether the tax be a fixed sum of money for a given quantity of the commodity, or an *ad valorem* duty, will, as a general rule, raise the value and price of the commodity by at least the amount of the tax. There are few cases in which it does not raise them by more than that amount. In the first place, there are few taxes on production on account of which it is not found or deemed necessary to impose restrictive regulations on the manufacturers or dealers, in order to check evasions of the tax. These regulations are always sources of trouble and annoyance, and generally of expense, for all of which, being peculiar disadvantages, the producers or dealers must have compensation in the price of their commodity. These restrictions also frequently interfere with the processes of manufacture, requiring the producer to carry on his operations in the way most convenient to the revenue, though not the cheapest, or most efficient

for purposes of production. Any regulations whatever, enforced by law, make it difficult for the producer to adopt new and improved processes. Further, the necessity of advancing the tax obliges producers and dealers to carry on their business with larger capitals than would otherwise be necessary, on the whole of which they must receive the ordinary rate of profit, though a part only is employed in defraying the real expenses of production or importation. The price of the article must be such as to afford a profit on more than its natural value, instead of a profit on only its natural value. A part of the capital of the country, in short, is not employed in production, but in advances to the state, repaid in the price of goods; and the consumers must give an indemnity to the sellers, equal to the profit which they could have made on the same capital if really employed in production.[1] Neither ought it to be forgotten, that whatever renders a larger capital necessary in any trade or business, limits the competition in that business; and by giving something like a monopoly to a few dealers, may enable them either to keep up the price beyond what would afford the ordinary rate of profit, or to obtain the ordinary rate of profit with a less degree of exertion for improving and cheapening their commodity. In these several modes, taxes on commodities often cost to the consumer, through the increased price of the article, much more than they bring into the treasury of the state. There is still another consideration. The higher price necessitated by the tax, almost always checks the demand for the commodity; and since there are many improvements in production which, to make them practicable, require a certain extent of demand, such improvements are obstructed, and many of them prevented altogether. It is a well-known fact, that the branches of

---

[1] It is true, this does not constitute, as at first sight it appears to do, a case of taking more out of the pockets of the people than the state receives; since if the state needs the advance, and gets it in this manner, it can dispense with an equivalent amount of borrowing in stock or exchequer bills. But it is more economical that the necessities of the state should be supplied from the disposable capital in the hands of the lending class, than by an artificial addition to the expenses of one or several classes of producers or dealers.

production in which fewest improvements are made, are those with which the revenue officer interferes; and that nothing, in general, gives a greater impulse to improvements in the production of a commodity, than taking off a tax which narrowed the market for it.

3. Such are the effects of taxes on commodities, considered generally; but as there are some commodities (those composing the necessaries of the labourer) of which the values have an influence on the distribution of wealth among different classes of the community, it is requisite to trace the effects of taxes on those particular articles somewhat farther. If a tax be laid, say on corn, and the price rises in proportion to the tax, the rise of price may operate in two ways. First: it may lower the condition of the labouring classes; temporarily indeed it can scarcely fail to do so. If it diminishes their consumption of the produce of the earth, or makes them resort to a food which the soil produces more abundantly, and therefore more cheaply, it to that extent contributes to throw back agriculture upon more fertile lands or less costly processes, and to lower the value and price of corn; which therefore ultimately settles at a price, increased not by the whole amount of the tax, but by only a part of its amount. Secondly, however, it may happen that the dearness of the taxed food does not lower the habitual standard of the labourer's requirements, but that wages, on the contrary, through an action on population, rise, in a shorter or longer period, so as to compensate the labourers for their portion of the tax; the compensation being of course at the expense of profits. Taxes on necessaries must thus have one of two effects. Either they lower the condition of the labouring classes; or they exact from the owners of capital, in addition to the amount due to the state on their own necessaries, the amount due on those consumed by the labourers. In the last case, the tax on necessaries, like a tax on wages, is equivalent to a peculiar tax on profits; which is, like all other partial taxation, unjust, and is specially prejudicial to the increase of the national wealth.

It remains to speak of the effect on rent. Assuming (what is usually the fact,) that the consumption of food is not diminished, the same cultivation as before will be necessary to supply the wants of the community; the margin of cultivation, to use Dr Chalmers' expression, remains where it was; and the same land or capital which, as the least productive, already regulated the value and price of the whole produce, will continue to regulate them. The effect which a tax on agricultural produce will have on rent, depends on its affecting or not affecting the difference between the return to this least productive land or capital, and the returns to other lands and capitals. Now this depends on the manner in which the tax is imposed. If it is an *ad valorem* tax, or what is the same thing, a fixed proportion of the produce, such as tithe for example, it evidently lowers corn-rents. For it takes more corn from the better lands than from the worse; and exactly in the degree in which they are better; land of twice the productiveness paying twice as much to the tithe. Whatever takes more from the greater of two quantities than from the less, diminishes the difference between them. The imposition of a tithe on corn would take a tithe also from corn-rent: for if we reduce a series of numbers by a tenth each, the differences between them are reduced one-tenth.

For example, let there be five qualities of land, which severally yield, on the same extent of ground, and with the same expenditure, 100, 90, 80, 70, and 60 bushels of wheat; the last of these being the lowest quality which the demand for food renders it necessary to cultivate. The rent of these lands will be as follows:

The land producing 100 bushels will yield a rent of 100–60, or 40 bushels.

That producing 90 bushels will yield a rent of 90–60, or 30 bushels.

That producing 80 bushels will yield a rent of 80–60, or 20 bushels.

That producing 70 bushels will yield a rent of 70–60, or 10 bushels.

That producing 60 bushels will yield no rent.

Now let a tithe be imposed, which takes from these five pieces of land 10, 9, 8, 7, and 6 bushels respectively, the fifth quality still being the one which regulates the price, but returning to the farmer, after payment of tithe, no more than 54 bushels:

The land producing } 100 bushels reduced to 90, will yield a rent of 90–54, or 36 bushels.

That producing } 90 bushels reduced to 81, will yield a rent of 81–54, or 27 bushels.

That producing } 80 bushels reduced to 72, will yield a rent of 72–54, or 18 bushels.

That producing } 70 bushels reduced to 63, will yield a rent of 63–54, or 9 bushels,

and that producing 60 bushels, reduced to 54, will yield, as before, no rent. So that the rent of the first quality of land has lost four bushels; of the second, three; of the third, two; and of the fourth, one: that is, each has lost exactly one-tenth. A tax, therefore, of a fixed proportion of the produce, lowers, in the same proportion, corn-rent.

But it is only corn-rent that is lowered, and not rent estimated in money, or in any other commodity. For, in the same proportion as corn-rent is reduced in quantity, the corn composing it is raised in value. Under the tithe, 54 bushels will be worth in the market what 60 were before; and nine-tenths will in all cases sell for as much as the whole ten-tenths previously sold for. The landlords will therefore be compensated in value and price for what they lose in quantity; and will suffer only so far as they consume their rent in kind, or after receiving it in money, expend it in agricultural produce: that is, they only suffer as consumers of agricultural produce, and in common with all the other consumers. Considered as landlords, they have the same income as before; the tithe, therefore, falls on the consumer, and not on the landlord.

The same effect would be produced on rent, if the tax, instead of being a fixed proportion of the produce, were a fixed sum per quarter or per bushel. A tax which takes a shilling for every bushel, takes more shillings from one field than from another, just in proportion as it produces more bushels; and operates exactly like tithe, except that tithe is not only the same proportion on all lands, but is also the same proportion at all times, while a fixed sum of money per bushel will amount to a greater or a less proportion, according as corn is cheap or dear.

There are other modes of taxing agriculture, which would affect rent differently. A tax proportioned to the rent would fall wholly on the rent, and would not at all raise the price of corn, which is regulated by the portion of the produce that pays no rent. A fixed tax of so much per cultivated acre, without distinction of value, would have effects directly the reverse. Taking no more from the best qualities of land than from the worst, it would leave the differences the same as before, and consequently the same corn-rents, and the landlords would profit to the full extent of the rise of price. To put the thing in another manner; the price must rise sufficiently to enable the worst land to pay the tax; thus enabling all lands which produce more than the worst, to pay not only the tax, but also an increased rent to the landlords. These, however, are not so much taxes on the produce of land, as taxes on the land itself. Taxes on the produce, properly so called, whether fixed or *ad valorem*, do not affect rent, but fall on the consumer: profits, however, generally bearing either the whole or the greatest part of the portion which is levied on the consumption of the labouring classes.

4. The preceding is, I apprehend, a correct statement of the manner in which taxes on agricultural produce operate when first laid on. When, however, they are of old standing, their effect may be different, as was first pointed out, I believe, by Mr Senior. It is, as we have seen, an almost infallible consequence of any reduction of profits, to retard the rate of accumulation. Now the effect of accumulation, when attended by its usual accompaniment, an increase of population, is to increase the value and price of food, to raise rent, and to lower profits: that is, to do precisely what

is done by a tax on agricultural produce, except that this does not raise rent. The tax, therefore, merely anticipates the rise of price, and fall of profits, which would have taken place ultimately through the mere progress of accumulation; while it at the same time prevents, or at least retards, that progress. If the rate of profit was such, previous to the imposition of a tithe, that the effect of the tithe reduces it to the practical minimum, the tithe will put a stop to all further accumulation, or cause it to take place out of the country; and the only effect which the tithe will then have had on the consumer, is to make him pay earlier the price which he would have had to pay somewhat later—part of which, indeed, in the gradual progress of wealth and population, he would have almost immediately begun to pay. After a lapse of time which would have admitted of a rise of one-tenth through the natural progress of wealth, the consumer will be paying no more than he would have paid if the tithe had never existed; he will have ceased to pay any portion of it, and the person who will really pay it is the landlord, whom it deprives of the increase of rent which would by that time have accrued to him. At every successive point in this interval of time, less of the burthen will rest on the consumer, and more of it on the landlord: and in the ultimate result, the minimum of profits will be reached with a smaller capital and population, and a lower rental, than if the course of things had not been disturbed by the imposition of the tax. If, on the other hand, the tithe or other tax on agricultural produce does not reduce profits to the minimum, but to something above the minimum, accumulation will not be stopped, but only slackened: and if population also increases, the two-fold increase will continue to produce its effects—a rise of the price of corn, and an increase of rent. These consequences, however, will not take place with the same rapidity as if the higher rate of profit had continued. At the end of twenty years the country will have a smaller population and capital, than, but for the tax, it would by that time have had; the landlords will have a smaller rent; and the price of corn, having increased less rapidly than it would otherwise have done, will not be so much as a tenth higher than what, if there had been no tax, it would by that time have become. A part of the tax, therefore, will already have ceased to fall on the consumer, and devolved upon the landlord; and the proportion will become greater and greater by lapse of time.

Mr Senior illustrates this view of the subject by likening the effects of tithes, or other taxes on agricultural produce to those of natural sterility of soil. If the land of a country without access to foreign supplies, were suddenly smitten with a permanent deterioration of quality, to an extent which would make a tenth more labour necessary to raise the existing produce, the price of corn would undoubtedly rise one-tenth. But it cannot hence be inferred that if the soil of the country had from the beginning been one-tenth worse than it is, corn would at present have been one-tenth dearer than we find it. It is far more probable, that the smaller return to labour and capital, ever since the first settlement of the country, would have caused in each successive generation a less rapid increase than has taken place: that the country would now have contained less capital, and maintained a smaller population, so that notwithstanding the inferiority of the soil, the price of corn would not have been higher, nor profits lower, than at present; rent alone would certainly have been lower. We may suppose two islands, which, being alike in extent, in natural fertility, and industrial advancement, have up to a certain time been equal in population and capital, and have had equal rentals, and the same price of corn. Let us imagine a tithe imposed in one of these islands, but not in the other. There will be immediately a difference in the price of corn, and therefore probably in profits. While profits are not tending downwards in either country, that is, while improvements in the production of necessaries fully keep pace with the increase of population, this difference of prices and profits between the islands may continue. But if, in the untithed island, capital increases, and population along with it, more than enough to counterbalance any improvements which take place, the price of corn will gradually rise, profits will fall, and rent will increase; while in the tithed island capital and population will either not increase (beyond what is balanced by the improvements), or if they do, will increase in a less degree; so that rent and the price of corn will either not rise at all, or rise more slowly. Rent, therefore, will soon be higher in the untithed than in the tithed island, and profits not so much higher, nor corn so much cheaper, as they were on the first imposition of the tithe. These effects will be progressive. At the end of every ten years there will be a greater difference between the rentals and between the aggregate wealth and population of the two islands, and a less difference in profits and in the price of corn.

At what point will these last differences entirely cease, and the temporary effect of taxes on agricultural produce, in raising the price, have entirely given place to the ultimate effect, that of limiting the total produce of the country? Though the untithed island is always verging towards the point at which the price of food would overtake that in the tithed island, its progress towards that point naturally slackens as it draws nearer to attaining it; since—the difference between the two islands in the rapidity of accumulation depending upon the difference in the rates of profit —in proportion as these approximate, the movement which draws them closer together, abates of its force. The one may not actually overtake the other, until both islands reach the minimum of profits: up to that point, the tithed island may continue more or less ahead of the untithed island in the price of corn: considerably ahead if it is far from the minimum, and is therefore accumulating rapidly; very little ahead if it is near the minimum, and accumulating slowly.

But whatever is true of the tithed and untithed islands in our hypothetical case, is true of any country having a tithe, compared with the same country if it had never had a tithe.

In England the great emigration of capital, and the almost periodical occurrence of commercial crises through the speculations occasioned by the habitually low rate of profit, are indications that profit has attained the practical, though not the ultimate minimum, and that all the savings which take place (beyond what improvements, tending to the cheapening of necessaries, make room for) are either sent abroad for investment, or periodically swept away. There can therefore, I think, be little doubt that if England had never had a tithe, or any tax on agricultural produce, the price of corn would have been by this time as high, and the rate of profits as low, as at present. Independently of the more rapid accumulation which would have taken place if profits had not been prematurely lowered by these imposts; the mere saving of a part of the capital which has been wasted in unsuccessful speculations, and the keeping at home a part of that which has been sent abroad, would have been quite sufficient to produce the effect. I think, therefore, with Mr Senior, that the tithe, even before its commutation, had ceased to be a cause of high prices or low profits, and had become a mere deduction from rent; its other effects being, that it caused the country to have no greater capital, no larger production, and no more numerous population than if it had been one-tenth less fertile than it is; or let us rather say one-twentieth (considering how great a portion of the land of Great Britain was tithe-free).

But though tithes and other taxes on agricultural produce, when of long standing, either do not raise the price of food and lower profits at all, or if at all, not in proportion to the tax; yet the abrogation of such taxes, when they exist, does not the less diminish price, and, in general, raise the rate of profit. The abolition of a tithe takes one-tenth from the cost of production, and consequently from the price, of all agricultural produce; and unless it permanently raises the labourer's requirements, it lowers the cost of labour, and raises profits. Rent, estimated in money or in commodities, generally remains as before; estimated in agricultural produce, it is raised. The country adds as much by the repeal of a tithe, to the margin which intervenes between it and the stationary state, as is cut off from that margin by a tithe when first imposed. Accumulation is greatly accelerated; and if population also increases, the price of corn immediately begins to recover itself, and rent to rise; thus gradually transferring the benefit of the remission, from the consumer to the landlord.

The effects which thus result from abolishing tithe, result equally from what has been done by the arrangements under the Commutation Act for converting it into a rent-charge. When the tax, instead of being levied on the whole produce of the soil, is levied only from the portions which pay rent, and does not touch any fresh extension of cultivation, the tax no longer forms any part of the cost of production of the portion of the produce which regulates the price of all the rest. The land or capital which pays no rent, can now send its produce to market one-tenth cheaper. The commutation of tithe ought therefore to have produced a considerable fall in the average price of corn. If it had not come so gradually into operation, and if the price of corn had not during the same period been under the influence of several other causes of change, the effect would probably have been markedly conspicuous. As it is, there can be no doubt that this circumstance has had its share in the fall which has taken place in the cost of production and in the price of home-grown produce; though the effects of the great agricultural improvements which have been simultaneously advancing, and of the free admission of agricultural produce from foreign countries, have masked those of the other cause. This fall of price would not in itself have any tendency injurious to the landlord, since corn-rents are increased in the same ratio in which the price of corn is diminished. But neither does it in any way tend to increase his income. The rent-charge, therefore, which is substituted for tithe, is a dead loss to him at the expiration of existing leases: and the commutation of tithe was not a mere alteration in the mode in which the landlord bore an existing burthen, but the imposition of a new one; relief being afforded to the consumer at the expense of the landlord, who, however, begins immediately to receive progressive indemnification at the consumer's expense, by the impulse given to accumulation and population.

5. We have hitherto inquired into the effects of taxes on commodities, on the assumption that they are levied impartially on every mode in which the commodity can be

produced or brought to market. Another class of considerations is opened, if we suppose that this impartiality is not
maintained, and that the tax is imposed, not on the commodity, but on some particular mode of obtaining it.

Suppose that a commodity is capable of being made by
two different processes; as a manufactured commodity may
be produced either by hand or by steam-power; sugar may
be made either from the sugar-cane or from beet-root, cattle
fattened either on hay and green crops, or on oil-cake and
the refuse of breweries. It is the interest of the community,
that of the two methods, producers should adopt that which
produces the best article at the lowest price. This being also
the interest of the producers, unless protected against competition, and shielded from the penalties of indolence; the
process most advantageous to the community is that which,
if not interfered with by government, they ultimately find it
to their advantage to adopt. Suppose however that a tax is
laid on one of the processes, and no tax at all, or one of
smaller amount, on the other. If the taxed process is the one
which the producers would not have adopted, the measure is
simply nugatory. But if the tax falls, as it is of course
intended to do, upon the one which they would have
adopted, it creates an artificial motive for preferring the untaxed process, though the inferior of the two. If, therefore,
it has any effect at all, it causes the commodity to be
produced of worse quality, or at a greater expense of
labour; it causes so much of the labour of the community
to be wasted, and the capital employed in supporting and
remunerating the labour to be expended as uselessly, as if it
were spent in hiring men to dig holes and fill them up again.
This waste of labour and capital constitutes an addition to
the cost of production of the commodity, which raises its
value and price in a corresponding ratio, and thus the
owners of the capital are indemnified. The loss falls on the
consumers; though the capital of the country is also eventually diminished, by the diminution of their means of saving,
and in some degree, of their inducements to save.

The kind of tax, therefore, which comes under the general
denomination of a discriminating duty, transgresses the rule

that taxes should take as little as possible from the tax-payer beyond what they bring into the treasury of the state. A discriminating duty makes the consumer pay two distinct taxes, only one of which is paid to the government, and that frequently the less onerous of the two. If a tax were laid on sugar produced from the cane, leaving the sugar from beet-root untaxed, then in so far as cane sugar continued to be used, the tax on it would be paid to the treasury, and might be as unobjectionable as most other taxes; but if cane sugar, having previously been cheaper than beet-root sugar, was now dearer, and beet-root sugar was to any consider-able amount substituted for it, and fields laid out and manufactories established in consequence, the government would gain no revenue from the beet-root sugar, while the consumers of it would pay a real tax. They would pay for beet-root sugar more than they had previously paid for cane sugar, and the difference would go to indemnify producers for a portion of the labour of the country actually thrown away, in producing by the labour of (say) three hundred men, what could be obtained by the other process with the labour of two hundred.

One of the commonest cases of discriminating duties, is that of a tax on the importation of a commodity capable of being produced at home, unaccompanied by an equivalent tax on the home production. A commodity is never perman-ently imported, unless it can be obtained from abroad at a smaller cost of labour and capital on the whole, than is necessary for producing it. If, therefore, by a duty on the importation, it is rendered cheaper to produce the article than to import it, an extra quantity of labour and capital is expended, without any extra result. The labour is useless, and the capital is spent in paying people for laboriously doing nothing. All custom duties which operate as an en-couragement to the home production of the taxed article, are thus an eminently wasteful mode of raising a revenue.

This character belongs in a peculiar degree to custom duties on the produce of land, unless countervailed by excise duties on the home production. Such taxes bring less into the public treasury, compared with what they take from the consumers, than any other imposts to which civilized nations are usually subject. If the wheat produced in a country is twenty millions of quarters, and the consumption twenty-one millions, a million being annually imported, and if on this million a duty is laid which raises the price ten shillings per quarter, the price which is raised is not that of the million only, but of the whole twenty-one millions. Taking the most favourable, but extremely improbable supposition, that the importation is not at all checked, nor the home production enlarged, the state gains a revenue of only half a million, while the consumers are taxed ten millions and a half; the ten millions being a contribution to the home growers, who are forced by competition to resign it all to the landlords. The consumer thus pays to the owners of land an additional tax, equal to twenty times that which he pays to the state. Let us now suppose that the tax really checks importation. Suppose importation stopped altogether in ordinary years; it being found that the million of quarters can be obtained, by a more elaborate cultivation, or by breaking up inferior land, at a less advance than ten shillings upon the previous price—say, for instance, five shillings a quarter. The revenue now obtains nothing, except from the extraordinary imports which may happen to take place in a season of scarcity. But the consumers pay every year a tax of five shillings on the whole twenty-one millions of quarters, amounting to $5\frac{1}{4}$ millions sterling. Of this the odd £250,000 goes to compensate the growers of the last million of quarters for the labour and capital wasted under the compulsion of the law. The remaining five millions go to enrich the landlords as before.

Such is the operation of what are technically termed Corn Laws, when first laid on; and such continues to be their operation, so long as they have any effect at all in raising the price of corn. But I am by no means of opinion that in the long run they keep up either prices or rents in the degree which these considerations might lead us to suppose. What we have said respecting the effect of tithes and other taxes on agricultural produce, applies in a great degree to corn laws: they anticipate artificially a rise of price and of rent, which would at all events have taken place through the increase of population and of production. The difference between a country without corn laws, and a country which has long had corn laws, is not so much that the last has a higher price or a larger rental, but that it has the same price and the same rental with a smaller aggregate capital and a smaller population. The imposition of corn laws raises rents, but retards that progress of accumulation which would in no long period have raised them fully as much. The repeal of corn laws tends to lower rents, but it unchains a force which, in a progressive state of capital and population, restores and even increases the former amount. There is every reason to expect that under the virtually free importation of agricultural produce, at last extorted from the ruling powers of this country, the price of food, if population goes on increasing, will gradually but steadily rise; though this effect may for a time be postponed by the strong current which in this country has set in (and the impulse is extending itself to other countries) towards the improvement of agricultural science, and its increased application to practice.

What we have said of duties on importation generally, is equally applicable to discriminating duties which favour importation from one place or in one particular manner, in contradistinction to others: such as the preference given to the produce of a colony, or of a country with which there is a commercial treaty: or the higher duties formerly imposed by our navigation laws on goods imported in other than British shipping. Whatever else may be alleged in favour of such distinctions, whenever they are not nugatory, they are economically wasteful. They induce a resort to a more costly mode of obtaining a commodity, in lieu of one less costly, and thus cause a portion of the labour which the country employs in providing itself with foreign commodities, to be sacrificed without return.

6. There is one more point relating to the operation of taxes on commodities conveyed from one country to

another, which requires notice: the influence which they exert on international exchanges. Every tax on a commodity tends to raise its price, and consequently to lessen the demand for it in the market in which it is sold. All taxes on international trade tend, therefore, to produce a disturbance and a re-adjustment of what we have termed the Equation of International Demand. This consideration leads to some rather curious consequences, which have been pointed out in the separate essay* on International Commerce, already several times referred to in this treatise.

Taxes on foreign trade are of two kinds—taxes on imports, and on exports. On the first aspect of the matter it would seem that both these taxes are paid by the consumers of the commodity; that taxes on exports consequently fall entirely on foreigners, taxes on imports wholly on the home consumer. The true state of the case, however, is much more complicated.

'By taxing exports, we may, in certain circumstances, produce a division of the advantage of the trade more favourable to ourselves. In some cases we may draw into our coffers, at the expense of foreigners, not only the whole tax, but more than the tax: in other cases, we should gain exactly the tax; in others, less than the tax. In this last case, a part of the tax is borne by ourselves: possibly the whole, possibly even, as we shall show, more than the whole.'

Reverting to the suppositious case employed in the Essay, of a trade between Germany and England in broadcloth and linen, 'suppose that England taxes her export of cloth, the tax not being supposed high enough to induce Germany to produce cloth for herself. The price at which cloth can be sold in Germany is augmented by the tax. This will probably diminish the quantity consumed. It may diminish it so much that, even at the increased price, there will not be required so great a money value as before. Or it may not diminish it at all, or so little, that in consequence of the higher price, a greater money value will be purchased than before. In this last case, England will gain, at the expense of Germany, not only the whole amount of the duty, but more; for, the money value of her exports to Germany being increased, while her imports remain the same, money will flow into England from Germany. The price of cloth will rise in England, and consequently in Germany; but the price of linen will fall in Germany, and consequently in England. We shall export less cloth, and import more linen, till the equilibrium is restored. It thus appears (what is at first sight somewhat remarkable) that by taxing her exports, England would, in some conceivable circumstances, not only gain from her foreign customers the whole amount of the tax, but would also get her imports cheaper. She would get them cheaper in two ways; for she would obtain them for less money, and would have more money to purchase them with. Germany, on the other hand, would suffer doubly: she would have to pay for her cloth a price increased not only by the duty, but by the influx of money into England, while the same change in the distribution of the circulating medium would leave her less money to purchase it with.

'This, however, is only one of three possible cases. If, after the imposition of the duty, Germany requires so diminished a quantity of cloth, that its total value is exactly the same as before, the balance of trade would be undisturbed; England will gain the duty, Germany will lose it, and nothing more. If, again, the imposition of the duty occasions such a falling off in the demand that Germany requires a less pecuniary value than before, our exports will no longer pay for our imports; money must pass from England into Germany; and Germany's share of the advantage of the trade will be increased. By the change in the distribution of money, cloth will fall in England; and therefore it will, of course, fall in Germany. Thus Germany will not pay the whole of the tax. From the same cause, linen will rise in Germany, and consequently in England. When this alteration of prices has so adjusted the demand, that the cloth and the linen again pay for one another, the result is that Germany has paid only a part of the tax, and the remainder of what has been received into our treasury has come indirectly out of the pockets of our own consumers of linen, who pay a higher price for that imported commodity in consequence of the tax on our exports, while at the same time they, in consequence of the efflux of money and the fall of prices, have smaller money incomes wherewith to pay for the linen at that advanced price.

'It is not an impossible supposition that by taxing our exports we might not only gain nothing from the foreigner, the tax being paid out of our own pockets, but might even compel our own people to pay a second tax to the foreigner. Suppose, as before, that the demand of Germany for cloth falls off so much on the imposition of the duty, that she requires a smaller money value than before, but that the case is so different with linen in England, that when the price rises the demand either does not fall off at all, or so little that the money value required is greater than before. The first effect of laying on the duty is, as before, that the cloth exported will no longer pay for the linen imported. Money will therefore flow out of England into Germany. One effect is to raise the price of linen in Germany, and consequently in England. But this, by the supposition, instead of stopping the efflux of money, only makes it greater, because the higher the price, the greater the money value of the linen consumed. The balance, therefore, can only be restored by the other effect, which is going on at the same time, namely, the fall of cloth in the English and consequently in the German market. Even when cloth has fallen so low that its price with the duty is only equal to what its price without the duty was at first, it is not a necessary consequence that the fall will stop; for the same amount of exportation as before will not now suffice to pay the increased money value of the imports; and although the German consumers have now not only cloth at the old price, but likewise increased money incomes, it is not certain that they will be inclined to employ the increase of their incomes in increasing their purchases of cloth. The price of cloth, therefore, must perhaps fall, to restore the equilibrium, more than the whole amount of the duty; Germany may be enabled to import cloth at a lower price when it is taxed, than when it was untaxed: and this gain she will acquire at the expense of the English consumers of linen, who, in addition, will be the real payers of the whole of what is received at their own custom-house under the name of duties on the export of cloth.'

It is almost unnecessary to remark that cloth and linen are here merely representatives of exports and imports in general; and that the effect which a tax on exports might have in increasing the cost of imports, would affect the imports from all countries, and not peculiarly the articles which might be imported from the particular country to which the taxed exports were sent.

'Such are the extremely various effects which may result to ourselves and to our customers from the imposition of taxes on our exports; and the determining circumstances are of a nature so imperfectly ascertainable, that it must be almost impossible to decide with any certainty, even after the tax has been imposed, whether we have been gainers by it or losers.' In general however there could be little doubt that a country which imposed such taxes would succeed in making foreign countries contribute something to its revenue; but unless the taxed article be one for which their demand is extremely urgent, they will seldom pay the whole of the amount which the tax brings in.[1] 'In any case, whatever we gain is lost by somebody else, and there is the expense of the collection besides: if international morality, therefore, were rightly understood and acted upon, such taxes, as being contrary to the universal weal, would not exist.'

Thus far of duties on exports. We now proceed to the more ordinary case of duties on imports. 'We have had an example of a tax on exports, that is, on foreigners, falling in part on ourselves. We shall therefore not be surprised if we find a tax on imports, that is, on ourselves, partly falling upon foreigners.

'Instead of taxing the cloth which we export, suppose that we tax the linen which we import. The duty which we are now supposing must not be what is termed a protecting

---

[1] Probably the strongest known instance of a large revenue raised from foreigners by a tax on exports, is the opium trade with China. The high price of the article under the Government monopoly (which is equivalent to a high export duty) has so little effect in discouraging its consumption, that it is said to have been occasionally sold in China for as much as its weight in silver.

duty, that is, a duty sufficiently high to induce us to produce the article at home. If it had this effect, it would destroy entirely the trade both in cloth and in linen, and both countries would lose the whole of the advantage which they previously gained by exchanging those commodities with one another. We suppose a duty which might diminish the consumption of the article, but which would not prevent us from continuing to import, as before, whatever linen we did consume.

'The equilibrium of trade would be disturbed if the imposition of the tax diminished, in the slightest degree, the quantity of linen consumed. For, as the tax is levied at our own custom-house, the German exporter only receives the same price as formerly, though the English consumer pays a higher one. If, therefore, there be any diminution of the quantity bought, although a larger sum of money may be actually laid out in the article, a smaller one will be due from England to Germany: this sum will no longer be an equivalent for the sum due from Germany to England for cloth, the balance therefore must be paid in money. Prices will fall in Germany and rise in England; linen will fall in the German market; cloth will rise in the English. The Germans will pay a higher price for cloth, and will have smaller money incomes to buy it with; while the English will obtain linen cheaper, that is, its price will exceed what it previously was by less than the amount of the duty, while their means of purchasing it will be increased by the increase of their money incomes.

'If the imposition of the tax does not diminish the demand, it will leave the trade exactly as it was before. We shall import as much, and export as much; the whole of the tax will be paid out of our own pockets.

'But the imposition of a tax on a commodity almost always diminishes the demand more or less; and it can never, or scarcely ever, increase the demand. It may, therefore, be laid down as a principle, that a tax on imported commodities, when it really operates as a tax, and not as a prohibition either total or partial, almost always falls in part upon the foreigners who consume our goods; and that this is a mode in which a nation may appropriate to itself, at the expense of foreigners, a larger share than would otherwise belong to it of the increase in the general product-iveness of the labour and capital of the world, which results from the interchange of commodities among nations.'

Those are, therefore, in the right who maintain that taxes on imports are partly paid by foreigners; but they are mistaken when they say, that it is by the foreign producer. It is not on the person from whom we buy, but on all those who buy from us, that a portion of our custom-duties spontaneously falls. It is the foreign consumer of our ex-ported commodities, who is obliged to pay a higher price for them because we maintain revenue duties on foreign goods.

There are but two cases in which duties on commodities can in any degree, or in any manner, fall on the producer. One is, when the article is a strict monopoly, and at a scarcity price. The price in this case being only limited by the desires of the buyer; the sum obtained from the re-stricted supply being the utmost which the buyers would consent to give rather than go without it; if the treasury interprets a part of this, the price cannot be further raised to compensate for the tax, and it must be paid from the monopoly profits. A tax on rare and high-priced wines will fall wholly on the growers, or rather, on the owners of the vineyards. The second case in which the producer some-times bears a portion of the tax, is more important: the case of duties on the produce of land or of mines. These might be so high as to diminish materially the demand for the produce, and compel the abandonment of some of the inferior qualities of land or mines. Supposing this to be the effect, the consumers, both in the country itself and in those which dealt with it, would obtain the produce at smaller cost; and a part only, instead of the whole, of the duty would fall on the purchaser, who would be indemnified chiefly at the expense of the landowners or mine-owners in the producing country.

Duties on importation may, then, be divided 'into two classes: those which have the effect of encouraging some particular branch of domestic industry, and those which have not. The former are purely mischievous, both to the country imposing them, and to those with whom it trades. They prevent a saving of labour and capital, which, if permitted to be made, would be divided in some proportion or other between the importing country and the countries which buy what that country does or might export.

'The other class of duties are those which do not encourage one mode of procuring an article at the expense of another, but allow interchange to take place just as if the duty did not exist, and to produce the saving of labour which constitutes the motive to international, as to all other commerce. Of this kind are duties on the importation of any commodity which could not by any possibility be produced at home; and duties not sufficiently high to counterbalance the difference of expense between the production of the article at home and its importation. Of the money which is brought into the treasury of any country by taxes of this last description, a part only is paid by the people of that country; the remainder by the foreign consumers of their goods.

'Nevertheless, this latter kind of taxes are in principle as ineligible as the former, though not precisely on the same ground. A protecting duty can never be a cause of gain, but always and necessarily of loss, to the country imposing it, just so far as it is efficacious to its end. A non-protecting duty, on the contrary, would in most cases be a source of gain to the country imposing it, in so far as throwing part of the weight of its taxes upon other people is a gain; but it would be a means which it could seldom be advisable to adopt, being so easily counteracted by a precisely similar proceeding on the other side.

'If England, in the case already supposed, sought to obtain for herself more than her natural share of the advantage of the trade with Germany, by imposing a duty upon linen, Germany would only have to impose a duty upon cloth, sufficient to diminish the demand for that article about as much as the demand for linen had been diminished in England by the tax. Things would then be as before, and each country would pay its own tax. Unless, indeed, the sum of the two duties exceeded the entire advantage of the trade; for in that case the trade, and its advantage, would cease entirely.

'There would be no advantage, therefore, in imposing duties of this kind, with a view to gain by them in the manner which has been pointed out. But when any part of the revenue is derived from taxes on commodities, these may often be as little objectionable as the rest. It is evident, too, that considerations of reciprocity, which are quite unessential when the matter in debate is a protecting duty, are of material importance when the repeal of duties of this other description is discussed. A country cannot be expected to renounce the power of taxing foreigners, unless foreigners will in return practise towards itself the same forbearance. The only mode in which a country can save itself from being a loser by the revenue duties imposed by other countries on its commodities, is to impose corresponding revenues duties on theirs. Only it must take care that those duties be not so high as to exceed all that remains of the advantage of the trade, and put an end to importation altogether, causing the article to be either produced at home, or imported from another and dearer market.'

V

OF SOME OTHER TAXES

1. Besides direct taxes on income, and taxes on consumption, the financial systems of most countries comprise a variety of miscellaneous imposts, not strictly included in either class. The modern European systems retain many such taxes, though in much less number and variety than those semi-barbarous governments which European influence has not yet reached. In some of these, scarcely any incident of life has escaped being made an excuse for some fiscal exaction; hardly any act, not belonging to daily routine, can be performed by any one, without obtaining leave from some agent of government, which is only granted in consideration of a payment: especially when the act requires the aid or the peculiar guarantee of a public authority. In the present treatise we may confine our attention to such taxes as lately existed, or still exist, in countries usually classed as civilized.

In almost all nations a considerable revenue is drawn from taxes on contracts. These are imposed in various forms. One expedient is that of taxing the legal instrument which serves as evidence of the contract, and which is commonly the only evidence legally admissible. In England, scarcely any contract is binding unless executed on stamped paper, which has paid a tax to government; and until very lately, when the contract related to property the tax was proportionally much heavier on the smaller than on the larger transactions; which is still true of some of those taxes. There are also stamp-duties on the legal instruments which are evidence of the fulfilment of contracts; such as acknowledgments of receipt, and deeds of release. Taxes on contracts are not always levied by means of stamps. The duty on sales by auction, abrogated by Sir Robert Peel, was an instance in point. The taxes on transfers of landed property, in France, are another: in England there are stamp-duties. In some countries, contracts of many kinds are not valid unless registered, and their registration is made an occasion for a tax.

Of taxes on contracts, the most important are those on the transfer of property; chiefly on purchases and sales. Taxes on the sale of consumable commodities are simply taxes on those commodities. If they affect only some particular commodities, they raise the prices of those commodities, and are paid by the consumer. If the attempt were made to tax all purchases and sales, which, however absurd, was for centuries the law of Spain, the tax, if it could be enforced, would be equivalent to a tax on all commodities, and would not affect prices: if levied from the sellers, it would be a tax on profits, if from the buyers, a tax on consumption; and neither class could throw the burthen upon the other. If confined to some one mode of sale, as for example by auction, it discourages recourse to that mode, and if of any material amount, prevents it from being adopted at all, unless in a case of emergency; in which case as the seller is under a necessity to sell, but the buyer under no necessity to buy, the tax falls on the seller; and this was the strongest of the objections to the auction duty: it almost always fell on a necessitous person, and in the crisis of his necessities.

Taxes on the purchase and sale of land are, in most countries, liable to the same objection. Landed property in old countries is seldom parted with, except from reduced circumstances, or some urgent need: the seller, therefore, must take what he can get, while the buyer, whose object is an investment, makes his calculations on the interest which he can obtain for his money in other ways, and will not buy if he is charged with a government tax on the transaction.[1] It has indeed been objected, that this argument would not apply if all modes of permanent investment, such as the purchase of government securities, shares in joint-stock

---

[1] The statement in the text requires modification in the case of countries where the land is owned in small portions. These, being neither a badge of importance, nor in general an object of local attachment, are readily parted with at a small advance on their original cost, with the intention of buying elsewhere; and the desire of acquiring land even on disadvantageous terms is so great, as to be little checked by even a high rate of taxation.

companies, mortgages, and the like, were subject to the same tax. But even then, if paid by the buyer, it would be equivalent to a tax on interest: if sufficiently heavy to be of any importance, it would disturb the established relation between interest and profit; and the disturbance would redress itself by a rise in the rate of interest, and a fall of the price of land and of all securities. It appears to me, therefore, that the seller is the person by whom such taxes, unless under peculiar circumstances, will generally be borne.

All taxes must be condemned which throw obstacles in the way of the sale of land, or other instruments of production. Such sales tend naturally to render the property more productive. The seller, whether moved by necessity or choice, is probably some one who is either without the means, or without the capacity, to make the most advantageous use of the property for productive purposes; while the buyer, on the other hand, is at any rate not needy, and is frequently both inclined and able to improve the property, since, as it is worth more to such a person than to any other, he is likely to offer the highest price for it. All taxes, therefore, and all difficulties and expenses, annexed to such contracts, are decidedly detrimental; especially in the case of land, the source of subsistence, and the original foundation of all wealth, on the improvement of which, therefore, so much depends. Too great facilities cannot be given to enable land to pass into the hands, and assume the modes of aggregation or division, most conducive to its productiveness. If landed properties are too large, alienation should be free, in order that they may be subdivided; if too small, in order that they may be united. All taxes on the transfer of landed property should be abolished; but, as the landlords have no claim to be relieved from any reservation which the state has hitherto made in its own favour from the amount of their rent, an annual impost equivalent to the average produce of these taxes should be distributed over the land generally, in the form of a land-tax.

Some of the taxes on contracts are very pernicious, imposing a virtual penalty upon transactions which it ought to be the policy of the legislator to encourage. Of this sort is the stamp-duty on leases, which in a country of large properties are an essential condition of good agriculture; and the taxes on insurances, a direct discouragement to prudence and forethought.

2. Nearly allied to the taxes on contracts are those on communication. The principal of these is the postage tax; to which may be added taxes on advertisements, and on newspapers, which are taxes on the communication of information.

The common mode of levying a tax on the conveyance of letters, is by making the government the sole authorized carrier of them, and demanding a monopoly price. When this price is so moderate as it is in this country under the uniform penny postage, scarcely if at all exceeding what would be charged under the freest competition by any private company, it can hardly be considered as taxation, but rather as the profits of a business; whatever excess there is above the ordinary profits of stock being a fair result of the saving of expense, caused by having only one establishment and one set of arrangements for the whole country, instead of many competing ones. The business, too, being one which both can and ought to be conducted on fixed rules, is one of the few businesses which it is not unsuitable to a government to conduct. The post office, therefore, is at present one of the best of the sources from which this country derives its revenue. But a postage much exceeding what would be paid for the same service in a system of freedom, is not a desirable tax. Its chief weight falls on letters of business, and increases the expense of mercantile relations between distant places. It is like an attempt to raise a large revenue by heavy tolls: it obstructs all operations by which goods are conveyed from place to place, and discourages the production of commodities in one place for consumption in another; which is not only in itself one of the greatest sources of economy of labour, but is a necessary condition of almost all improvements in production, and one of the strongest stimulants to industry, and promoters of civilization.

The tax on advertisements was not free from the same objection, since in whatever degree advertisements are useful to business, by facilitating the coming together of the dealer or producer and the consumer, in that same degree, if the tax be high enough to be a serious discouragement to advertising, it prolongs the period during which goods remain unsold, and capital locked up in idleness.

A tax on newspapers is objectionable, not so much where it does fall as where it does not, that is, where it prevents newspapers from being used. To the generality of those who buy them, newspapers are a luxury which they can as well afford to pay for as any other indulgence, and which is as unexceptionable a source of revenue. But to that large part of the community who have been taught to read, but have received little other intellectual education, newspapers are the source of nearly all the general information which they possess, and of nearly all their acquaintance with the ideas and topics current among mankind; and an interest is more easily excited in newspapers, than in books or other more recondite sources of instruction. Newspapers contribute so little, in a direct way to the origination of useful ideas, that many persons undervalue the importance of their office in disseminating them. They correct many prejudices and superstitions, and keep up a habit of discussion, and interest in public concerns, the absence of which is a great cause of the stagnation of mind usually found in the lower and middle, if not in all, ranks, of those countries where newspapers of an important or interesting character do not exist. There ought to be no taxes (as in this country there now are not) which render this great diffuser of information, of mental excitement, and mental exercise, less accessible to that portion of the public which most needs to be carried into a region of ideas and interests beyond its own limited horizon.

3. In the enumeration of bad taxes, a conspicuous place must be assigned to law taxes; which extract a revenue for the state from the various operations involved in an application to the tribunals. Like all needless expenses attached to

law proceedings, they are a tax on redress, and therefore a premium on injury. Although such taxes have been abolished in this country as a general source of revenue, they still exist in the form of fees of court, for defraying the expense of the courts of justice; under the idea, apparently, that those may fairly be required to bear the expenses of the administration of justice, who reap the benefit of it. The fallacy of this doctrine was powerfully exposed by Bentham. As he remarked, those who are under the necessity of going to law, are those who benefit least, not most, by the law and its administration. To them the protection which the law affords has not been complete, since they have been obliged to resort to a court of justice to ascertain their rights, or maintain those rights against infringement: while the remainder of the public have enjoyed the immunity from injury conferred by the law and the tribunals, without the inconvenience of an appeal to them.

4. Besides the general taxes of the State, there are in all or most countries local taxes, to defray any expenses of a public nature which it is thought best to place under the control or management of a local authority. Some of these expenses are incurred for purposes in which the particular locality is solely or chiefly interested; as the paving, cleansing, and lighting of the streets; or the making and repairing of roads and bridges, which may be important to people from any part of the country, but only in so far as they, or goods in which they have an interest, pass along the roads or over the bridges. In other cases again, the expenses are of a kind as nationally important as any others, but are defrayed locally because supposed more likely to be well administered by local bodies; as, in England, the relief of the poor, and the support of gaols, and in some other countries, of schools. To decide for what public objects local superintendence is best suited, and what are those which should be kept immediately under the central government, or under a mixed system of local management and central superintendence, is a question not of political economy, but of administration. It is an important principle,

however, that taxes imposed by a local authority, being less amenable to publicity and discussion than the acts of the government, should always be special—laid on for some definite service, and not exceeding the expense actually incurred in rendering the service. Thus limited, it is desirable, whenever practicable, that the burthen should fall on those to whom the service is rendered; that the expense, for instance, of roads and bridges, should be defrayed by a toll on passengers and goods conveyed by them, thus dividing the cost between those who use them for pleasure or convenience, and the consumers of the goods which they enable to be brought to and from the market at a diminished expense. When, however, the tolls have repaid with interest the whole of the expenditure, the road or bridge should be thrown open free of toll, that it may be used also by those to whom, unless open gratuitously, it would be valueless; provision being made for repairs either from the funds of the state, or by a rate levied on the localities which reap the principal benefit.

In England, almost all local taxes are direct, (the coal duty of the City of London, and a few similar imposts, being the chief exceptions,) though the greatest part of the taxation for general purposes is indirect. On the contrary, in France, Austria, and other countries where direct taxation is much more largely employed by the state, the local expenses of towns are principally defrayed by taxes levied on commodities when entering them. These indirect taxes are much more objectionable in towns than on the frontier, because the things which the country supplies to the towns are chiefly the necessaries of life and the materials of manufacture, while, of what a country imports from foreign countries, the greater part usually consists of luxuries. An octroi cannot produce a large revenue, without pressing severely upon the labouring classes of the towns; unless their wages rise proportionally, in which case the tax falls in a great measure on the consumers of town produce, whether residing in town or country, since capital will not remain in the towns if its profits fall below their ordinary proportion as compared with the rural districts.

VI

COMPARISON BETWEEN
DIRECT AND INDIRECT TAXATION

1. Are direct or indirect taxes the most eligible? This question, at all times interesting, has of late excited a considerable amount of discussion. In England there is a popular feeling, of old standing, in favour of indirect, or it should rather be said in opposition to direct, taxation. The feeling is not grounded on the merits of the case, and is of a puerile kind. An Englishman dislikes, not so much the payment, as the act of paying. He dislikes seeing the face of the tax-collector, and being subjected to his peremptory demand. Perhaps, too, the money which he is required to pay directly out of his pocket is the only taxation which he is quite sure that he pays at all. That a tax of one shilling per pound on tea, or of two shillings per bottle on wine, raises the price of each pound of tea and bottle of wine which he consumes, by that and more than that amount, cannot indeed be denied; it is the fact, and is intended to be so, and he himself, at times, is perfectly aware of it; but it makes hardly any impression on his practical feelings and associations, serving to illustrate the distinction between what is merely known to be true and what is felt to be so. The unpopularity of direct taxation, contrasted with the easy manner in which the public consent to let themselves be fleeced in the prices of commodities, has generated in many friends of improvement a directly opposite mode of thinking to the foregoing. They contend that the very reason which makes direct taxation disagreeable, makes it preferable. Under it, every one knows how much he really pays; and if he votes for a war, or any other expensive national luxury, he does so with his eyes open to what it costs him. If all taxes were direct, taxation would be much more perceived than at present; and there would be a security which now there is not, for economy in the public expenditure.

Although this argument is not without force, its weight is likely to be constantly diminishing. The real incidence of indirect taxation is every day more generally understood and more familiarly recognised: and whatever else may be said of the changes which are taking place in the tendencies of the human mind, it can scarcely, I think, be denied, that things are more and more estimated according to their calculated value, and less according to their non-essential accompaniments. The mere distinction between paying money directly to the tax-collector, and contributing the same sum through the intervention of the tea-dealer or the wine-merchant, no longer makes the whole difference between dislike or opposition, and passive acquiescence. But further, while any such infirmity of the popular mind subsists, the argument grounded on it tells partly on the other side of the question. If our present revenue of about seventy millions were all raised by direct taxes, an extreme dissatisfaction would certainly arise at having to pay so much; but while men's minds are so little guided by reason, as such a change of feeling from so irrelevant a cause would imply, so great an aversion to taxation might not be an unqualified good. Of the seventy millions in question, nearly thirty are pledged, under the most binding obligations, to those whose property has been borrowed and spent by the state: and while this debt remains unredeemed, a greatly increased impatience of taxation would involve no little danger of a breach of faith, similar to that which, in the defaulting states of America,* has been produced, and in some of them still continues, from the same cause. That part, indeed, of the public expenditure, which is devoted to the maintenance of civil and military establishments, (that is, all except the interest of the national debt,) affords, in many of its details, ample scope for retrenchment. But while much of the revenue is wasted under the mere pretence of public service, so much of the most important business of government is left undone, that whatever can be rescued from useless expenditure is urgently required for useful. Whether the object be education; a more efficient and accessible administration of justice; reforms of any kind which, like the Slave Emancipation, require compensation to individual interests; or what is as important as any of these, the entertainment of a sufficient staff of able and educated public servants, to conduct in a better than the present awkward manner the business of legislation and administration; every one of these things implies considerable expense, and many of them have again and again been prevented by the reluctance which existed to apply to Parliament for an increased grant of public money, though (besides that the existing means would probably be sufficient if applied to the proper purposes) the cost would be repaid, often a hundredfold, in mere pecuniary advantage to the community generally. If so great an addition were made to the public dislike of taxation as might be the consequence of confining it to the direct form, the classes who profit by the misapplication of public money might probably succeed in saving that by which they profit, at the expense of that which would only be useful to the public.

There is, however, a frequent plea in support of indirect taxation, which must be altogether rejected, as grounded on a fallacy. We are often told that taxes on commodities are less burthensome than other taxes, because the contributor can escape from them by ceasing to use the taxed commodity. He certainly can, if that be his object, deprive the government of the money: but he does so by a sacrifice of his own indulgences, which (if he chose to undergo it) would equally make up to him for the same amount taken from him by direct taxation. Suppose a tax laid on wine, sufficient to add five pounds to the price of the quantity of wine which he consumes in a year. He has only (we are told) to diminish his consumption of wine by £5, and he escapes the burthen. True: but if the £5, instead of being laid on wine, had been taken from him by an income tax, he could, by expending £5 less in wine, equally save the amount of the tax, so that the difference between the two cases is really illusory. If the government takes from the contributor five pounds a year, whether in one way or another, exactly that amount must be retrenched from his consumption to leave him as well off as before; and in either way the same amount of sacrifice, neither more nor less, is imposed on him.

On the other hand, it is some advantage on the side of indirect taxes, that what they exact from the contributor is taken at a time and in a manner likely to be convenient to him. It is paid at a time when he has at any rate a payment to make; it causes, therefore, no additional trouble, nor (unless the tax be on necessaries) any inconvenience but what is inseparable from the payment of the amount. He can also, except in the case of very perishable articles, select his own time for laying in a stock of the commodity, and consequently for payment of the tax. The producer or dealer who advances these taxes, is, indeed, sometimes subjected to inconvenience; but, in the case of imported goods, this inconvenience is reduced to a minimum by what is called the Warehousing System, under which, instead of paying the duty at the time of importation, he is only required to do so when he takes out the goods for consumption, which is seldom done until he has either actually found, or has the prospect of immediately finding, a purchaser.

The strongest objection, however, to raising the whole or the greater part of a large revenue by direct taxes, is the impossibility of assessing them fairly without a conscientious co-operation on the part of the contributors, not to be hoped for in the present low state of public morality. In the case of an income tax, we have already seen that unless it be found practicable to exempt savings altogether from the tax, the burthen cannot be apportioned with any tolerable approach to fairness upon those whose incomes are derived from business or professions; and this is in fact admitted by most of the advocates of direct taxation, who, I am afraid, generally get over the difficulty by leaving those classes untaxed, and confining their projected income tax to 'realized property', in which form it certainly has the merit of being a very easy form of plunder. But enough has been said in condemnation of this expedient. We have seen, however, that a house tax is a form of direct taxation not liable to the same objections as an income tax, and indeed liable to as few objections of any kind as perhaps any of our indirect taxes. But it would be impossible to raise by a house tax alone, the greatest part of the revenue of Great Britain, without producing a very objectionable over-crowding of the population, through the strong motive which all persons would have to avoid the tax by restricting their house accommodation. Besides, even a house tax has inequalities, and consequent injustices; no tax is exempt from them, and it is neither just nor politic to make all the inequalities fall in the same places, by calling upon one tax to defray the whole or the chief part of the public expenditure. So much of the local taxation, in this country, being already in the form of a house tax, it is probable that ten millions a year would be fully as much as could beneficially be levied, through this medium, for general purposes.

A certain amount of revenue may, as we have seen, be obtained without injustice by a peculiar tax on rent. Besides the present land-tax, and an equivalent for the revenue now derived from stamp duties on the conveyance of land, some further taxation might, I have contended, at some future period be imposed, to enable the state to participate in the progressive increase of the incomes of landlords from natural causes. Legacies and inheritances, we have also seen, ought to be subjected to taxation sufficient to yield a considerable revenue. With these taxes, and a house tax of suitable amount, we should, I think, have reached the prudent limits of direct taxation, save in a national emergency so urgent as to justify the government in disregarding the amount of inequality and unfairness which may ultimately be found inseparable from an income tax. The remainder of the revenue would have to be provided by taxes on consumption, and the question is, which of these are the least objectionable.

2. There are some forms of indirect taxation which must be peremptorily excluded. Taxes on commodities, for revenue purposes, must not operate as protecting duties, but must be levied impartially on every mode in which the articles can be obtained, whether produced in the country itself, or

imported. An exclusion must also be put upon all taxes on the necessaries of life, or on the materials or instruments employed in producing those necessaries. Such taxes are always liable to encroach on what should be left untaxed, the incomes barely sufficient for healthful existence; and on the most favourable supposition, namely, that wages rise to compensate the labourers for the tax, it operates as a peculiar tax on profits, which is at once unjust, and detrimental to national wealth.[1] What remain are taxes on luxuries. And these have some properties which strongly recommend them. In the first place, they can never, by any possibility, touch those whose whole income is expended on necessaries; while they do reach those by whom what is required for necessaries, is expended on indulgences. In the next place, they operate in some cases as an useful, and the only useful, kind of sumptuary law. I disclaim all asceticism, and by no means wish to see discouraged, either by law or opinion, any indulgence (consistent with the means and obligations of the person using it) which is sought from a genuine inclination for, and enjoyment of, the thing itself; but a great portion of the expenses of the higher and middle classes in most countries, and the greatest in this, is not incurred for the sake of the pleasure afforded by the things on which the money is spent, but from regard to opinion, and an idea that certain expenses are expected from them, as an appendage of station; and I cannot but think that expenditure of this sort is a most desirable subject of taxation. If taxation discourages it, some good is done, and if not, no harm; for in so far as taxes are levied on things which are desired and possessed from motives of this description, nobody is the worse for them. When a thing is

[1] Some argue that the materials and instruments of all production should be exempt from taxation; but these, when they do not enter into the production of necessaries, seem as proper subjects of taxation as the finished article. It is chiefly with reference to foreign trade, that such taxes have been considered injurious. Internationally speaking, they may be looked upon as export duties, and, unless in cases in which an export duty is advisable, they should be accompanied with an equivalent drawback on exportation. But there is no sufficient reason against taxing the materials and instruments used in the production of anything which is itself a fit object of taxation.

bought not for its use but for its costliness, cheapness is no recommendation. As Sismondi remarks, the consequence of cheapening articles of vanity, is not that less is expended on such things, but that the buyers substitute for the cheapened article some other which is more costly, or a more elaborate quality of the same thing; and as the inferior quality answered the purpose of vanity equally well when it was equally expensive, a tax on the article is really paid by nobody: it is a creation of public revenue by which nobody loses.[1]

3. In order to reduce as much as possible the inconveniences, and increase the advantages, incident to taxes on commodities, the following are the practical rules which suggest themselves. 1. To raise as large a revenue as conveniently may be, from those classes of luxuries which have most connexion with vanity, and least with positive enjoyment; such as the more costly qualities of all kinds of personal equipment and ornament. 2. Whenever possible, to demand the tax, not from the producer, but directly from the consumer, since when levied on the producer it raises the price always by more, and often by much more, than the mere amount of the tax. Most of the minor assessed taxes in this country are recommended by both these considerations. But with regard to horses and carriages, as there are many persons to whom, from health or constitution, these are not so much luxuries as necessaries, the tax paid by those who have but one riding horse, or but one carriage, especially of the cheaper descriptions, should be low; while taxation should rise very rapidly with the number of horses and carriages, and with their costliness. 3. But as the only indirect taxes which yield a large revenue are those which fall on articles of universal or very general consumption, and as it is therefore necessary to have some taxes on real luxuries, that is, on things which afford pleasure in themselves, and are valued on that account rather than for their cost; these taxes should, if possible, be so adjusted as to fall

---

[1] [Note omitted.]

with the same proportional weight on small, on moderate, and on large incomes. This is not an easy matter; since the things which are the subjects of the more productive taxes, are in proportion more largely consumed by the poorer members of the community than by the rich. Tea, coffee, sugar, tobacco, fermented drinks, can hardly be so taxed that the poor shall not bear more than their due share of the burthen. Something might be done by making the duty on the superior qualities, which are used by the richer consumers, much higher in proportion to the value (instead of much lower, as is almost universally the practice, under the present English system); but in some cases the difficulty of at all adjusting the duty to the value, so as to prevent evasion, is said, with what truth I know not, to be insuperable; so that it is thought necessary to levy the same fixed duty on all the qualities alike: a flagrant injustice to the poorer class of contributors, unless compensated by the existence of other taxes from which, as from the present income tax, they are altogether exempt. 4. As far as is consistent with the preceding rules, taxation should rather be concentrated on a few articles than diffused over many, in order that the expenses of collection may be smaller, and that as few employments as possible may be burthensomely and vexatiously interfered with. 5. Among luxuries of general consumption, taxation should by preference attach itself to stimulants, because these, though in themselves as legitimate indulgences as any others, are more liable than most to be used in excess, so that the check to consumption, naturally arising from taxation, is on the whole better applied to them than to other things. 6. As far as other considerations permit, taxation should be confined to imported articles, since these can be taxed with a less degree of vexatious interference, and with fewer incidental bad effects, than when a tax is levied on the field or on the workshop. Custom-duties are, *ceteris paribus*, much less objectionable than excise: but they must be laid only on things which either cannot, or at least will not, be produced in the country itself; or else their production there must be prohibited (as in England is the case with tobacco), or subjected to an excise duty of equivalent amount. 7. No tax ought to be kept so high as to furnish a motive to its evasion, too strong to be counteracted by ordinary means of prevention: and especially no commodity should be taxed so highly as to raise up a class of lawless characters, smugglers, illicit distillers, and the like.

Of the excise and custom duties lately existing in this country, all which are intrinsically unfit to form part of a good system of taxation, have, since the last reforms by Mr Gladstone, been got rid of. Among these are all duties on ordinary articles of food, whether for human beings or for cattle; those on timber, as falling on the materials of lodging, which is one of the necessaries of life; all duties on the metals, and on implements made of them; taxes on soap, which is a necessary of cleanliness, and on tallow, the material both of that and of some other necessaries; the tax on paper, an indispensable instrument of almost all business and of most kinds of instruction. The duties which now yield nearly the whole of the customs and excise revenue, those on sugar, coffee, tea, wine, beer, spirits, and tobacco, are in themselves, where a large amount of revenue is necessary, extremely proper taxes; but at present grossly unjust, from the disproportionate weight with which they press on the poorer classes; and some of them (those on spirits and tobacco) are so high as to cause a considerable amount of smuggling. It is probable that most of these taxes might bear a great reduction without any material loss of revenue. In what manner the finer articles of manufacture, consumed by the rich, might most advantageously be taxed, I must leave to be decided by those who have the requisite practical knowledge. The difficulty would be, to effect it without an inadmissible degree of interference with production. In countries which, like the United States, import the principal part of the finer manufactures which they consume, there is little difficulty in the matter: and even where nothing is imported but the raw material, that may be taxed, especially the qualities of it which are exclusively employed for the fabrics used by the richer class of consumers. Thus, in England a high custom-duty on raw silk would be consistent with principle; and it might perhaps be practicable to tax the finer qualities of cotton or linen yarn, whether spun in the country itself or imported.

248   PRINCIPLES OF POLITICAL ECONOMY

with the debt besides, and with its interest in perpetuity.
The system of public loans, in such circumstances, may be
pronounced the very worst which, in the present state of
civilization, is advisable as a resource of financial
expedient.

VII

OF A NATIONAL DEBT

1. The question must now be considered, how far it is
right or expedient to raise money for the purposes of
government, not by laying on taxes to the amount required,
but by taking a portion of the capital of the country in the
form of a loan, and charging the public revenue with only
the interest. Nothing needs be said about providing for
temporary wants by taking up money; for instance, by an
issue of exchequer bills, destined to be paid off, at furthest
in a year or two, from the proceeds of the existing taxes.
This is a convenient expedient, and when the government
does not possess a treasure or hoard, is often a necessary
one, on the occurrence of extraordinary expenses, or of a
temporary failure in the ordinary sources of revenue. What
we have to discuss is the propriety of contracting a national
debt of a permanent character; defraying the expenses of a
war, or of any season of difficulty, by loans, to be redeemed
either very gradually and at a distant period, or not at all.

This question has already been touched upon in the First
Book.[1] We remarked, that if the capital taken in loans is
abstracted from funds either engaged in production, or
destined to be employed in it, their diversion from that
purpose is equivalent to taking the amount from the wages
of the labouring classes. Borrowing, in this case, is not a
substitute for raising the supplies within the year. A government which borrows does actually take the amount within
the year, and that too by a tax exclusively on the labouring
classes: than which it could have done nothing worse, if it
had supplied its wants by avowed taxation; and in that case
the transaction, and its evils, would have ended with the
emergency; while by the circuitous mode adopted, the value
exacted from the labourers is gained, not by the state, but
by the employers of labour, the state remaining charged

[1] [Bk I, Ch. V. 8. Not included in present edn.]

with the debt besides, and with its interest in perpetuity. The system of public loans, in such circumstances, may be pronounced the very worst which, in the present state of civilization, is still included in the catalogue of financial expedients.

We however remarked that there are other circumstances in which loans are not chargeable with these pernicious consequences: namely, first, when what is borrowed is foreign capital, the overflowings of the general accumulation of the world; or, secondly, when it is capital which either would not have been saved at all unless this mode of investment had been open to it, or after being saved, would have been wasted in unproductive enterprises, or sent to seek employment in foreign countries. When the progress of accumulation has reduced profits either to the ultimate or to the practical minimum,—to the rate, less than which would either put a stop to the increase of capital, or send the whole of the new accumulations abroad; government may annually intercept these new accumulations, without trenching on the employment or wages of the labouring classes in the country itself, or perhaps in any other country. To this extent, therefore, the loan system may be carried, without being liable to the utter and peremptory condemnation which is due to it when it overpasses this limit. What is wanted is an index to determine whether, in any given series of years, as during the last great war for example, the limit has been exceeded or not.

Such an index exists, at once a certain and an obvious one. Did the government, by its loan operations, augment the rate of interest? If it only opened a channel for capital which would not otherwise have been accumulated, or which, if accumulated, would not have been employed within the country; this implies that the capital, which the government took and expended, could not have found employment at the existing rate of interest. So long as the loans do no more than absorb this surplus, they prevent any tendency to a fall of the rate of interest, but they cannot occasion any rise. When they do raise the rate of interest, as they did in a most extraordinary degree during the French war, this is positive proof that the government is a competitor for capital with the ordinary channels of productive investment, and is carrying off, not merely funds which would not, but funds which would, have found productive employment within the country. To the full extent, therefore, to which the loans of government, during the war, caused the rate of interest to exceed what it was before, and what it has been since, those loans are chargeable with all the evils which have been described. If it be objected that interest only rose because profits rose, I reply that this does not weaken, but strengthens, the argument. If the government loans produced the rise of profits by the great amount of capital which they absorbed, by what means can they have had this effect, unless by lowering the wages of labour? It will perhaps be said, that what kept profits high during the war was not the drafts made on the national capital by the loans, but the rapid progress of industrial improvements. This, in a great measure, was the fact; and it no doubt alleviated the hardship to the labouring classes, and made the financial system which was pursued less actively mischievous, but not less contrary to principle. These very improvements in industry, made room for a larger amount of capital; and the government, by draining away a great part of the annual accumulations, did not indeed prevent that capital from existing ultimately, (for it started into existence with great rapidity after the peace,) but prevented it from existing at the time, and subtracted just so much, while the war lasted, from distribution among productive labourers. If the government had abstained from taking this capital by loan, and had allowed it to reach the labourers, but had raised the supplies which it required by a direct tax on the labouring classes, it would have produced (in every respect but the expense and inconvenience of collecting the tax) the very same economical effects which it did produce, except that we should not now have had the debt. The course it actually took was therefore worse than the very worst mode which it could possibly have adopted of raising the supplies within the year: and the only excuse, or justification, which it admits of, (so far as that excuse could be truly pleaded,) was hard necessity; the impossibility of raising so enormous an annual sum by taxation, without resorting to taxes which from their odiousness, or from the facility of evasion, it would have been found impracticable to enforce.

When government loans are limited to the overflowings of the national capital, or to those accumulations which would not take place at all unless suffered to overflow, they are at least not liable to this grave condemnation: they occasion no privation to any one at the time, except by the payment of the interest, and may even be beneficial to the labouring class during the term of their expenditure, by employing in the direct purchase of labour, as that of soldiers, sailors, etc., funds which might otherwise have quitted the country altogether. In this case therefore the question really is, what it is commonly supposed to be in all cases, namely, a choice between a great sacrifice at once, and a small one indefinitely prolonged. On this matter it seems rational to think, that the prudence of a nation will dictate the same conduct as the prudence of an individual; to submit to as much of the privation immediately, as can easily be borne, and only when any further burthen would distress or cripple them too much, to provide for the remainder by mortgaging their future income. It is an excellent maxim to make present resources suffice for present wants; the future will have its own wants to provide for. On the other hand, it may reasonably be taken into consideration that in a country increasing in wealth, the necessary expenses of government do not increase in the same ratio as capital or population; any burthen, therefore, is always less and less felt: and since those extraordinary expenses of government which are fit to be incurred at all, are mostly beneficial beyond the existing generation, there is no injustice in making posterity pay a part of the price, if the inconvenience would be extreme of defraying the whole of it by the exertions and sacrifices of the generation which first incurred it.

2. When a country, wisely or unwisely, has burthened itself with a debt, is it expedient to take steps for redeeming that debt? In principle it is impossible not to maintain the

affirmative. It is true that the payment of the interest, when the creditors are members of the same community, is no national loss, but a mere transfer. The transfer, however, being compulsory, is a serious evil, and the raising a great extra revenue by any system of taxation necessitates so much expense, vexation, disturbance of the channels of industry, and other mischiefs over and above the mere payment of the money wanted by the government, that to get rid of the necessity of such taxation is at all times worth a considerable effort. The same amount of sacrifice which would have been worth incurring to avoid contracting the debt, it is worth while to incur, at any subsequent time, for the purpose of extinguishing it.

Two modes have been contemplated of paying off a national debt: either at once by a general contribution, or gradually by a surplus revenue. The first would be incomparably the best, if it were practicable; and it would be practicable if it could justly be done by assessment on property alone. If property bore the whole interest of the debt, property might, with great advantage to itself, pay it off; since this would be merely surrendering to a creditor the principal sum, the whole annual proceeds of which were already his by law; and would be equivalent to what a landowner does when he sells part of his estate, to free the remainder from a mortgage. But property, it needs hardly be said, does not pay, and cannot justly be required to pay, the whole interest of the debt. Some indeed affirm that it can, on the plea that the existing generation is only bound to pay the debts of its predecessors from the assets it has received from them, and not from the produce of its own industry. But has no one received anything from previous generations except those who have succeeded to property? Is the whole difference between the earth as it is, with its clearings and improvements, its roads and canals, its towns and manufactories, and the earth as it was when the first human being set foot on it, of no benefit to any but those who are called the owners of the soil? Is the capital accumulated by the labour and abstinence of all former generations, of no advantage to any but those who have succeeded to the legal ownership of part of it? And have we not inherited a mass of acquired knowledge, both scientific and empirical, due to the sagacity and industry of those who preceded us, the benefits of which are the common wealth of all? Those who are born to the ownership of property have, in addition to these common benefits, a separate inheritance, and to this difference it is right that advertence should be had in regulating taxation. It belongs to the general financial system of the country to take due account of this principle, and I have indicated, as in my opinion a proper mode of taking account of it, a considerable tax on legacies and inheritances. Let it be determined directly and openly what is due from property to the state, and from the state to property, and let the institutions of the state be regulated accordingly. Whatever is the fitting contribution from property to the general expenses of the state, in the same and in no greater proportion should it contribute towards either the interest or the repayment of the national debt.

This, however, if admitted, is fatal to any scheme for the extinction of the debt by a general assessment on the community. Persons of property could pay their share of the amount by a sacrifice of property, and have the same net income as before; but if those who have no accumulations, but only incomes, were required to make up by a single payment the equivalent of the annual charge laid on them by the taxes maintained to pay the interest of the debt, they could only do so by incurring a private debt equal to their share of the public debt; while, from the insufficiency, in most cases, of the security which they could give, the interest would amount to a much larger annual sum than their share of that now paid by the state. Besides, a collective debt defrayed by taxes, has over the same debt parcelled out among individuals, the immense advantage, that it is virtually a mutual insurance among the contributors. If the fortune of a contributor diminishes, his taxes diminish; if he is ruined, they cease altogether, and his portion of the debt is wholly transferred to the solvent members of the community. If it were laid on him as a private obligation, he would still be liable to it even when penniless.

When the state possesses property, in land or otherwise, which there are not strong reasons of public utility for its retaining at its disposal, this should be employed, as far as it will go, in extinguishing debt. Any casual gain, or god-send, is naturally devoted to the same purpose. Beyond this, the only mode which is both just and feasible, of extinguishing or reducing a national debt, is by means of surplus revenue.

3. The desirableness, *per se*, of maintaining a surplus for this purpose, does not, I think, admit of a doubt. We sometimes, indeed, hear it said that the amount should rather be left to 'fructify in the pockets of the people.' This is a good argument, as far as it goes, against levying taxes unnecessarily for purposes of unproductive expenditure, but not against paying off a national debt. For, what is meant by the word fructify? If it means anything, it means product-ive employment; and as an argument against taxation, we must understand it to assert, that if the amount were left with the people they would save it, and convert it into capital. It is probable, indeed, that they would save a part, but extremely improbable that they would save the whole: while if taken by taxation, and employed in paying off debt, the whole is saved, and made productive. To the fund-holder who receives the payment it is already capital, not revenue, and he will make it 'fructify', that it may continue to afford him an income. The objection, therefore, is not only groundless, but the real argument is on the other side: the amount is much more certain of fructifying if it is not 'left in the pockets of the people'.

It is not, however, advisable in all cases to maintain a surplus revenue for the extinction of debt. The advantage of paying off the national debt of Great Britain, for instance, is that it would enable us to get rid of the worse half of our taxation. But of this worse half some portions must be worse than others, and to get rid of those would be a greater benefit proportionally than to get rid of the rest. If renoun-cing a surplus revenue would enable us to dispense with a tax, we ought to consider the very worst of all our taxes as precisely the one which we are keeping up for the sake of ultimately abolishing taxes not so bad as itself. In a country advancing in wealth, whose increasing revenue gives it the power of ridding itself from time to time of the most inconvenient portions of its taxation, I conceive that the increase of revenue should rather be disposed of by taking off taxes, than by liquidating debt, as long as any very objectionable imposts remain. In the present state of England, therefore, I hold it to be good policy in the government, when it has a surplus of an apparently permanent character, to take off taxes, provided these are rightly selected. Even when no taxes remain but such as are not unfit to form part of a permanent system, it is wise to continue the same policy by experimental reductions of those taxes, until the point is discovered at which a given amount of revenue can be raised with the smallest pressure on the contributors. After this, such surplus revenue as might arise from any further increase of the produce of the taxes, should not, I conceive, be remitted, but applied to the redemption of debt. Eventually, it might be expedient to appropriate the entire produce of particular taxes to this purpose; since there would be more assurance that the liquidation would be persisted in, if the fund destined to it were kept apart, and not blended with the general revenues of the state. The succession duties would be peculiarly suited to such a purpose, since taxes paid as they are, out of capital, would be better employed in reimbursing capital than in defraying current expenditure. If this separate appropriation were made, any surplus afterwards arising from the increasing produce of the other taxes, and from the saving of interest on the successive portions of debt paid off, might form a ground for a remission of taxation.

It has been contended that some amount of national debt is desirable, and almost indispensable, as an investment for the savings of the poorer or more inexperienced part of the community. Its convenience in that respect is undeniable; but (besides that the progress of industry is gradually affording other modes of investment almost as safe and untroublesome, such as the shares or obligations of great public companies) the only real superiority of an investment in the funds consists in the national guarantee, and this could be afforded by other means than that of a public debt, involving compulsory taxation. One mode which would answer the purpose, would be a national bank of deposit and discount, with ramifications throughout the country; which might receive any money confided to it, and either fund it at a fixed rate of interest, or allow interest on a floating balance, like the joint stock banks; the interest given being of course lower than the rate at which individuals can borrow, in proportion to the greater security of a government investment; and the expenses of the establishment being defrayed by the difference between the interest which the bank would pay, and that which it would obtain, by lending its deposits on mercantile, landed, or other security. There are no insuperable objections in principle, nor, I should think, in practice, to an institution of this sort, as a means of supplying the same convenient mode of investment now afforded by the public funds. It would constitute the state a great insurance company, to insure that part of the community who live on the interest of their property, against the risk of losing it by the bankruptcy of those to whom they might otherwise be under the necessity of confiding it.

VIII

OF THE ORDINARY FUNCTIONS
OF GOVERNMENT, CONSIDERED AS TO
THEIR ECONOMICAL EFFECTS

1. Before we discuss the line of demarcation between the things with which government should, and those with which they should not, directly interfere, it is necessary to consider the economical effects, whether of a bad or of a good complexion, arising from the manner in which they acquit themselves of the duties which devolve on them in all societies, and which no one denies to be incumbent on them.

The first of these is the protection of person and property. There is no need to expatiate on the influence exercised over the economical interests of society by the degree of completeness with which this duty of government is performed. Insecurity of person and property, is as much as to say, uncertainty of the connexion between all human exertions or sacrifice, and the attainment of the ends for the sake of which they are undergone. It means, uncertainty whether they who sow shall reap, whether they who produce shall consume, and they who spare to-day shall enjoy to-morrow. It means, not only that labour and frugality are not the road to acquisition, but that violence is. When person and property are to a certain degree insecure, all the possessions of the weak are at the mercy of the strong. No one can keep what he has produced, unless he is more capable of defending it, than others who give no part of their time and exertions to useful industry are of taking it from him. The productive classes, therefore, when the insecurity surpasses a certain point, being unequal to their own protection against the predatory population, are obliged to place themselves individually in a state of dependence on some member of the predatory class, that it may be his interest to shield them from all depredation except his own. In this manner, in the Middle Ages, allodial property generally became feudal, and numbers of the poorer freemen voluntarily made themselves and their posterity serfs of some military lord.

Nevertheless, in attaching to this great requisite, security of person and property, the importance which is justly due to it, we must not forget that even for economical purposes there are other things quite as indispensable, the presence of which will often make up for a very considerable degree of imperfection in the protective arrangements of government. As was observed in a previous chapter,[1] the free cities of Italy, Flanders, and the Hanseatic league, were habitually in a state of such internal turbulence, varied by such destructive external wars, that person and property enjoyed very imperfect protection; yet during several centuries they increased rapidly in wealth and prosperity, brought many of the industrial arts to a high degree of advancement, carried on distant and dangerous voyages of exploration and commerce with extraordinary success, became an over-match in power for the greatest feudal lords, and could defend themselves even against the sovereigns of Europe: because in the midst of turmoil and violence, the citizens of those towns enjoyed a certain rude freedom, under conditions of union and co-operation, which, taken together, made them a brave, energetic, and high-spirited people, and fostered a great amount of public spirit and patriotism. The prosperity of these and other free states in a lawless age, shows that a certain degree of insecurity, in some combinations of circumstances, has good as well as bad effects, by making energy and practical ability the conditions of safety. Insecurity paralyzes, only when it is such in nature and in degree, that no energy of which mankind in general are capable, affords any tolerable means of self-protection. And this is a main reason why oppression by the government, whose power is generally irresistible by any efforts that can be made by individuals, has so much more baneful an effect on the springs of national prosperity, than almost any degree of lawlessness and turbulence under free institutions.

[1] [Bk. I, Ch. VII. 6. Not included in present edn.]

Nations have acquired some wealth, and made some progress in improvement, in states of social union so imperfect as to border on anarchy: but no countries in which the people were exposed without limit to arbitrary exactions from the officers of government, ever yet continued to have industry or wealth. A few generations of such a government never fail to extinguish both. Some of the fairest, and once the most prosperous, regions of the earth, have, under the Roman and afterwards under the Turkish dominion, been reduced to a desert, solely by that cause. I say solely, because they would have recovered with the utmost rapidity, as countries always do, from the devastations of war, or any other temporary calamities. Difficulties and hardships are often but an incentive to exertion: what is fatal to it, is the belief that it will not be suffered to produce its fruits.

2. Simple over-taxation by government, though a great evil, is not comparable in the economical part of its mischiefs to exactions much more moderate in amount, which either subject the contributor to the arbitrary mandate of government officers, or are so laid on as to place skill, industry, and frugality at a disadvantage. The burthen of taxation in our own country is very great, yet as every one knows its limit, and is seldom made to pay more than he expects and calculates on, and as the modes of taxation are not of such a kind as much to impair the motives to industry and economy, the sources of prosperity are little diminished by the pressure of taxation; they may even, as some think, be increased, by the extra exertions made to compensate for the pressure of the taxes. But in the barbarous despotisms of many countries of the East, where taxation consists in fastening upon those who have succeeded in acquiring something, in order to confiscate it, unless the possessor buys its release by submitting to give some large sum as a compromise, we cannot expect to find voluntary industry, or wealth derived from any source but plunder. And even in comparatively civilized countries, bad modes of raising a revenue have had effects similar in kind, though in an inferior degree. French writers before the Revolution

represented the *taille** a main cause of the backward state of agriculture, and of the wretched condition of the rural population; not from its amount, but because, being proportioned to the visible capital of the cultivator, it gave him a motive for appearing poor, which sufficed to turn the scale in favour of indolence. The arbitrary powers also of fiscal officers, of *intendants* and *subdélégués*,* were more destructive of prosperity than a far larger amount of exactions, because they destroyed security: there was a marked superiority in the condition of the *pays d'états** which were exempt from this scourge. The universal venality ascribed to Russian functionaries, must be an immense drag on the capabilities of economical improvement possessed so abundantly by the Russian empire: since the emoluments of public officers must depend on the success with which they can multiply vexations, for the purpose of being bought off by bribes.

Yet mere excess of taxation, even when not aggravated by uncertainty, is, independently of its injustice, a serious economical evil. It may be carried so far as to discourage industry by insufficiency of reward. Very long before it reaches this point, it prevents or greatly checks accumulation, or causes the capital accumulated to be sent for investment to foreign countries. Taxes which fall on profits, even though that kind of income may not pay more than its just share, necessarily diminish the motive to any saving, except for investment in foreign countries where profits are higher. Holland, for example, seems to have long ago reached the practical minimum of profits: already in the last century her wealthy capitalists had a great part of their fortunes invested in the loans and joint-stock speculations of other countries: and this low rate of profit is ascribed to the heavy taxation, which had been in some measure forced on her by the circumstances of her position and history. The taxes indeed, besides their great amount, were many of them on necessaries, a kind of tax peculiarly injurious to industry and accumulation. But when the aggregate amount of taxation is very great, it is inevitable that recourse must be had for part of it to taxes of an objectionable character.

And any taxes on consumption, when heavy, even if not operating on profits, have something of the same effect, by driving persons of moderate means to live abroad, often taking their capital with them. Although I by no means join with those political economists who think no state of national existence desirable in which there is not a rapid increase of wealth, I cannot overlook the many disadvantages to an independent nation from being brought prematurely to a stationary state, while the neighbouring countries continue advancing.

3. The subject of protection to person and property, considered as afforded by government, ramifies widely, into a number of indirect channels. It embraces, for example, the whole subject of the perfection or inefficiency of the means provided for the ascertainment of rights and the redress of injuries. Persons and property cannot be considered secure where the administration of justice is imperfect, either from defect of integrity or capacity in the tribunals, or because the delay, vexation, and expense accompanying their operation impose a heavy tax on those who appeal to them, and make it preferable to submit to any endurable amount of the evils which they are designed to remedy. In England there is no fault to be found with the administration of justice, in point of pecuniary integrity; a result which the progress of social improvement may also be supposed to have brought about in several other nations of Europe. But legal and judicial imperfections of other kinds are abundant; and, in England especially, are a large abatement from the value of the services which the government renders back to the people in return for our enormous taxation. In the first place, the incognoscibility (as Bentham termed it) of the law, and its extreme uncertainty, even to those who best know it, render a resort to the tribunals often necessary for obtaining justice, when, there being no dispute as to facts, no litigation ought to be required. In the next place, the procedure of the tribunals is so replete with delay, vexation, and expense, that the price at which justice is at last obtained is an evil outweighing a very considerable amount

of injustice; and the wrong side, even that which the law considers such, has many chances of gaining its point, through the abandonment of litigation by the other party for want of funds, or through a compromise in which a sacrifice is made of just rights to terminate the suit, or through some technical quirk, whereby a decision is obtained on some other ground than the merits. This last detestable incident often happens without blame to the judge, under a system of law, of which a great part rests on no rational principles adapted to the present state of society, but was originally founded partly on a kind of whims and conceits, and partly on the principles and incidents of feudal tenure, (which now survive only as legal fictions;) and has only been very imperfectly adapted, as cases arose, to the changes which had taken place in society. Of all parts of the English legal system, the Court of Chancery,* which has the best substantive law, has been incomparably the worst as to delay, vexation, and expense; and this is the only tribunal for most of the classes of cases which are in their nature the most complicated, such as cases of partnership, and the great range and variety of cases which come under the denomination of trust. The recent reforms in this Court have abated the mischief, but are still far from having removed it.

Fortunately for the prosperity of England, the greater part of the mercantile law is comparatively modern, and was made by the tribunals, by the simple process of recognizing and giving force of law to the usages which, from motives of convenience, had grown up among merchants themselves: so that this part of the law, at least, was substantially made by those who were most interested in its goodness: while the defects of the tribunals have been the less practically pernicious in reference to commerical transactions, because the importance of credit, which depends on character, renders the restraints of opinion (though, as daily experience proves, an insufficient) yet a very powerful, protection against those forms of mercantile dishonesty which are generally recognized as such.

The imperfections of the law, both in its substance and in its procedure, fall heaviest upon the interests connected with what is technically called *real* property; in the general language of European jurisprudence, immoveable property. With respect to all this portion of the wealth of the community, the law fails egregiously in the protection which it undertakes to provide. It fails, first, by the uncertainty, and the maze of technicalities, which make it impossible for any one, at however great an expense, to possess a title to land which he can positively know to be unassailable. It fails, secondly, in omitting to provide due evidence of transactions, by a proper registration of legal documents. It fails, thirdly, by creating a necessity for operose and expensive instruments and formalities (independently of fiscal burthens) on occasion of the purchase and sale, or even the lease or mortgage, of immoveable property. And, fourthly, it fails by the intolerable expense and delay of law proceedings, in almost all cases in which real property is concerned. There is no doubt that the greatest sufferers by the defects of the higher courts of civil law are the landowners. Legal expenses, either those of actual litigation, or of the preparation of legal instruments, form, I apprehend, no inconsiderable item in the annual expenditure of most persons of large landed property, and the saleable value of their land is greatly impaired, by the difficulty of giving to the buyer complete confidence in the title; independently of the legal expenses which accompany the transfer. Yet the landowners, though they have been masters of the legislation of England, to say the least since 1688, have never made a single move in the direction of law reform, and have been strenuous opponents of some of the improvements of which they would more particularly reap the benefit; especially that great one of a registration of contracts affecting land, which when proposed by a Commission of eminent real property lawyers, and introduced into the House of Commons by Lord Campbell, was so offensive to the general body of landlords, and was rejected by so large a majority, as to have long discouraged any repetition of the attempt.[1] This

---

[1] Lord Westbury's recent Act is a material mitigation of this grievous defect in English law, and will probably lead to further improvements.

irrational hostility to improvement, in a case in which their own interest would be the most benefited by it, must be ascribed to an intense timidity on the subject of their titles, generated by the defects of the very law which they refuse to alter; and to a conscious ignorance, and incapacity of judgment, on all legal subjects, which makes them helplessly defer to the opinion of their professional advisers, heedless of the fact that every imperfection of the law, in proportion as it is burthensome to them, brings gain to the lawyer.

In so far as the defects of legal arrangements are a mere burthen on the landowner, they do not much affect the sources of production; but the uncertainty of the title under which land is held, must often act as a great discouragement to the expenditure of capital in its improvement; and the expense of making transfers, operates to prevent land from coming into the hands of those who would use it to most advantage; often amounting, in the case of small purchases, to more than the price of the land, and tantamount, therefore, to a prohibition of the purchase and sale of land in small portions, unless in exceptional circumstances. Such purchases, however, are almost everywhere extremely desirable, there being hardly any country in which landed property is not either too much or too little subdivided, requiring either that great estates should be broken down, or that small ones should be bought up and consolidated. To make land as easily transferable as stock, would be one of the greatest economical improvements which could be bestowed on a country; and has been shown, again and again, to have no insuperable difficulty attending it.

Besides the excellences or defects that belong to the law and judicature of a country as a system of arrangements for attaining direct practical ends, much also depends, even in an economical point of view, upon the moral influence of the law. Enough has been said in a former place,[1] on the degree in which both the industrial and all other combined operations of mankind depend for efficiency on their being able to rely on one another for probity and fidelity to

---

[1] [Bk. I, Ch. VII. 5. Not included in present edn.]

engagements; from which we see how greatly even the economical prosperity of a country is liable to be affected, by anything in its institutions by which either integrity and trustworthiness, or the contrary qualities, are encouraged. The law everywhere ostensibly favours at least pecuniary honesty and the faith of contracts; but if it affords facilities for evading those obligations, by trick and chicanery, or by the unscrupulous use of riches in instituting unjust or resisting just litigation; if there are ways and means by which persons may attain the ends of roguery, under the apparent sanction of the law; to that extent the law is demoralizing, even in regard to pecuniary integrity. And such cases are, unfortunately, frequent under the English system. If, again, the law, by a misplaced indulgence, protects idleness or prodigality against their natural consequences, or dismisses crime with inadequate penalties, the effect, both on the prudential and on the social virtues, is unfavourable. When the law, by its own dispensations and injunctions, establishes injustice between individual and individual; as all laws do which recognise any form of slavery, as the laws of all countries do, though not all in the same degree, in respect to the family relations; and as the laws of many countries do, though in still more unequal degrees, as between rich and poor; the effect on the moral sentiments of the people is still more disastrous. But these subjects introduce considerations so much larger and deeper than those of political economy, that I only advert to them in order not to pass wholly unnoticed, things superior in importance to those of which I treat.

IX

THE SAME SUBJECT CONTINUED

1. Having spoken thus far of the effects produced by the excellences or defects of the general system of the law, I shall now touch upon those resulting from the special character of particular parts of it. As a selection must be made, I shall confine myself to a few leading topics. The portions of the civil law of a country which are of most importance economically (next to those which determine the status of the labourer, as slave, serf, or free), are those relating to the two subjects of Inheritance and Contract. Of the laws relating to contract, none are more important economically, than the laws of partnership, and those of insolvency. It happens that on all these three points, there is just ground for condemning some of the provisions of the English law.

With regard to Inheritance, I have, in an early chapter, considered the general principles of the subject, and suggested what appear to me to be, putting all prejudice apart, the best dispositions which the law could adopt. Freedom of bequest as the general rule, but limited by two things: first, that if there are descendants, who, being unable to provide for themselves, would become burthensome to the state, the equivalent of whatever the state would accord to them should be reserved from the property for their benefit; and secondly, that no one person should be permitted to acquire, by inheritance, more than the amount of a moderate independence. In case of intestacy, the whole property to escheat to the state: which should be bound to make a just and reasonable provision for descendants, that is, such a provision as the parent or ancestor ought to have made, their circumstances, capacities, and mode of bringing up being considered.

The laws of inheritance, however, have probably several phases of improvement to go through, before ideas so far removed from present modes of thinking will be taken into serious consideration: and as, among the recognized modes of determining the succession to property, some must be better and others worse, it is necessary to consider which of them deserves the preference. As an intermediate course, therefore, I would recommend the extension to all property, of the present English law of inheritance affecting personal property (freedom of bequest, and in case of intestacy, equal division): except that no rights should be acknowledged in collaterals, and that the property of those who have neither descendants nor ascendants, and make no will, should escheat to the state.

The laws of existing nations deviate from these maxims in two opposite ways. In England, and in most of the countries where the influence of feudality is still felt in the laws, one of the objects aimed at in respect to land and other immoveable property, is to keep it together in large masses: accordingly, in cases of intestacy, it passes, generally speaking (for the local custom of a few places is different), exclusively to the eldest son. And though the rule of primogeniture is not binding on testators, who in England have nominally the power of bequeathing their property as they please, any proprietor may so exercise this power as to deprive his immediate successor of it, by entailing the property on one particular line of his descendants: which, besides preventing it from passing by inheritance in any other than the prescribed manner, is attended with the incidental consequence of precluding it from being sold; since each successive possessor, having only a life interest in the property, cannot alienate it for a longer period than his own life. In some other countries, such as France, the law, on the contrary, compels division of inheritances; not only, in case of intestacy, sharing the property, both real and personal, equally among all the children, or (if there are no children) among all relatives in the same degree of propinquity; but also not recognising any power of bequest, or recognising it over only a limited portion of the property, the remainder being subjected to compulsory equal division.

Neither of these systems, I apprehend, was introduced, or is perhaps maintained, in the countries where it exists, from any general considerations of justice, or any foresight of economical consequences, but chiefly from political motives; in the one case to keep up large hereditary fortunes, and a landed aristocracy; in the other, to break these down, and prevent their resurrection. The first object, as an aim of national policy, I conceive to be eminently undesirable: with regard to the second, I have pointed out what seems to me a better mode of attaining it. The merit, or demerit, however, of either purpose, belongs to the general science of politics, not to the limited department of that science which is here treated of. Each of the two systems is a real and efficient instrument for the purpose intended by it; but each, as it appears to me, achieves that purpose at the cost of much mischief.

2. There are two arguments of an economical character, which are urged in favour of primogeniture. One is, the stimulus applied to the industry and ambition of younger children, by leaving them to be the architects of their own fortunes. This argument was put by Dr Johnson* a manner more forcible than complimentary to an hereditary aristocracy, when he said, by way of recommendation of primogeniture, that it 'makes but one fool in a family'. It is curious that a defender of aristocratic institutions should be the person to assert that to inherit such a fortune as takes away any necessity for exertion, is generally fatal to activity and strength of mind: in the present state of education, however, the proposition, with some allowance for exaggeration, may be admitted to be true. But whatever force there is in the argument, counts in favour of limiting the eldest, as well as all the other children, to a mere provision, and dispensing with even the 'one fool' whom Dr Johnson was willing to tolerate. If unearned riches are so pernicious to the character, one does not see why, in order to withhold the poison from the junior members of a family, there should be no way but to unite all their separate potions, and administer them in the largest possible dose to one selected victim. It cannot be necessary to inflict this great evil on the eldest son, for want of knowing what else to do with a large fortune.

Some writers, however, look upon the effect of primogeniture in stimulating industry, as depending, not so much on the poverty of the younger children, as on the contrast between that poverty and the riches of the elder; thinking it indispensable to the activity and energy of the hive, that there should be a huge drone here and there, to impress the working bees with a due sense of the advantages of honey. 'Their inferiority in point of wealth', says Mr M'Culloch, speaking of the younger children, 'and their desire to escape from this lower station, and to attain to the same level with their elder brothers, inspires them with an energy and vigour they could not otherwise feel. But the advantage of preserving large estates from being frittered down by a scheme of equal division, is not limited to its influence over the younger children of their owners. It raises universally the standard of competence, and gives new force to the springs which set industry in motion. The manner of living among the great landlords is that in which every one is ambitious of being able to indulge; and their habits of expense, though sometimes injurious to themselves, act as powerful incentives to the ingenuity and enterprise of the other classes, who never think their fortunes sufficiently ample, unless they will enable them to emulate the splendour of the richest landlords; so that the custom of primogeniture seems to render all classes more industrious, and to augment at the same time, the mass of wealth and the scale of enjoyment.'[1]

The portion of truth, I can hardly say contained in these observations, but recalled by them, I apprehend to be, that a state of complete equality of fortunes would not be favourable to active exertion for the increase of wealth. Speaking of the mass, it is as true of wealth as of most other distinctions—of talent, knowledge, virtue—that those who already have, or think they have, as much of it as their neighbours, will seldom exert themselves to acquire more.

[1] *Principles of Political Economy* (1843), 264. There is much more to the same effect in the more recent treatise by the same author, 'On the Succession to Property Vacant by Death.'

But it is not therefore necessary that society should provide a set of persons with large fortunes, to fulfil the social duty of standing to be looked at, with envy and admiration, by the aspiring poor. The fortunes which people have acquired for themselves, answer the purpose quite as well, indeed much better; since a person is more powerfully stimulated by the example of somebody who has earned a fortune, than by the mere sight of somebody who possesses one; and the former is necessarily an example of prudence and frugality as well as industry, while the latter much oftener sets an example of profuse expense, which spreads, with pernicious effect, to the very class on whom the sight of riches is supposed to have so beneficial an influence, namely, those whose weakness of mind, and taste for ostentation, makes 'the splendour of the richest landlords' attract them with the most potent spell. In America there are few or no hereditary fortunes; yet industrial energy, and the ardour of accumulation, are not supposed to be particularly backward in that part of the world. When a country has once fairly entered into the industrial career, which is the principal occupation of the modern, as war was that of the ancient and medieval world, the desire of acquisition by industry needs no factitious stimulus: the advantages naturally inherent in riches, and the character they assume of a test by which talent and success in life are habitually measured, are an ample security for their being pursued with sufficient intensity and zeal. As to the deeper consideration, that the diffusion of wealth, and not its concentration, is desirable, and that the more wholesome state of society is not that in which immense fortunes are possessed by a few and coveted by all, but that in which the greatest possible numbers possess and are contented with a moderate competency, which all may hope to acquire: I refer to it in this place, only to show, how widely separated, on social questions, is the entire mode of thought of the defenders of primogeniture, from that which is partially promulgated in the present treatise.

The other economical argument in favour of primogeniture, has special reference to landed property. It is contended that the habit of dividing inheritances equally, or with an approach to equality, among children, promotes the sub-division of land into portions too small to admit of being cultivated in an advantageous manner. This argument, eternally reproduced, has again and again been refuted by English and Continental writers. It proceeds on a supposition entirely at variance with that on which all the theorems of political economy are grounded. It assumes that mankind in general will habitually act in a manner opposed to their immediate and obvious pecuniary interest. For the division of the inheritance does not necessarily imply division of the land; which may be held in common, as is not unfrequently the case in France and Belgium; or may become the property of one of the coheirs, being charged with the shares of the others by way of mortgage; or they may sell it outright, and divide the proceeds. When the division of the land would diminish its productive power, it is the direct interest of the heirs to adopt some one of these arrangements. Supposing, however, what the argument assumes, that either from legal difficulties or from their own stupidity and barbarism, they would not, if left to themselves, obey the dictates of this obvious interest, but would insist upon cutting up the land bodily into equal parcels, with the effect of impoverishing themselves; this would be an objection to a law such as exists in France, of compulsory divison, but can be no reason why testators should be discouraged from exercising the right of bequest in general conformity to the rule of equality, since it would always be in their power to provide that the division of the inheritance should take place without dividing the land itself. That the attempts of the advocates of primogeniture to make out a case by facts against the custom of equal division, are equally abortive, has been shown in a former place. In all countries, or parts of countries, in which the division of inheritance is accompanied by small holdings, it is because small holdings are the general system of the country, even on the estates of the great proprietors.

Unless a strong case of social utility can be made out for primogeniture, it stands sufficiently condemned by the general principles of justice; being a broad distinction in the treatment of one person and of another, grounded solely on an accident. There is no need, therefore, to make out any case of economical evil *against* primogeniture. Such a case, however, and a very strong one, may be made. It is a natural effect of primogeniture to make the landlords a needy class. The object of the institution, or custom, is to keep the land together in large masses, and this it commonly accomplishes; but the legal proprietor of a large domain is not necessarily the bona fide owner of the whole income which it yields. It is usually charged, in each generation, with provisions for the other children. It is often charged still more heavily by the imprudent expenditure of the proprietor. Great landowners are generally improvident in their expenses; they live up to their incomes when at the highest, and if any change of circumstances diminishes their resources, some time elapses before they make up their minds to retrench. Spendthrifts in other classes are ruined, and disappear from society; but the spendthrift landlord usually holds fast to his land, even when he has become a mere receiver of its rents for the benefit of creditors. The same desire to keep up the 'splendour' of the family, which gives rise to the custom of primogeniture, indisposes the owner to sell a part in order to set free the remainder; their apparent are therefore habitually greater than their real means, and they are under a perpetual temptation to proportion their expenditure to the former rather than to the latter. From such causes as these, in almost all countries of great landowners, the majority of landed estates are deeply mortgaged; and instead of having capital to spare for improvements, it requires all the increased value of land, caused by the rapid increase of the wealth and population of the country, to preserve the class from being impoverished.

3. To avert this impoverishment, recourse was had to the contrivance of entails, whereby the order of succession was irrevocably fixed, and each holder, having only a life interest, was unable to burthen his successor. The land thus passing, free from debt, into the possession of the heir, the family could not be ruined by the improvidence of its

existing representative. The economical evils arising from this disposition of property were partly of the same kind, partly different, but on the whole greater, than those arising from primogeniture. The possessor could not now ruin his successors, but he could still ruin himself: he was not at all more likely than in the former case to have the means necessary for improving the property: while, even if he had, he was still less likely to employ them for that purpose, when the benefit was to accrue to a person whom the entail made independent of him, while he had probably younger children to provide for, in whose favour he could not now charge the estate. While thus disabled from being himself an improver, neither could he sell the estate to somebody who would; since entail precludes alienation. In general he has even been unable to grant leases beyond the term of his own life; 'for,' says Blackstone, 'if such leases had been valid, then, under cover of long leases, the issue might have been virtually disinherited'; and it has been necessary in Great Britain to relax, by statute, the rigour of entails, in order to allow either of long leases, or of the execution of improvements at the expense of the estate. It may be added that the heir of entail, being assured of succeeding to the family property, however underserving of it, and being aware of this from his earliest years, has much more than the ordinary chances of growing up idle, dissipated, and profligate.

In England, the power of entail is more limited by law, than in Scotland and in most other countries where it exists. A landowner can settle his property upon any number of persons successively who are living at the time, and upon one unborn person, on whose attaining the age of twenty-one, the entail expires, and the land becomes his absolute property. An estate may in this manner be transmitted through a son, or a son and grandson, living when the deed is executed, to an unborn child of that grandson. It has been maintained that this power of entail is not sufficiently extensive to do any mischief: in truth, however, it is much larger than it seems. Entails very rarely expire; the first heir of entail, when of age, joins with the existing possessor in resettling the estate, so as to prolong the entail for a further term. Large properties, therefore, are rarely free for any considerable period, from the restraints of a strict settlement; though the mischief is in one respect mitigated, since in the renewal of the settlement for one more generation, the estate is usually charged with a provision for younger children.

In an economical point of view, the best system of landed property is that in which land is most completely an object of commerce; passing readily from hand to hand when a buyer can be found to whom it is worth while to offer a greater sum for the land, than the value of the income drawn from it by its existing possessor. This of course is not meant of ornamental property, which is a source of expense, not profit; but only of land employed for industrial uses, and held for the sake of the income which it affords. Whatever facilitates the sale of land, tends to make it a more productive instrument of the community at large; whatever prevents or restricts its sale, subtracts from its usefulness. Now, not only has entail this effect, but primogeniture also. The desire to keep land together in large masses, from other motives than that of promoting its productiveness, often prevents changes and alienations which would increase its efficiency as an instrument.

4. On the other hand, a law which, like the French, restricts the power of bequest to a narrow compass, and compels the equal division of the whole or the greater part of the property among the children, seems to me, though on different grounds, also very seriously objectionable. The only reason for recognizing in the children any claim at all to more than a provision, sufficient to launch them in life, and enable them to find a livelihood, is grounded on the expressed or presumed wish of the parent; whose claim to dispose of what is actually his own, cannot be set aside by any pretensions of others to receive what is not theirs. To control the rightful owner's liberty of gift, by creating in the children a legal right superior to it, is to postpone a real claim to an imaginary one. To this great and paramount

objection to the law, numerous secondary ones may be added. Desirable as it is that the parent should treat the children with impartiality, and not make an eldest son or a favourite, impartial division is not always synonymous with equal division. Some of the children may, without fault of their own, be less capable than others of providing for themselves: some may, by other means than their own exertions, be already provided for: and impartiality may therefore require that the rule observed should not be one of equality, but of compensation. Even when equality is the object, there are sometimes better means of attaining it, than the inflexible rules by which law must necessarily proceed. If one of the coheirs, being of a quarrelsome or litigious disposition, stands upon his utmost rights, the law cannot make equitable adjustments; it cannot apportion the property as seems best for the collective interest of all concerned; if there are several parcels of land, and the heirs cannot agree about their value, the law cannot give a parcel to each, but every separate parcel must be either put up to sale or divided: if there is a residence, or a park or pleasure-ground, which would be destroyed, as such, by subdivision, it must be sold, perhaps at a great sacrifice both of money and of feeling. But what the law could not do, the parent could. By means of the liberty of bequest, all these points might be determined according to reason and the general interest of the persons concerned; and the spirit of the principle of equal division might be the better observed, because the testator was emancipated from its letter. Finally, it would not then be necessary, as under the compulsory system it is, that the law should interfere authoritatively in the concerns of individuals, not only on the occurrence of a death, but throughout life, in order to guard against the attempts of parents to frustrate the legal claims of their heirs, under colour of gifts and other alienations *inter vivos*.

In conclusion; all owners of property should, I conceive, have power to dispose by will of every part of it, but not to determine the person who should succeed to it after the death of all who were living when the will was made. Under what restrictions it should be allowable to bequeath property to one person for life, with remainder to another person already in existence, is a question belonging to general legislation, not to political economy. Such settlements would be no greater hindrance to alienation than any case of joint ownership, since the consent of persons actually in existence is all that would be necessary for any new arrangement respecting the property.

5. From the subject of Inheritance I now pass to that of Contracts, and among these, to the important subject of the Laws of Partnership. How much of good or evil depends upon these laws, and how important it is that they should be the best possible, is evident to all who recognise in the extension of the co-operative principle in the larger sense of the term, the great economical necessity of modern industry. The progress of the productive arts requiring that many sorts of industrial occupation should be carried on by larger and larger capitals, the productive power of industry must suffer by whatever impedes the formation of large capitals through the aggregation of smaller ones. Capitals of the requisite magnitude belonging to single owners, do not, in most countries, exist in the needful abundance, and would be still less numerous if the laws favoured the diffusion instead of the concentration of property: while it is most undesirable that all those improved processes, and those means of efficiency and economy in production, which depend on the possession of large funds, should be monopolies in the hands of a few rich individuals, through the difficulties experienced by persons of moderate or small means in associating their capital. Finally, I must repeat my conviction, that the industrial economy which divides society absolutely into two portions, the payers of wages and the receivers of them, the first counted by thousands and the last by millions, is neither fit for, nor capable of, indefinite duration: and the possibility of changing this system for one of combination without dependence, and unity of interest instead of organized hostility, depends altogether upon the future developments of the Partnership principle.

Yet there is scarcely any country whose laws do not throw great, and in most cases, intentional obstacles in the way of the formation of any numerous partnership. In England it is already a serious discouragement, that differences among partners are, practically speaking, only capable of adjudication by the Court of Chancery: which is often worse than placing such questions out of the pale of all law; since any one of the disputant parties, who is either dishonest or litigious, can involve the others at his pleasure in the expense, trouble, and anxiety, which are the unavoidable accompaniments of a Chancery suit, without their having the power of freeing themselves from the infliction even by breaking up the association.[1] Besides this, it required, until lately, a separate Act of the legislature before any joint-stock association could legally constitute itself, and be empowered to act as one body. By a statute passed a few years ago, this necessity is done away; but the statute in question is described by competent authorities as a 'mass of confusion', of which they say that there 'never was such an infliction' on persons entering into partnership.[2] When a number of persons, whether few or many, freely desire to unite their funds for a common undertaking, not asking any peculiar privilege, nor the power to dispossess any one

---

[1] Mr Cecil Fane, the Commissioner of the Bankruptcy Court, in his evidence before the Committee on the Law of Partnership, says: 'I remember a short time ago reading a written statement by two eminent solicitors, who said that they had known many partnership accounts go into Chancery, but that they never knew one come out. . . . Very few of the persons who would be disposed to engage in partnerships of this kind' (co-operative associations of working men) 'have any idea of the truth, namely, that the decision of questions arising amongst partners is really impracticable.

'Do they not know that one partner may rob the other without any possibility of his obtaining redress?—The fact is so; but whether they know it or not, I cannot undertake to say.'

This flagrant injustice is, in Mr Fane's opinion, wholly attributable to the defects of the tribunal. 'My opinion is, that if there is one thing more easy than another, it is the settlement of partnership questions, and for the simple reason, that everything which is done in a partnership is entered in the books; the evidence therefore is at hand; if therefore a rational mode of proceeding were once adopted, the difficulty would altogether vanish.'—Minutes of Evidence annexed to the Report of the Select Committee on the Law of Partnership (1851), 85₂-7.

[2] Report, *ut supra*, p. 167.

of property, the law can have no good reason for throwing difficulties in the way of the realization of the project. On compliance with a few simple conditions of publicity, any body of persons ought to have the power of constituting themselves into a joint-stock company, or *société en nom collectif*,* without asking leave either of any public officer or of parliament. As an association of many partners must practically be under the management of a few, every facility ought to be afforded to the body for exercising the necessary control and check over those few, whether they be themselves members of the association, or merely its hired servants: and in this point the English system is still at a lamentable distance from the standard of perfection.

6. Whatever facilities, however, English law might give to associations formed on the principles of ordinary partnership, there is one sort of joint-stock association which until the year 1855 it absolutely disallowed, and which could only be called into existence by a special act either of the legislature or of the crown. I mean, associations with limited liability.

Associations with limited liability are of two kinds: in one, the liability of all the partners is limited, in the other that of some of them only. The first is the *société anonyme*,* of the French law, which in England had until lately no other name than that of 'chartered company': meaning thereby a joint-stock company whose shareholders, by a charter from the crown or a special enactment of the legislature, stood exempted from any liability for the debts of the concern, beyond the amount of their subscriptions. The other species of limited partnership is that known to the French law under the name of *commandite*,* of this, which in England is still unrecognized and illegal, I shall speak presently.

If a number of persons choose to associate for carrying on any operation of commerce or industry, agreeing among themselves and announcing to those with whom they deal that the members of the association do not undertake to be responsible beyond the amount of the subscribed capital; is there any reason that the law should raise objections to this proceeding, and should impose on them the unlimited responsibility which they disclaim? For whose sake? Not for that of the partners themselves; for it is they whom the limitation of responsibility benefits and protects. It must therefore be for the sake of third parties; namely, those who may have transactions with the association, and to whom it may run in debt beyond what the subscribed capital suffices to pay. But nobody is obliged to deal with the association: still less is any one obliged to give it unlimited credit. The class of persons with whom such associations have dealings are in general perfectly capable of taking care of themselves, and there seems no reason that the law should be more careful of their interests than they will themselves be; provided no false representation is held out, and they are aware from the first what they have to trust to. The law is warranted in requiring from all joint-stock associations with limited responsibilities, not only that the amount of capital on which they profess to carry on business should either be actually paid up or security given for it (if, indeed, with complete publicity, such a requirement would be necessary), but also that such accounts should be kept, accessible to individuals, and if needful, published to the world, as shall render it possible to ascertain at any time the existing state of the company's affairs, and to learn whether the capital which is the sole security for the engagements into which they enter, still subsists unimpaired: the fidelity of such accounts being guarded by sufficient penalties. When the law has thus afforded to individuals all practicable means of knowing the circumstances which ought to enter into their prudential calculations in dealing with the company, there seems no more need for interfering with individual judgment in this sort of transactions, than in any other part of the private business of life.

The reason usually urged for such interference is, that the managers of an association with limited responsibility, not risking their whole fortunes in the event of loss, while in case of gain they might profit largely, are not sufficiently interested in exercising due circumspection, and are under the temptation of exposing the funds of the association to improper hazards. It is, however, well ascertained that associations with unlimited responsibility, if they have rich shareholders, can obtain, even when known to be reckless in their transactions, improper credit to an extent far exceeding what would be given to companies equally ill-conducted whose creditors had only the subscribed capital to rely on.[1] To whichever side the balance of evil inclines, it is a consideration of more importance to the share-holders themselves than to third parties; since, with proper securities for publicity, the capital of an association with limited liability could not be engaged in hazards beyond those ordinarily incident to the business it carries on, without the facts being known, and becoming the subject of comments by which the credit of the body would be likely to be affected in quite as great a degree as the circumstances would justify. If, under securities for publicity, it were found in practice that companies, formed on the principle of unlimited responsibility, were more skilfully and more cautiously managed, companies with limited liability would be unable to maintain an equal competition with them; and would therefore rarely be formed, unless when such limitation was the only condition on which the necessary amount of capital could be raised: and in that case it would be very unreasonable to say that their formation ought to be prevented.

It may further be remarked, that although, with equality of capital, a company of limited liability offers a somewhat less security to those who deal with it, than one in which every shareholder is responsible with his whole fortune, yet even the weaker of these two securities is in some respects stronger than that which an individual capitalist can afford. In the case of an individual, there is such security as can be founded on his unlimited liability, but not that derived from publicity of transactions, or from a known and large amount of paid-up capital. This topic is well treated in an able paper

[1] See the Report already referred to, pp. 145–58.

by M. Coquelin, published in the Revue des Deux Mondes for July 1843.[1]

'While third parties who trade with individuals', says this writer, 'scarcely ever know, except by approximation, and even that most vague and uncertain, what is the amount of capital responsible for the performance of contracts made with them, those who trade with a *société anonyme* can obtain full information if they seek it, and perform their operations with a feeling of confidence that cannot exist in the other case. Again, nothing is easier than for an individual trader to conceal the extent of his engagements, as no one can know it certainly but himself. Even his confidential clerk may be ignorant of it, as the loans he finds himself compelled to make may not all be of a character to require that they be entered in his day-book. It is a secret confined to himself; one which transpires rarely, and always slowly; one which is unveiled only when the catastrophe has occurred. On the contrary, the *société anonyme* neither can nor ought to borrow, without the fact becoming known to all the world—directors, clerks, shareholders, and the public. Its operations partake in some respects, of the nature of those of governments. The light of day penetrates in every direction, and there can be no secrets from those who seek for information. Thus all is fixed, recorded, known, of the capital and debts in the case of the *société anonyme*, while all is uncertain and unknown in the case of the individual trader. Which of the two, we would ask the reader, presents the most favourable aspect, or the surest guarantee, to the view of those who trade with them?

'Again, availing himself of the obscurity in which his affairs are shrouded, and which he desires to increase, the private trader is enabled, so long as his business appears prosperous, to produce impressions in regard to his means far exceeding the reality, and thus to establish a credit not justified by those means. When losses occur, and he sees himself threatened with bankruptcy, the world is still ignor-

---

[1] The quotation is from a translation published by Mr H. C. Carey, in an American periodical, *Hunt's Merchant's Magazine*, for May and June 1845.

ant of his condition, and he finds himself enabled to contract debts far beyond the possibility of payment. The fatal day arrives, and the creditors find a debt much greater than had been anticipated, while the means of payment are as much less. Even this is not all. The same obscurity which has served him so well thus far, when desiring to magnify his capital and increase his credit, now affords him the opportunity of placing a part of that capital beyond the reach of his creditors. It becomes diminished, if not annihilated. It hides itself, and not even legal remedies, nor the activity of creditors, can bring it forth from the dark corners in which it is placed. . . . Our readers can readily determine for themselves if practices of this kind are equally easy in the case of the *société anonyme*. We do not doubt that such things are possible, but we think that they will agree with us that from its nature, its organization, and the necessary publicity that attends all its actions, the liability to such occurrences is very greatly diminished.'

The laws of most countries, England included, have erred in a twofold manner with regard to joint-stock companies. While they have been most unreasonably jealous of allowing such associations to exist, especially with limited responsibility, they have generally neglected the enforcement of publicity; the best security to the public against any danger which might arise from this description of partnerships; and a security quite as much required in the case of those associations of the kind in question, which, by an exception from their general practice, they suffered to exist. Even in the instance of the Bank of England, which holds a monopoly from the legislature, and has had partial control over a matter of so much public interest as the state of the circulating medium, it is only within these few years that any publicity has been enforced; and the publicity was at first of an extremely incomplete character, though now, for most practical purposes, probably at length sufficient.

7. The other kind of limited partnership which demands our attention, is that in which the managing partner or partners are responsible with their whole fortunes for the

engagements of the concern, but have others associated with them who contribute only definite sums, and are not liable for anything beyond, though they participate in the profits according to any rule which may be agreed on. This is called partnership *en commandite*: and the partners with limited liability (to whom, by the French law, all interference in the management of the concern is interdicted) are known by the name *commanditaires*. Such partnerships are not allowed by English law: in all private partnerships, whoever shares in the profits is liable for the debts, to as plenary an extent as the managing partner.

For such prohibition no satisfactory defence has ever, so far as I am aware, been made. Even the insufficient reason given against limiting the responsibility of shareholders in a joint-stock company, does not apply here; there being no diminution of the motives to circumspect management, since all who take any part in the direction of the concern are liable with their whole fortunes. To third parties, again, the security is improved by the existence of commandite; since the amount subscribed by commanditaires is all of it available to creditors, the commanditaires losing their whole investment before any creditor can lose anything; while, if instead of becoming partners to that amount, they had lent the sum at an interest equal to the profit they derived from it, they would have shared with the other creditors in the residue of the estate, diminishing pro rata the dividend obtained by all. While the practice of commandite thus conduces to the interest of creditors, it is often highly desirable for the contracting parties themselves. The managers are enabled to obtain the aid of a much greater amount of capital than they could borrow on their own security; and persons are induced to aid useful undertakings, by embarking limited portions of capital in them, when they would not, and often could not prudently, have risked their whole fortunes on the chances of the enterprise.

It may perhaps be thought that where due facilities are afforded to joint-stock companies, commandite partnerships are not required. But there are classes of cases to which the commandite principle must always be better adapted than the joint-stock principle. 'Suppose', says M. Coquelin, 'an inventor seeking for a capital to carry his invention into practice. To obtain the aid of capitalists, he must offer them a share of the anticipated benefit; they must associate themselves with him in the chances of its success. In such a case, which of the forms would he select? Not a common partnership, certainly'; for various reasons, and especially the extreme difficulty of finding a partner with capital, willing to risk his whole fortune on the success of the invention.[1] 'Neither would he select the *société anonyme*', or any other form of joint-stock company, 'in which he might be superseded as manager. He would stand, in such an association, on no better footing than any other shareholder, and he might be lost in the crowd; whereas, the association existing, as it were, by and for him, the management would appear to belong to him as a matter of right. Cases occur in which a merchant or a manufacturer, without being precisely an inventor, has undeniable claims to the management of an undertaking, from the possession of qualities peculiarly calculated to promote its success. So great, indeed', continues M. Coquelin, 'is the necessity, in

---

[1] 'There has been a great deal of commiseration professed', says Mr Duncan, solicitor, 'towards the poor inventor; he has been oppressed by the high cost of patents; but his chief oppression has been the partnership law, which prevents his getting any one to help him to develop his invention. He is a poor man, and therefore cannot give security to a creditor; no one will lend him money; the rate of interest offered, however high it may be, is not an attraction. But if by the alteration of the law he could allow capitalists to take an interest with him and share the profits, while the risk should be confined to the capital they embarked, there is very little doubt at all that he would frequently get assistance from capitalists; whereas at the present moment, with the law as it stands, he is completely destroyed, and his invention is useless to him; he struggles month after month; he applies again and again to the capitalist without avail. I know it practically in two or three cases of patented inventions; especially one where parties with capital were desirous of entering into an undertaking of great moment in Liverpool, but five or six different gentlemen were deterred from doing so, all feeling the strongest objection to what each one called the cursed partnership law.' Report, p. 155.
Mr Fane says, 'In the course of my professional life, as a Commissioner of the Court of Bankruptcy, I have learned that the most unfortunate man in the world is an inventor. The difficulty which an inventor finds in getting at capital involves him in all sorts of embarrassments, and he ultimately is for the most part a ruined man, and somebody else gets possession of his invention.' Ibid. 82.

many cases, for the limited partnership, that it is difficult to conceive how we could dispense with or replace it': and in reference to his own country he is probably in the right.

Where there is so great a readiness as in England, on the part of the public, to form joint-stock associations, even without the encouragement of a limitation of responsibility; commandite partnership, though its prohibition is in principle quite indefensible, cannot be deemed to be, in a merely economical point of view, of the imperative necessity which M. Coquelin ascribes to it. Yet the inconveniences are not small, which arise indirectly from those provisions of the law by which every one who shares in the profits of a concern is subject to the full liabilities of an unlimited partnership. It is impossible to say how many or what useful modes of combination are rendered impracticable by this state of the law. It is sufficient for its condemnation that, unless in some way relaxed, it is inconsistent with the payment of wages in part by a percentage on profits; in other words, the association of the operatives as virtual partners with the capitalist.[1]

It is, above all, with reference to the improvement and elevation of the working classes that complete freedom in the conditions of partnership is indispensable. Combinations such as the associations of workpeople, described in a former chapter, are the most powerful means of effecting the social emancipation of the labourers through their own moral qualities. Nor is the liberty of association important solely for its examples of success, but fully as much so for the sake of attempts which would not succeed; but by their failure would give instruction more impressive than can be afforded by anything short of actual experience. Every theory of social improvement, the worth of which is capable of being brought to an experimental test, should be permitted, and even encouraged, to submit itself to that test. From such experiments the active portion of the working classes would derive lessons, which they would be slow to

[1] It is considered possible to effect this through the Limited Liability Act, by erecting the capitalist and his workpeople into a Limited Company; as proposed by Messrs. Briggs [*supra*, Bk. IV, Ch. VII. 5].

learn from the teaching of persons supposed to have interests and prejudices adverse to their good; would obtain the means of correcting, at no cost to society, whatever is now erroneous in their notions of the means of establishing their independence; and of discovering the conditions, moral, intellectual, and industrial, which are indispensably necessary for effecting without injustice, or for effecting at all, the social regeneration they aspire to.[1]

The French law of partnership is superior to the English in permitting commandite; and superior, in having no such unmanageable instrument as the Court of Chancery, all cases arising from commercial transactions being adjudicated in a comparatively cheap and expeditious manner by a tribunal of merchants. In other respects the French system is far worse than the English. A joint-stock company with limited responsibility cannot be formed without the express authorization of the department of government called the *Conseil d'État*, a body of administrators, generally entire strangers to industrial transactions, who have no interest in promoting enterprises, and are apt to think that the purpose of their institution is to restrain them; whose consent cannot in any case be obtained without an amount of time and labour which is a very serious hindrance to the commencement of an enterprise, while the extreme uncertainty of obtaining that consent at all is a great discouragement to capitalists who would be willing to subscribe. In regard to joint-stock companies without limitation of responsibility, which in England exist in such numbers and are formed with such facility, these associations cannot, in France, exist at all; for, in cases of unlimited partnership, the French law does not permit the division of the capital into transferable shares.

---

[1] By an Act of the year 1852, called the Industrial and Provident Societies Act, for which the nation is indebted to the public-spirited exertions of Mr Slaney, industrial associations of working people are admitted to the statutory privileges of Friendly Societies. This not only exempts them from the formalities applicable to joint-stock companies, but provides for the settlement of disputes among the partners without recourse to the Court of Chancery. There are still some defects in the provisions of this Act, which hamper the proceedings of the Societies in several respects; as is pointed out in the Almanack of the Rochdale Equitable Pioneers for 1861.

The best existing laws of partnership appear to be those of the New England States. According to Mr Carey,[1]* 'nowhere is association so little trammelled by regulations as in New England; the consequence of which is, that it is carried to a greater extent there, and particularly in Massachusetts and Rhode Island, than in any other part of the world. In these states, the soil is covered with *compagnies anonymes*—chartered companies—for almost every conceivable purpose. Every town is a corporation for the management of its roads, bridges, and schools: which are, therefore, under the direct control of those who pay for them, and are consequently well managed. Academies and churches, lyceums and libraries, saving-fund societies, and trust companies, exist in numbers proportioned to the wants of the people, and all are corporations. Every district has its local bank, of a size to suit its wants, the stock of which is owned by the small capitalists of the neighbourhood, and managed by themselves; the consequence of which is, that in no part of the world is the system of banking so perfect—so little liable to vibration in the amount of loans—the necessary effect of which is, that in none is the value of property so little affected by changes in the amount or value of the currency resulting from the movements of *their own* banking institutions. In the two states to which we have particularly referred, they are almost two hundred in number. Massachusetts, alone, offers to our view fifty-three insurance offices, of various forms, scattered through the state, and all incorporated. Factories are incorporated, and are owned in shares; and every one that has any part in the management of their concerns, from the purchase of the raw material to the sale of the manufactured article, is a part owner; while every one employed in them has a prospect of becoming one, by the use of prudence, exertion, and economy. Charitable associations exist in large numbers, and all are incorporated. Fishing vessels are owned in shares by those who navigate them; and the sailors of a whaling ship depend in a great degree, if not altogether, upon the success of the

---

[1] In a note appended to his translation of M. Coquelin's paper.

voyage for their compensation. Every master of a vessel trading in the Southern Ocean is a part owner, and the interest he possesses is a strong inducement to exertion and economy, by aid of which the people of New England are rapidly driving out the competition of other nations for the trade of that part of the world. Wherever settled, they exhibit the same tendency to combination of action. In New York they are the chief owners of the lines of packet ships, which are divided into shares, owned by the shipbuilders, the merchants, the master, and the mates; which last generally acquire the means of becoming themselves masters, and to this is due their great success. The system is the most perfectly democratic of any in the world. It affords to every labourer, every sailor, every operative, male or female, the prospect of advancement; and its results are precisely such as we should have reason to expect. In no part of the world are talent, industry, and prudence, so certain to be largely rewarded.'

The cases of insolvency and fraud on the part of chartered companies in America, which have caused so much loss and so much scandal in Europe, did not occur in the part of the Union to which this extract refers, but in other States, in which the right of association is much more fettered by legal restrictions, and in which, accordingly, joint-stock associations are not comparable in number or variety to those of New England. Mr Carey adds, 'A careful examination of the systems of the several states, can scarcely, we think, fail to convince the reader of the advantage resulting from permitting men to determine among themselves the terms upon which they will associate, and allowing the associations that may be formed to contract with the public as to the terms upon which they will trade together, whether of the limited or unlimited liability of the partners.' This principle has been adopted as the foundation of all recent English legislation on the subject.

8. I proceed to the subject of Insolvency Laws.

Good laws on this subject are important, first and principally, on the score of public morals; which are on no point more under the influence of the law, for good and evil, than in a matter belonging so pre-eminently to the province of law as the preservation of pecuniary integrity. But the subject is also, in a merely economical point of view, of great importance. First, because the economical well-being of a people, and of mankind, depends in an especial manner upon their being able to trust each other's engagements. Secondly, because one of the risks, or expenses, of industrial operations is the risk or expense of what are commonly called bad debts, and every saving which can be effected in this liability is a diminution of cost of production; by dispensing with an item of outlay which in no way conduces to the desired end, and which must be paid for either by the consumer of the commodity, or from the general profits of capital, according as the burthen is peculiar or general.

The laws and practice of nations on this subject have almost always been in extremes. The ancient laws of most countries were all severity to the debtor. They invested the creditor with a power of coercion, more or less tyrannical, which he might use against his insolvent debtor, either to extort the surrender of hidden property, or to obtain satisfaction of a vindictive character, which might console him for the non-payment of the debt. This arbitrary power has extended, in some countries, to making the insolvent debtor serve the creditor as his slave: in which plan there were at least some grains of common sense, since it might possibly be regarded as a scheme for making him work out the debt by his labour. In England the coercion assumed the milder form of ordinary imprisonment. The one and the other were the barbarous expedients of a rude age, repugnant to justice, as well as to humanity. Unfortunately the reform of them, like that of the criminal law generally, has been taken in hand as an affair of humanity only, not of justice: and the modish humanity of the present time, which is essentially a thing of one idea, has in this as in other cases, gone into a violent reaction against the ancient severity, and might almost be supposed to see in the fact of having lost or squandered other people's property, a peculiar title to indulgence. Everything in the law which attached disagreeable consequences to that fact, was gradually relaxed, or entirely got rid of: until the demoralizing effects of this laxity became so evident as to determine, by more recent legislation, a salutary though very insufficient movement in the reverse direction.

The indulgence of the laws to those who have made themselves unable to pay their just debts, is usually defended, on the plea that the sole object of the law should be, in case of insolvency, not to coerce the person of the debtor, but to get at his property, and distribute it fairly among the creditors. Assuming that this is and ought to be the sole object, the mitigation of the law was in the first instance carried so far as to sacrifice that object. Imprisonment at the discretion of a creditor was really a powerful engine for extracting from the debtor any property which he had concealed or otherwise made away with; and it remains to be shown by experience whether, in depriving creditors of this instrument, the law, even as last amended, has furnished them with a sufficient equivalent. But the doctrine, that the law has done all that ought to be expected from it, when it has put the creditors in possession of the property of an insolvent, is in itself a totally inadmissible piece of spurious humanity. It is the business of law to prevent wrong-doing, and not simply to patch up the consequences of it when it has been committed. The law is bound to take care that insolvency shall not be a good pecuniary speculation; that men shall not have the privilege of hazarding other people's property without their knowledge or consent, taking the profits of the enterprise if it is successful, and if it fails throwing the loss upon the rightful owners; and that they shall not find it answer to make themselves unable to pay their just debts, by spending the money of their creditors in personal indulgence. It is admitted that what is technically called fraudulent bankruptcy, the false pretence of inability to pay, is, when detected, properly subject to punishment. But does it follow that insolvency is not the consequence of misconduct because the inability to pay may be real? If a man has been a spendthrift, or a gambler, with property on which his creditors had a prior claim, shall he pass scot-free because the mischief is consummated and the money gone? Is there any very material difference in point of morality between this conduct, and those other kinds of dishonesty which go by the names of fraud and embezzlement?

Such cases are not a minority, but a large majority among insolvencies. The statistics of bankruptcy prove the fact. 'By far the greater part of all insolvencies arise from notorious misconduct; the proceedings of the Insolvent Debtors Court and of the Bankruptcy Court will prove it. Excessive and unjustifiable overtrading, or most absurd speculation in commodities, merely because the poor speculator "thought they would get up", but why he thought so he cannot tell; speculation in hops, in tea, in silk, in corn—things with which he is altogether unacquainted; wild and absurd investments in foreign funds, or in joint-stocks; these are among the most innocent causes of bankruptcy.'[1] The experienced and intelligent writer from whom I quote, corroborates his assertion by the testimony of several of the official assignees of the Bankruptcy Court. One of them says, 'As far as I can collect from the books and documents furnished by the bankrupts, it seems to me that' in the whole number of cases which occurred during a given time in the court to which he was attached, 'fourteen have been ruined by speculations in things with which they were unacquainted; three by neglecting book-keeping; ten by trading beyond their capital and means, and the consequent loss and expense of accommodation-bills; forty-nine by expending more than they could reasonably hope their profits would be, though their business yielded a fair return; none by any general distress, or the falling off of any particular branch of trade.' Another of these officers says that, during a period of eighteen months, 'fifty-two cases of bankruptcy have come under my care. It is my opinion that thirty-two of these have arisen from an imprudent expenditure, and five partly from that cause, and partly from a

---

[1] From a volume published in 1845, entitled, 'Credit the Life of Commerce', by Mr J. H. Elliott [London, 48–50].

pressure on the business in which the bankrupts were employed. Fifteen I attribute to improvident speculations, combined in many instances with an extravagant mode of life.'

To these citations the author adds the following statements from his personal means of knowledge. 'Many insolvencies are produced by tradesmen's indolence; they keep no books, or at least imperfect ones, which they never balance; they never take stock; they employ servants, if their trade be extensive, whom they are too indolent even to supervise, and then become insolvent. It is not too much to say, that one-half of all the persons engaged in trade, even in London, never take stock at all: they go on year after year without knowing how their affairs stand, and at last, like the child at school, they find to their surprise, but one halfpenny left in their pocket. I will venture to say that not one-fourth of all the persons in the provinces, either manufacturers, tradesmen, or farmers, ever take stock; nor in fact does one-half of them ever keep account-books, deserving any other name than memorandum books. I know sufficient of the concerns of five hundred small tradesmen in the provinces, to be enabled to say, that not one-fifth of them ever take stock, or keep even the most ordinary accounts. I am prepared to say of such tradesmen, from carefully prepared tables, giving every advantage where there has been any doubt as to the causes of their insolvency, that where nine happen from extravagance or dishonesty, one' at most 'may be referred to misfortune alone'.[1]

Is it rational to expect among the trading classes any high sense of justice, honour, or integrity, if the law enables men who act in this manner to shuffle off the consequences of their misconduct upon those who have been so unfortunate as to trust them; and practically proclaims that it looks upon insolvency thus produced, as a 'misfortune', not an offence?

It is, of course, not denied, that insolvencies do arise from causes beyond the control of the debtor, and that, in many more cases, his culpability is not of a high order; and the law ought to make a distinction in favour of such cases, but not without a searching investigation; nor should the case ever be let go without having ascertained, in the most complete manner practicable, not the fact of insolvency only, but the cause of it. To have been trusted with money or money's worth, and to have lost or spent it, is prima facie evidence of something wrong: and it is not for the creditor to prove, which he cannot do in one case out of ten, that there has been criminality, but for the debtor to rebut the presumption, by laying open the whole state of his affairs, and showing either that there has been no misconduct, or that the misconduct has been of an excusable kind. If he fail in this, he ought never to be dismissed without a punishment proportioned to the degree of blame which seems justly imputable to him; which punishment, however, might be shortened or mitigated in proportion as he appeared likely to exert himself in repairing the injury done.

It is a common argument with those who approve a relaxed system of insolvency laws, that credit, except in the great operations of commerce, is an evil; and that to deprive creditors of legal redress is a judicious means of preventing credit from being given. That which is given by retail dealers to unproductive consumers is, no doubt, to the excess to which it is carried, a considerable evil. This, however, is only true of large, and especially of long, credits; for there is credit whenever goods are not paid for before they quit the shop, or, at least, the custody of the seller; and there would be much inconvenience in putting an end to this sort of credit. But a large proportion of the debts on which insolvency laws take effect, are those due by small tradesmen to the dealers who supply them: and on no class of debts does the demoralization occasioned by a bad state of the law, operate more perniciously. These are commercial credits, which no one wishes to see curtailed; their existence is of great importance to the general industry of the country, and to numbers of honest, well-conducted persons of small means, to whom it would be a great injury that they should be prevented from obtaining the accommodation they need, and would not abuse, through the omission of the law to provide just remedies against dishonest or reckless borrowers.

But though it were granted that retail transactions, on any footing but that of ready money payment, are an evil, and their entire suppression a fit object for legislation to aim at; a worse mode of compassing that object could scarcely be invented, than to permit those who have been trusted by others to cheat and rob them with impunity. The law does not generally select the vices of mankind as the appropriate instrument for inflicting chastisement on the comparatively innocent. When it seeks to discourage any course of action, it does so by applying inducements of its own, not by outlawing those who act in the manner it deems objectionable, and letting loose the predatory instincts of the worthless part of mankind to feed upon them. If a man has committed murder, the law condemns him to death; but it does not promise impunity to anybody who may kill him for the sake of taking his purse. The offence of believing another's word, even rashly, is not so heinous that for the sake of discouraging it, the spectacle should be brought home to every door, of triumphant rascality, with the law on its side, mocking the victims it has made. This pestilent example has been very widely exhibited since the relaxation of the insolvency laws. It is idle to expect that, even by absolutely depriving creditors of all legal redress, the kind of credit which is considered objectionable would really be very much checked. Rogues and swindlers are still an exception among mankind, and people will go on trusting each other's promises. Large dealers, in abundant business, would refuse credit, as many of them already do: but in the eager competition of a great town, or the dependent position of a village shopkeeper, what can be expected from the tradesman to whom a single customer is of importance, the beginner, perhaps, who is striving to get into business? He will take the risk, even if it were still greater; he is ruined if he cannot sell his goods, and he can but be ruined if he is defrauded. Nor does it avail to say, that he ought to make proper inquiries, and ascertain the character of those to

whom he supplies goods on trust. In some of the most
flagrant cases of profligate debtors which have come
before the Bankruptcy Court, the swindler had been able to
give, and had given, excellent references.[1]

[1] The following extracts from the French Code de Commerce, (the translation
is that of Mr Fane [*Bankruptcy Reform* (London, 1838), 44–7]) show the great
extent to which the just distinctions are made, and the proper investigations
provided for, by French law. The word *banqueroute*, which can only be translated
by bankruptcy, is, however, confined in France to *culpable* insolvency, which is
distinguished into *simple* bankruptcy and *fraudulent* bankruptcy. The following
are cases of simple bankruptcy:

'Every insolvent who, in the investigation of his affairs, shall appear chargeable
with one or more of the following offences, shall be proceeded against as a simple
bankrupt.

'If his house expenses, which he is bound to enter regularly in a day-book,
appear excessive.

'If he has spent considerable sums at play, or in operations of pure hazard.

'If it shall appear that he has borrowed largely, or resold merchandize at a loss,
or below the current price, after it appeared by his last account-taking that his
debts exceeded his assets by one-half.

'If he has issued negotiable securities to three times the amount of his available
assets, according to his last account-taking.

'The following *may* also be proceeded against as simple bankrupts:

'He who has not declared his own insolvency in the manner prescribed by law:

'He who has not come in and surrendered within the time limited, having no
legitimate excuse for his absence:

'He who either produces no books at all, or produces such as have been
irregularly kept, and this although the irregularities may not indicate fraud.'

The penalty for 'simple bankruptcy' is imprisonment for a term of not less than
one month, nor more than two years. The following are cases of fraudulent
bankruptcy, of which the punishment is *travaux forcés* (the galleys) for a term:

'If he has attempted to account for his property by fictitious expenses and
losses, or if he does not fully account for all his receipts:

'If he has fraudulently concealed any sum of money or any debt due to him, or
any merchandize or other movables:

'If he has made fraudulent sales or gifts of his property:

'If he has allowed fictitious debts to be proved against his estate:

'If he has been entrusted with property, either merely to keep, or with special
directions as to its use, and has nevertheless appropriated it to his own use:

'If he has purchased real property in a borrowed name:

'If he has concealed his books.

'The following *may* also be proceeded against in a similar way:

'He who has not kept books, or whose books shall not exhibit his real situation
as regards his debts and credits:

'He who, having obtained a protection (*sauf-conduit*), shall not have duly
attended.'

These various provisions relate only to commercial insolvency. The laws in
regard to ordinary debts are considerably more rigorous to the debtor.

X

OF INTERFERENCES OF GOVERNMENT
GROUNDED ON ERRONEOUS THEORIES

1. From the necessary functions of government, and the effects produced on the economical interests of society by their good or ill discharge, we proceed to the functions which belong to what I have termed, for want of a better designation, the optional class; those which are sometimes assumed by governments and sometimes not, and which it is not unanimously admitted that they ought to exercise.

Before entering on the general principles of the question, it will be advisable to clear from our path all those cases, in which government interference works ill because grounded on false views of the subject interfered with. Such cases have no connexion with any theory respecting the proper limits of interference. There are some things with which governments ought not to meddle, and other things with which they ought; but whether right or wrong in itself, the interference must work for ill, if government, not understanding the subject which it meddles with, meddles to bring about a result which would be mischievous. We will therefore begin by passing in review various false theories, which have from time to time formed the ground of acts of government more or less economically injurious.

Former writers on political economy have found it needful to devote much trouble and space to this department of their subject. It has now happily become possible, at least in our own country, greatly to abridge this purely negative part of our discussions. The false theories of political economy which have done so much mischief in times past, are entirely discredited among all who have not lagged behind the general progress of opinion; and few of the enactments which were once grounded on those theories still help to deform the statute-book. As the principles on which their condemnation rests have been fully set forth in other parts of this Treatise, we may here content ourselves with a few brief indications.

Of these false theories, the most notable is the doctrine of Protection to Native Industry; a phrase meaning the prohibition, or the discouragement by heavy duties, of such foreign commodities as are capable of being produced at home. If the theory involved in this system had been correct, the practical conclusions grounded on it would not have been unreasonable. The theory was, that to buy things produced at home was a national benefit, and the introduction of foreign commodities generally a national loss. It being at the same time evident that the interest of the consumer is to buy foreign commodities in preference to domestic whenever they are either cheaper or better, the interest of the consumer appeared in this respect to be contrary to the public interest; he was certain, if left to his own inclinations, to do what according to the theory was injurious to the public.

It was shown, however, in our analysis of the effects of international trade, as it had been often shown by former writers, that the importation of foreign commodities, in the common course of traffic, never takes place, except when it is, economically speaking, a national good, by causing the same amount of commodities to be obtained at a smaller cost of labour and capital to the country. To prohibit, therefore, this importation, or impose duties which prevent it, is to render the labour and capital of the country less efficient in production than they would otherwise be; and compel a waste, of the difference between the labour and capital necessary for the home production of the commodity, and that which is required for producing the things with which it can be purchased from abroad. The amount of national loss thus occasioned is measured by the excess of the price at which the commodity is produced over that at which it could be imported. In the case of manufactured goods, the whole difference between the two prices is absorbed in indemnifying the producers for waste of labour, or of the capital which supports that labour. Those who are supposed to be benefited, namely, the makers of the protected articles, (unless they form an exclusive company, and have a monopoly against their own countrymen as well as against foreigners,) do not obtain higher profits than other people. All is sheer loss, to the country as well as to the consumer. When the protected article is a product of agriculture—the waste of labour not being incurred on the whole produce, but only on what may be called the last instalment of it—the extra price is only in part an indemnity for waste, the remainder being a tax paid to the landlords.

The restrictive and prohibitory policy was originally grounded on what is called the Mercantile System, which representing the advantage of foreign trade to consist solely in bringing money into the country, gave artificial encouragement to exportation of goods, and discountenanced their importation. The only exceptions to the system were those required by the system itself. The materials and instruments of production were the subjects of a contrary policy, directed however to the same end; they were freely imported, and not permitted to be exported, in order that manufacturers, being more cheaply supplied with the requisites of manufacture, might be able to sell cheaper, and therefore to export more largely. For a similar reason, importation was allowed and even favoured, when confined to the productions of countries which were supposed to take from the country still more than it took from them, thus enriching it by a favourable balance of trade. As part of the same system, colonies were founded, for the supposed advantage of compelling them to buy our commodities, or at all events not to buy those of any other country: in return for which restriction, we were generally willing to come under an equivalent obligation with respect to the staple productions of the colonists. The consequences of the theory were pushed so far, that it was not unusual even to give bounties on exportation, and induce foreigners to buy from us rather than from other countries, by a cheapness which we artificially produced, by paying part of the price for them out of our own taxes. This is a stretch beyond the point yet reached by any private tradesman in his competition for business. No shopkeeper, I should think, ever made a practice of bribing customers by selling goods to them at a permanent loss, making it up to himself from other funds in his possession.

The principle of the Mercantile Theory is now given up even by writers and governments who still cling to the restrictive system. Whatever hold that system has over men's minds, independently of the private interests exposed to real or apprehended loss by its abandonment, is derived from fallacies other than the old notion of the benefits of heaping up money in the country. The most effective of these is the specious plea of employing our own countrymen and our national industry, instead of feeding and supporting the industry of foreigners. The answer to this, from the principles laid down in former chapters, is evident. Without reverting to the fundamental theorem discussed in an early part of the present treatise,[1] respecting the nature and sources of employment for labour, it is sufficient to say, what has usually been said by the advocates of free trade, that the alternative is not between employing our own people and foreigners, but between employing one class and another of our own people. The imported commodity is always paid for, directly or indirectly, with the produce of our own industry: that industry being, at the same time rendered more productive, since, with the same labour and outlay, we are enabled to possess ourselves of a greater quantity of the article. Those who have not well considered the subject are apt to suppose that our exporting an equivalent in our own produce, for the foreign articles we consume, depends on contingencies—on the consent of foreign countries to make some corresponding relaxation of their own restrictions, or on the question whether those from whom we buy are induced by that circumstance to buy more from us; and that, if these things, or things equivalent to them, do not happen, the payment must be made in money. Now, in the first place, there is nothing more objectionable in a money payment than in payment by any other medium, if the state of the market makes it the most

[1] [Bk. I, Ch. V. 9. Not included in present edn.]

advantageous remittance; and the money itself was first acquired, and would again be replenished, by the export of an equivalent value of our own products. But, in the next place, a very short interval of paying in money would so lower prices as either to stop a part of the importation, or raise up a foreign demand for our produce, sufficient to pay for the imports. I grant that this disturbance of the equation of international demand would be in some degree to our disadvantage, in the purchase of other imported articles; and that a country which prohibits some foreign commodities, does, *ceteris paribus*, obtain those which it does not prohibit, at a less price than it would otherwise have to pay. To express the same thing in other words; a country which destroys or prevents altogether certain branches of foreign trade, thereby annihilating a general gain to the world, which would be shared in some proportion between itself and other countries—does, in some circumstances, draw to itself, at the expense of foreigners, a larger share than would else belong to it of the gain arising from that portion of its foreign trade which it suffers to subsist. But even this it can only be enabled to do, if foreigners do not maintain equivalent prohibitions or restrictions against its commodities. In any case, the justice or expediency of destroying one of two gains, in order to engross a rather larger share of the other, does not require much discussion: the gain, too, which is destroyed, being, in proportion to the magnitude of the transactions, the larger of the two, since it is the one which capital, left to itself, is supposed to seek by preference.

Defeated as a general theory, the Protectionist doctrine finds support in some particular cases, from considerations which, when really in point, involve greater interests than mere saving of labour; the interests of national subsistence and of national defence. The discussions on the Corn Laws have familiarized everybody with the plea, that we ought to be independent of foreigners for the food of the people; and the Navigation Laws were grounded, in theory and profession, on the necessity of keeping up a 'nursery of seamen' for the navy. On this last subject I at once admit, that the object is worth the sacrifice; and that a country exposed to invasion by sea, if it cannot otherwise have sufficient ships and sailors of its own to secure the means of manning on an emergency an adequate fleet, is quite right in obtaining those means, even at an economical sacrifice in point of cheapness of transport. When the English Navigation Laws were enacted, the Dutch, from their maritime skill and their low rate of profit at home, were able to carry for other nations, England included, at cheaper rates than those nations could carry for themselves: which placed all other countries at a great comparative disadvantage in obtaining experienced seamen for their ships of war. The Navigation Laws, by which this deficiency was remedied, and at the same time a blow struck against the maritime power of a nation with which England was then frequently engaged in hostilities, were probably, though economically disadvantageous, politically expedient. But English ships and sailors can now navigate as cheaply as those of any other country; maintaining at least an equal competition with the other maritime nations even in their own trade. The ends which may once have justified Navigation Laws, require them no longer, and afforded no reason for maintaining this invidious exception to the general rule of free trade.

With regard to subsistence, the plea of the Protectionists has been so often and so triumphantly met, that it requires little notice here. That country is the most steadily as well as the most abundantly supplied with food, which draws its supplies from the largest surface. It is ridiculous to found a general system of policy on so improbable a danger as that of being at war with all the nations of the world at once; or to suppose that, even if inferior at sea, a whole country could be blockaded like a town, or that the growers of food in other countries would not be as anxious not to lose an advantageous market, as we should be not to be deprived of their corn. On the subject, however, of subsistence, there is one point which deserves more especial consideration. In cases of actual or apprehended scarcity, many countries of Europe are accustomed to stop the exportation of food. Is this, or not, sound policy? There can be no doubt that in the present state of international morality, a people cannot, any more than an individual, be blamed for not starving itself to feed others. But if the greatest amount of good to mankind on the whole, were the end aimed at in the maxims of international conduct, such collective churlishness would certainly be condemned by them. Suppose that in ordinary circumstances the trade in food were perfectly free, so that the price in one country could not habitually exceed that in any other by more than the cost of carriage, together with a moderate profit to the importer. A general scarcity ensues, affecting all countries, but in unequal degrees. If the price rose in one country more than in others, it would be a proof that in that country the scarcity was severest, and that by permitting food to go freely thither from any other country, it would be spared from a less urgent necessity to relieve a greater. When the interests, therefore, of all countries are considered, free exportation is desirable. To the exporting country considered separately, it may, at least on the particular occasion, be an inconvenience: but taking into account that the country which is now the giver, will in some future season be the receiver, and the one that is benefited by the freedom, I cannot but think that even to the apprehension of food rioters it might be made apparent, that in such cases they should do to others what they would wish done to themselves.

In countries in which the Protection theory is declining, but not yet given up, such as the United States, a doctrine has come into notice which is a sort of compromise between free trade and restriction, namely, that protection for protection's sake is improper, but that there is nothing objectionable in having as much protection as may incidentally result from a tariff framed solely for revenue. Even in England, regret is sometimes expressed that a 'moderate fixed duty' was not preserved on corn, on account of the revenue it would yield. Independently, however, of the general impolicy of taxes on the necessaries of life, this doctrine overlooks the fact, that revenue is received only on the quantity imported, but that the tax is paid on the entire quantity consumed. To make the public pay much that the treasury may receive a little, is not an eligible mode of obtaining a revenue. In the case of manufactured articles the doctrine involves a palpable inconsistency. The object of the duty as a means of revenue, is inconsistent with its affording, even incidentally, any protection. It can only operate as protection in so far as it prevents importation; and to whatever degree it prevents importation, it affords no revenue.

The only case in which, on mere principles of political economy, protecting duties can be defensible, is when they are imposed temporarily (especially in a young and rising nation) in hopes of naturalizing a foreign industry, in itself perfectly suitable to the circumstances of the country. The superiority of one country over another in a branch of production, often arises only from having begun it sooner. There may be no inherent advantage on one part, or disadvantage on the other, but only a present superiority of acquired skill and experience. A country which has this skill and experience yet to acquire, may in other respects be better adapted to the production than those which were earlier in the field: and besides, it is a just remark of Mr Rae,* that nothing has a greater tendency to promote improvements in any branch of production, than its trial under a new set of conditions. But it cannot be expected that individuals should, at their own risk, or rather to their certain loss, introduce a new manufacture, and bear the burthen of carrying it on until the producers have been educated up to the level of those with whom the processes are traditional. A protecting duty, continued for a reasonable time, might sometimes be the least inconvenient mode in which the nation can tax itself for the support of such an experiment. But it is essential that the protection should be confined to cases in which there is good ground of assurance that the industry which it fosters will after a time be able to dispense with it; nor should the domestic producers ever be allowed to expect that it will be continued to them beyond the time necessary for a fair trial of what they are capable of accomplishing.

The only writer, of any reputation as a political economist, who now adheres to the Protectionist doctrine, Mr

H. C. Carey, rests its defence, in an economic point of view, principally on two reasons. One is, the great saving in cost of carriage, consequent on producing commodities at or very near to the place where they are to be consumed. The whole of the cost of carriage, both on the commodities imported and on those exported in exchange for them, he regards as a direct burthen on the producers, and not, as is obviously the truth, on the consumers. On whomsoever it falls, it is, without doubt, a burthen on the industry of the world. But it is obvious (and that Mr Carey does not see it, is one of the many surprising things in his book) that the burthen is only borne for a more than equivalent advantage. If the commodity is bought in a foreign country with domestic produce in spite of the double cost of carriage, the fact proves that, heavy as that cost may be, the saving in cost of production outweighs it, and the collective labour of the country is on the whole better remunerated than if the article were produced at home. Cost of carriage is a natural protecting duty, which free trade has no power to abrogate: and unless America gained more by obtaining her manufactures through the medium of her corn and cotton than she loses in cost of carriage, the capital employed in producing corn and cotton in annually increased quantities for the foreign market, would turn to manufactures instead. The natural advantages attending a mode of industry in which there is less cost of carriage to pay, can at most be only a justification for a temporary and merely tentative protection. The expenses of production being always greatest at first, it may happen that the home production, though really the most advantageous, may not become so until after a certain duration of pecuniary loss, which it is not to be expected that private speculators should incur in order that their successors may be benefited by their ruin. I have therefore conceded that in a new country a temporary protecting duty may sometimes be economically defensible; on condition, however, that it be strictly limited in point of time, and provision be made that during the latter part of its existence it be on a gradually decreasing scale. Such temporary protection is of the same nature as a patent, and should be governed by similar conditions.

The remaining argument of Mr Carey in support of the economic benefits of Protectionism, applies only to countries whose exports consist of agricultural produce. He argues, that by a trade of this description they actually send away their soil: the distant consumers not giving back to the land of the country, as home consumers would do, the fertilizing elements which they abstract from it. This argument deserves attention on account of the physical truth on which it is founded; a truth which has only lately come to be understood, but which is henceforth destined to be a permanent element in the thoughts of statesmen, as it must always have been in the destinies of nations. To the question of Protectionism, however, it is irrelevant. That the immense growth of raw produce in America to be consumed in Europe, is progressively exhausting the soil of the Eastern, and even of the older Western States, and that both are already far less productive than formerly, is credible in itself, even if no one bore witness to it. But what I have already said respecting cost of carriage, is true also of the cost of manuring. Free trade does not compel America to export corn: she would cease to do so if it ceased to be to her advantage. As, then, she would not persist in exporting raw produce and importing manufactures, any longer than the labour she saved by doing so exceeded what the carriage cost her, so when it became necessary for her to replace in the soil the elements of fertility which she had sent away, if the saving in cost of production were more than equivalent to the cost of carriage and of manure together, manure would be imported; and if not, the export of corn would cease. It is evident that one of these two things would already have taken place, if there had not been near at hand a constant succession of new soils, not yet exhausted of their fertility, the cultivation of which enables her, whether judiciously or not, to postpone the question of manure. As soon as it no longer answers better to break up new soils than to manure the old, America will either become a regular importer of manure, or will, without protecting duties, grow corn for herself only, and manufacturing for herself, will make her manure, as Mr Carey desires, at home.[1]

For these obvious reasons, I hold Mr Carey's economic arguments for Protectionism to be totally invalid. The economic, however, is far from being the strongest point of his case. American Protectionists often reason extremely ill; but it is an injustice to them to suppose that their Protectionist creed rests upon nothing superior to an economic blunder. Many of them have been led to it, much more by consideration for the higher interests of humanity, than by purely economic reasons. They, and Mr Carey at their head, deem it a necessary condition of human improvement that towns should abound; that men should combine their labour, by means of interchange—with near neighbours, with people of pursuits, capacities, and mental cultivation different from their own, sufficiently close at hand for mutual sharpening of wits and enlarging of ideas—rather than with people on the opposite side of the globe. They believe that a nation all engaged in the same, or nearly the same, pursuit—a nation all agricultural—cannot attain a high state of civilization and culture. And for this there is a great foundation of reason. If the difficulty can be overcome, the United States, with their free institutions, their universal schooling, and their omnipresent press, are the people to do it; but whether this is possible or not is still a problem. So far, however, as it is an object to check the excessive dispersion of the population, Mr Wakefield has pointed out

---

[1] To this Mr Carey would reply (indeed he has already so replied in advance) that of all commodities manure is the least susceptible of being conveyed to a distance. This is true of sewage, and of stable manure, but not true of the ingredients to which those manures owe their efficiency. These, on the contrary, are chiefly substances containing great fertilizing power in small bulk; substances of which the human body requires but a small quantity, and hence peculiarly susceptible of being imported; the mineral alkalies and the phosphates. The question indeed mainly concerns the phosphates, for of the alkalies, soda is procurable everywhere; while potass, being one of the constituents of granite and the other feldspathic rocks, exists in many subsoils, by whose progressive decomposition it is renewed, a large quantity also being brought down in the deposits of rivers. As for the phosphates, they, in the very convenient form of pulverized bones, are a regular article of commerce, largely imported into England; as they are sure to be into any country where the conditions of industry make it worth while to pay the price.

a better way; to modify the existing method of disposing of the unoccupied lands, by raising the price, instead of lowering it, or giving away the land gratuitously, as is largely done since the passing of the Homestead Act.* To cut the knot in Mr Carey's fashion, by Protectionism, it would be necessary that Ohio and Michigan should be protected against Massachusetts as well as against England: for the manufactories of New England, no more than those of the old country, accomplish his desideratum of bringing a manufacturing population to the doors of the Western farmer. Boston and New York do not supply the want of local towns to the Western prairies, any better than Manchester; and it is as difficult to get back the manure from the one place as from the other.

There is only one part of the Protectionist scheme which requires any further notice: its policy towards colonies, and foreign dependencies; that of compelling them to trade exclusively with the dominant country. A country which thus secures to itself an extra foreign demand for its commodities, undoubtedly gives itself some advantage in the distribution of the general gains of the commercial world. Since, however, it causes the industry and capital of the colony to be diverted from channels, which are proved to be the most productive, inasmuch as they are those into which industry and capital spontaneously tend to flow; there is a loss, on the whole, to the productive powers of the world, and the mother country does not gain so much as she makes the colony lose. If, therefore, the mother country refuses to acknowledge any reciprocity of obligation, she imposes a tribute on the colony in an indirect mode, greatly more oppressive and injurious than the direct. But if, with a more equitable spirit, she submits herself to corresponding restrictions for the benefit of the colony, the result of the whole transaction is the ridiculous one, that each party loses much, in order that the other may gain a little.

2. Next to the system of Protection, among mischievous interferences with the spontaneous course of industrial transactions, may be noticed certain interferences with contracts.

One instance is that of the Usury Laws. These originated in a religious prejudice against receiving interest on money, derived from that fruitful source of mischief in modern Europe, the attempted adaptation to Christianity of doctrines and precepts drawn from the Jewish law. In Mahomedan nations the receiving of interest is formally interdicted, and rigidly abstained from: and Sismondi has noticed, as one among the causes of the industrial inferiority of the Catholic, compared with the Protestant parts of Europe, that the Catholic Church in the middle ages gave its sanction to the same prejudice; which subsists, impaired but not destroyed, wherever that religion is acknowledged. Where law or conscientious scruples prevent lending at interest, the capital which belongs to persons not in business is lost to productive purposes, or can be applied to them only in peculiar circumstances of personal connexion, or by a subterfuge. Industry is thus limited to the capital of the undertakers, and to what they can borrow from persons not bound by the same laws or religion as themselves. In Mussulman countries the bankers and money dealers are either Hindoos, Armenians, or Jews.

In more improved countries, legislation no longer discountenances the receipt of an equivalent for money lent; but it has everywhere interfered with the free agency of the lender and borrowers, by fixing a legal limit to the rate of interest, and making the receipt of more than the appointed maximum a penal offence. This restriction, though approved by Adam Smith, has been condemned by all enlightened persons since the triumphant onslaught made upon it by Bentham in his 'Letters on Usury', which may still be referred to as the best extant writing on the subject.

Legislators may enact and maintain Usury Laws from one of two motives: ideas of public policy, or concern for the interest of the parties in the contract; in this case, of one party only, the borrower. As a matter of policy, the notion may possibly be, that it is for the general good that interest should be low. It is however a misapprehension of the causes which influence commercial transactions, to suppose that the rate of interest is really made lower by law, than it would be made by the spontaneous play of supply and demand. If the competition of borrowers, left unrestrained, would raise the rate of interest to six per cent, this proves that at five there would be a greater demand for loans, than there is capital in the market to supply. If the law in these circumstances permits no interest beyond five per cent, there will be some lenders, who not choosing to disobey the law, and not being in a condition to employ their capital otherwise, will content themselves with the legal rate: but others, finding that in a season of pressing demand, more may be made of their capital by other means than they are permitted to make by lending it, will not lend it at all; and the loanable capital, already too small for the demand, will be still further diminished. Of the disappointed candidates there will be many at such periods, who must have their necessities supplied at any price, and these will readily find a third section of lenders, who will not be averse to join in a violation of the law, either by circuitous transactions partaking of the nature of fraud, or by relying on the honour of the borrower. The extra expense of the roundabout mode of proceeding, and an equivalent for the risk of non-payment and of legal penalties, must be paid by the borrower, over and above the extra interest which would have been required of him by the general state of the market. The laws which were intended to lower the price paid by him for pecuniary accommodation, end thus in greatly increasing it. These laws have also a directly demoralizing tendency. Knowing the difficulty of detecting an illegal pecuniary transaction between two persons, in which no third person is involved, so long as it is the interest of both to keep the secret, legislators have adopted the expedient of tempting the borrower to become the informer, by making the annulment of the debt a part of the penalty for the offence; thus rewarding men for first obtaining the property of others by false promises, and then not only refusing payment, but invoking legal penalties on those who have helped them in their need. The moral sense of mankind very rightly infamizes those who resist an otherwise just claim on the ground of usury, and tolerates such a plea only when resorted to as the best legal defence available against an attempt really considered as partaking of fraud or extortion. But this very severity of public opinion renders the enforcement of the laws so difficult, and the infliction of the penalties so rare, that when it does occur it merely victimizes an individual, and has no effect on general practice.

In so far as the motive of the restriction may be supposed to be, not public policy, but regard for the interest of the borrower, it would be difficult to point out any case in which such tenderness on the legislator's part is more misplaced. A person of sane mind, and of the age at which persons are legally competent to conduct their own concerns, must be presumed to be a sufficient guardian of his pecuniary interests. If he may sell an estate, or grant a release, or assign away all his property, without control from the law, it seems very unnecessary that the only bargain which he cannot make without its intermeddling, should be a loan of money. The law seems to presume that the money-lender, dealing with necessitous persons, can take advantage of their necessities, and exact conditions limited only by his own pleasure. It might be so if there were only one money-lender within reach. But when there is the whole monied capital of a wealthy community to resort to, no borrower is placed under any disadvantage in the market merely by the urgency of his need. If he cannot borrow at the interest paid by other people, it must be because he cannot give such good security: and competition will limit the extra demand to a fair equivalent for the risk of his proving insolvent. Though the law intends favour to the borrower, it is to him above all that injustice is, in this case, done by it. What can be more unjust than that a person who cannot give perfectly good security, should be prevented from borrowing of persons who are willing to lend money to him, by their not being permitted to receive the rate of interest which would be a just equivalent for their risk? Through the mistaken kindness of the law, he must either go without the money which is perhaps necessary to save him from much greater losses, or be driven to expedients of a far more ruinous description, which the law either has not found it possible, or has not happened, to interdict.

Adam Smith rather hastily expressed the opinion, that only two kinds of persons, 'prodigals and projectors', could require to borrow money at more than the market rate of interest. He should have included all persons who are in any pecuniary difficulties, however temporary their necessities may be. It may happen to any person in business, to be disappointed of the resources on which he had calculated for meeting some engagement, the non-fulfilment of which on a fixed day would be bankruptcy. In periods of commercial difficulty, this is the condition of many prosperous mercantile firms, who become competitors for the small amount of disposable capital which, in a time of general distrust, the owners are willing to part with. Under the English usury laws, now happily abolished, the limitations imposed by those laws were felt as a most serious aggravation of every commercial crisis. Merchants who could have obtained the aid they required at an interest of seven or eight per cent for short periods, were obliged to give 20 or 30 per cent, or to resort to forced sales of goods at a still greater loss. Experience having obtruded these evils on the notice of Parliament, the sort of compromise took place, of which English legislation affords so many instances, and which helps to make our laws and policy the mass of inconsistency that they are. The law was reformed as a person reforms a tight shoe, who cuts a hole in it where it pinches hardest, and continues to wear it. Retaining the erroneous principle as a general rule, Parliament allowed an exception in the case in which the practical mischief was most flagrant. It left the usury laws unrepealed, but exempted bills of exchange, of not more than three months date, from their operation. Some years afterwards the laws were repealed in regard to all other contracts, but left in force as to all those which relate to land. Not a particle of reason could be given for making this extraordinary distinction: but the 'agricultural mind' was of opinion that the interest on mortgages, though it hardly ever came up to the permitted point, would come up to a still higher point; and the usury laws were maintained that the landlords might as they thought, be enabled to borrow below the market rate, as the corn-laws were kept up that the same class might be able to sell corn above the market rate. The modesty of the pretension was quite worthy of the intelligence which could think that the end aimed at was in any way forwarded by the means used.

With regard to the 'prodigals and projectors' spoken of by Adam Smith; no law can prevent a prodigal from ruining himself, unless it lays him or his property under actual restraint, according to the unjustifiable practice of the Roman Law and some of the Continental systems founded on it. The only effect of usury laws upon a prodigal, is to make his ruin rather more expeditious, by driving him to a disreputable class of money-dealers, and rendering the conditions more onerous by the extra risk created by the law. As for projectors, (a term, in its unfavourable sense, rather unfairly applied to every person who has a project); such laws may put a veto upon the prosecution of the most promising enterprise, when planned, as it generally is, by a person who does not possess capital adequate to its successful completion. Many of the greatest improvements were at first looked shyly on by capitalists, and had to wait long before they found one sufficiently adventurous to be the first in a new path: many years elapsed before Stephenson could convince even the enterprising mercantile public of Liverpool and Manchester, of the advantage of substituting railways for turnpike roads; and plans on which great labour and large sums have been expended with little visible result, (the epoch in their progress when predictions of failure are most rife,) may be indefinitely suspended, or altogether dropped, and the outlay all lost, if, when the original funds are exhausted, the law will not allow more to be raised on the terms on which people are willing to expose it to the chances of an enterprise not yet secure of success.

3. Loans are not the only kind of contract, of which governments have thought themselves qualified to regulate the conditions better than the persons interested. There is

scarcely any commodity which they have not, at some place or time, endeavoured to make either dearer or cheaper than it would be if left to itself. The most plausible case for artificially cheapening a commodity, is that of food. The desirableness of the object is in this case undeniable. But since the average price of food, like that of other things, conforms to the cost of production, with the addition of the usual profit; if this price is not expected by the farmer, he will, unless compelled by law, produce no more than he requires for his own consumption: and the law, therefore, if absolutely determined to have food cheaper, must substitute, for the ordinary motives to cultivation, a system of penalties. If it shrinks from doing this, it has no resource but that of taxing the whole nation, to give a bounty or premium to the grower or importer of corn, thus giving everybody cheap bread at the expense of all: in reality a largess to those who do not pay taxes, at the expense of those who do; one of the forms of a practice essentially bad, that of converting the working classes into unworking classes by making them a present of subsistence.

It is not however so much the general or average price of food, as its occasional high price in times of emergency, which governments have studied to reduce. In some cases, as for example the famous 'maximum' of the revolutionary government of 1793* the compulsory regulation was an attempt by the ruling powers to counteract the necessary consequences of their own acts; to scatter an indefinite abundance of the circulating medium with one hand, and keep down prices with the other; a thing manifestly impossible under any régime except one of unmitigated terror. In case of actual scarcity, governments are often urged, as they were in the Irish emergency of 1847,* to take measures of some sort for moderating the price of food. But the price of a thing cannot be raised by deficiency of supply, beyond what is sufficient to make a corresponding reduction of the consumption; and if a government prevents this reduction from being brought about by a rise of price, there remains no mode of effecting it unless by taking possession of all the food, and serving it out in rations, as in a besieged town. In a real scarcity, nothing can afford general relief, except a determination by the richer classes to diminish their own consumption. If they buy and consume their usual quantity of food, and content themselves with giving money, they do no good. The price is forced up until the poorest competitors have no longer the means of competing, and the privation of food is thrown exclusively upon the indigent, the other classes being only affected pecuniarily. When the supply is insufficient, somebody must consume less, and if every rich person is determined not to be that somebody, all they do by subsidizing their poorer competitors is to force up the price so much the higher, with no effect but to enrich the corn-dealers, the very reverse of what is desired by those who recommend such measures. All that governments can do in these emergencies, is to counsel a general moderation in consumption, and to interdict such kinds of it as are not of primary importance. Direct measures at the cost of the state, to procure food from a distance, are expedient when from peculiar reasons the thing is not likely to be done by private speculation. In any other case they are a great error. Private speculators will not, in such cases, venture to compete with the government; and though a government can do more than any one merchant, it cannot do nearly so much as all merchants.

4. Governments, however, are oftener chargeable with having attempted, too successfully, to make things dear, than with having aimed by wrong means at making them cheap. The usual instrument for producing artificial dearness is monopoly. To confer a monopoly upon a producer or dealer, or upon a set of producers or dealers not too numerous to combine, is to give them the power of levying any amount of taxation on the public, for their individual benefit, which will not make the public forego the use of the commodity. When the sharers in the monopoly are so numerous and so widely scattered that they are prevented from combining, the evil is considerably less: but even then the competition is not so active among a limited as among an unlimited number. Those who feel assured of a fair

average proportion in the general business, are seldom eager to get a larger share by foregoing a portion of their profits. A limitation of competition, however partial, may have mischievous effects quite disproportioned to the apparent cause. The mere exclusion of foreigners, from a branch of industry open to the free competition of every native, has been known, even in England, to render that branch a conspicuous exception to the general industrial energy of the country. The silk manufacture of England remained far behind that of other countries of Europe, so long as the foreign fabrics were prohibited. In addition to the tax levied for the profit, real or imaginary, of the monopolists, the consumer thus pays an additional tax for their laziness and incapacity. When relieved from the immediate stimulus of competition, producers and dealers grow indifferent to the dictates of their ultimate pecuniary interest; preferring to the most hopeful prospects, the present ease of adhering to routine. A person who is already thriving, seldom puts himself out of his way to commence even a lucrative improvement, unless urged by the additional motive of fear lest some rival should supplant him by getting possession of it before him.

The condemnation of monopolies ought not to extend to patents, by which the originator of an improved process is allowed to enjoy, for a limited period, the exclusive privilege of using his own improvement. This is not making the commodity dear for his benefit, but merely postponing a part of the increased cheapness which the public owe to the inventor, in order to compensate and reward him for the service. That he ought to be both compensated and rewarded for it, will not be denied, and also that if all were at once allowed to avail themselves of his ingenuity, without having shared the labours or the expenses which he had to incur in bringing his idea into a practical shape, either such expenses and labours would be undergone by nobody except very opulent and very public-spirited persons, or the state must put a value on the service rendered by an inventor, and make him a pecuniary grant. This has been done in some instances, and may be done without inconvenience in cases of very conspicuous public benefit; but in general an exclusive privilege, of temporary duration, is preferable; because it leaves nothing to any one's discretion; because the reward conferred by it depends upon the invention's being found useful, and the greater the usefulness the greater the reward; and because it is paid by the very persons to whom the service is rendered, the consumers of the commodity. So decisive, indeed, are these considerations, that if the system of patents were abandoned for that of rewards by the state, the best shape which these could assume would be that of a small temporary tax, imposed for the inventor's benefit, on all persons making use of the invention. To this, however, or to any other system which would vest in the state the power of deciding whether an inventor should derive any pecuniary advantage from the public benefit which he confers, the objections are evidently stronger and more fundamental than the strongest which can possibly be urged against patents. It is generally admitted that the present Patent Laws need much improvement; but in this case, as well as in the closely analogous one of Copyright, it would be a gross immorality in the law to set everybody free to use a person's work without his consent, and without giving him an equivalent. I have seen with real alarm several recent attempts, in quarters carrying some authority, to impugn the principle of patents altogether; attempts which, if practically successful, would enthrone free stealing under the prostituted name of free trade, and make the men of brains, still more than at present, the needy retainers and dependents of the men of money-bags.

5. I pass to another kind of government interference, in which the end and the means are alike odious, but which existed in England until not more than a generation ago, and in France up to the year 1864. I mean the laws against combinations of workmen to raise wages; laws enacted and maintained for the declared purpose of keeping wages low, as the famous Statute of Labourers* was passed by a legislature of employers, to prevent the labouring class, when its numbers had been thinned by a pestilence, from

taking advantage of the diminished competition to obtain higher wages. Such laws exhibit the infernal spirit of the slave master, when to retain the working classes in avowed slavery has ceased to be practicable.

If it were possible for the working classes, by combining among themselves, to raise or keep up the general rate of wages, it needs hardly be said that this would be a thing not to be punished, but to be welcomed and rejoiced at. Unfortunately the effect is quite beyond attainment by such means. The multitudes who compose the working class are too numerous and too widely scattered to combine at all, much more to combine effectually. If they could do so, they might doubtless succeed in diminishing the hours of labour, and obtaining the same wages for less work. They would also have a limited power of obtaining, by combination, an increase of general wages at the expense of profits. But the limits of this power are narrow; and were they to attempt to strain it beyond those limits, this could only be accomplished by keeping a part of their number permanently out of employment. As support from public charity would of course be refused to those who could get work and would not accept it, they would be thrown for support upon the trades union of which they were members; and the workpeople collectively would be no better off than before, having to support the same numbers out of the same aggregate wages. In this way, however, the class would have its attention forcibly drawn to the fact of a superfluity of numbers, and to the necessity, if they would have high wages, of proportioning the supply of labour to the demand.

Combinations to keep up wages are sometimes successful, in trades where the workpeople are few in number, and collected in a small number of local centres. It is questionable if combinations ever had the smallest effect on the permanent remuneration of spinners or weavers; but the journeymen type-founders, by a close combination, are able, it is said, to keep up a rate of wages much beyond that which is usual in employments of equal hardness and skill; and even the tailors, a much more numerous class, are understood to have had, to some extent, a similar success.

A rise of wages, thus confined to particular employments, is not (like a rise of general wages) defrayed from profits, but raises the value and price of the particular article, and falls on the consumer; the capitalist who produces the commodity being only injured in so far as the high price tends to narrow the market; and not even then, unless it does so in a greater ratio than that of the rise of price: for though, at higher wages, he employs, with a given capital, fewer workpeople, and obtains less of the commodity, yet if he can sell the whole of this diminished quantity at the higher price, his profits are as great as before.

This partial rise of wages, if not gained at the expense of the remainder of the working class, ought not to be regarded as an evil. The consumer, indeed, must pay for it; but cheapness of goods is desirable only when the cause of it is that their production costs little labour, and not when occasioned by that labour's being ill remunerated. It may appear, indeed, at first sight, that the high wages of the type-founders (for example) are obtained at the general cost of the labouring class. This high remuneration either causes fewer persons to find employment in the trade, or if not, must lead to the investment of more capital in it, at the expense of other trades: in the first case, it throws an additional number of labourers on the general market; in the second, it withdraws from that market a portion of the demand: effects, both of which are injurious to the working classes. Such, indeed, would really be the result of a successful combination in a particular trade or trades, for some time after its formation; but when it is a permanent thing, the principles so often insisted upon in this treatise, show that it can have no such effect. The habitual earnings of the working classes at large can be affected by nothing but the habitual requirements of the labouring people: these indeed may be altered, but while they remain the same, wages never fall permanently below the standard of these requirements, and do not long remain above that standard. If there had been no combinations in particular trades, and the wages of those trades had never been kept above the common level, there is no reason to suppose that the common level would

have been at all higher than it now is. There would merely have been a greater number of people altogether, and a
smaller number of exceptions to the ordinary low rate of
wages.

If, therefore, no improvement were to be hoped for in the
general circumstances of the working classes, the success of
a portion of them, however small, in keeping their wages by
combination above the market rate, would be wholly a
matter of satisfaction. But when the elevation of the character and condition of the entire body has at last become a
thing not beyond the reach of rational effort, it is time that
the better paid classes of skilled artisans should seek their
own advantage in common with, and not by the exclusion
of, their fellow-labourers. While they continue to fix their
hopes on hedging themselves in against competition, and
protecting their own wages by shutting out others from
access to their employment, nothing better can be expected
from them than that total absence of any large and generous aims, that almost open disregard of all other objects
than high wages and little work for their own small body,
which were so deplorably evident in the proceedings and
manifestoes of the Amalgamated Society of Engineers during their quarrel with their employers. Success, even if
attainable, in raising up a protected class of working people,
would now be a hindrance, instead of a help, to the
emancipation of the working classes at large.

But though combinations to keep up wages are seldom
effectual, and when effectual, are, for the reasons which I
have assigned, seldom desirable, the right of making the
attempt is one which cannot be refused to any portion of
the working population without great injustice, or without
the probability of fatally misleading them respecting the
circumstances which determine their condition. So long as
combinations to raise wages were prohibited by law, the law
appeared to the operatives to be the real cause of the low
wages which there was no denying that it had done its best
to produce. Experience of strikes has been the best teacher
of the labouring classes on the subject of the relation
between wages and the demand and supply of labour: and

it is most important that this course of instruction should not be disturbed.

It is a great error to condemn, *per se* and absolutely, either trades unions or the collective action of strikes. Even assuming that a strike must inevitably fail whenever it attempts to raise wages above that market rate which is fixed by the demand and supply; demand and supply are not physical agencies, which thrust a given amount of wages into a labourer's hand without the participation of his own will and actions. The market rate is not fixed for him by some self-acting instrument, but is the result of bargaining between human beings—of what Adam Smith calls 'the higgling of the market'; and those who do not 'higgle' will long continue to pay, even over a counter, more than the market price for their purchases. Still more might poor labourers who have to do with rich employers, remain long without the amount of wages which the demand for their labour would justify, unless, in vernacular phrase, they stood out for it: and how can they stand out for terms without organized concert? What chance would any labourer have, who struck singly for an advance of wages? How could he even know whether the state of the market admitted of a rise, except by consultation with his fellows, naturally leading to concerted action? I do not hesitate to say that associations of labourers, of a nature similar to trades unions, far from being a hindrance to a free market for labour, are the necessary instrumentality of that free market; the indispensable means of enabling the sellers of labour to take due care of their own interests under a system of competition. There is an ulterior consideration of much importance, to which attention was for the first time drawn by Professor Fawcett,* in an article in the *Westminster Review.*[1] Experience has at length enabled the more intelligent trades to take a tolerably correct measure of the circumstances on which the success of a strike for an advance of wages depends. The workmen are now nearly as

---

[1] ['Strikes, Their Tendencies and Remedies', *Westminster Review*, NS 18 (July, 1860), 1–23.]

well informed as the master, of the state of the market for his commodities; they can calculate his gains and his expenses, they know when his trade is or is not prosperous, and only when it is, are they ever again likely to strike for higher wages; which wages their known readiness to strike makes their employers for the most part willing, in that case, to concede. The tendency, therefore, of this state of things is to make a rise of wages in any particular trade usually consequent upon a rise of profits, which, as Mr Fawcett observes, is a commencement of that regular participation of the labourers in the profits derived from their labour, every tendency to which, for the reasons stated in a previous chapter,[1] it is so important to encourage, since to it we have chiefly to look for any radical improvement in the social and economical relations between labour and capital. Strikes, therefore, and the trade societies which render strikes possible, are for these various reasons not a mischievous, but on the contrary, a valuable part of the existing machinery of society.

It is, however, an indispensable condition of tolerating combinations, that they should be voluntary. No severity, necessary to the purpose, is too great to be employed against attempts to compel workmen to join a union, or take part in a strike by threats or violence. Mere moral compulsion, by the expression of opinion, the law ought not to interfere with; it belongs to more enlightened opinion to restrain it, by rectifying the moral sentiments of the people. Other questions arise when the combination, being voluntary, proposes to itself objects really contrary to the public good. High wages and short hours are generally good objects, or, at all events, may be so: but in many trades unions, it is among the rules that there shall be no task work, or no difference of pay between the most expert workmen and the most unskilful, or that no member of the union shall earn more than a certain sum per week, in order that there may be more employment for the rest; and the abolition of piece work, under more or less of modification,

---

[1] *Supra,* Bk. V, Ch. VII.

held a conspicuous place among the demands of the Amalgamated Society. These are combinations to effect objects which are pernicious. Their success, even when only partial, is a public mischief; and were it complete, would be equal in magnitude to almost any of the evils arising from bad economical legislation. Hardly anything worse can be said of the worst laws on the subject of industry and its remuneration, consistent with the personal freedom of the labourer, than that they place the energetic and the idle, the skilful and the incompetent, on a level: and this, in so far as it is in itself possible, it is the direct tendency of the regulations of these unions to do. It does not, however, follow as a consequence that the law would be warranted in making the formation of such associations illegal and punishable. Independently of all considerations of constitutional liberty, the best interests of the human race imperatively require that all economical experiments, voluntarily undertaken, should have the fullest licence, and that force and fraud should be the only means of attempting to benefit themselves, which are interdicted to the less fortunate classes of the community.[1]

6. Among the modes of undue exercise of the power of government, on which I have commented in this chapter, I have included only such as rest on theories which have still more or less of footing in the most enlightened countries. I have not spoken of some which have done still greater mischief in times not long past, but which are now generally given up, at least in theory, though enough of them still remains in practice to make it impossible as yet to class them among exploded errors.

[1] Whoever desires to understand the question of Trade Combinations as seen from the point of view of the working people, should make himself acquainted with a pamphlet published in 1860, under the title 'Trades Unions and Strikes, their Philosophy and Intention; by T. J. Dunning, Secretary to the London Consolidated Society of Bookbinders.' There are many opinions in this able tract in which I only partially, and some in which I do not at all, coincide. But there are also many sound arguments, and an instructive exposure of the common fallacies of opponents. Readers of other classes will see with surprise, not only how great a portion of truth the Unions have on their side, but how much less flagrant and condemnable even their errors appear, when seen under the aspect in which it is only natural that the working classes should themselves regard them.

The notion, for example, that a government should choose opinions for the people, and should not suffer any doctrines in politics, morals, law, or religion, but such as it approves, to be printed or publicly professed, may be said to be altogether abandoned as a general thesis. It is now well understood that a régime of this sort is fatal to all prosperity, even of an economical kind: that the human mind when prevented either by fear of the law or by fear of opinion from exercising its faculties freely on the most important subjects, acquires a general torpidity and imbecility, by which, when they reach a certain point, it is disqualified from making any considerable advances even in the common affairs of life, and which, when greater still, make it gradually lose even its previous attainments. There cannot be a more decisive example than Spain and Portugal, for two centuries after the Reformation. The decline of those countries in national greatness, and even in material civilization, while almost all the other nations of Europe were uninterruptedly advancing, has been ascribed to various causes, but there is one which lies at the foundation of them all: the Holy Inquisition, and the system of mental slavery of which it is the symbol.

Yet although these truths are very widely recognized, and freedom both of opinion and of discussion is admitted as an axiom in all free countries, this apparent liberality and tolerance has acquired so little of the authority of a principle, that it is always ready to give way to the dread or horror inspired by some particular sort of opinions. Within the last fifteen or twenty years several individuals have suffered imprisonment, for the public profession, sometimes in a very temperate manner, of disbelief in religion; and it is probable that both the public and the government, at the first panic which arises on the subject of Chartism or Communism, will fly to similar means for checking the propagation of democratic or anti-property doctrines. In this country, however, the effective restraints on mental freedom proceed much less from the law or the government, than from the intolerant temper of the national mind; arising no longer from even as respectable a source as bigotry or fanaticism, but rather from the general habit, both in opinion and conduct, of making adherence to custom the rule of life, and enforcing it, by social penalties, against all persons who, without a party to back them, assert their individual independence.

bigotry of Institutions, but rather from the general habit both in opinion and conduct, of making adherence to custom the rule of life, and enforcing it, by social penalties against all —————————————— back from asserting their —————————————

XI

OF THE GROUNDS AND LIMITS
OF THE *LAISSEZ-FAIRE* OR
NON-INTERFERENCE PRINCIPLE

1. We have now reached the last part of our undertaking; the discussion, so far as suited to this treatise (that is, so far as it is a question of principle, not detail) of the limits of the province of government: the question, to what objects governmental intervention in the affairs of society may or should extend, over and above those which necessarily appertain to it. No subject has been more keenly contested in the present age: the contest, however, has chiefly taken place round certain select points, with only flying excursions into the rest of the field. Those indeed who have discussed any particular question of government interference, such as state education (spiritual or secular), regulation of hours of labour, a public provision for the poor, etc., have often dealt largely in general arguments, far outstretching the special application made of them, and have shown a sufficiently strong bias either in favour of letting things alone, or in favour of meddling; but have seldom declared, or apparently decided in their own minds, how far they would carry either principle. The supporters of interference have been content with asserting a general right and duty on the part of government to intervene, wherever its intervention would be useful: and when those who have been called the *laissez-faire* school* have attempted any definite limitation of the province of government, they have usually restricted it to the protection of person and property against force and fraud; a definition to which neither they nor any one else can deliberately adhere, since it excludes, as has been shown in a preceding chapter,[1] some of the most indispensable and unanimously recognised of the duties of government.

------

[1] *Supra*, Bk. V, Ch. I.

Without professing entirely to supply this deficiency of a general theory, on a question which does not, as I conceive, admit of any universal solution, I shall attempt to afford some little aid towards the resolution of this class of questions as they arise, by examining, in the most general point of view in which the subject can be considered, what are the advantages, and what the evils or inconveniences, of government interference.

We must set out by distinguishing between two kinds of intervention by the government, which, though they may relate to the same subject, differ widely in their nature and effects, and require, for their justification, motives of a very different degree of urgency. The intervention may extend to controlling the free agency of individuals. Government may interdict all persons from doing certain things; or from doing them without its authorization; or may prescribe to them certain things to be done, or a certain manner of doing things which it is left optional with them to do or to abstain from. This is the *authoritative* interference of government. There is another kind of intervention which is not authoritative: when a government, instead of issuing a command and enforcing it by penalties, adopts the course so seldom resorted to by governments, and of which such important use might be made, that of giving advice, and promulgating information; or when, leaving individuals free to use their own means of pursuing any object of general interest, the government, not meddling with them, but not trusting the object solely to their care, establishes, side by side with their arrangements, an agency of its own for a like purpose. Thus, it is one thing to maintain a Church Establishment, and another to refuse toleration to other religions, or to persons professing no religion. It is one thing to provide schools or colleges, and another to require that no person shall act as an instructor of youth without a government licence. There might be a national bank, or a government manufactory, without any monopoly against private banks and manufactories. There might be a post-office, without penalties against the conveyance of letters by other means. There may be a corps of government engineers for civil purposes, while the profession of a civil engineer is free to be adopted by every one. There may be public hospitals, without any restriction upon private medical or surgical practice.

2. It is evident, even at first sight, that the authoritative form of government intervention has a much more limited sphere of legitimate action than the other. It requires a much stronger necessity to justify it in any case; while there are large departments of human life from which it must be unreservedly and imperiously excluded. Whatever theory we adopt respecting the foundation of the social union, and under whatever political institutions we live, there is a circle around every individual human being, which no government, be it that of one, of a few, or of the many, ought to be permitted to overstep: there is a part of the life of every person who has come to years of discretion, within which the individuality of that person ought to reign uncontrolled either by any other individual or by the public collectively. That there is, or ought to be, some space in human existence thus entrenched around, and sacred from authoritative intrusion, no one who professes the smallest regard to human freedom or dignity will call in question: the point to be determined is, where the limit should be placed; how large a province of human life this reserved territory should include. I apprehend that it ought to include all that part which concerns only the life, whether inward or outward, of the individual, and does not affect the interests of others, or affects them only through the moral influence of example. With respect to the domain of the inward consciousness, the thoughts and feelings, and as much of external conduct as is personal only, involving no consequences, none at least of a painful or injurious kind, to other people; I hold that it is allowable in all, and in the more thoughtful and cultivated often a duty, to assert and promulgate, with all the force they are capable of, their opinion of what is good or bad, admirable or contemptible, but not to compel others to conform to that opinion; whether the force used is that of extra-legal coercion, or exerts itself by means of the law.

Even in those portions of conduct which do affect the interest of others, the onus of making out a case always lies on the defenders of legal prohibitions. It is not a merely constructive or presumptive injury to others, which will justify the interference of law with individual freedom. To be prevented from doing what one is inclined to, or from acting according to one's own judgment of what is desirable, is not only always irksome, but always tends, *pro tanto*, to starve the development of some portion of the bodily or mental faculties, either sensitive or active; and unless the conscience of the individual goes freely with the legal restraint, it partakes, either in a great or in a small degree, of the degradation of slavery. Scarcely any degree of utility, short of absolute necessity, will justify a prohibitory regulation, unless it can also be made to recommend itself to the general conscience; unless persons of ordinary good intentions either believe already, or can be induced to believe, that the thing prohibited is a thing which they ought not to wish to do.

It is otherwise with governmental interferences which do not restrain individual free agency. When a government provides means for fulfilling a certain end, leaving individuals free to avail themselves of different means if in their opinion preferable, there is no infringement of liberty, no irksome or degrading restraint. One of the principal objections to government interference is then absent. There is, however, in almost all forms of government agency, one thing which is compulsory; the provision of the pecuniary means. These are derived from taxation; or, if existing in the form of an endowment derived from public property, they are still the cause of as much compulsory taxation as the sale or the annual proceeds of the property would enable to be dispensed with.[1] And the objection necessarily attaching

---

[1] The only cases in which government agency involves nothing of a compulsory nature, are the rare cases in which, without any artificial monopoly, it pays its own expenses. A bridge built with public money, on which tolls are collected sufficient to pay not only all current expenses, but the interest of the original outlay, is one case in point. The government railways in Belgium and Germany are another example. The Post Office, if its monopoly were abolished, and it still paid its expenses, would be another.

to compulsory contributions, is almost always greatly aggravated by the expensive precautions and onerous restrictions, which are indispensable to prevent evasion of a compulsory tax.

3. A second general objection to government agency, is that every increase of the functions devolving on the government is an increase of its power, both in the form of authority, and still more, in the indirect form of influence. The importance of this consideration, in respect to political freedom, has in general been quite sufficiently recognized, at least in England; but many, in latter times, have been prone to think that limitation of the powers of the government is only essential when the government itself is badly constituted; when it does not represent the people, but is the organ of a class, or coalition of classes: and that a government of sufficiently popular constitution might be trusted with any amount of power over the nation, since its power would be only that of the nation over itself. This might be true, if the nation, in such cases, did not practically mean a mere majority of the nation, and if minorities were only capable of oppressing, but not of being oppressed. Experience, however, proves that the depositaries of power who are mere delegates of the people, that is of a majority, are quite as ready (when they think they can count on popular support) as any organs of oligarchy, to assume arbitrary power, and encroach unduly on the liberty of private life. The public collectively is abundantly ready to impose, not only its generally narrow views of its interests, but its abstract opinions, and even its tastes, as laws binding upon individuals. And the present civilization tends so strongly to make the power of persons acting in masses the only substantial power in society, that there never was more necessity for surrounding individual independence of thought, speech, and conduct, with the most powerful defences, in order to maintain that originality of mind and individuality of character, which are the only source of any real progress, and of most of the qualities which make the human race much superior to any herd of animals. Hence it is no less

important in a democratic than in any other government, that all tendency on the part of public authorities to stretch their interference, and assume a power of any sort which can easily be dispensed with, should be regarded with unremitting jealousy. Perhaps this is even more important in a democracy than in any other form of political society; because where public opinion is sovereign, an individual who is oppressed by the sovereign does not, as in most other states of things, find a rival power to which he can appeal for relief, or, at all events, for sympathy.

4. A third general objection to government agency, rests on the principle of the division of labour. Every additional function undertaken by the government, is a fresh occupation imposed upon a body already overcharged with duties. A natural consequence is that most things are ill done; much not done at all, because the government is not able to do it without delays which are fatal to its purpose; that the more troublesome, and less showy, of the functions undertaken, are postponed or neglected, and an excuse is always ready for the neglect; while the heads of the administration have their minds so fully taken up with official details, in however perfunctory a manner superintended, that they have no time or thought to spare for the great interests of the state, and the preparation of enlarged measures of social improvement.

But these inconveniences, though real and serious, result much more from the bad organization of governments, than from the extent and variety of the duties undertaken by them. Government is not a name for some one functionary, or definite number of functionaries: there may be almost any amount of division of labour within the administrative body itself. The evil in question is felt in great magnitude under some of the governments of the Continent, where six or eight men, living at the capital and known by the name of ministers, demand that the whole public business of the country shall pass, or to be supposed to pass, under their individual eye. But the inconvenience would be reduced to a very manageable compass, in a country in which there was a proper distribution of functions between the central and local officers of government, and in which the central body was divided into a sufficient number of departments. When Parliament thought it expedient to confer on the government an inspecting and partially controlling authority over railways, it did not add railways to the department of the Home Minister, but created a Railway Board. When it determined to have a central superintending authority for pauper administration, it established the Poor Law Commission. There are few countries in which a greater number of functions are discharged by public officers, than in some states of the American Union, particularly the New England States: but the division of labour in public business is extreme; most of these officers being not even amenable to any common superior, but performing their duties freely, under the double check of election by their townsmen, and civil as well as criminal responsibility to the tribunals.

It is, no doubt, indispensable to good government that the chiefs of the administration, whether permanent or temporary, should extend a commanding, though general, view over the *ensemble** of all the interests confided, in any degree, to the responsibility of the central power. But with a skilful internal organization of the administrative machine, leaving to subordinates, and as far as possible, to local subordinates, not only the execution, but to a great degree the control, of details; holding them accountable for the results of their acts rather than for the acts themselves, except where these come within the cognizance of the tribunals; taking the most effectual securities for honest and capable appointments; opening a broad path to promotion from the inferior degrees of the administrative scale to the superior; leaving, at each step, to the functionary, a wider range in the origination of measures, so that, in the highest grade of all, deliberation might be concentrated on the great collective interests of the country in each department; if all this were done, the government would not probably be overburthened by any business, in other respects fit to be undertaken by it; though the overburthening would remain as a serious addition to the inconveniences incurred by its undertaking any which was unfit.

5. But though a better organization of governments would greatly diminish the force of the objection to the mere multiplication of their duties, it would still remain true that in all the more advanced communities, the great majority of things are worse done by the intervention of government, than the individuals most interested in the matter would do them, or cause them to be done, if left to themselves. The grounds of this truth are expressed with tolerable exactness in the popular dictum, that people understand their own business and their own interests better, and care for them more, than the government does, or can be expected to do. This maxim holds true throughout the greatest part of the business of life, and wherever it is true we ought to condemn every kind of government intervention that conflicts with it. The inferiority of government agency, for example, in any of the common operations of industry or commerce, is proved by the fact, that it is hardly ever able to maintain itself in equal competition with individual agency, where the individuals possess the requisite degree of industrial enterprise, and can command the necessary assemblage of means. All the facilities which a government enjoys of access to information; all the means which it possesses of remunerating, and therefore of commanding, the best available talent in the market—are not an equivalent for the one great disadvantage of an inferior interest in the result.

It must be remembered, besides, that even if a government were superior in intelligence and knowledge to any single individual in the nation, it must be inferior to all the individuals of the nation taken together. It can neither possess in itself, nor enlist in its service, more than a portion of the acquirements and capacities which the country contains, applicable to any given purpose. There must be many persons equally qualified for the work with those whom the government employs, even if it selects its instruments with no reference to any consideration but their fitness. Now these are the very persons into whose hands, in the cases of most common occurrence, a system of individual agency naturally tends to throw the work, because they are capable of doing it better or on cheaper terms than any other person. So far as this is the case, it is evident that government, by excluding or even by superseding individual agency, either substitutes a less qualified instrumentality for one better qualified, or at any rate substitutes its own mode of accomplishing the work, for all the variety of modes which would be tried by a number of equally qualified persons aiming at the same end; a competition by many degrees more propitious to the progress of improvement, than any uniformity of system.

6. I have reserved for the last place one of the strongest of the reasons against the extension of government agency. Even if the government could comprehend within itself, in each department, all the most eminent intellectual capacity and active talent of the nation, it would not be the less desirable that the conduct of a large portion of the affairs of the society should be left in the hands of the persons immediately interested in them. The business of life is an essential part of the practical education of a people; without which, book and school instruction, though most necessary and salutary, does not suffice to qualify them for conduct, and for the adaptation of means to ends. Instruction is only one of the desiderata of mental improvement; another, almost as indispensable, is a vigorous exercise of the active energies; labour, contrivance, judgment, self-control: and the natural stimulus to these is the difficulties of life. This doctrine is not to be confounded with the complacent optimism, which represents the evils of life as desirable things, because they call forth qualities adapted to combat with evils. It is only because the difficulties exist, that the qualities which combat with them are of any value. As practical beings it is our business to free human life from as many as possible of its difficulties, and not to keep up a stock of them as hunters preserve game, for the exercise of pursuing it. But since the need of active talent and practical judgment in the affairs of life can only be diminished, and not, even on the most favourable supposition, done away with, it is important that those endowments should be cultivated not merely in a select few, but in all, and that the

cultivation should be more varied and complete than most persons are able to find in the narrow sphere of their merely individual interests. A people among whom there is no habit of spontaneous action for a collective interest—who look habitually to their government to command or prompt them in all matters of joint concern—who expect to have everything done for them, except what can be made an affair of mere habit and routine—have their faculties only half developed; their education is defective in one of its most important branches.

Not only is the cultivation of the active faculties by exercise, diffused through the whole community, in itself one of the most valuable of national possessions: it is rendered, not less, but more, necessary, when a high degree of that indispensable culture is systematically kept up in the chiefs and functionaries of the state. There cannot be a combination of circumstances more dangerous to human welfare, than that in which intelligence and talent are maintained at a high standard within a governing corporation, but starved and discouraged outside the pale. Such a system, more completely than any other, embodies the idea of despotism, by arming with intellectual superiority as an additional weapon, those who have already the legal power. It approaches as nearly as the organic difference between human beings and other animals admits, to the government of sheep by their shepherd, without anything like so strong an interest as the shepherd has in the thriving condition of the flock. The only security against political slavery, is the check maintained over governors, by the diffusion of intelligence, activity, and public spirit among the governed. Experience proves the extreme difficulty of permanently keeping up a sufficiently high standard of those qualities; a difficulty which increases, as the advance of civilization and security removes one after another of the hardships, embarrassments, and dangers against which individuals had formerly no resource but in their own strength, skill, and courage. It is therefore of supreme importance that all classes of the community, down to the lowest, should have much to do for themselves; that as great a demand should be made upon their intelligence and virtue as it is in any respect equal to; that the government should not only leave as far as possible to their own faculties the conduct of whatever concerns themselves alone, but should suffer them, or rather encourage them, to manage as many as possible of their joint concerns by voluntary co-operation; since this discussion and management of collective interests is the great school of that public spirit, and the great source of that intelligence of public affairs, which are always regarded as the distinctive character of the public of free countries.

A democratic constitution, not supported by democratic institutions in detail, but confined to the central government, not only is not political freedom, but often creates a spirit precisely the reverse, carrying down to the lowest grade in society the desire and ambition of political domination. In some countries the desire of the people is for not being tyrannized over, but in others it is merely for an equal chance to everybody of tyrannizing. Unhappily this last state of the desires is fully as natural to mankind as the former, and in many of the conditions even of civilized humanity, is far more largely exemplified. In proportion as the people are accustomed to manage their affairs by their own active intervention, instead of leaving them to the government, their desires will turn to repelling tyranny, rather than to tyrannizing: while in proportion as all real initiative and direction resides in the government, and individuals habitually feel and act as under its perpetual tutelage, popular institutions develope in them not the desire of freedom, but an unmeasured appetite for place and power; diverting the intelligence and activity of the country from its principal business, to a wretched competition for the selfish prizes and the petty vanities of office.

7. The preceding are the principal reasons, of a general character, in favour of restricting to the narrowest compass the intervention of a public authority in the business of the community: and few will dispute the more than sufficiency of these reasons, to throw, in every instance, the burthen of making out a strong case, not on those who resist, but on

those who recommend, government interference. *Laissez-
faire*, in short, should be the general practice: every departure from it, unless required by some great good, is a certain
evil.

The degree in which the maxim, even in the cases to which
it is most manifestly applicable, has heretofore been in-
fringed by governments, future ages will probably have
difficulty in crediting. Some idea may be formed of it from
the description of M. Dunoyer[1] of the restraints imposed on
the operations of manufacture under the old government of
France, by the meddling and regulating spirit of legislation.

'La société exerçait sur la fabrication la juridiction la plus
illimitée et la plus arbitraire: elle disposait sans scrupule des
facultés des fabricants; elle décidait qui pourrait travailler,
quelle chose on pourrait faire, quels matériaux on devrait
employer, quels procédés il faudrait suivre, quelles formes
on donnerait aux produits, etc. Il ne suffisait pas de faire
bien, de faire mieux, il fallait faire suivant les règles. Qui ne
connaît ce règlement de 1670, qui préscrivait de saisir et de
clouer au poteau, avec le nom des auteurs, les marchandises
non conformes aux règles tracées, et qui, à la seconde
récidive, voulait que les fabricants y fussent attachés eux-
mêmes? Il ne s'agissait pas de consulter le goût des consom-
mateurs, mais de se conformer aux volontés de la loi. Des
légions d'inspecteurs, de commissaires, de contrôleurs, de
jurés, de gardes, étaient chargés de les faire exécuter; on
brisait les métiers, on brûlait les produits qui n'y étaient pas
conformes: les améliorations étaient punies; on mettait les
inventeurs à l'amende. On soumettait à des règles différen-
tes la fabrication des objets destinés à la consommation
intérieure et celle des produits destinés au commerce étranger.
Un artisan n'était pas le maître de choisir le lieu de son
établissement, ni de travailler en toute saison, ni de travailler
pour tout le monde. Il existe un décret du 30 Mars 1700, qui
borne à dix-huit villes le nombre des lieux où l'on pourra
faire des bas au métier; un arrêt du 18 Juin 1723 enjoint aux
fabricants de Rouen de suspendre leurs travaux du 1er

---

[1] *De la Liberté du Travail*, ii. 353-4.

Juillet au 15 Septembre, afin de faciliter ceux de la récolte; Louis XIV., quand il voulut entreprendre la colonnade du Louvre, défendit aux particuliers d'employer des ouvriers sans sa permission, sous peine de 10,000 livres d'amende, et aux ouvriers de travailler pour les particuliers, sous peine, pour la première fois, de la prison, et pour la seconde, des galères.'*

That these and similar regulations were not a dead letter, and that the officious and vexatious meddling was prolonged down to the French Revolution, we have the testimony of Roland, the Girondist minister.[1] 'I have seen', says he, 'eighty, ninety, a hundred pieces of cotton or woollen stuff cut up, and completely destroyed. I have witnessed similar scenes every week for a number of years. I have seen manufactured goods confiscated; heavy fines laid on the manufacturers; some pieces of fabric were burnt in public places, and at the hours of market: others were fixed to the pillory, with the name of the manufacturer inscribed upon them, and he himself was threatened with the pillory, in case of a second offence. All this was done under my eyes, at Rouen, in conformity with existing regulations, or ministerial orders. What crime deserved so cruel a punishment? Some defects in the materials employed, or in the texture of the fabric, or even in some of the threads of the warp.

'I have frequently seen manufacturers visited by a band of satellites who put all in confusion in their establishments, spread terror in their families, cut the stuffs from the frames, tore off the warp from the looms, and carried them away as proofs of infringement; the manufacturers were summoned, tried, and condemned: their goods confiscated; copies of their judgment of confiscation posted up in every public place; fortune, reputation, credit, all was lost and destroyed. And for what offence? Because they had made of worsted, a kind of cloth called shag, such as the English used to manufacture, and even sell in France, while the French regulations stated that that kind of cloth should be

---

[1] I quote at second hand, from Mr Carey's *Essay on the Rate of Wages* [Philadelphia, 1835], 195–6.

made with mohair. I have seen other manufacturers treated in the same way, because they had made camlets of a particular width, used in England and Germany, for which there was a great demand from Spain, Portugal, and other countries, and from several parts of France, while the French regulations prescribed other widths for camlets.'

The time is gone by, when such applications as these of the principle of 'paternal government' would be attempted, in even the least enlightened country of the European commonwealth of nations. In such cases as those cited, all the general objections to government interference are valid, and several of them in nearly their highest degree. But we must now turn to the second part of our task, and direct our attention to cases, in which some of those general objections are altogether absent, while those which can never be got rid of entirely, are overruled by counter-considerations of still greater importance.

We have observed that, as a general rule, the business of life is better performed when those who have an immediate interest in it are left to take their own course, uncontrolled either by the mandate of the law or by the meddling of any public functionary. The persons, or some of the persons, who do the work, are likely to be better judges than the government, of the means of attaining the particular end at which they aim. Were we to suppose, what is not very probable, that the government has possessed itself of the best knowledge which had been acquired up to a given time by the persons most skilled in the occupation; even then, the individual agents have so much stronger and more direct an interest in the result, that the means are far more likely to be improved and perfected if left to their uncontrolled choice. But if the workman is generally the best selector of means, can it be affirmed with the same universality, that the consumer, or person served, is the most competent judge of the end? Is the buyer always qualified to judge of the commodity? If not, the presumption in favour of the competition of the market does not apply to the case; and if the commodity be one, in the quality of which society has much at stake, the balance of advantages may be in favour of some mode and degree of intervention, by the authorized representatives of the collective interest of the state.

8. Now, the proposition that the consumer is a competent judge of the commodity, can be admitted only with numerous abatements and exceptions. He is generally the best judge (though even this is not true universally) of the material objects produced for his use. These are destined to supply some physical want, or gratify some taste or inclination, respecting which wants or inclinations there is no appeal from the person who feels them; or they are the means and appliances of some occupation, for the use of the persons engaged in it, who may be presumed to be judges of the things required in their own habitual employment. But there are other things, of the worth of which the demand of the market is by no means a test; things of which the utility does not consist in ministering to inclinations, nor in serving the daily uses of life, and the want of which is least felt where the need is greatest. This is peculiarly true of those things which are chiefly useful as tending to raise the character of human beings. The uncultivated cannot be competent judges of cultivation. Those who most need to be made wiser and better, usually desire it least, and if they desired it, would be incapable of finding the way to it by their own lights. It will continually happen, on the voluntary system, that, the end not being desired, the means will not be provided at all, or that, the persons requiring improvement having an imperfect or altogether erroneous conception of what they want, the supply called forth by the demand of the market will be anything but what is really required. Now any well-intentioned and tolerably civilized government may think, without presumption, that it does or ought to possess a degree of cultivation above the average of the community which it rules, and that it should therefore be capable of offering better education and better instruction to the people, than the greater number of them would spontaneously demand. Education, therefore, is one of those things which it is admissible in principle that a government should provide for the people. The case is one

to which the reasons of the non-interference principle do not necessarily or universally extend.[1]

With regard to elementary education, the exception to ordinary rules may, I conceive, justifiably be carried still further. There are certain primary elements and means of knowledge, which it is in the highest degree desirable that all human beings born into the community should acquire during childhood. If their parents, or those on whom they depend, have the power of obtaining for them this instruction, and fail to do it, they commit a double breach of duty, towards the children themselves, and towards the members of the community generally, who are all liable to suffer seriously from the consequences of ignorance and want of education in their fellow-citizens. It is therefore an allowable exercise of the powers of government, to impose on parents the legal obligation of giving elementary instruction

[1] In opposition to these opinions, a writer, with whom on many points I agree, but whose hostility to government intervention seems to me too indiscriminate and unqualified, M. Dunoyer, observes, that instruction, however good in itself, can only be useful to the public in so far as they are willing to receive it, and that the best proof that the instruction is suitable to their wants is its success as a pecuniary enterprise. This argument seems no more conclusive respecting instruction for the mind, than it would be respecting medicine for the body. No medicine will do the patient any good if he cannot be induced to take it; but we are not bound to admit as a corollary from this, that the patient will select the right medicine without assistance. Is it not probable that a recommendation, from any quarter which he respects, may induce him to accept a better medicine than he would spontaneously have chosen? This is, in respect to education, the very point in debate. Without doubt, instruction which is so far in advance of the people that they cannot be induced to avail themselves of it, is to them of no more worth than if it did not exist. But between what they spontaneously choose, and what they will refuse to accept when offered, there is a breadth of interval proportioned to their deference for the recommender. Besides, a thing of which the public are bad judges, may require to be shown to them and pressed on their attention for a long time, and to prove its advantages by long experience, before they learn to appreciate it, yet they may learn at last; which they might never have done, if the thing had not been thus obtruded upon them in act, but only recommended in theory. Now, a pecuniary speculation cannot wait years, or perhaps generations for success; it must succeed rapidly, or not at all. Another consideration which M. Dunoyer seems to have overlooked, is, that institutions and modes of tuition which never could be made sufficiently popular to repay, with a profit, the expenses incurred on them, may be invaluable to the many by giving the highest quality of education to the few, and keeping up the perpetual succession of superior minds, by whom knowledge is advanced, and the community urged forward in civilization.

to children. This, however, cannot fairly be done, without taking measures to insure that such instruction shall be always accessible to them, either gratuitously or at a trifling expense.

It may indeed be objected that the education of children is one of those expenses which parents, even of the labouring class, ought to defray; that it is desirable that they should feel it incumbent on them to provide by their own means for the fulfilment of their duties, and that by giving education at the cost of others, just as much as by giving subsistence, the standard of necessary wages is proportionally lowered, and the springs of exertion and self-restraint in so much relaxed. This argument could, at best, be only valid if the question were that of substituting a public provision for what individuals would otherwise do for themselves; if all parents in the labouring class recognised and practised the duty of giving instruction to their children at their own expense. But inasmuch as parents do not practise this duty, and do not include education among those necessary expenses which their wages must provide for, therefore the general rate of wages is not high enough to bear those expenses, and they must be borne from some other source. And this is not one of the cases in which the tender of help perpetuates the state of things which renders help necessary. Instruction, when it is really such, does not enervate, but strengthens as well as enlarges the active faculties: in whatever manner acquired, its effect on the mind is favourable to the spirit of independence: and when, unless had gratuitously, it would not be had at all, help in this form has the opposite tendency to that which in so many other cases makes it objectionable; it is help towards doing without help.

In England, and most European countries, elementary instruction cannot be paid for, at its full cost, from the common wages of unskilled labour, and would not if it could. The alternative, therefore, is not between government and private speculation, but between a government provision and voluntary charity: between interference by government, and interference by associations of individuals, subscribing their own money for the purpose, like the two great School Societies. It is, of course, not desirable that anything should be done by funds derived from compulsory taxation, which is already sufficiently well done by individual liberality. How far this is the case with school instruction, is, in each particular instance, a question of fact. The education provided in this country on the voluntary principle has of late been so much discussed, that it is needless in this place to criticise it minutely, and I shall merely express my conviction, that even in quantity it is, and is likely to remain, altogether insufficient, while in quality, though with some slight tendency to improvement, it is never good except by some rare accident, and generally so bad as to be little more than nominal. I hold it therefore the duty of the government to supply the defect, by giving pecuniary support to elementary schools, such as to render them accessible to all the children of the poor, either freely, or for a payment too inconsiderable to be sensibly felt.

One thing must be strenuously insisted on; that the government must claim no monopoly for its education, either in the lower or in the higher branches; must exert neither authority nor influence to induce the people to resort to its teachers in preference to others, and must confer no peculiar advantages on those who have been instructed by them. Though the government teachers will probably be superior to the average of private instructors, they will not embody all the knowledge and sagacity to be found in all instructors taken together, and it is desirable to leave open as many roads as possible to the desired end. It is not endurable that a government should, either *de jure* or *de facto*, have a complete control over the education of the people. To possess such a control, and actually exert it, is to be despotic. A government which can mould the opinions and sentiments of the people from their youth upwards, can do with them whatever it pleases. Though a government, therefore, may, and in many cases ought to, establish schools and colleges, it must neither compel nor bribe any person to come to them; nor ought the power of individuals to set up rival establishments, to depend in any degree upon its authorization. It would be justified in requiring from all the people that they shall possess instruction in certain things, but not in prescribing to them how or from whom they shall obtain it.

9. In the matter of education, the intervention of government is justifiable, because the case is not one in which the interest and judgment of the consumer are a sufficient security for the goodness of the commodity. Let us now consider another class of cases, where there is no person in the situation of a consumer, and where the interest and judgment to be relied on are those of the agent himself; as in the conduct of any business in which he is exclusively interested, or in entering into any contract or engagement by which he himself is to be bound.

The ground of the practical principle of non-interference must here be, that most persons take a juster and more intelligent view of their own interest, and of the means of promoting it, than can either be prescribed to them by a general enactment of the legislature, or pointed out in the particular case by a public functionary. The maxim is unquestionably sound as a general rule; but there is no difficulty in perceiving some very large and conspicuous exceptions to it. These may be classed under several heads.

First:—The individual who is presumed to be the best judge of his own interests may be incapable of judging or acting for himself; may be a lunatic, an idiot, an infant: or though not wholly incapable, may be of immature years and judgment. In this case the foundation of the *laissez-faire* principle breaks down entirely. The person most interested is not the best judge of the matter, nor a competent judge at all. Insane persons are everywhere regarded as proper objects of the care of the state.[1] In the case of children and

---

[1] The practice of the English law with respect to insane persons, especially on the all-important point of the ascertainment of insanity, most urgently demands reform. At present no persons, whose property is worth coveting, and whose nearest relations are unscrupulous, or on bad terms with them, are secure against a commission of lunacy. At the instance of the persons who would profit by their

young persons, it is common to say, that though they cannot judge for themselves, they have their parents or other relatives to judge for them. But this removes the question into a different category; making it no longer a question whether the government should interfere with individuals in the direction of their own conduct and interests, but whether it should leave absolutely in their power the conduct and interests of somebody else. Parental power is as susceptible of abuse as any other power, and is, as a matter of fact, constantly abused. If laws do not succeed in preventing parents from brutally ill-treating, and even from murdering their children, far less ought it to be presumed that the interests of children will never be sacrificed, in more commonplace and less revolting ways, to the selfishness or the ignorance of their parents. Whatever it can be clearly seen that parents ought to do or forbear for the interest of children, the law is warranted, if it is able, in compelling to be done or forborne, and is generally bound to do so. To take an example from the peculiar province of political economy; it is right that children, and young persons not yet arrived at maturity, should be protected, so far as the eye and hand of the state can reach, from being over-worked. Labouring for too many hours in the day, or on work beyond their strength, should not be permitted to them, for if permitted it may always be compelled. Freedom of contract, in the case of children, is but

---

being declared insane, a jury may be impanelled and an investigation held at the expense of the property, in which all their personal peculiarities, with all the additions made by the lying gossip of low servants, are poured into the credulous ears of twelve petty shopkeepers, ignorant of all ways of life except those of their own class, and regarding every trait of individuality in character or taste as eccentricity, and all eccentricity as either insanity or wickedness. If this sapient tribunal gives the desired verdict, the property is handed over to perhaps the last persons whom the rightful owner would have desired or suffered to possess it. Some recent instances of this kind of investigation have been a scandal to the administration of justice. Whatever other changes in this branch of law may be made, two at least are imperative: first, that, as in other legal proceedings, the expenses should not be borne by the person on trial, but by the promoters of the inquiry, subject to recovery of costs in case of success: and secondly, that the property of a person declared insane, should in no case be made over to heirs while the proprietor is alive, but should be managed by a public officer until his death or recovery.

another word for freedom of coercion. Education also, the best which circumstances admit of their receiving, is not a thing which parents or relatives, from indifference, jealousy, or avarice, should have it in their power to withhold.

The reasons for legal intervention in favour of children, apply not less strongly to the case of those unfortunate slaves and victims of the most brutal part of mankind, the lower animals. It is by the grossest misunderstanding of the principles of liberty, that the infliction of exemplary punishment on ruffianism practised towards these defence-less creatures, has been treated as a meddling by government with things beyond its province; an interference with domestic life. The domestic life of domestic tyrants is one of the things which it is the most imperative on the law to interfere with; and it is to be regretted that metaphysical scruples respecting the nature and source of the authority of government, should induce many warm supporters of laws against cruelty to animals, to seek for a justification of such laws in the incidental consequences of the indulgence of ferocious habits to the interests of human beings, rather than in the intrinsic merits of the case itself. What it would be the duty of human being, possessed of the requisite physical strength, to prevent by force if attempted in his presence, it cannot be less incumbent on society generally to repress. The existing laws of England on the subject are chiefly defective in the trifling, often almost nominal, maximum, to which the penalty even in the worst cases is limited.

Among those members of the community whose freedom of contract ought to be controlled by the legislature for their own protection, on account (it is said) of their depend-ent position, it is frequently proposed to include women: and in the existing Factory Acts, their labour, in common with that of young persons, has been placed under peculiar restrictions. But the classing together, for this and other purposes, of women and children, appears to me both indefensible in principle and mischievous in practice. Chil-dren below a certain age *cannot* judge or act for themselves; up to a considerably greater age they are inevitably more or

less disqualified for doing so; but women are as capable as
men of appreciating and managing their own concerns, and
the only hindrance to their doing so arises from the injustice
of their present social position. When the law makes everything which the wife acquires, the property of the husband,
while by compelling her to live with him it forces her to
submit to almost any amount of moral and even physical
tyranny which he may choose to inflict, there is some ground
for regarding every act done by her as done under coercion:
but it is the great error of reformers and philanthropists in
our time, to nibble at the consequences of unjust power,
instead of redressing the injustice itself. If women had a
absolute a control as men have, over their own persons and
their own patrimony or acquisitions, there would be no plea
for limiting their hours of labouring for themselves, in order
that they might have time to labour for the husband, in
what is called, by the advocates of restriction, *his* home.
Women employed in factories are the only women in the
labouring rank of life whose position is not that of slaves
and drudges; precisely because they cannot easily be compelled to work and earn wages in factories against their
will. For improving the condition of women, it should, on
the contrary, be an object to give them the readiest access
to independent industrial employment, instead of closing,
either entirely or partially, that which is already open
to them.

10. A second exception to the doctrine that individuals
are the best judges of their own interest, is when an
individual attempts to decide irrevocably now, what will be
best for his interest at some future and distant time. The
presumption in favour of individual judgment is only legitimate, where the judgment is grounded on actual, and
especially on present, personal experience; not where it is
formed antecedently to experience, and not suffered to be
reversed even after experience has condemned it. When
persons have bound themselves by a contract, not simply to
do some one thing, but to continue doing something for
ever or for a prolonged period, without any power of

revoking the engagement, the presumption which their perseverance in that course of conduct would otherwise raise in favour of its being advantageous to them, does not exist; and any such presumption which can be grounded on their having voluntarily entered into the contract, perhaps at an early age, and without any real knowledge of what they undertook, is commonly next to null. The practical maxim of leaving contracts free, is not applicable without great limitations in case of engagements in perpetuity; and the law should be extremely jealous of such engagements; should refuse its sanction to them, when the obligations they impose are such as the contracting party cannot be a competent judge of; if it ever does sanction them, it should take every possible security for their being contracted with foresight and deliberation; and in compensation for not permitting the parties themselves to revoke their engagement, should grant them a release from it, on a sufficient case being made out before an impartial authority. These considerations are eminently applicable to marriage, the most important of all cases of engagement for life.

11. The third exception which I shall notice, to the doctrine that government cannot manage the affairs of individuals as well as the individuals themselves, has reference to the great class of cases in which the individuals can only manage the concern by delegated agency, and in which the so-called private management is, in point of fact, hardly better entitled to be called management by the persons interested, than administration by a public officer. Whatever, if left to spontaneous agency, can only be done by joint-stock associations, will often be as well, and sometimes better done, as far as the actual work is concerned, by the state. Government management is, indeed, proverbially jobbing, careless, and ineffective, but so likewise has generally been joint-stock management. The directors of a joint-stock company, it is true, are always shareholders; but also the members of a government are invariably taxpayers; and in the case of directors, no more than in that of govern-

ments, is their proportional share of the benefits of good management, equal to the interest they may possibly have in mismanagement, even without reckoning the interest of their ease. It may be objected, that the shareholders, in their collective character, exercise a certain control over the directors, and have almost always full power to remove them from office. Practically, however, the difficulty of exercising this power is found to be so great, that it is hardly ever exercised except in cases of such flagrantly unskilful, or, at least, unsuccessful management, as would generally produce the ejection from office of managers appointed by the government. Against the very ineffectual security afforded by meetings of shareholders, and by their individual inspection and inquiries, may be placed the greater publicity and more active discussion and comment, to be expected in free countries with regard to affairs in which the general government takes part. The defects, therefore, of government management, do not seem to be necessarily much greater, if necessarily greater at all, than those of management by joint-stock.

The true reasons in favour of leaving to voluntary associations all such things as they are competent to perform, would exist in equal strength if it were certain that the work itself would be as well or better done by public officers. These reasons have been already pointed out: the mischief of overloading the chief functionaries of government with demands on their attention, and diverting them from duties which they alone can discharge, to objects which can be sufficiently well attained without them; the danger of unnecessarily swelling the direct power and indirect influence of government, and multiplying occasions of collision between its agents and private citizens; and the inexpediency of concentrating in a dominant bureaucracy, all the skill and experience in the management of large interests, and all the power of organized action, existing in the community; a practice which keeps the citizens in a relation to the government like that of children to their guardians, and is a main cause of the inferior capacity for political life which has hitherto characterized the over-governed countries of the

Continent, whether with or without the forms of representative government.[1]

But although, for these reasons, most things which are likely to be even tolerably done by voluntary associations, should, generally speaking, be left to them; it does not follow that the manner in which those associations perform their work should be entirely uncontrolled by the government. There are many cases in which the agency, of whatever nature, by which a service is performed, is certain, from the nature of the case, to be virtually single; in which a practical monopoly, with all the power it confers of taxing the community, cannot be prevented from existing. I have already more than once adverted to the case of the gas and water companies, among which, though perfect freedom is allowed to competition, none really takes place, and practically they are found to be even more irresponsible, and unapproachable by individual complaints, than the government. There are the expenses without the advantages of plurality of agency; and the charge made for services which cannot be dispensed with, is, in substance, quite as much compulsory taxation as if imposed by law; there are few householders who make any distinction between their 'water rate' and their other local taxes. In the case of these particular services, the reasons preponderate in favour of their being performed, like the paving and cleansing of the streets, not certainly by the general government of the state, but by the municipal authorities of the town, and the expense defrayed, as even now it in fact is, by a local rate. But in the many analogous cases which it is best to resign

---

[1] A parallel case may be found in the distaste for politics, and absence of public spirit, by which women, as a class, are characterized in the present state of society, and which is often felt and complained of by political reformers, without, in general, making them willing to recognize, or desirous to remove, its cause. It obviously arises from their being taught, both by institutions and by the whole of their education, to regard themselves as entirely apart from politics. Wherever they have been politicians, they have shown as great interest in the subject, and as great aptitude for it, according to the spirit of their time, as the men with whom they were cotemporaries: in that period of history (for example) in which Isabella of Castile and Elizabeth of England were, not rare exceptions, but merely brilliant examples of a spirit and capacity very largely diffused among women of high station and cultivation in Europe.

to voluntary agency, the community needs some other security for the fit performance of the service than the interest of the managers; and it is the part of government, either to subject the business to reasonable conditions for the general advantage, or to retain such power over it, that the profits of the monopoly may at least be obtained for the public. This applies to the case of a road, a canal, or a railway. These are always, in a great degree, practical monopolies; and a government which concedes such monopoly unreservedly to a private company, does much the same thing as if it allowed an individual or an association to levy any tax they chose, for their own benefit, on all the malt produced in the country, or on all the cotton imported into it. To make the concession for a limited time is generally justifiable, on the principle which justifies patents for inventions: but the state should either reserve to itself a reversionary property in such public works, or should retain, and freely exercise, the right of fixing a maximum of fares and charges, and, from time to time, varying that maximum. It is perhaps necessary to remark, that the state may be the proprietor of canals or railways without itself working them; and that they will almost always be better worked by means of a company, renting the railway or canal for a limited period from the state.

12. To a fourth case of exception I must request particular attention, it being one to which, as it appears to me, the attention of political economists has not yet been sufficiently drawn. There are matters in which the interference of law is required, not to overrule the judgment of individuals respecting their own interest, but to give effect to that judgment: they being unable to give effect to it except by concert, which concert again cannot be effectual unless it receives validity and sanction from the law. For illustration, and without prejudging the particular point, I may advert to the question of diminishing the hours of labour. Let us suppose, what is at least supposable, whether it be the fact or not—that a general reduction of the hours of factory labour, say from ten to nine, would be for the advantage of

the work-people: that they would receive as high wages, or nearly as high, for nine hours' labour as they receive for ten. If this would be the result, and if the operatives generally are convinced that it would, the limitation, some may say, will be adopted spontaneously. I answer, that it will not be adopted unless the body of operatives bind themselves to one another to abide by it. A workman who refused to work more than nine hours while there were others who worked ten, would either not be employed at all, or if employed, must submit to lose one-tenth of his wages. However convinced, therefore, he may be that it is the interest of the class to work short time, it is contrary to his own interest to set the example, unless he is well assured that all or most others will follow it. But suppose a general agreement of the whole class: might not this be effectual without the sanction of law? Not unless enforced by opinion with a rigour practically equal to that of law. For however beneficial the observance of the regulation might be to the class collectively, the immediate interest of every individual would lie in violating it: and the more numerous those were who adhered to the rule, the more would individuals gain by departing from it. If nearly all restricted themselves to nine hours, those who chose to work for ten would gain all the advantages of the restriction, together with the profit of infringing it; they would get ten hours' wages for nine hours' work, and an hour's wages besides. I grant that if a large majority adhered to the nine hours, there would be no harm done: the benefit would be, in the main, secured to the class, while those individuals who preferred to work harder and earn more, would have an opportunity of doing so. This certainly would be the state of things to be wished for; and assuming that a reduction of hours without any diminution of wages could take place without expelling the commodity from some of its markets—which is in every particular instance a question of fact, not of principle—the manner in which it would be most desirable that this effect should be brought about, would be by a quiet change in the general custom of the trade; short hours becoming, by spontaneous choice, the general practice, but those who chose to deviate from it having the fullest liberty to do so. Probably, however, so many would prefer the ten hours' work on the improved terms, that the limitation could not be maintained as a general practice: what some did from choice, others would soon be obliged to do from necessity, and those who had chosen long hours for the sake of increased wages, would be forced in the end to work long hours for no greater wages than before. Assuming then that it really would be the interest of each to work only nine hours if he could be assured that all others would do the same, there might be no means of their attaining this object but by converting their supposed mutual agreement into an engagement under penalty, by consenting to have it enforced by law. I am not expressing any opinion in favour of such an enactment, which has never in this country been demanded, and which I certainly should not, in present circumstances, recommend: but it serves to exemplify the manner in which classes of persons may need the assistance of law, to give effect to their deliberate collective opinion of their own interest, by affording to every individual a guarantee that his competitors will pursue the same course, without which he cannot safely adopt it himself.

Another exemplification of the same principle is afforded by what is known as the Wakefield system of colonization. This system is grounded on the important principle, that the degree of productiveness of land and labour depends on their being in a due proportion to one another; that if a few persons in a newly-settled country attempt to occupy and appropriate a large district, or if each labourer becomes too soon an occupier and cultivator of land, there is a loss of productive power, and a great retardation of the progress of the colony in wealth and civilization: that nevertheless the instinct (as it may almost be called) of appropriation, and the feelings associated in old countries with landed proprietorship, induce almost every emigrant to take possession of as much land as he has the means of acquiring, and every labourer to become at once a proprietor, cultivating his own land with no other aid than that of his family. If this propensity to the immediate possession of land could be in some degree restrained, and each labourer induced to work a certain number of years on hire before he became a landed proprietor, a perpetual stock of hired labourers could be maintained, available for roads, canals, works of irrigation, etc., and for the establishment and carrying on of the different branches of town industry; whereby the labourer, when he did at last become a landed proprietor, would find his land much more valuable, through access to markets, and facility of obtaining hired labour. Mr Wakefield therefore proposed to check the premature occupation of land, and dispersion of the people, by putting upon all unappropriated lands a rather high price, the proceeds of which were to be expended in conveying emigrant labourers from the mother country.

This salutary provision, however, has been objected to, in the name and on the authority of what was represented as the great principle of political economy, that individuals are the best judges of their own interest. It was said, that when things are left to themselves, land is appropriated and occupied by the spontaneous choice of individuals, in the quantities and at the times most advantageous to each person, and therefore to the community generally; and that to interpose artificial obstacles to their obtaining land, is to prevent them from adopting the course which in their own judgment is most beneficial to them, from a self-conceited notion of the legislator, that he knows what is most for their interest, better than they do themselves. Now this is a complete misunderstanding, either of the system itself, or of the principle with which it is alleged to conflict. The oversight is similar to that which we have just seen exemplified on the subject of hours of labour. However beneficial it might be to the colony in the aggregate, and to each individual composing it, that no one should occupy more land than he can properly cultivate, nor become a proprietor until there are other labourers ready to take his place in working for hire; it can never be the interest of an individual to exercise this forbearance, unless he is assured that others will do so too. Surrounded by settlers who have each their thousand acres, how is he benefited by restricting himself to

fifty? or what does a labourer gain by deferring the acquisition altogether for a few years, if all other labourers rush to
convert their first earnings into estates in the wilderness,
several miles apart from one another? If they, by seizing on
land, prevent the formation of a class of labourers for
wages, he will not, by postponing the time of his becoming
a proprietor, be enabled to employ the land with any greater
advantage when he does obtain it; to what end therefore
should he place himself in what will appear to him and others
a position of inferiority, by remaining a hired labourer,
when all around him are proprietors? It is the interest of
each to do what is good for all, but only if others will do
likewise.

The principle that each is the best judge of his own
interest, understood as these objectors understand it, would
prove that governments ought not to fulfil any of their
acknowledged duties—ought not, in fact, to exist at all. It
is greatly the interest of the community, collectively and
individually, not to rob or defraud one another: but there is
not the less necessity for laws to punish robbery and fraud;
because, though it is the interest of each that nobody should
rob or cheat, it is not any one's interest to refrain from
robbing and cheating others when all others are permitted
to rob and cheat him. Penal laws exist at all, chiefly for this
reason—because even an unanimous opinion that a certain
line of conduct is for the general interest, does not always
make it people's individual interest to adhere to that line of
conduct.

13. Fifthly; the argument against governmental interference grounded on the maxim that individuals are the best
judges of their own interest, cannot apply to the very large
class of cases, in which those acts of individuals with which
the government claims to interfere, are not done by those
individuals for their own interest, but for the interest of
other people. This includes, among other things, the important and much agitated subject of public charity. Though
individuals should, in general, be left to do for themselves
whatever it can reasonably be expected that they should be

capable of doing, yet when they are at any rate not to be left to themselves, but to be helped by other people, the question arises whether it is better that they should receive this help exclusively from individuals, and therefore uncertainly and casually, or by systematic arrangements, in which society acts through its organ, the state.

This brings us to the subject of Poor Laws; a subject which would be of very minor importance if the habits of all classes of the people were temperate and prudent, and the diffusion of property satisfactory; but of the greatest moment in a state of things so much the reverse of this, in both points, as that which the British islands present.

Apart from any metaphysical considerations respecting the foundation of morals or of the social union, it will be admitted to be right that human beings should help one another; and the more so, in proportion to the urgency of the need: and none needs help so urgently as one who is starving. The claim to help, therefore, created by destitution, is one of the strongest which can exist; and there is prima facie the amplest reason for making the relief of so extreme an exigency as certain to those who require it, as by any arrangements of society it can be made.

On the other hand, in all cases of helping, there are two sets of consequences to be considered; the consequences of the assistance itself, and the consequences of relying on the assistance. The former are generally beneficial, but the latter, for the most part, injurious; so much so, in many cases, as greatly to outweigh the value of the benefit. And this is never more likely to happen than in the very cases where the need of help is the most intense. There are few things for which it is more mischievous that people should rely on the habitual aid of others, than for the means of subsistence, and unhappily there is no lesson which they more easily learn. The problem to be solved is therefore one of peculiar nicety as well as importance; how to give the greatest amount of needful help, with the smallest encouragement to undue reliance on it.

Energy and self-dependence are, however, liable to be impaired by the absence of help, as well as by its excess. It is even more fatal to exertion to have no hope of succeeding by it, than to be assured of succeeding without it. When the condition of any one is so disastrous that his energies are paralyzed by discouragement, assistance is a tonic, not a sedative: it braces instead of deadening the active faculties: always provided that the assistance is not such as to dispense with self-help, by substituting itself for the person's own labour, skill, and prudence, but is limited to affording him a better hope of attaining success by those legitimate means. This accordingly is a test to which all plans of philanthropy and benevolence should be brought, whether intended for the benefit of individuals or of classes, and whether conducted on the voluntary or on the government principle.

In so far as the subject admits of any general doctrine or maxim, it would appear to be this—that if assistance is given in such a manner that the condition of the person helped is as desirable as that of the person who succeeds in doing the same thing without help, the assistance, if capable of being previously calculated on, is mischievous: but if, while available to everybody, it leaves to every one a strong motive to do without it if he can, it is then for the most part beneficial. This principle, applied to a system of public charity, is that of the Poor Law of 1834.* If the condition of a person receiving relief is made as eligible as that of the labourer who supports himself by his own exertions, the system strikes at the root of all individual industry and self-government; and, if fully acted up to, would require as its supplement an organized system of compulsion, for governing and setting to work like cattle, those who had been removed from the influence of the motives that act on human beings. But if, consistently with guaranteeing all persons against absolute want, the condition of those who are supported by legal charity can be kept considerably less desirable than the condition of those who find support for themselves, none but beneficial consequences can arise from a law which renders it impossible for any person, except by his own choice, to die from insufficiency of food. That in England at least this supposition can be realized, is proved by the experience of a long period preceding the close of the last century, as well as by that of many highly pauperized districts in more recent times, which have been dispauperized by adopting strict rules of poor-law administration, to the great and permanent benefit of the whole labouring class. There is probably no country in which, by varying the means suitably to the character of the people, a legal provision for the destitute might not be made compatible with the observance of the conditions necessary to its being innocuous.

Subject to these conditions, I conceive it to be highly desirable, that the certainty of subsistence should be held out by law to the destitute able-bodied, rather than that their relief should depend on voluntary charity. In the first place, charity almost always does too much or too little: it lavishes its bounty in one place, and leaves people to starve in another. Secondly, since the state must necessarily provide subsistence for the criminal poor while undergoing punishment, not to do the same for the poor who have not offended is to give a premium on crime. And lastly, if the poor are left to individual charity, a vast amount of mendicity is inevitable. What the state may and should abandon to private charity, is the task of distinguishing between one case of real necessity and another. Private charity can give more to the more deserving. The state must act by general rules. It cannot undertake to discriminate between the deserving and the undeserving indigent. It owes no more than subsistence to the first, and can give no less to the last. What is said about the injustice of a law which has no better treatment for the merely unfortunate poor than for the ill-conducted, is founded on a misconception of the province of law and public authority. The dispensers of public relief have no business to be inquisitors. Guardians and overseers are not fit to be trusted to give or withhold other people's money according to their verdict on the morality of the person soliciting it; and it would show much ignorance of the ways of mankind to suppose that such persons, even in the almost impossible case of their being qualified, will take the trouble of ascertaining and sifting the past conduct of a person in distress, so as to form a rational judgment on it. Private charity can make these distinctions; and in bestowing its own money, is entitled to do so according to its own judgment. It should understand that this is its peculiar and appropriate province, and that it is commendable or the contrary, as it exercises the function with more or less discernment. But the administrators of a public fund ought not to be required to do more for anybody, than that minimum which is due even to the worst. If they are, the indulgence very speedily becomes the rule, and refusal the more or less capricious or tyrannical exception.

14. Another class of cases which fall within the same general principle as the case of public charity, are those in which the acts done by individuals, though intended solely for their own benefit, involve consequences extending indefinitely beyond them, to interests of the nation or of posterity, for which society in its collective capacity is alone able, and alone bound, to provide. One of these cases is that of Colonization. If it is desirable, as no one will deny it to be, that the planting of colonies should be conducted, not with an exclusive view to the private interests of the first founders, but with a deliberate regard to the permanent welfare of the nations afterwards to arise from these small beginnings; such regard can only be secured by placing the enterprise, from its commencement, under regulations constructed with the foresight and enlarged views of philosophical legislators; and the government alone has power either to frame such regulations, or to enforce their observance.

The question of government intervention in the work of Colonization involves the future and permanent interests of civilization itself, and far outstretches the comparatively narrow limits of purely economical considerations. But even with a view to those considerations alone, the removal of population from the overcrowded to the unoccupied parts of the earth's surface is one of those works of eminent social usefulness, which most require, and which at the same time best repay, the intervention of government.

To appreciate the benefits of colonization, it should be considered in its relation, not to a single country, but to the collective economical interests of the human race. The question is in general treated too exclusively as one of distribution; of relieving one labour market and supplying another. It is this, but it is also a question of production, and of the most efficient employment of the productive resources of the world. Much has been said of the good economy of importing commodities from the place where they can be bought cheapest; while the good economy of producing them where they can be produced cheapest, is comparatively little thought of. If to carry consumable goods from the places where they are superabundant to those where they are scarce, is a good pecuniary speculation, is it not an equally good speculation to do the same thing with regard to labour and instruments? The exportation of labourers and capital from old to new countries, from a place where their productive power is less, to a place where it is greater, increases by so much the aggregate produce of the labour and capital of the world. It adds to the joint wealth of the old and the new country, what amounts in a short period to many times the mere cost of effecting the transport. There needs be no hesitation in affirming that Colonization, in the present state of the world, is the best affair of business, in which the capital of an old and wealthy country can engage.

It is equally obvious, however, that Colonization on a great scale can be undertaken, as an affair of business, only by the government, or by some combination of individuals in complete understanding with the government; except under such very peculiar circumstances as those which succeeded the Irish famine. Emigration on the voluntary principle rarely has any material influence in lightening the pressure of population in the old country, though as far as it goes it is doubtless a benefit to the colony. Those labouring persons who voluntarily emigrate are seldom the very poor; they are small farmers with some little capital, or labourers who have saved something, and who, in removing only their own labour from the crowded labour-market, withdraw from the capital of the country a fund which maintained and employed more labourers than themselves. Besides, this portion of the community is so limited in number, that it might be removed entirely, without making any sensible impression upon the numbers of the population, or even upon the annual increase. Any considerable emigration of labour is only practicable, when its cost is defrayed, or at least advanced, by others than the emigrants themselves. Who then is to advance it? Naturally, it may be said, the capitalists of the colony, who require the labour, and who intend to employ it. But to this there is the obstacle, that a capitalist, after going to the expense of carrying out labourers, has no security that he shall be the person to derive any benefit from them. If all the capitalists of the colony were to combine, and bear the expense by subscription, they would still have no security that the labourers, when there, would continue to work for them. After working for a short time and earning a few pounds, they always, unless prevented by the government, squat on unoccupied land, and work only for themselves. The experiment has been repeatedly tried whether it was possible to enforce contracts for labour, or the repayment of the passage money of emigrants to those who advanced it, and the trouble and expense have always exceeded the advantage. The only other resource is the voluntary contributions of parishes or individuals, to rid themselves of surplus labourers who are already, or who are likely to become, locally chargeable on the poor-rate. Were this speculation to become general, it might produce a sufficient amount of emigration to clear off the existing unemployed population, but not to raise the wages of the employed: and the same thing would require to be done over again in less than another generation.

One of the principal reasons why Colonization should be a national undertaking, is that in this manner alone, save in highly exceptional cases, can emigration be self-supporting. The exportation of capital and labour to a new country being, as before observed, one of the best of all affairs of business, it is absurd that it should not, like other affairs of business, repay its own expenses. Of the great addition which it makes to the produce of the world, there can be no reason why a sufficient portion should not be intercepted, and employed in reimbursing the outlay incurred in effecting it. For reasons already given, no individual, or body of individuals, can reimburse themselves for the expense; the government, however, can. It can take from the annual increase of wealth, caused by the emigration, the fraction which suffices to repay with interest what the emigration has cost. The expenses of emigration to a colony ought to be borne by the colony; and this, in general, is only possible when they are borne by the colonial government.

Of the modes in which a fund for the support of colonization can be raised in the colony, none is comparable in advantage to that which was first suggested, and so ably and perseveringly advocated, by Mr Wakefield: the plan of putting a price on all unoccupied land, and devoting the proceeds to emigration. The unfounded and pedantic objections to this plan have been answered in a former part of this chapter: we have now to speak of its advantages. First, it avoids the difficulties and discontents incident to raising a large annual amount by taxation; a thing which it is almost useless to attempt with a scattered population of settlers in the wilderness, who, as experience proves, can seldom be compelled to pay direct taxes, except at a cost exceeding their amount; while in an infant community indirect taxation soon reaches its limit. The sale of lands is thus by far the easiest mode of raising the requisite funds. But it has other and still greater recommendations. It is a beneficial check upon the tendency of a population of colonists to adopt the tastes and inclinations of savage life, and to disperse so widely as to lose all the advantages of commerce, of markets, of separation of employments, and combination of labour. By making it necessary for those who emigrate at the expense of the fund, to earn a considerable sum before they can become landed proprietors, it keeps up a perpetual succession of labourers for hire, who in every country are a most important auxiliary even to peasant proprietors: and by diminishing the eagerness of agricultural speculators to add to their domain, it keeps the settlers within reach of each other for purposes of co-operation, arranges a numerous body of them within easy distance of each centre of foreign commerce and non-agricultural industry, and insures the formation and rapid growth of towns and town products. This concentration, compared with the dispersion which uniformly occurs when unoccupied land can be had for nothing, greatly accelerates the attainment of prosperity, and enlarges the fund which may be drawn upon for further emigration. Before the adoption of the Wakefield system, the early years of all new colonies were full of hardship and difficulty: the last colony founded on the old principle, the Swan River settlement, being one of the most characteristic instances. In all subsequent colonization, the Wakefield principle has been acted upon, though imperfectly, a part only of the proceeds of the sale of land being devoted to emigration: yet wherever it has been introduced at all, as in South Australia, Victoria, and New Zealand, the restraint put upon the dispersion of the settlers, and the influx of capital caused by the assurance of being able to obtain hired labour, has, in spite of many difficulties and much mismanagement, produced a suddenness and rapidity of prosperity more like fable than reality.[1]

The self-supporting system of colonization, once established, would increase in efficiency every year; its effect would tend to increase in geometrical progression: for since every able-bodied emigrant, until the country is fully peopled, adds in a very short time to its wealth, over and above his own consumption, as much as would defray the expense of bringing out another emigrant, it follows that the greater the number already sent, the greater number might continue

[1] The objections which have been made, with so much virulence, in some of these colonies, to the Wakefield system, apply, in so far as they have any validity, not to the principle, but to some provisions which are no part of the system, and have been most unnecessarily and improperly engrafted on it; such as the offering only a limited quantity of land for sale, and that by auction, and in lots of not less than 640 acres, instead of selling all land which is asked for, and allowing to the buyer unlimited freedom of choice, both as to quantity and situation, at a fixed price.

to be sent, each emigrant laying the foundation of a succession of other emigrants at short intervals without fresh expense, until the colony is filled up. It would therefore be worth while, to the mother country, to accelerate the early stages of this progression, by loans to the colonies for the purpose of emigration, repayable from the fund formed by the sales of land. In thus advancing the means of accomplishing a large immediate emigration, it would be investing that amount of capital in the mode, of all others, most beneficial to the colony; and the labour and savings of these emigrants would hasten the period at which a large sum would be available from sales of land. It would be necessary, in order not to overstock the labour market, to act in concert with the persons disposed to remove their own capital to the colony. The knowledge that a large amount of hired labour would be available, in so productive a field of employment, would insure a large emigration of capital from a country, like England, of low profits and rapid accumulation: and it would only be necessary not to send out a greater number of labourers at one time, than this capital could absorb and employ at high wages.

Inasmuch as, on this system, any given amount of expenditure, once incurred, would provide not merely a single emigration, but a perpetually flowing stream of emigrants, which would increase in breadth and depth as it flowed on; this mode of relieving overpopulation has a recommendation, not possessed by any other plan ever proposed for making head against the consequences of increase without restraining the increase itself: there is an element of indefiniteness in it; no one can perfectly foresee how far its influence, as a vent for surplus population, might possibly reach. There is hence the strongest obligation on the government of a country like our own, with a crowded population, and unoccupied continents under its command, to build, as it were, and keep open, in concert with the colonial governments, a bridge from the mother country to those continents, by establishing the self-supporting system of colonization on such a scale, that as great an amount of emigration as the colonies can at the time accomodate, may at all times be able to take place without cost to the emigrants themselves.

The importance of these considerations, as regards the British islands, has been of late considerably diminished by the unparalleled amount of spontaneous emigration from Ireland; an emigration not solely of small farmers, but of the poorest class of agricultural labourers, and which is at once voluntary and self-supporting, the succession of emigrants being kept up by funds contributed from the earnings of their relatives and connexions who had gone before. To this has been added a large amount of voluntary emigration to the seats of the gold discoveries, which has partly supplied the wants of our most distant colonies, where, both for local and national interests, it was most of all required. But the stream of both these emigrations has already considerably slackened, and though that from Ireland has since partially revived, it is not certain that the aid of government in a systematic form, and on the self-supporting principle, will not again become necessary to keep the communication open between the hands needing work in England, and the work which needs hands elsewhere.

15. The same principle which points out colonization, and the relief of the indigent, as cases to which the principal objection to government interference does not apply, extends also to a variety of cases, in which important public services are to be performed, while yet there is no individual specially interested in performing them, nor would any adequate remuneration naturally or spontaneously attend their performance. Take for instance a voyage of geographical or scientific exploration. The information sought may be of great public value, yet no individual would derive any benefit from it which would repay the expense of fitting out the expedition; and there is no mode of intercepting the benefit on its way to those who profit by it, in order to levy a toll for the remuneration of its authors. Such voyages are, or might be, undertaken by private subscription; but this is a rare and precarious resource. Instances are more frequent in which the expense has been borne by public companies

or philanthropic associations; but in general such enterprises have been conducted at the expense of government,
which is thus enabled to entrust them to the persons in its
judgment best qualified for the task. Again, it is a proper
office of government to build and maintain lighthouses,
establish buoys, etc. for the security of navigation: for since
it is impossible that the ships at sea which are benefited by
a lighthouse, should be made to pay a toll on the occasion
of its use, no one would build lighthouses from motives of
personal interest, unless indemnified and rewarded from a
compulsory levy made by the state. There are many scientific researches, of great value to a nation and to mankind,
requiring assiduous devotion of time and labour, and not
unfrequently great expense, by persons who can obtain a
high price for their services in other ways. If the government
had no power to grant indemnity for expense, and remuneration for time and labour thus employed, such researches
could only be undertaken by the very few persons who, with
an independent fortune, unite technical knowledge, labori-
ous habits, and either great public spirit, or an ardent desire
of scientific celebrity.

Connected with this subject is the question of providing,
by means of endowments or salaries, for the maintenance
of what has been called a learned class. The cultivation of
speculative knowledge, though one of the most useful of all
employments, is a service rendered to a community collectively, not individually, and one consequently for which it is,
prima facie, reasonable that the community collectively
should pay; since it gives no claim on any individual for a
pecuniary remuneration; and unless a provision is made for
such services from some public fund, there is not only no
encouragement to them, but there is as much discouragement as is implied in the impossibility of gaining a living by
such pursuits, and the necessity consequently imposed on
most of those who would be capable of them, to employ the
greatest part of their time in gaining a subsistence. The evil,
however, is greater in appearance than in reality. The
greatest things, it has been said, have generally been done
by those who had the least time at their disposal; and the

occupation of some hours every day in a routine employment, has often been found compatible with the most brilliant achievements in literature and philosophy. Yet there are investigations and experiments which require not only a long but a continuous devotion of time and attention: there are also occupations which so engross and fatigue the mental faculties, as to be inconsistent with any vigorous employment of them upon other subjects, even in intervals of leisure. It is highly desirable, therefore, that there should be a mode of insuring to the public the services of scientific discoverers, and perhaps of some other classes of savants, by affording them the means of support consistently with devoting a sufficient portion of time to their peculiar pursuits. The fellowships of the Universities are an institution excellently adapted for such a purpose; but are hardly ever applied to it, being bestowed, at the best, as a reward for past proficiency, in committing to memory what has been done by others, and not as the salary of future labours in the advancement of knowledge. In some countries, Academies of science, antiquities, history, etc., have been formed, with emoluments annexed. The most effectual plan, and at the same time least liable to abuse, seems to be that of conferring Professorships, with duties of instruction attached to them. The occupation of teaching a branch of knowledge, at least in its higher departments, is a help rather than an impediment to the systematic cultivation of the subject itself. The duties of a professorship almost always leave much time for original researches; and the greatest advances which have been made in the various sciences, both moral and physical, have originated with those who were public teachers of them; from Plato and Aristotle to the great names of the Scotch, French, and German Universities. I do not mention the English, because until very lately their professorships have been, as is well known, little more than nominal. In the case, too, of a lecturer in a great institution of education, the public at large has the means of judging, if not the quality of the teaching, at least the talents and industry of the teacher; and it is more difficult to misemploy the power of appointment to such an office, than to job in pensions and salaries to persons not so directly before the public eye.

It may be said generally, that anything which it is desirable should be done for the general interests of mankind or of future generations, or for the present interests of those members of the community who require external aid, but which is not of a nature to remunerate individuals or associations for undertaking it, is in itself a suitable thing to be undertaken by government: though, before making the work their own, governments ought always to consider if there be any rational probability of its being done on what is called the voluntary principle, and if so, whether it is likely to be done in a better or more effectual manner by government agency, than by the zeal and liberality of individuals.

16. The preceding heads comprise, to the best of my judgment, the whole of the exceptions to the practical maxim, that the business of society can be best performed by private and voluntary agency. It is, however, necessary to add, that the intervention of government cannot always practically stop short at the limit which defines the cases intrinsically suitable for it. In the particular circumstances of a given age or nation, there is scarcely anything really important to the general interest, which it may not be desirable, or even necessary, that the government should take upon itself, not because private individuals cannot effectually perform it, but because they will not. At some times and places, there will be no roads, docks, harbours, canals, works of irrigation, hospitals, schools, colleges, printing-presses, unless the government establishes them; the public being either too poor to command the necessary resources, or too little advanced in intelligence to appreciate the ends, or not sufficiently practised in joint action to be capable of the means. This is true, more or less, of all countries inured to despotism, and particularly of those in which there is a very wide distance in civilization between the people and the government: as in those which have been conquered and are retained in subjection by a more energetic and more cultivated people. In many parts of the

world, the people can do nothing for themselves which requires large means and combined action: all such things are left undone, unless done by the state. In these cases, the mode in which the government can most surely demonstrate the sincerity with which it intends the greatest good of its subjects, is by doing the things which are made incumbent on it by the helplessness of the public, in such a manner as shall tend not to increase and perpetuate, but to correct, that helplessness. A good government will give all its aid in such a shape, as to encourage and nurture any rudiments it may find of a spirit of individual exertion. It will be assiduous in removing obstacles and discouragements to voluntary enterprise, and in giving whatever facilities and whatever direction and guidance may be necessary: its pecuniary means will be applied, when practicable, in aid of private efforts rather than in supersession of them, and it will call into play its machinery of rewards and honours to elicit such efforts. Government aid, when given merely in default of private enterprise, should be so given as to be as far as possible a course of education for the people in the art of accomplishing great objects by individual energy and voluntary co-operation.

I have not thought it necessary here to insist on that part of the functions of government which all admit to be indispensable, the function of prohibiting and punishing such conduct on the part of individuals in the exercise of their freedom, as is clearly injurious to other persons, whether the case be one of force, fraud, or negligence. Even in the best state which society has yet reached, it is lamentable to think how great a proportion of all the efforts and talents in the world are employed in merely neutralizing one another. It is the proper end of government to reduce this wretched waste to the smallest possible amount, by taking such measures as shall cause the energies now spent by mankind in injuring one another, or in protecting themselves against injury, to be turned to the legitimate employment of the human faculties, that of compelling the powers of nature to be more and more subservient to physical and moral good.

world, the people can do nothing for themselves which requires large means and combined action; all such things are left undone, unless done by the state. In these cases, the mode in which the government can most safely demonstrate the sincerity with which it intends the greatest good of its subjects, is by doing the things which are made incumbent on it by the helplessness of the public, in such a manner as shall tend not to increase and perpetuate, but to correct, that helplessness. A good government will give all its aid in such a shape as to encourage and nurture any rudiments it may find of a spirit of individual exertion. It will be assiduous in removing obstacles and discouragements to voluntary enterprise, and in giving whatever facilities and whatever direction and guidance may be necessary: its pecuniary means will be applied, when practicable, in aid of private efforts rather than in supersession of them, and it will call into play its machinery of rewards and honours to elicit such efforts. Government aid, when given merely in default of private enterprise, should be so given as to be as far as possible a course of education for the people in the art of accomplishing great objects by individual energy and voluntary co-operation.

I have not thought it necessary here to insist on that part of the functions of government, which all admit to be indispensable, the function of prohibiting and punishing such conduct on the part of individuals in the exercise of their freedom, as is clearly injurious to other persons, whether the case be one of force, fraud, or negligence. Even in the best state, which society has yet reached, it is lamentable to think how great a proportion of all the efforts and talents in the world are employed in merely neutralizing one another. It is the proper end of government to reduce this wretched waste to the smallest possible amount, by taking such measures as shall cause the energies now spent by mankind in injuring one another, or in protecting themselves against injury, to be turned to the legitimate employment of the human faculties, that of compelling the powers of nature to be more and more subservient to physical and moral good

CHAPTERS ON SOCIALISM

CHAPTERS ON SOCIALISM

Preliminary Notice

IT was in the year 1869 that, impressed with the degree in which, even during the last twenty years, when the world seemed so wholly occupied with other matters, the socialist ideas of speculative thinkers had spread among the workers in every civilised country, Mr Mill formed the design of writing a book on Socialism. Convinced that the inevitable tendencies of modern society must be to bring the questions involved in it always more and more to the front, he thought it of great practical consequence that they should be thoroughly and impartially considered, and the lines pointed out by which the best speculatively-tested theories might, without prolongation of suffering on the one hand, or unnecessary disturbance on the other, be applied to the existing order of things. He therefore planned a work which should go exhaustively through the whole subject, point by point; and the four chapters now printed are the first rough drafts thrown down towards the foundation of that work. These chapters might not, when the work came to be completely written out and then re-written, according to the author's habit, have appeared in the present order; they might have been incorporated into different parts of the work. It has not been without hesitation that I have yielded to the urgent wish of the editor of this Review to give these chapters to the world; but I have complied with his request because, while they appear to me to possess great intrinsic value as well as special application to the problems now forcing themselves on public attention, they will not, I believe, detract even from the mere literary reputation of their author, but will rather form an example of the patient labour with which good work is done.

HELEN TAYLOR

January, 1879

Introductory

IN the great country beyond the Atlantic, which is now well-nigh the most powerful country in the world, and will soon be indisputably so, manhood suffrage prevails.* Such is also the political qualification of France since 1848, and has become that of the German Confederation, though not of all the several states composing it. In Great Britain the suffrage is not yet so widely extended, but the last Reform Act* admitted within what is called the pale of the Constitution so large a body of those who live on weekly wages, that as soon and as often as these shall choose to act together as a class, and exert for any common object the whole of the electoral power which our present institutions give them, they will exercise, though not a complete ascendancy, a very great influence on legislation. Now these are the very class which, in the vocabulary of the higher ranks, are said to have no stake in the country. Of course they have in reality the greatest stake, since their daily bread depends on its prosperity. But they are not engaged (we may call it bribed) by any peculiar interest of their own, to the support of property as it is, least of all to the support of inequalities of property. So far as their power reaches, or may hereafter reach, the laws of property have to depend for support upon considerations of a public nature, upon the estimate made of their conduciveness to the general welfare, and not upon motives of a mere personal character operating on the minds of those who have control over the Government.

It seems to me that the greatness of this change is as yet by no means completely realised, either by those who opposed, or by those who effected our last constitutional reform. To say the truth, the perceptions of Englishmen are of late somewhat blunted as to the tendencies of political changes. They have seen so many changes made, from which, while only in prospect, vast expectations were entertained, both of evil and of good, while the results of either kind that actually followed seemed far short of what had been predicted, that they have come to feel as if it were the nature of political changes not to fulfil expectation, and have fallen into a habit of half-unconscious belief that such changes, when they take place without a violent revolution, do not much or permanently disturb in practice the course of things habitual to the country. This, however, is but a superficial view either of the past or of the future. The various reforms of the last two generations have been at least as fruitful in important consequences as was foretold. The predictions were often erroneous as to the suddenness of the effects, and sometimes even as to the kind of effect. We laugh at the vain expectations of those who thought that Catholic emancipation would tranquillise Ireland, or reconcile it to British rule. At the end of the first ten years of the Reform Act of 1832,* few continued to think either that it would remove every important practical grievance, or that it had opened the door to universal suffrage. But five-and-twenty years more of its operation have given scope for a large development of its indirect working, which is much more momentous than the direct. Sudden effects in history are generally superficial. Causes which go deep down into the roots of future events produce the most serious parts of their effect only slowly, and have, therefore, time to become a part of the familiar order of things before general attention is called to the changes they are producing; since, when the changes do become evident, they are often not seen, by cursory observers, to be in any peculiar manner connected with the cause. The remoter consequences of a new political fact are seldom understood when they occur, except when they have been appreciated beforehand.

This timely appreciation is particularly easy in respect to the tendencies of the change made in our institutions by the Reform Act of 1867. The great increase of electoral power which the Act places within the reach of the working classes is permanent. The circumstances which have caused them, thus far, to make a very limited use of that power, are essentially temporary. It is known even to the most inobservant, that the working classes have, and are likely to have, political objects which concern them as working classes, and on which they believe, rightly or wrongly, that the interests and opinions of the other powerful classes are opposed to theirs. However much their pursuit of these objects may be for the present retarded by want of electoral organization, by dissensions among themselves, or by their not having reduced as yet their wishes into a sufficiently definite practical shape, it is as certain as anything in politics can be, that they will before long find the means of making their collective electoral power effectively instrumental to the promotion of their collective objects. And when they do so, it will not be in the disorderly and ineffective way which belongs to a people not habituated to the use of legal and constitutional machinery, nor will it be by the impulse of a mere instinct of levelling. The instruments will be the press, public meetings and associations, and the return to Parliament of the greatest possible number of persons pledged to the political aims of the working classes.* The political aims will themselves be determined by definite political doctrines; for politics are now scientifically studied from the point of view of the working classes, and opinions conceived in the special interest of those classes are organized into systems and creeds which lay claim to a place on the platform of political philosophy, by the same right as the systems elaborated by previous thinkers. It is of the utmost importance that all reflecting persons should take into early consideration what these popular political creeds are likely to be, and that every single article of them should be brought under the fullest light of investigation and discussion, so that, if possible, when the time shall be ripe, whatever is right in them may be adopted, and what is wrong rejected by general consent, and that instead of a hostile conflict, physical or only moral, between the old and the new, the best parts of both may be combined in a renovated social fabric. At the ordinary pace of those great social changes which are not effected by physical violence, we have before us an interval of about a generation, on the due employment of which it depends whether the accommodation of social institutions to the altered state of human society, shall be the work of wise foresight, or of a conflict of opposite prejudices. The future of mankind will be gravely imperilled,* if great questions are left to be fought over between ignorant change and ignorant opposition to change.

And the discussion that is now required is one that must go down to the very first principles of existing society. The fundamental doctrines which were assumed as incontestable by former generations, are now put again on their trial. Until the present age, the institution of property in the shape in which it has been handed down from the past, had not, except by a few speculative writers, been brought seriously into question, because the conflicts of the past have always been conflicts between classes, both of which had a stake in the existing constitution of property. It will not be possible to go on longer in this manner. When the discussion includes classes who have next to no property of their own, and are only interested in the institution so far as it is a public benefit, they will not allow anything to be taken for granted—certainly not the principle of private property, the legitimacy and utility of which are denied by many of the reasoners who look out from the standpoint of the working classes. Those classes will certainly demand that the subject, in all its parts, shall be reconsidered from the foundation; that all proposals for doing without the institution, and all modes of modifying it which have the appearance of being favourable to the interest of the working classes, shall receive the fullest consideration and discussion before it is decided that the subject must remain as it is. As far as this country is concerned, the dispositions of the working classes have as yet manifested themselves hostile only to certain outlying portions of the proprietary system. Many of them desire to withdraw questions of wages from the freedom of contract, which is one of the ordinary attributions of private property. The more aspiring of them deny that land is a proper subject for private appropriation, and have commenced an agitation for its resumption by the State. With this is combined, in the speeches of some of the agitators, a denunciation of what they term usury, but without any definition of what they mean by the name; and the cry does not seem to be of home origin, but to have been

caught up from the intercourse which has recently commenced through the Labour Congresses and the International
Society,* with the Continental Socialists who object to all
interest on money, and deny the legitimacy of deriving an
income in any form from property apart from labour. This
doctrine does not as yet show signs of being widely preval-
ent in Great Britain, but the soil is well prepared to receive
the seeds of this description which are widely scattered from
those foreign countries where large, general theories, and
schemes of vast promise, instead of inspiring distrust, are
essential to the popularity of a cause. It is in France, Germany,
and Switzerland that anti-property doctrines in the widest
sense have drawn large bodies of working men to rally
round them. In these countries nearly all those who aim at
reforming society in the interest of the working classes
profess themselves Socialists, a designation under which
schemes of very diverse character are comprehended and
confounded, but which implies at least a remodelling generally approaching to abolition of the institution of private
property. And it would probably be found that even in
England the more prominent and active leaders of the
working classes are usually in their private creed Socialists
of one order or another, though being, like most English
politicians, better aware than their Continental brethren
that great and permanent changes in the fundamental ideas
of mankind are not to be accomplished by a *coup de main*,*
they direct their practical efforts towards ends which seem
within easier reach, and are content to hold back all
extreme theories until there has been experience of the
operation of the same principles on a partial scale. While
such continues to be the character of the English working
classes, as it is of Englishmen in general, they are not likely
to rush headlong into the reckless extremities of some of the
foreign Socialists, who, even in sober Switzerland, proclaim
themselves content to begin by simple subversion, leaving
the subsequent reconstruction to take care of itself; and by
subversion they mean not only the annihilation of all
government, but getting all property of all kinds out of the
hands of the possessors to be used for the general benefit;

but in what mode it will, they say, be time enough afterwards to decide.

The avowal of this doctrine by a public newspaper, the
organ of an association (*La Solidarité*, published at Neuchâtel*), is one of the most curious signs of the times. The
leaders of the English working men—whose delegates at
the congresses of Geneva and Bâle contributed much the
greatest part of such practical common sense as was shown
there—are not likely to begin deliberately by anarchy, without having formed any opinion as to what form of society
should be established in the room of the old. But it is evident
that whatever they do propose can only be properly judged,
and the grounds of the judgment made convincing to the
general mind, on the basis of a previous survey of the two
rival theories, that of private property and that of Socialism, one or other of which must necessarily furnish most of
the premises in the discussion. Before, therefore, we can
usefully discuss this class of questions in detail, it will be
advisable to examine from their foundations the general
questions raised by Socialism. And this examination should
be made without any hostile prejudice. However irrefutable
the arguments in favour of the laws of property may appear
to those to whom they have the double prestige of immemo-
rial custom and of personal interest, nothing is more natural
than that a working man who has begun to speculate on
politics, should regard them in a very different light. Having,
after long struggles, attained in some countries, and nearly
attained in others, the point at which for them, at least,
there is no further progress to make in the department of
purely political rights, is it possible that the less fortunate
classes among the 'adult males' should not ask themselves
whether progress ought to stop there? Notwithstanding all
that has been done, and all that seems likely to be done, in
the extension of franchises, a few are born to great riches,
and the many to a penury, made only more grating by
contrast. No longer enslaved or made dependent by force of
law, the great majority are so by force of poverty; they are
still chained to a place, to an occupation, and to conformity
with the will of an employer, and debarred by the accident

of birth both from the enjoyments, and from the mental and moral advantages, which others inherit without exertion and independently of desert. That this is an evil equal to almost any of those against which mankind have hitherto struggled, the poor are not wrong in believing. Is it a necessary evil? They are told so by those who do not feel it—by those who have gained the prizes in the lottery of life. But it was also said that slavery, that despotism, that all the privileges of oligarchy were necessary. All the successive steps that have been made by the poorer classes, partly won from the better feelings of the powerful, partly extorted from their fears, and partly bought with money, or attained in exchange for support given to one section of the powerful in its quarrels with another, had the strongest prejudices opposed to them beforehand; but their acquisition was a sign of power gained by the subordinate classes, a means to those classes of acquiring more; it consequently drew to those classes a certain share of the respect accorded to power, and produced a corresponding modification in the creed of society respecting them; whatever advantages they succeeded in acquiring came to be considered their due, while, of those which they had not yet attained, they continued to be deemed unworthy. The classes, therefore, which the system of society makes subordinate, have little reason to put faith in any of the maxims which the same system of society may have established as principles. Considering that the opinions of mankind have been found so wonderfully flexible, have always tended to consecrate existing facts, and to declare what did not yet exist, either pernicious or impracticable, what assurance have those classes that the distinction of rich and poor is grounded on a more imperative necessity than those other ancient and long-established facts, which, having been abolished, are now condemned even by those who formerly profited by them? This cannot be taken on the word of an interested party. The working classes are entitled to claim that the whole field of social institutions should be re-examined, and every question considered as if it now arose for the first time; with the idea constantly in view that the persons who are to be convinced are not those who owe their ease and importance to the present system, but persons who have no other interest in the matter than abstract justice and the general good of the community.* It should be the object to ascertain what institutions of property would be established by an unprejudiced legislator, absolutely impartial between the possessors of property and the non-possessors; and to defend and justify them by the reasons which would really influence such a legislator, and not by such as have the appearance of being got up to make out a case for what already exists. Such rights or privileges of property as will not stand this test will, sooner or later, have to be given up. An impartial hearing ought, moreover, to be given to all objections against property itself. All evils and inconveniences attaching to the institution in its best form ought to be frankly admitted, and the best remedies or palliatives applied which human intelligence is able to devise. And all plans proposed by social reformers, under whatever name designated, for the purpose of attaining the benefits aimed at by the institution of property without its inconveniences, should be examined with the same candour, not prejudged as absurd or impracticable.

Socialist Objections to the Present Order of Society

As in all proposals for change there are two elements to be considered—that which is to be changed, and that which it is to be changed to—so in Socialism considered generally, and in each of its varieties taken separately, there are two parts to be distinguished, the one negative and critical, the other constructive. There is, first, the judgment of Socialism on existing institutions and practices and on their results; and secondly, the various plans which it has propounded for doing better. In the former all the different schools of Socialism are at one. They agree almost to identity in the faults which they find with the economical order of existing society. Up to a certain point also they entertain the same general conception of the remedy to be provided for those faults; but in the details, notwithstanding this general agreement, there is a wide disparity. It will be both natural and convenient, in attempting an estimate of their doctrines, to begin with the negative portion which is common to them all, and to postpone all mention of their differences until we arrive at that second part of their undertaking, in which alone they seriously differ.

The first part of our task is by no means difficult; since it consists only in an enumeration of existing evils. Of these there is no scarcity, and most of them are by no means obscure or mysterious. Many of them are the veriest commonplaces of moralists, though the roots even of these lie deeper than moralists usually attempt to penetrate. So various are they that the only difficulty is to make any approach to an exhaustive catalogue. We shall content ourselves for the present with mentioning a few of the principal. And let one thing be remembered by the reader. When item after item of the enumeration passes before him, and he finds one fact after another which he has been accustomed to include among the necessities of nature urged as an accusation against social institutions, he is not entitled to cry unfairness, and to protest that the evils complained of are inherent in Man and Society, and are such as no arrangements can remedy. To assert this would be to beg the very question at issue.* No one is more ready than Socialists to admit—they affirm it indeed much more decidedly than truth warrants—that the evils they complain of are irremediable in the present constitution of society. They propose to consider whether some other form of society may be devised which would not be liable to those evils, or would be liable to them in a much less degree. Those who object to the present order of society, considered as a whole, and who accept as an alternative the possibility of a total change, have a right to set down all the evils which at present exist in society as part of their case, whether these are apparently attributable to social arrangements or not, provided they do not flow from physical laws which human power is not adequate, or human knowledge has not yet learned, to counteract. Moral evils, and such physical evils as would be remedied if all persons did as they ought, are fairly chargeable against the state of society which admits of them; and are valid as arguments until it is shown that any other state of society would involve an equal or greater amount of such evils. In the opinion of Socialists, the present arrangements of society in respect to Property and the Production and Distribution of Wealth, are, as means to the general good, a total failure. They say that there is an enormous mass of evil which these arrangements do not succeed in preventing; that the good, either moral or physical, which they realise is wretchedly small compared with the amount of exertion employed, and that even this small amount of good is brought about by means which are full of pernicious consequences, moral and physical.

First among existing social evils may be mentioned the evil of Poverty. The institution of Property is upheld and commended principally as being the means by which labour and frugality are insured their reward, and mankind enabled to emerge from indigence. It may be so; most Socialists allow that it has been so in earlier periods of history. But if the institution can do nothing more or better in this respect than it has hitherto done, its capabilities, they affirm, are very insignificant. What proportion of the population, in the most civilized countries of Europe, enjoy in their own persons anything worth naming of the benefits of property? It may be said, that but for property in the hands of their employers they would be without daily bread; but, though this be conceded, at least their daily bread is all that they have; and that often in insufficient quantity; almost always of inferior quality; and with no assurance of continuing to have it at all; an immense proportion of the industrious classes being at some period or other of their lives (and all being liable to become) dependent, at least temporarily, on legal or voluntary charity. Any attempt to depict the miseries of indigence, or to estimate the proportion of mankind who in the most advanced countries are habitually given up during their whole existence to its physical and moral sufferings, would be superfluous here.

This may be left to philanthropists, who have painted these miseries in colours sufficiently strong. Suffice it to say that the condition of numbers in civilized Europe, and even in England and France, is more wretched than that of most tribes of savages who are known to us.

It may be said that of this hard lot no one has any reason to complain, because it befalls those only who are outstripped by others, from inferiority of energy or of prudence. This, even were it true, would be a very small alleviation of the evil. If some Nero or Domitian were to require a hundred persons to run a race for their lives, on condition that the fifty or twenty who came in hindmost should be put to death, it would not be any diminution of the injustice that the strongest or nimblest would, except through some untoward accident, be certain to escape. The misery and the crime would be that any were put to death at all. So in the economy of society; if there be any who suffer physical privation or moral degradation, whose bodily necessities are either not satisfied or satisfied in a manner which only brutish creatures can be content with, this, though not necessarily the crime of society, is *pro tanto* a failure of the social arrangements. And to assert as a mitigation of the evil that those who thus suffer are the weaker members of the community, morally or physically, is to add insult to misfortune. Is weakness a justification of suffering? Is it not, on the contrary, an irresistible claim upon every human being for protection against suffering? If the minds and feelings of the prosperous were in a right state, would they accept their prosperity if for the sake of it even one person near them was, for any other cause than voluntary fault, excluded from obtaining a desirable existence?

One thing there is, which if it could be affirmed truly, would relieve social institutions from any share in the responsibility of these evils. Since the human race has no means of enjoyable existence, or of existence at all, but what it derives from its own labour and abstinence, there would be no ground for complaint against society if every one who was willing to undergo a fair share of this labour and abstinence could attain a fair share of the fruits. But is this the fact? Is it not the reverse of the fact? The reward, instead of being proportioned to the labour and abstinence of the individual, is almost in an inverse ratio to it: those who receive the least, labour and abstain the most. Even the idle, reckless, and ill-conducted poor, those who are said with most justice to have themselves to blame for their condition, often undergo much more and severer labour, not only than those who are born to pecuniary independence, but than almost any of the more highly remunerated of those who earn their subsistence; and even the inadequate self-control exercised by the industrious poor costs them more sacrifice and more effort than is almost ever required from the more favoured members of society. The very idea of distributive justice, or of any proportionality between success and merit, or between success and exertion, is in the present state of society so manifestly chimerical as to be relegated to the regions of romance. It is true that the lot of individuals is not wholly independent of their virtue and intelligence; these do really tell in their favour, but far less than many other things in which there is no merit at all. The most powerful of all the determining circumstances is birth. The great majority are what they were born to be. Some are born rich without work, others are born to a position in which they can become rich *by* work, the great majority are born to hard work and poverty throughout life, numbers to indigence. Next to birth the chief cause of success in life is accident and opportunity. When a person not born to riches succeeds in acquiring them, his own industry and dexterity have generally contributed to the result; but industry and dexterity would not have sufficed unless there had been also a concurrence of occasions and chances which falls to the lot of only a small number. If persons are helped in their worldly career by their virtues, so are they, and perhaps quite as often, by their vices: by servility and sycophancy, by hard-hearted and close-fisted selfishness, by the permitted lies and tricks of trade, by gambling speculations, not seldom by downright knavery. Energies and talents are of much more avail for success in life than virtues; but if one man succeeds by employing energy and talent in something generally useful, another thrives by exercising the same qualities in out-generalling and ruining a rival. It is as much as any moralist ventures to assert, that, other circumstances being given, honesty is the best policy, and that with parity of advantages an honest person has better chances than a rogue. Even this in many stations and circumstances of life is questionable; anything more than this is out of the question. It cannot be pretended that honesty, as a means of success, tells for as much as a difference of one single step on the social ladder. The connection between fortune and conduct is mainly this, that there is a degree of bad conduct, or rather of some kinds of bad conduct, which suffices to ruin any amount of good fortune; but the converse is not true: in the situation of most people no degree whatever of good conduct can be counted upon for raising them in the world, without the aid of fortunate accidents.

These evils, then—great poverty, and that poverty very little connected with desert—are the first grand failure of the existing arrangements of society. The second is human misconduct; crime, vice, and folly, with all the sufferings which follow in their train. For, nearly all the forms of misconduct, whether committed towards ourselves or towards others, may be traced to one of three causes: Poverty and its temptations in the many; Idleness and *désœuvrement*** in the few whose circumstances do not compel them to work; bad education, or want of education, in both. The first two must be allowed to be at least failures in the social arrangements, the last is now almost universally admitted to be the fault of those arrangements—it may almost be said the crime. I am speaking loosely and in the rough, for a minuter analysis of the sources of faults of character and errors of conduct would establish far more conclusively the filiation which connects them with a defective organization of society, though it would also show the reciprocal dependence of that faulty state of society on a backward state of the human mind.*

At this point, in the enumeration of the evils of society, the mere levellers of former times usually stopped: but their more far-sighted successors, the present Socialists, go farther. In their eyes the very foundation of human life as at present constituted, the very principle on which the production and repartition of all material products is now carried on, is essentially vicious and anti-social. It is the principle of individualism, competition, each one for himself and against all the rest. It is grounded on opposition of interests, not harmony of interests, and under it every one is required to find his place by a struggle, by pushing others back or being pushed back by them. Socialists consider this system of private war* (as it may be termed) between every one and every one, especially fatal in an economical point of view and in a moral. Morally considered, its evils are obvious. It is the parent of envy, hatred, and all uncharitableness; it makes every one the natural enemy of all others who cross his path, and every one's path is constantly liable to be crossed. Under the present system hardly any one can gain except by the loss or disappointment of one or of many others. In a well-constituted community every one would be a gainer by every other person's successful exertions; while now we gain by each other's loss and lose by each other's gain, and our greatest gains come from the worst source of all, from death, the death of those who are nearest and should be dearest to us. In its purely economical operation the principle of individual competition receives as unqualified condemnation from the social reformers as in its moral. In the competition of labourers they see the cause of low wages; in the competition of producers the cause of ruin and bankruptcy; and both evils, they affirm, tend constantly to increase as population and wealth make progress; no person (they conceive) being benefited except the great proprietors of land, the holders of fixed money incomes, and a few great capitalists, whose wealth is gradually enabling them to undersell all other producers, to absorb the whole of the operations of industry into their own sphere, to drive from the market all employers of labour except themselves, and to convert the labourers into a kind of slaves or serfs, dependent on them for the means of support, and compelled to accept these on such terms as they choose to offer. Society, in short, is travelling onward, according to these speculators, towards a new feudality, that of the great capitalists.

As I shall have ample opportunity in future chapters to state my own opinion on these topics, and on many others connected with and subordinate to them, I shall now, without further preamble, exhibit the opinions of distinguished Socialists on the present arrangements of society, in a selection of passages from their published writings. For the present I desire to be considered as a mere reporter of the opinions of others. Hereafter it will appear how much of what I cite agrees or differs with my own sentiments.

The clearest, the most compact, and the most precise and specific statement of the case of the Socialists generally against the existing order of society in the economical department of human affairs, is to be found in the little work of M. Louis Blanc, *Organisation du Travail.* My first extracts, therefore, on this part of the subject, shall be taken from that treatise.

Competition is for the people a system of extermination. Is the poor man a member of society, or an enemy to it? We ask for an answer.

All around him he finds the soil preoccupied. Can he cultivate the earth for himself? No; for the right of the first occupant has become a right of property. Can he gather the fruits which the hand of God ripens on the path of man? No; for, like the soil, the fruits have been *appropriated*. Can he hunt or fish? No; for that is a right which is dependent upon the government. Can he draw water from a spring enclosed in a field? No; for the proprietor of the field is, in virtue of his right to the field, proprietor of the fountain. Can he, dying of hunger and thirst, stretch out his hands for the charity of his fellow creatures? No; for there are laws against begging. Can he, exhausted by fatigue and without a refuge, lie down to sleep upon the pavement of the streets? No; for there are laws against vagabondage. Can he, flying from the cruel native land where everything is denied him, seek the means of living far from the place where life was given him? No; for it is not permitted to change your country except on certain conditions which the poor man cannot fulfil.

What, then, can the unhappy man do? He will say, 'I have hands to work with, I have intelligence, I have youth, I have strength;

take all this, and in return give me a morsel of bread.' This is what the working men do say. But even here the poor man may be answered, 'I have no work to give you.' What is he to do then?

What is competition from the point of view of the workman? It is work put up to auction. A contractor wants a workman: three present themselves.—How much for your work?—Half-a-crown: I have a wife and children.—Well; and how much for yours?—Two shillings: I have no children, but I have a wife.—Very well; and now how much for you?—One and eightpence are enough for me; I am single. Then you shall have the work. It is done; the bargain is struck. And what are the other two workmen to do? It is to be hoped they will die quietly of hunger. But what if they take to thieving? Never fear; we have the police. To murder? We have got the hangman. As for the lucky one, his triumph is only temporary. Let a fourth workman make his appearance, strong enough to fast every other day, and his price will run down still lower; then there will be a new outcast, a new recruit for the prison perhaps!

Will it be said that these melancholy results are exaggerated; that at all events they are only possible when there is not work enough for the hands that seek employment? But I ask, in answer, Does the principle of competition contain, by chance, within itself any method by which this murderous disproportion is to be avoided? If one branch of industry is in want of hands, who can answer for it that, in the confusion created by universal competition, another is not overstocked? And if, out of thirty-four millions of men, twenty are really reduced to theft for a living, this would suffice to condemn the principle.

But who is so blind as not to see that under the system of unlimited competition, the continual fall of wages is no exceptional circumstance, but a necessary and general fact? Has the population a limit which it cannot exceed? Is it possible for us to say to industry—industry given up to the accidents of individual egotism and fertile in ruin—can we say, 'Thus far shalt thou go, and no farther?' The population increases constantly: tell the poor mother to become sterile, and blaspheme the God who made her fruitful, for if you do not the lists will soon become too narrow for the combatants. A machine is invented: command it to be broken, and anathematize science, for if you do not, the thousand workmen whom the new machine deprives of work will knock at the door of the neighbouring workshop, and lower the wages of their companions. Thus systematic lowering of wages, ending in the driving out of a certain number of workmen, is the inevitable effect of unlimited competition. It is an industrial system by means of which the working classes are forced to exterminate one another.

If there is an undoubted fact, it is that the increase of population is much more rapid among the poor than among the rich. According to the *Statistics of European Population*, the births at Paris are only one-thirty-second of the population in the rich quarters, while in the others they rise to one-twenty-sixth. This disproportion is a general fact, and M. de Sismondi, in his work on Political Economy,* has explained it by the impossibility for the workmen of hopeful prudence. Those only who feel themselves assured of the morrow can regulate the number of their children according to their income; he who lives from day to day is under the yoke of a mysterious fatality, to which he sacrifices his children as he was sacrificed to it himself. It is true the workhouses exist, menacing society with an inundation of beggars—what way is there of escaping from the cause? . . . It is clear that any society where the means of subsistence increase less rapidly than the numbers of the population, is a society on the brink of an abyss. . . . Competition produces destitution; this is a fact shown by statistics. Destitution is fearfully prolific; this is shown by statistics. The fruitfulness of the poor throws upon society unhappy creatures who have need of work and cannot find it; this is shown by statistics. At this point society is reduced to a choice between killing the poor or maintaining them gratuitously—between atrocity or folly.[1]

So much for the poor. We now pass to the middle classes.

According to the political economists of the school of Adam Smith and Léon Say, *cheapness* is the word in which may be summed up the advantages of unlimited competition. But why persist in considering the effect of cheapness with a view only to the momentary advantage of the consumer? Cheapness is advantageous to the consumer at the cost of introducing the seeds of ruinous anarchy among the producers. Cheapness is, so to speak, the hammer with which the rich among the producers crush their poorer rivals. Cheapness is the trap into which the daring speculators entice the hard-workers. Cheapness is the sentence of death to the producer on a small scale who has no money to invest in the purchase of machinery that his rich rivals can easily procure.

[1] See Louis Blanc, 'Organisation du Travail', 4me édition [Paris, 1845], pp. 6, 11, 53, 57.

Cheapness is the great instrument in the hands of monopoly; it absorbs the small manufacturer, the small shopkeeper, the small proprietor; it is, in one word, the destruction of the middle classes for the advantage of a few industrial oligarchs.

Ought we, then, to consider cheapness as a curse? No one would attempt to maintain such an absurdity. But it is the speciality of wrong principles to turn good into evil and to corrupt all things. Under the system of competition cheapness is only a provisional and fallacious advantage. It is maintained only so long as there is a struggle; no sooner have the rich competitors driven out their poorer rivals than prices rise. Competition leads to monopoly, for the same reason cheapness leads to high prices. Thus, what has been made use of as a weapon in the contest between the producers, sooner or later becomes a cause of impoverishment among the consumers. And if to this cause we add the others we have already enumerated, first among which must be ranked the inordinate increase of the population, we shall be compelled to recognise the impoverishment of the mass of the consumers as a direct consequence of competition.

But, on the other hand, this very competition which tends to dry up the sources of demand, urges production to over-supply. The confusion produced by the universal struggle prevents each producer from knowing the state of the market. He must work in the dark and trust to chance for a sale. Why should he check the supply, especially as he can throw any loss on the workman whose wages are so pre-eminently liable to rise and fall? Even when production is carried on at a loss the manufacturers still often carry it on, because they will not let their machinery, etc., stand idle, or risk the loss of raw material, or lose their customers; and because productive industry as carried on under the competitive system being nothing else than a game of chance, the gambler will not lose his chance of a lucky stroke.

Thus, and we cannot too often insist upon it, competition necessarily tends to increase supply and to diminish consumption; its tendency therefore is precisely the opposite of what is sought by economic science; hence it is not merely oppressive but foolish as well.

And in all this, in order to avoid dwelling on truths which have become commonplaces and sound declamatory from their very truth, we have said nothing of the frightful moral corruption which industry, organized, or more properly speaking disorganized as it is at the present day, has introduced among the middle classes. Everything has become venal, and competition invades even the domain of thought.

The factory crushing the workshop; the showy establishment absorbing the humble shop; the artisan who is his own master replaced by the day-labourer; cultivation by the plough superseding that by the spade, and bringing the poor man's field under disgraceful homage to the money-lender; bankrupticies multiplied; manufacturing industry transformed by the ill-regulated extension of credit into a system of gambling where no one, not even the rogue, can be sure of winning; in short a vast confusion calculated to arouse jealousy, mistrust, and hatred, and to stifle, little by little, all generous aspirations, all faith, self-sacrifice, and poetry— such is the hideous but only too faithful picture of the results obtained by the application of the principle of competition.[1]

The Fourierists, through their principal organ, M. Considérant,* enumerate the evils of the existing civilization in the following order:

1. It employs an enormous quantity of labour and of human power unproductively, or in the work of destruction.

In the first place there is the army, which in France, as in all other countries, absorbs the healthiest and strongest men, a large number of the most talented and intelligent, and a considerable part of the public revenue .... The existing state of society develops in its impure atmosphere innumerable outcasts, whose labour is not merely unproductive, but actually destructive: adventurers, prostitutes, people with no acknowledged means of living, beggars, convicts, swindlers, thieves, and others whose number tends rather to increase than to diminish. ...

To the list of unproductive labour fostered by our state of Society must be added that of the judicature and of the bar, of the courts of law and magistrates, the police, gaolers, executioners, etc.—functions indispensable to the state of society as it is.

Also people of what is called 'good society'; those who pass their lives in doing nothing; idlers of all ranks.

Also the numberless custom-house officials, tax-gatherers, bailiffs, excisemen; in short, all that army of men which overlooks, brings to account, takes, but produces nothing.

Also the labours of sophists, philosophers, metaphysicians, political men, working in mistaken directions, who do nothing to

[1] [Ibid. 58–61, 65–6.]

advance science, and produce nothing but disturbance and sterile discussions; the verbiage of advocates, pleaders, witnesses, etc.

And finally all the operations of commerce, from those of the bankers and brokers, down to those of the grocer behind his counter.[1]

Secondly, they assert that even the industry and powers which in the present system are devoted to production, do not produce more than a small portion of what they might produce if better employed and directed:

Who with any good-will and reflection will not see how much the want of coherence—the disorder, the want of combination, the parcelling out of labour and leaving it wholly to individual action without any organization, without any large or general views—are causes which limit the possibilities of production and destroy, or at least waste, our means of action? Does not disorder give birth to poverty, as order and good management give birth to riches? Is not want of combination a source of weakness, as combination is a source of strength? And who can say that industry, whether agricultural, domestic, manufacturing, scientific, artistic, or commercial, is organized at the present day either in the state or in municipalities? Who can say that all the work which is carried on in any of these departments is executed in subordination to any general views, or with foresight, economy, and order? Or, again, who can say that it is possible in our present state of society to develop, by a good education, all the faculties bestowed by nature on each of its members; to employ each one in functions which he would like, which he would be the most capable of, and which, therefore, he could carry on with the greatest advantage to himself and to others? Has it even been so much as attempted to solve the problems presented by varieties of character so as to regulate and harmonize the varieties of employments in accordance with natural aptitudes? Alas! The Utopia of the most ardent philanthropists is to teach reading and writing to twenty-five millions of the French people! And in the present state of things we may defy them to succeed even in that!

And is it not a strange spectacle, too, and one which cries out in condemnation of us, to see this state of society where the soil is badly cultivated, and sometimes not cultivated at all; where man is ill lodged, ill clothed, and yet where whole masses are continually

[1] [See V. Considérant, 'Destinée Sociale', 3ᵐᵉ édition (Paris 1848), i. 35, 36, 37.]

in need of work, and pining in misery because they cannot find it? Of a truth we are forced to acknowledge that if the nations are poor and starving it is not because nature has denied the means of producing wealth, but because of the anarchy and disorder in our employment of those means; in other words, it is because society is wretchedly constituted and labour unorganized.

But this is not all, and you will have but a faint conception of the evil if you do not consider that to all these vices of society, which dry up the sources of wealth and prosperity, must be added the struggle, the discord, the war, in short, under many names and many forms which society cherishes and cultivates between the individuals that compose it. These struggles and discords correspond to radical oppositions—deep-seated antinomies between the various interests. Exactly in so far as you are able to establish classes and categories within the nation; in so far, also, you will have opposition of interests and internal warfare either avowed or secret, even if you take into consideration the industrial system only.[1]

One of the leading ideas of this school is the wastefulness and at the same time the immorality of the existing arrangements for distributing the produce of the country among the various consumers, the enormous superfluity in point of number of the agents of distribution, the merchants, dealers, shopkeepers and their innumerable employés, and the depraving character of such a distribution of occupations.

It is evident that the interest of the trader is opposed to that of the consumer and of the producer. Has he not bought cheap and undervalued as much as possible in all his dealings with the producer, the very same article which, vaunting its excellence, he sells to you as dear as he can? Thus the interest of the commercial body, collectively and individually, is contrary to that of the producer and of the consumer—that is to say, to the interest of the whole body of society.

The trader is a go-between, who profits by the general anarchy and the non-organization of industry. The trader buys up products, he buys up everything; he owns and detains everything, in such sort that:

1stly. He holds both Production and Consumption *under his yoke*, because both must come to him either finally for the products to be consumed, or at first for the raw materials to be worked up. Commerce with all its methods of buying, and of raising and lowering prices, its innumerable devices, and its holding everything in the hands of *middle-men*, levies toll right and left: it despotically gives the law to Production and Consumption, of which it ought to be only the subordinate.

2ndly. It robs society by its *enormous profits*—profits levied upon the consumer and the producer, and altogether out of proportion to the services rendered, for which a twentieth of the persons actually employed would be sufficient.

3rdly. It robs society by the subtraction of its productive forces; taking off from productive labour nineteen-twentieths of the agents of trade who are mere parasites. Thus, not only does commerce rob society by appropriating an exorbitant share of the common wealth, but also by considerably diminishing the productive energy of the human beehive. The great majority of traders would return to productive work if a rational system of commercial organization were substituted for the inextricable chaos of the present state of things.

4thly. It robs society by the *adulteration* of products, pushed at the present day beyond all bounds. And in fact, if a hundred grocers establish themselves in a town where before there were only twenty, it is plain that people will not begin to consume five times as many groceries. Hereupon the hundred virtuous grocers have to dispute between them the profits which before were honestly made by the twenty; competition obliges them to make it up at the expense of the consumer, either by raising the prices as sometimes happens, or by adulterating the goods as always happens. In such a state of things there is an end to good faith. Inferior or adulterated goods are sold for articles of good quality whenever the credulous customer is not too experienced to be deceived. And when the customer has been thoroughly imposed upon, the trading conscience consoles itself by saying, 'I state my price; people can take or leave; no one is obliged to buy.' The losses imposed on the consumers by the bad quality or the adulteration of goods are incalculable.

5thly. It robs society by *accumulations*, artificial or not, in consequence of which vast quantities of goods, collected in one place, are damaged and destroyed for want of a sale. Fourier (Th. des Quat. Mouv., p. 334, 1st ed.) says: 'The fundamental principle of the commercial systems, that of *leaving full liberty to the merchants*, gives them absolute right of property over the goods in which they deal; they have the right to withdraw them altogether, to withhold or even to burn them, as happened more than once with the Oriental Company of Amsterdam, which publicly burnt stores of cinnamon in order to raise the price. What it did with cinnamon it would have done with corn; but for the fear of being stoned by the populace, it would have burnt some corn in order to sell the rest at four times its value. Indeed, it actually is of daily occurrence in ports, for provisions of grains to be thrown into the sea because the merchants have allowed them to rot while waiting for a rise. I myself, when I was a clerk, have had to superintend these infamous proceedings, and in one day caused to be thrown into the sea some forty thousand bushels of rice, which might have been sold at a fair profit had the withholder been less greedy of gain. It is society that bears the cost of this waste, which takes place daily under shelter of the philosophical maxim of *full liberty for the merchants.*'

6thly. Commerce robs society, moreover, by all the loss, damage, and waste that follows from the extreme scattering of products in millions of shops, and by the multiplication and complication of carriage.

7thly. It robs society by shameless and unlimited *usury*—usury absolutely appalling. The trader carries on operations with fictitious capital, much higher in amount that his real capital. A trader with a capital of twelve hundred pounds will carry on operations, by means of bills and credit, on a scale of four, eight, or twelve thousand pounds. Thus he draws from capital *which he does not possess*, usurious interest, out of all proportion with the capital he actually owns.

8thly. It robs society by innumerable *bankruptcies*, for the daily accidents of our commercial system, political events, and any kind of disturbance, must usher in a day when the trader, having incurred obligations beyond his means, is no longer able to meet them; his failure, whether fraudulent or not, must be a severe blow to his creditors. The bankruptcy of some entails that of others, so that bankruptcies follow one upon another, causing widespread ruin. And it is always the producer and the consumer who suffer; for commerce, considered as a whole, does not produce wealth, and invests very little in proportion to the wealth which passes through its hands. How many are the manufactures crushed by these blows! how many fertile sources of wealth dried up by these devices, with all their disastrous consequences!

The producer furnishes the goods, the consumer the money. Trade furnishes credit, founded on little or no actual capital, and the different members of the commercial body are in no way responsible for one another. This, in a few words, is the whole theory of the thing.

9thly. Commerce robs society by the *independence* and *irresponsibility* which permits it to buy at the epochs when the producers are forced to sell and compete with one another, in order to procure money for their rent and necessary expenses of production. When the markets are overstocked and goods cheap, trade purchases. Then it creates a rise, and by this simple manœuvre despoils both producer and consumer.

10thly. It robs society by a considerable *drawing off* of *capital*, which will return to productive industry when commerce plays its proper subordinate part, and is only an agency carrying on transactions between the producers (more or less distant) and the great centres of consumption—the communistic societies. Thus the capital engaged in the speculations of commerce (which, small as it is, compared to the immense wealth which passes through its hands, consists nevertheless of sums enormous in themselves), would return to stimulate production if commerce was deprived of the intermediate property in goods, and their distribution became a matter of administrative organization. Stock-jobbing is the most odious form of this vice of commerce.

11thly. It robs society by the *monopolising* or buying up of raw materials. 'For' (says Fourier, Th. des Quat. Mouv., p. 359, 1st ed.), 'the rise in price on articles that are bought up, is borne ultimately by the consumer, although in the first place by the manufacturers, who, being obliged to keep up their establishments, must make pecuniary sacrifices, and manufacture at small profits in the hope of better days; and it is often long before they can repay themselves the rise in prices which the monopoliser has compelled them to support in the first instance. . . .'

In short, all these vices, besides many others which I omit, are multiplied by the extreme complication of mercantile affairs; for products do not pass once only through the greedy clutches of commerce; there are some which pass and repass twenty or thirty times before reaching the consumer. In the first place, the raw material passes through the grasp of commerce before reaching the manufacturer who first works it up; then it returns to commerce to be sent out again to be worked up in a second form; and so on until it receives its final shape. Then it passes into the hands of merchants, who sell to the wholesale dealers, and these to the great retail dealers of towns, and these again to the little dealers and to the country shops; and each time that it changes hands, it leaves something behind it.

. . . One of my friends who was lately exploring the Jura, where much working in metal is done, had occasion to enter the house of a peasant who was a manufacturer of shovels. He asked the price. 'Let us come to an understanding,' answered the poor labourer, not an economist at all, but a man of common sense; 'I sell them for 8*d.* to the trade, which retails them at 1*s.* 8*d.* in the towns. If you could find a means of opening a direct communication between the workman and the consumer, you might have them for 1*s.* 2*d.*, and we should each gain 6*d.* by the transaction.'[1]

To a similar effect Owen, in the *Book of the New Moral World,** part 2, chap. iii.

The principle now in practice is to induce a large portion of society to devote their lives to distribute wealth upon a large, a medium, and a small scale, and to have it conveyed from place to place in larger or smaller quantities, to meet the means and wants of various divisions of society and individuals, as they are now situated in cities, towns, villages, and country places. This principle of distribution makes a class in society whose business it is to *buy from* some parties and to *sell to* others. By this proceeding they are placed under circumstances which induce them to endeavour to buy at what appears at the time a low price in the market, and to sell again at the greatest permanent profit which they can obtain. Their real object being to get as much profit as gain between the seller to, and the buyer from them, as can be effected in their transactions.

There are innumerable errors in principle and evils in practice which necessarily proceed from this mode of distributing the wealth of society.

1st. A general class of distributers is formed, whose interest is separated from, and apparently opposed to, that of the individual from whom they buy and to whom they sell.

2nd. Three classes of distributers are made, the small, the medium, and the large buyers and sellers; or the retailers, the wholesale dealers, and the extensive merchants.

3rd. Three classes of buyers thus created constitute the small, the medium, and the large purchasers.

By this arrangement into various classes of buyers and sellers, the parties are easily trained to learn that they have separate and

[1] [Ibid. 43–51.]

opposing interests, and different ranks and stations in society. An inequality of feeling and condition is thus created and maintained, with all the servility and pride which these unequal arrangements are sure to produce. The parties are regularly trained in a general system of deception, in order that they may be the more successful in buying cheap and selling dear.

The smaller sellers acquire habits of injurious idleness, waiting often for hours for customers. And this evil is experienced to a considerable extent even amongst the class of wholesale dealers.

There are, also, by this arrangement, many more establishments for selling than are necessary in the villages, towns, and cities; and a very large capital is thus wasted without benefit to society. And from their number opposed to each other all over the country to obtain customers, they endeavour to undersell each other, and are therefore continually endeavouring to injure the producer by the establishment of what are called cheap shops and warehouses; and to support their character the master or his servants must be continually on the watch to buy bargains, that is, to procure wealth for less than the cost of its production.

The distributers, small, medium, and large, have all to be supported by the producers, and the greater the number of the former compared with the latter, the greater will be the burden which the producer has to sustain; for as the number of distributers increases, the accumulation of wealth must decrease, and more must be required from the producer.

The distributers of wealth, under the present system, are a dead weight upon the producers, and are most active demoralisers of society. Their dependent condition, at the commencement of their task, teaches or induces them to be servile to their customers, and to continue to be so as long as they are accumulating wealth by their cheap buying and dear selling. But when they have secured sufficient to be what they imagine to be an independence—to live without business—they are too often filled with a most ignorant pride, and become insolent to their dependents.

The arrangement is altogether a most improvident one for society, whose interest it is to produce the greatest amount of wealth of the best qualities; while the existing system of distribution is not only to withdraw great numbers from producing to become distributers, but to add to the cost of the consumer all the expense of a most wasteful and extravagant distribution; the distribution costing to the consumer many times the price of the original cost of the wealth purchased.

Then, by the position in which the seller is placed by his created desire for gain on the one hand, and the competition he meets with from opponents selling similar productions on the other, he is strongly tempted to deteriorate the articles which he has for sale; and when these are provisions, either of home production or of foreign importation, the effects upon the health, and consequent comfort and happiness of the consumers, are often most injurious, and productive of much premature death, especially among the working classes, who, in this respect, are perhaps made to be the greatest sufferers, by purchasing the inferior or low-priced articles. . . .

The expense of thus distributing wealth in Great Britain and Ireland, including transit from place to place, and all the agents directly and indirectly engaged in this department, is, perhaps, little short of one hundred millions annually, without taking into consideration the deterioration of the quality of many of the articles constituting this wealth, by carriage, and by being divided into small quantities, and kept in improper stores and places, in which the atmosphere is unfavourable to the keeping of such articles in a tolerably good, and much less in the best, condition for use.

In further illustration of the contrariety of interests between person and person, class and class, which pervades the present constitution of society, M. Considérant adds:

If the wine-growers wish for free trade, this freedom ruins the producer of corn, the manufacturers of iron, of cloth, of cotton, and—we are compelled to add—the smuggler and the customs' officer. If it is the interest of the consumer that machines should be invented which lower prices by rendering production less costly, these same machines throw out of work thousands of workmen who do not know how to, and cannot at once, find other work. Here, then, again is one of the innumerable *vicious circles* of civilisation . . . for there are a thousand facts which prove cumulatively that in our existing social system the introduction of any good brings always along with it some evil.

In short, if we go lower down and come to vulgar details, we find that it is the interest of the tailor, the shoemaker, and the hatter that coats, shoes, and hats should be soon worn out; that the glazier profits by the hail-storms which break windows; that the mason and the architect profit by fires; the lawyer is enriched by law-suits; the doctor by disease; the wine-seller by drunkenness; the prostitute by debauchery. And what a disaster would it be for the judges, the police, and the gaolers, as well as for the barristers and the solicitors, and all the lawyers' clerks, if crimes, offences, and law-suits were all at once to come to an end![1]

The following is one of the cardinal points of this school:

Add to all this, that civilisation, which sows dissension and war on every side; which employs a great part of its powers in unproductive labour, or even in destruction; which furthermore diminishes the public wealth by the unnecessary friction and discord it introduces into industry; add to all this, I say, that this same social system has for its special characteristic to produce a repugnance for work—a disgust for labour.

Everywhere you hear the labourer, the artisan, the clerk complain of his position and his occupation, while they long for the time when they can retire from work imposed upon them by necessity. To be repugnant, to have for its motive and pivot nothing but the fear of starvation, is the great, the fatal, characteristic of civilised labour. The civilised workman is condemned to penal servitude. So long as productive labour is so organized that instead of being associated with pleasure it is associated with pain, weariness and dislike, it will alway happen that all will avoid it who are able. With few exceptions, those only will consent to work who are compelled to it by want. Hence the most numerous classes, the artificers of social wealth, the active and direct creators of all comfort and luxury, will always be condemned to touch closely on poverty and hunger; they will always be the slaves to ignorance and degradation; they will continue to be always that huge herd of mere beasts of burden whom we see ill-grown, decimated by disease, bowed down in the great workshop of society over the plough or over the counter, that they may prepare the delicate food, and the sumptuous enjoyments of the upper and idle classes.

So long as no method of attractive labour has been devised, it will continue to be true that 'there must be many poor in order that there may be a few rich;' a mean and hateful saying, which we hear every day quoted as an eternal truth from the mouths of people who call themselves Christians or philosophers! It is very easy to understand that oppression, trickery, and especially poverty, are the permanent and fatal appanage of every state of society characterized by the dislike of work, for, in this case, there

[1] [Ibid. 59–60.]

is nothing but poverty that will force men to labour. And the proof of this is, that if every one of all the workers were to become suddenly rich, nineteen-twentieths of all the work now done would be abandoned.[1]

In the opinion of the Fourierists, the tendency of the present order of society is to a concentration of wealth in the hands of a comparatively few immensely rich individuals or companies, and the reduction of all the rest of the community into a complete dependence on them. This was termed by Fourier *la féodalité industrielle.**

This feudalism [says M. Considérant], would be constituted as soon as the largest part of the industrial and territorial property of the nation belongs to a minority which absorbs all its revenues, while the great majority, chained to the work-bench or labouring on the soil, must be content to gnaw the pittance which is cast to them.[2]

This disastrous result is to be brought about partly by the mere progress of competition, as sketched in our previous extract by M. Louis Blanc; assisted by the progress of national debts, which M. Considérant regards as mortgages of the whole land and capital of the country, of which 'les capitalistes prêteurs' become, in a greater and greater measure, co-proprietors, receiving without labour or risk an increasing portion of the revenues.

The Socialist Objections to the Present Order of Society Examined

It is impossible to deny that the considerations brought to notice in the preceding chapter make out a frightful case either against the existing order of society, or against the position of man himself in this world. How much of the evils should be referred to the one, and how much to the other, is the principal theoretic question which has to be resolved. But the strongest case is susceptible of exaggeration; and it

[1] Ibid. 60–1. [2] Ibid. 134.

will have been evident to many readers, even from the passages I have quoted, that such exaggeration is not wanting in the representations of the ablest and most candid Socialists. Though much of their allegations is unanswerable, not a little is the result of errors in political economy; by which, let me say once for all, I do not mean the rejection of any practical rules of policy which have been laid down by political economists, I mean ignorance of economic facts, and of the causes by which the economic phenomena of society as it is, are actually determined.

In the first place, it is unhappily true that the wages of ordinary labour, in all the countries of Europe, are wretchedly insufficient to supply the physical and moral necessities of the population in any tolerable measure. But, when it is further alleged that even this insufficient remuneration has a tendency to diminish; that there is, in the words of M. Louis Blanc, *une baisse continue des salaires;* * the assertion is in opposition to all accurate information, and to many notorious facts. It has yet to be proved that there is any country in the civilised world where the ordinary wages of labour, estimated either in money or in articles of consumption, are declining; while in many they are, on the whole, on the increase; and an increase which is becoming, not slower, but more rapid. There are, occasionally, branches of industry which are being gradually superseded by something else, and, in those, until production accommodates itself to demand, wages are depressed; which is an evil, but a temporary one, and would admit of great alleviation even in the present system of social economy. A diminution thus produced of the reward of labour in some particular employment is the effect and the evidence of increased remuneration, or of a new source of remuneration, in some other; the total and the average remuneration being undiminished, or even increased. To make out an appearance of diminution in the rate of wages in any leading branch of industry, it is always found necessary to compare some month or year of special and temporary depression at the present time, with the average rate, or even some exceptionally high rate, at an earlier time. The vicissitudes are no doubt a great evil, but they were as frequent and as severe in former periods of economical history as now. The greater scale of the transactions, and the greater number of persons involved in each fluctuation, may make the fluctuation appear greater, but though a larger population affords more sufferers, the evil does not weigh heavier on each of them individually. There is much evidence of improvement, and none, that is at all trustworthy, of deterioration, in the mode of living of the labouring population of the countries of Europe; when there is any appearance to the contrary it is local or partial, and can always be traced either to the pressure of some temporary calamity, or to some bad law or unwise act of government which admits of being corrected, while the permanent causes all operate in the direction of improvement.

M. Louis Blanc, therefore, while showing himself much more enlightened than the older school of levellers and democrats, inasmuch as he recognises the connection between low wages and the over-rapid increase of population, appears to have fallen into the same error which was at first committed by Malthus and his followers, that of supposing that because population has a greater power of increase than subsistence, its pressure upon subsistence must be always growing more severe. The difference is that the early Malthusians thought this an irrepressible tendency, while M. Louis Blanc thinks that it can be repressed, but only under a system of Communism. It is a great point gained for truth when it comes to be seen that the tendency to over-population is a fact which Communism, as well as the existing order of society, would have to deal with. And it is much to be rejoiced at that this necessity is admitted by the most considerable chiefs of all existing schools of Socialism. Owen and Fourier, no less than M. Louis Blanc, admitted it, and claimed for their respective systems a pre-eminent power of dealing with this difficulty. However this may be, experience shows that in the existing state of society the pressure of population on subsistence, which is the principal cause of low wages, though a great, is not an increasing evil; on the contrary, the progress of all that is called civilisation has a tendency to diminish it, partly by the more rapid increase of the means of employing and maintaining labour, partly by the increased facilities opened to labour for transporting itself to new countries and unoccupied fields of employment, and partly by a general improvement in the intelligence and prudence of the population. This progress, no doubt, is slow; but it is much that such progress should take place at all, while we are still only in the first stage of that public movement for the education of the whole people, which when more advanced must add greatly to the force of all the two causes of improvement specified above. It is, of course, open to discussion what form of society has the greatest power of dealing successfully with the pressure of population on subsistence, and on this question there is much to be said for Socialism; what was long thought to be its weakest point will, perhaps, prove to be one of its strongest. But it has no just claim to be considered as the sole means of preventing the general and growing degradation of the mass of mankind through the peculiar tendency of poverty to produce over-population. Society as at present constituted is not descending into that abyss, but gradually, though slowly, rising out of it, and this improvement is likely to be progressive if bad laws do not interfere with it.

Next, it must be observed that Socialists generally, and even the most enlightened of them, have a very imperfect and one-sided notion of the operation of competition.* They see half its effects, and overlook the other half; they regard it as an agency for grinding down every one's remuneration—for obliging every one to accept less wages for his labour, or a less price for his commodities, which would be true only if every one had to dispose of his labour or his commodities to some great monopolist, and the competition were all on one side. They forget that competition is a cause of high prices and values as well as of low; that the buyers of labour and of commodities compete with one another as well as the sellers; and that if it is competition which keeps the prices of labour and commodities as low as they are, it is competition which prevents them from falling still lower. In truth, when competition is perfectly free on both sides, its tendency is not specially either to raise or to lower the price of articles, but to equalise it; to level inequalities of remuneration, and to reduce all to a general average, a result which, in so far as realised (no doubt very imperfectly), is, on Socialistic principles, desirable. But if, disregarding for the time that part of the effects of competition which consists in keeping up prices, we fix our attention on its effect in keeping them down, and contemplate this effect in reference solely to the interest of the labouring classes, it would seem that if competition keeps down wages, and so gives a motive to the labouring classes to withdraw the labour market from the full influence of competition, if they can, it must on the other hand have credit for keeping down the prices of the articles on which wages are expended, to the great advantage of those who depend on wages. To meet this consideration Socialists, as we said in our quotation from M. Louis Blanc, are reduced to affirm that the low prices of commodities produced by competition are delusive, and lead in the end to higher prices than before, because when the richest competitor has got rid of all his rivals, he commands the market and can demand any price he pleases. Now, the commonest experience shows that this state of things, under really free competition, is wholly imaginary. The richest competitor neither does nor can get rid of all his rivals, and establish himself in exclusive possession of the market; and it is not the fact that any important branch of industry or commerce formerly divided among many has become, or shows any tendency to become, the monopoly of a few.

The kind of policy described is sometimes possible where, as in the case of railways, the only competition possible is between two or three great companies, the operations being on too vast a scale to be within the reach of individual capitalists; and this is one of the reasons why businesses which require to be carried on by great joint-stock enterprises cannot be trusted to competition, but, when not reserved by the State to itself, ought to be carried on under conditions prescribed, and, from time to time, varied by the

State, for the purpose of insuring to the public a cheaper supply of its wants than would be afforded by private interest in the absence of sufficient competition. But in the ordinary branches of industry no one rich competitor has it in his power to drive out all the smaller ones. Some businesses show a tendency to pass out of the hands of many small producers or dealers into a smaller number of larger ones; but the cases in which this happens are those in which the possession of a larger capital permits the adoption of more powerful machinery, more efficient by more expensive processes, or a better organized and more economical mode of carrying on business, and thus enables the large dealer legitimately and permanently to supply the commodity cheaper than can be done on the small scale; to the great advantage of the consumers, and therefore of the labouring classes, and diminishing, *pro tanto*, that waste of the resources of the community so much complained of by Socialists, the unnecessary multiplication of mere distributors, and of the various other classes whom Fourier calls the parasites of industry. When this change is effected, the larger capitalists, either individual or joint-stock, among which the business is divided, are seldom, if ever, in any considerable branch of commerce, so few as that competition shall not continue to act between them; so that the saving in cost, which enabled them to undersell the small dealers, continues afterwards, as at first, to be passed on, in lower prices, to their customers. The operation, therefore, of competition in keeping down the prices of commodities, including those on which wages are expended, is not illusive but real, and, we may add, is a growing, not a declining, fact.

But there are other respects, equally important, in which the charges brought by Socialists against competition do not admit of so complete an answer. Competition is the best security for cheapness, but by no means a security for quality. In former times, when producers and consumers were less numerous, it was a security for both. The market was not large enough nor the means of publicity sufficient to enable a dealer to make a fortune by continually attracting new customers: his success depended on his retaining those that he had; and when a dealer furnished good articles, or when he did not, the fact was soon known to those whom it concerned, and he acquired a character for honest or dishonest dealing of more importance to him than the gain that would be made by cheating casual purchasers. But on the great scale of modern transactions, with the great multiplication of competition and the immense increase in the quantity of business competed for, dealers are so little dependent on permanent customers that character is much less essential to them, while there is also far less certainty of their obtaining the character they deserve. The low prices which a tradesman advertises are known, to a thousand for one who has discovered for himself or learned from others, that the bad quality of the goods is more than an equivalent for their cheapness; while at the same time the much greater fortunes now made by some dealers excite the cupidity of all, and the greed of rapid gain substitutes itself for the modest desire to make a living by their business. In this manner, as wealth increases and greater prizes seem to be within reach, more and more of a gambling spirit is introduced into commerce; and where this prevails not only are the simplest maxims of prudence disregarded, but all, even the most perilous, forms of pecuniary improbity receive a terrible stimulus. This is the meaning of what is called the intensity of modern competition. It is further to be mentioned that when this intensity has reached a certain height, and when a portion of the producers of an article or the dealers in it have resorted to any of the modes of fraud, such as adulteration, giving short measure, etc., of the increase of which there is now so much complaint, the temptation is immense on these to adopt the fraudulent practices, who would not have originated them; for the public are aware of the low prices fallaciously produced by the frauds, but do not find out at first, if ever, that the article is not worth the lower price, and they will not go on paying a higher price for a better article, and the honest dealer is placed at a terrible disadvantage. Thus the frauds, begun by a few, become customs of the trade, and the morality of the trading classes is more and more deteriorated.

On this point, therefore, Socialists have really made out the existence not only of a great evil, but of one which grows and tends to grow with the growth of population and wealth. It must be said, however, that society has never yet used the means which are already in its power of grappling with this evil. The laws against commercial frauds are very defective, and their execution still more so. Laws of this description have no chance of being really enforced unless it is the special duty of some one to enforce them. They are specially in need of a public prosecutor. It is still to be discovered how far it is possible to repress by means of the criminal law a class of misdeeds which are now seldom brought before the tribunals, and to which, when brought, the judicial administration of this country is most unduly lenient. The most important class, however, of these frauds, to the mass of the people, those which affect the price or quality of articles of daily consumption, can be in a great measure overcome by the institution of co-operative stores. By this plan any body of consumers who form themselves into an association for the purpose, are enabled to pass over the retail dealers and obtain their articles direct from the wholesale merchants, or, what is better (now that wholesale co-operative agencies have been established), from the producers, thus freeing themselves from the heavy tax now paid to the distributing classes and at the same time eliminate the usual perpetrators of adulterations and other frauds. Distribution thus becomes a work performed by agents selected and paid by those who have no interest in anything but the cheapness and goodness of the article; and the distributors are capable of being thus reduced to the numbers which the quantity of work to be done really requires. The difficulties of the plan consist in the skill and trustworthiness required in the managers, and the imperfect nature of the control which can be exercised over them by the body at large. The great success and rapid growth of the system prove, however, that these difficulties are, in some tolerable degree, overcome. At all events, if the beneficial tendency of the competition of retailers in promoting cheapness is foregone, and has to be replaced by other securities, the mischievous tendency of the same competition in deteriorating quality is at any rate got rid of; and the prosperity of the co-operative stores shows that this benefit is obtained not only without detriment to cheapness, but with great advantage to it, since the profits of the concerns enable them to return to the consumers a large percentage on the price of every article supplied to them. So far, therefore, as this class of evils is concerned, an effectual remedy is already in operation, which, though suggested by and partly grounded on social-istic principles, is consistent with the existing constitution of property.

With regard to those greater and more conspicuous eco-nomical frauds, or malpractices equivalent to frauds, of which so many deplorable cases have become notorious— committed by merchants and bankers between themselves or between them and those who have trusted them with money, such a remedy as above described is not available, and the only resources which the present constitution of society affords against them are a sterner reprobation by opinion, and a more efficient repression by the law. Neither of these remedies has had any approach to an effectual trial. It is on the occurrence of insolvencies that these dishonest practices usually come to light; the perpetrators take their place, not in the class of malefactors, but in that of insol-vent debtors; and the laws of this and other countries were formerly so savage against simple insolvency, that by one of those reactions to which the opinions of mankind are liable, insolvents came to be regarded mainly as objects of compas-sion, and it seemed to be thought that the hand both of law and of public opinion could hardly press too lightly upon them. By an error in a contrary direction to the ordinary one of our law, which in the punishment of offences in general wholly neglects the question of reparation to the sufferer, our bankruptcy laws have for some time treated the recovery for creditors of what is left of their property as almost the sole object, scarcely any importance being at-tached to the punishment of the bankrupt for any misconduct which does not directly interfere with that primary purpose. For three or four years past there has been a slight counter-reaction, and more than one bankruptcy act has been passed, somewhat less indulgent to the bankrupt; but the primary object regarded has still been the pecuniary interest of the creditors, and criminality in the bankrupt himself, with the exception of a small number of well-marked offences, gets off almost with impunity. It may be confidently affirmed, therefore, that, at least in this country, society has not exerted the power it possesses of making mercantile dishonesty dangerous to the perpetrator. On the contrary, it is a gambling trick in which all the advantage is on the side of the trickster: if the trick succeeds it makes his fortune, or preserves it; if it fails, he is at most reduced to poverty, which was perhaps already impending when he determined to run the chance, and he is classed by those who have not looked closely into the matter, and even by many who have, not among the infamous but among the unfortunate. Until a more moral and rational mode of dealing with culpable insolvency has been tried and failed, commercial dishonesty cannot be ranked among evils the prevalence of which is inseparable from commercial competition.

Another point on which there is much misapprehension on the part of Socialists, as well as of Trades Unionists and other partisans of Labour against Capital, relates to the proportions in which the produce of the country is really shared and the amount of what is actually diverted from those who produce it, to enrich other persons. I forbear for the present to speak of the land, which is a subject apart. But with respect to capital employed in business, there is in the popular notions a great deal of illusion. When, for instance, a capitalist invests £20,000 in his business, and draws from it an income of (suppose) £2,000 a year, the common impression is as if he was the beneficial owner both of the £20,000 and of the £2,000, while the labourers own nothing but their wages. The truth, however, is that he only obtains the £2,000 on condition of applying no part of the £20,000 to his own use. He has the legal control over it, and might squander it if he chose, but if he did he would not have the £2,000 a year also. As long as he derives an income from his capital he has not the option of withholding it from the use of others. As much of his invested capital as consists of buildings, machinery and other instruments of production, are applied to production and are not applicable to the support or enjoyment of any one. What is so applicable (including what is laid out in keeping up or renewing the buildings and instruments) is paid away to labourers, forming their remuneration and their share in the division of the produce. For all personal purposes they have the capital and he has but the profits, which it only yields to him on condition that the capital itself is employed in satisfying not his own wants, but those of labourers. The proportion which the profits of capital usually bear to the capital itself (or rather to the circulating portion of it) is the ratio which the capitalist's share of the produce bears to the aggregate share of the labourers. Even of his own share a small part only belongs to him as the owner of capital. The portion of the produce which falls to capital merely as capital* is measured by the interest of money, since that is all that the owner of capital obtains when he contributes nothing to production except the capital itself. Now the interest of capital in the public funds, which are considered to be the best security, is at the present prices (which have not varied much for many years) about three and one-third per cent. Even in this investment there is some little risk—risk of repudiation, risk of being obliged to sell out at a low price in some commercial crisis.

Estimating these risks at $\frac{1}{3}$ per cent, the remaining 3 per cent may be considered as the remuneration of capital, apart from insurance against loss. On the security of a mortgage 4 per cent is generally obtained, but in this transaction there are considerably greater risks—the uncertainty of titles to land under our bad system of law; the chance of having to realize the security at a great cost in law charges; and liability to delay in the receipt of the interest, even when the principal is safe. When mere money independently of exertion yields a larger income, as it sometimes does, for example, by shares in railway or other companies, the surplus is hardly ever an equivalent for the risk of losing the whole, or part, of the capital by mismanagement, as in the case of the Brighton Railway, the dividend of which, after having been 6 per cent per annum, sunk to from nothing to $1\frac{1}{2}$ per cent, and shares which had been bought at 120 could not be sold for more than about 43. When money is lent at the high rates of interest one occasionally hears of, rates only given by spendthrifts and needy persons, it is because the risk of loss is so great that few who possess money can be induced to lend to them at all. So little reason is there for the outcry against 'usury' as one of the grievous burthens of the working classes. Of the profits, therefore, which a manufacturer or other person in business obtains from his capital no more than about 3 per cent can be set down to the capital itself. If he were able and willing to give up the whole of this to his labourers, who already share among them the whole of his capital as it is annually reproduced from year to year, the addition to their weekly wages would be inconsiderable. Of what he obtains beyond 3 per cent a great part is insurance against the manifold losses he is exposed to, and cannot safely be applied to his own use, but requires to be kept in reserve to cover those losses when they occur. The remainder is properly the remuneration of his skill and industry—the wages of his labour of superintendence. No doubt if he is very successful in business these wages of his are extremely liberal, and quite out of proportion to what the same skill and industry would command if offered for hire. But, on the other hand, he runs a worse risk than that of being out of employment; that of doing the work without earning anything by it, of having the labour and anxiety without the wages. I do not say that the drawbacks balance the privileges, or that he derives no advantage from the position which makes him a capitalist and employer of labour, instead of a skilled superintendent letting out his services to others; but the amount of his advantage must not be estimated by the great prizes alone. If we subtract from the gains of some the losses of others, and deduct from the balance a fair compensation for the anxiety, skill, and labour of both, grounded on the market price of skilled superintendence, what remains will be, no doubt, considerable, but yet, when compared to the entire capital of the country, annually reproduced and dispensed in wages, it is very much smaller than it appears to the popular imagination; and were the whole of it added to the share of the labourers it would make a less addition to that share than would be made by any important invention in machinery, or by the suppression of unnecessary distributors and other 'parasites of industry'. To complete the estimate, however, of the portion of the produce of industry which goes to remunerate capital we must not stop at the interest earned out of the produce by the capital actually employed in producing it, but must include that which is paid to the former owners of capital which has been unproductively spent and no longer exists, and is paid, of course, out of the produce of other capital. Of this nature is the interest of national debts, which is the cost a nation is burthened with for past difficulties and dangers, or for past folly or profligacy of its rulers, more or less shared by the nation itself. To this must be added the interest on the debts of landowners and other unproductive consumers; except so far as the money borrowed may have been spent in remunerative improvement of the productive powers of the land. As for landed property itself—the appropriation of the rent of land by private individuals—I reserve, as I have said, this question for discussion hereafter; for the tenure of land might be varied in any manner considered desirable, all the land might be declared the property of the State, without interfering with the right of property in anything which is the product of human labour and abstinence.

It seemed desirable to begin the discussion of the Socialist question by these remarks in abatement of Socialist exaggerations, in order that the true issues between Socialism and the existing state of society might be correctly conceived. The present system is not, as many Socialists believe, hurrying us into a state of general indigence and slavery from which only Socialism can save us. The evils and injustices suffered under the present system are great, but they are not increasing; on the contrary, the general tendency is towards their slow diminution. Moreover the inequalities in the distribution of the produce between capital and labour, however they may shock the feeling of natural justice, would not by their mere equalisation afford by any means so large a fund for raising the lower levels of remuneration as Socialists, and many besides Socialists, are apt to suppose. There is not any one abuse or injustice now prevailing in society by merely abolishing which the human race would pass out of suffering into happiness. What is incumbent on us is a calm comparison between two different systems of society, with a view of determining which of them affords the greatest resources for overcoming the inevitable difficulties of life. And if we find the answer to this question more difficult, and more dependent upon intellectual and moral conditions, than is usually thought, it is satisfactory to reflect that there is time before us for the question to work itself out on an experimental scale, by actual trial. I believe we shall find that no other test is possible of the practicability or beneficial operation of Socialist arrangements; but that the intellectual and moral grounds of Socialism deserve the most attentive study, as affording in many cases the guiding principles of the improvements necessary to give the present economic system of society its best chance.

The Difficulties of Socialism*

Among those who call themselves Socialists, two kinds of persons may be distinguished. There are, in the first place, those whose plans for a new order of society, in which private property and individual competition are to be superseded and other motives to action substituted, are on the scale of a village community or township, and would be applied to an entire country by the multiplication of such self-acting units; of this character are the systems of Owen, of Fourier, and the more thoughtful and philosophic Socialists generally. The other class, who are more a product of the Continent than of Great Britain and may be called the revolutionary Socialists, propose to themselves a much bolder stroke. Their scheme is the management of the whole productive resources of the country by one central authority, the general government. And with this view some of them avow as their purpose that the working classes, or somebody in their behalf, should take possession of all the property of the country, and administer it for the general benefit.

Whatever be the difficulties of the first of these two forms of Socialism, the second must evidently involve the same difficulties and many more. The former, too, has the great advantage that it can be brought into operation progressively, and can prove its capabilities by trial. It can be tried first on a select population and extended to others as their education and cultivation permit. It need not, and in the natural order of things would not, become an engine of subversion until it had shown itself capable of being also a means of reconstruction. It is not so with the other: the aim of that is to substitute the new rule for the old at a single stroke, and to exchange the amount of good realised under the present system, and its large possibilities of improvement, for a plunge without any preparation into the most extreme form of the problem of carrying on the whole round of the operations of social life without the motive power which has always hitherto worked the social machinery. It must be acknowledged that those who would play this game on the strength of their own private opinion, unconfirmed as yet by any experimental verification—who would forcibly deprive all who have now a comfortable physical existence of their only present means of preserving it, and would brave the frightful bloodshed and misery that would ensue if the attempt was resisted—must have a serene confidence in their own wisdom on the one hand and a recklessness of other people's sufferings on the other, which Robespierre and St Just, hitherto the typical instances of those united attributes, scarcely came up to. Nevertheless this scheme has great elements of popularity which the more cautious and reasonable form of Socialism has not; because what it professes to do it promises to do quickly, and holds out hope to the enthusiastic of seeing the whole of their aspirations realized in their own time and at a blow.

The peculiarities, however, of the revolutionary form of Socialism will be most conveniently examined after the considerations common to both the forms have been duly weighed.

The produce of the world could not attain anything approaching to its present amount, nor support anything approaching to the present number of its inhabitants, except upon two conditions: abundant and costly machinery, buildings, and other instruments of production; and the power of undertaking long operations and waiting a considerable time for their fruits. In other words, there must be a large accumulation of capital, both fixed in the implements and buildings, and circulating, that is, employed in maintaining the labourers and their families during the time which elapses before the productive operations are completed and the products come in. This necessity depends on physical laws, and is inherent in the condition of human life; but these requisites of production, the capital, fixed and circulating, of the country (to which has to be added the land, and all that is contained in it), may either be the collective property of those who use it, or may belong to individuals; and the question is, which of these arrangements is most conducive to human happiness. What is characteristic of Socialism is the joint ownership by all the members of the community of the instruments and means of production; which carries with it the consequence that the division of the produce among the body of owners must be a public act, performed according to rules laid down by the community. Socialism by no means excludes private ownership of articles of consumption; the exclusive right of each of his or her share of the produce when received, either to enjoy, to give, or to exchange it. The land, for example, might be wholly the property of the community for agricultural and other productive purposes, and might be cultivated on their joint account, and yet the dwelling assigned to each individual or family as part of their remuneration might be as exclusively theirs, while they continued to fulfil their share of the common labours, as any one's house now is; and not the dwelling only, but any ornamental ground which the circumstances of the association allowed to be attached to the house for purposes of enjoyment. The distinctive feature of Socialism is not that all things are in common, but that production is only carried on upon the common account, and that the instruments of production are held as common property. The *practicability* then of Socialism, on the scale of Mr Owen's or M. Fourier's villages, admits of no dispute. The attempt to manage the whole production of a nation by one central organization is a totally different matter; but a mixed agricultural and manufacturing association of from two thousand to four thousand inhabitants under any tolerable circumstances of soil and climate would be easier to manage than many a joint stock company. The question to be considered is, whether this joint management is likely to be as efficient and successful as the managements of private industry by private capital. And this question has to be considered in a double aspect; the efficiency of the directing mind, or minds, and that of the simple workpeople. And in order to state this question in its simplest form, we will suppose the form of Socialism to be simple Communism, i.e. equal division of the produce among all the sharers, or, according to M. Louis Blanc's still higher standard of justice, apportionment of it according to difference of need, but without making any difference of reward according to the nature of the duty nor according to the supposed merits or services of the individual. There are other forms of Socialism, particularly Fourierism, which do, on considerations of justice or expediency, allow differences of remuneration for different kinds or degrees of service to the community; but the consideration of these may be for the present postponed.

The difference between the motive powers in the economy of society under private property and under Communism would be greatest in the case of the directing minds. Under the present system, the direction being entirely in the hands of the person or persons who own (or are personally responsible for) the capital, the whole benefit of the difference between the best administration and the worst under which the business can continue to be carried on accrues to the person or persons who control the administration: they reap the whole profit of good management except so far as their self-interest or liberality induce them to share it with their subordinates; and they suffer the whole detriment of mismanagement except so far as this may cripple their subsequent power of employing labour. This strong personal motive to do their very best and utmost for the efficiency and economy of the operations, would not exist under Communism; as the managers would only receive out of the produce the same equal dividend as the other members of the association. What would remain would be the interest common to all in so managing affairs as to make the dividend as large as possible; the incentives of public spirit, of conscience, and of the honour and credit of the managers. The force of these motives, especially when combined, is great. But it varies greatly in different persons, and is much greater for some purposes than for others. The verdict of experience, in the imperfect degree of moral cultivation which mankind have yet reached, is that the motive of conscience and that of credit and reputation, even when they are of some strength, are, in the majority of cases, much stronger as restraining than as impelling forces—are more to be depended on for preventing wrong, than for calling forth the fullest energies in the pursuit of ordinary occupations. In the case of most men the only inducement which has been found sufficiently constant and unflagging to overcome the ever-present influence of indolence and love of ease, and induce men to apply themselves unrelaxingly to work for the most part in itself dull and unexciting, is the prospect of bettering their own economic condition and that of their family; and the closer the connection of every increase of exertion with a corresponding increase of its fruits, the more powerful is this motive. To suppose the contrary would be to imply that with men as they now are, duty and honour are more powerful principles of action than personal interest, not solely as to special acts and forbearances respecting which those sentiments have been exceptionally cultivated, but in the regulation of their whole lives; which no one, I suppose, will affirm. It may be said that this inferior efficacy of public and social feelings is not inevitable—is the result of imperfect education. This I am quite ready to admit, and also that there are even now many individual exceptions to the general infirmity. But before these exceptions can grow into a majority, or even into a very large minority, much time will be required. The education of human beings is one of the most difficult of all arts, and this is one of the points in which it has hitherto been least successful; moreover improvements in general education are necessarily very gradual, because the future generation is educated by the present, and the imperfections of the teachers set an invincible limit to the degree in which they can train their pupils to be better than themselves. We must therefore expect, unless we are operating upon a select portion of the population, that personal interest will for a long time be a more effective stimulus to the most vigorous and careful conduct of the industrial business of society than motives of a higher character. It will be said that at present the greed of personal gain by its very excess counteracts its own end by the stimulus it gives to reckless and often dishonest risks. This it does, and under Communism that source of evil would generally be absent. It is probable, indeed, that enterprise either of a bad or of a good kind would be a deficient element, and that business in general would fall very much under the dominion of routine; the rather, as the performance of duty in such communities has to be enforced by external sanctions, the more nearly each person's duty can be reduced to fixed rules, the easier it is to hold him to its performance. A circumstance which increases the probability of this result is the limited power which the managers would have of independent action. They would of course hold their authority from the choice of the community, by whom their function might at any time be withdrawn from them; and this would make it necessary for them, even if not so required by the constitution of the community, to obtain the general consent of the body before making any change in the established mode of carrying on the concern. The difficulty of persuading a numerous body to make a change in their accustomed mode of working, of which change the trouble is often great, and the risk more obvious to their minds than the advantage, would have a great tendency to keep things in their accustomed track. Against this it has to be set, that choice by the persons who are directly interested in the success of the work, and who have practical knowledge and opportunities of judgment, might be expected on the average to produce managers of greater skill than the chances of birth, which now so often determine who shall be the owner of the capital. This may be true; and though it may be replied that the capitalist by inheritance can also, like the community, appoint a manager more capable than himself, this would only place him on the same level of advantage as the community, not on a higher level. But it must be said on the other side that under the Communist system the persons most qualified for the management would be likely very often to hang back from undertaking it. At present the manager, even if he be a hired servant, has a very much larger remuneration than the other persons concerned in the business; and there are open to his ambition higher social positions to which his function of manager is a stepping-stone. On the Communist system none of these advantages would be possessed by him; he could obtain only the same dividend out of the produce of the community's labour as any other member of it; he would no longer have the chance of raising himself from a receiver of wages into the class of capitalists; and while he could be in no way better off than any other labourer, his responsibilities and anxieties would be so much greater that a large proportion of mankind would be likely to prefer the less onerous position. This difficulty was foreseen by Plato as an objection to the system proposed in his Republic of community of goods among a governing class; and the motive on which he relied for inducing the fit persons to take on themselves, in the absence of all the ordinary inducements, the cares and labours of government, was the fear of being governed by worse men.* This, in truth, is the motive which would have to be in the main depended upon; the persons most competent to the management would be prompted to undertake the office to prevent it from falling into less competent hands. And the motive would probably be effectual at times when there was an impression that by incompetent management the affairs of the community were going to ruin, or even only decidedly deteriorating. But this motive could not, as a rule, expect to be called into action by the less stringent inducement of merely promoting improvement; unless in the case of inventors or schemers eager to try some device from which they hoped for great and immediate fruits; and persons of this kind are very often unfitted by over-sanguine temper and imperfect judgment for the general conduct of affairs, while even when fitted for it they are precisely the kind of persons against whom the average man is apt to entertain a prejudice, and they would often be unable to overcome the preliminary difficulty of persuading the community both to adopt their project and to accept them as managers. Communistic management would thus be, in all probability, less favourable than private management to that striking out of new paths and making immediate sacrifices for distant and uncertain advantages, which, though seldom unattended with risk, is generally indispensable to great improvements in the economic condition of mankind, and even to keeping up the existing state in the face of a continual increase of the number of mouths to be fed.

We have thus far taken account only of the operation of motives upon the managing minds of the association. Let us now consider how the case stands in regard to the ordinary workers.

These, under Communism, would have no interest, except their share of the general interest, in doing their work honestly and energetically. But in this respect matters would be no worse than they now are in regard to the great majority of the producing classes. These, being paid by fixed wages, are so far from having any direct interest of their own in the efficiency of their work, that they have not even that share in the general interest which every worker would have in the Communistic organization. Accordingly, the inefficiency of hired labour, the imperfect manner in which it calls forth the real capabilities of the labourers, is matter of common remark. It is true that a character for being a good workman is far from being without its value, as it tends to give him a preference in employment, and sometimes obtains for him higher wages. There are also possibilities of rising to the position of foreman, or other subordinate administrative posts, which are not only more highly paid than ordinary labour, but sometimes open the way to ulterior advantages. But on the other side is to be set that under Communism the general sentiment of the community, composed of the comrades under whose eyes each person works, would be sure to be in favour of good and hard working, and unfavourable to laziness, carelessness, and waste. In the present system not only is this not the case, but the public opinion of the workman class often acts in the very opposite direction: the rules of some trade societies actually forbid their members to exceed a certain standard of efficiency, lest they should diminish the number of labourers required for the work; and for the same reason they often violently resist contrivances for economizing labour. The change from this to a state in which every person would have an interest in rendering every other person as industrious, skilful, and careful as possible (which would be the case under Communism), would be a change very much for the better.

It is, however, to be considered that the principal defects of the present system in respect to the efficiency of labour may be corrected, and the chief advantages of Communism in that respect may be obtained, by arrangements compatible with private property and individual competition. Considerable improvement is already obtained by piecework, in the kinds of labour which admit of it. By this the workman's personal interest is closely connected with the quantity of work he turns out—not so much with its quality, the security for which still has to depend on the employer's vigilance; neither does piece-work carry with it the public opinion of the workman class, which is often, on the contrary, strongly opposed to it, as a means of (as they think) diminishing the market for labourers. And there is really good ground for their dislike of piece-work, if, as is alleged, it is a frequent practice of employers, after using piece-work to ascertain the utmost which a good workman can do, to fix the price of piece-work so low that by doing that utmost he is not able to earn more than they would be obliged to give him as day wages for ordinary work.

But there is a far more complete remedy than piece-work for the disadvantages of hired labour, viz. what is now called industrial partnership—the admission of the whole body of labourers to a participation in the profits, by distributing among all who share in the work, in the form of a percentage on their earnings, the whole or a fixed portion of the gains after a certain remuneration has been allowed to the capitalist. This plan has been found of admirable efficacy, both in this country and abroad. It has enlisted the sentiments of the workmen employed on the side of the most careful regard by all of them to the general interest of the concern; and by its joint effect in promoting zealous exertion and checking waste, it has very materially increased the remuneration of every description of labour in the concerns in which it has been adopted. It is evident that this system of indefinite extension and of an indefinite increase in the share of profits assigned to the labourers, short of that which would leave to the managers less than the needful degree of personal interest in the success of the concern. It is even likely that when such arrangements become common, many of these concerns would at some period or another, on the death or retirement of the chiefs, pass, by arrangement, into the state of purely co-operative associations.

It thus appears that as far as concerns the motives to exertion in the general body, Communism has no advantage which may not be reached under private property, while as respects the managing heads it is at a considerable disadvantage. It has also some disadvantages which seem to be inherent in it, through the necessity under which it lies of deciding in a more or less arbitrary manner questions which, on the present system, decide themselves, often badly enough, but spontaneously.

It is a simple rule, and under certain aspects a just one, to give equal payment to all who share in the work. But this is a very imperfect justice unless the work also is apportioned equally. Now the many different kinds of work required in every society are very unequal in hardness and unpleasantness. To measure these against one another, so as to make quality equivalent to quantity, is so difficult that Communists generally propose that all should work by turns at every kind of labour. But this involves an almost complete sacrifice of the economic advantages of the division of employments, advantages which are indeed frequently over-estimated (or rather the counter-considerations are under-estimated) by political economists, but which are nevertheless, in the point of view of the productiveness of labour, very considerable, for the double reason that the co-operation of employment enables the work to distribute itself with some regard to the special capacities and qualifications of the worker, and also that every worker acquires greater skill and rapidity in one kind of work by confining himself to it. The arrangement, therefore, which is deemed indispensable to a just distribution would probably be a very considerable disadvantage in respect of production. But further, it is still a very imperfect standard of justice to demand the same amount of work from every one. People have unequal capacities of work, both mental and bodily, and what is a light task for one is an insupportable burthen to another. It is necessary, therefore, that there should be a dispensing power, an authority competent to grant exemptions from the ordinary amount of work, and to proportion tasks in some measure to capabilities. As long as there are any lazy or selfish persons who like better to be worked for by others than to work, there will be frequent attempts to obtain exemptions by favour or fraud, and the frustration of these attempts will be an affair of considerable difficulty, and will by no means be always successful. These inconveniences would be little felt, for some time at least, in communities composed of select persons, earnestly desirous of the success of the experiment; but plans for the regeneration of society must consider average human beings, and not only them but the large residuum of persons greatly below the average in the personal and social virtues. The squabbles and ill-blood which could not fail to be engendered by the distribution of work whenever such persons have to be dealt with, would be a great abatement from the harmony and unanimity which Communists hope would be found among the members of their association. That concord would, even in the most fortunate circumstances, be much more liable to disturbance than Communists suppose. The institution provides that there shall be no quarrelling about material interests; individualism is excluded from that department of affairs. But there are other departments from which no institutions can exclude it: there will still be rivalry for reputation and for personal power. When selfish ambition is excluded from the field in which, with most men, it chiefly exercises itself, that of riches and pecuniary interest, it would betake itself with greater intensity to the domain still open to it, and we may expect that the struggles for pre-eminence and for influence in the management would be of great bitterness when the personal passions, diverted from their ordinary channel, are driven to seek their principal gratification in that other direction. For these various reasons it is probable that a Communist association would frequently fail to exhibit the attractive picture of mutual love and unity of will and feeling which we are often told by Communists to expect, but would often be torn by dissension and not unfrequently broken up by it.

Other and numerous sources of discord are inherent in the necessity which the Communist principle involves, of deciding by the general voice questions of the utmost importance to every one, which on the present system can be and are left to individuals to decide, each for his own case. As an example, take the subject of education. All Socialists are strongly impressed with the all-importance of the training given to the young, not only for the reasons which apply universally, but because their demands being much greater than those of any other system upon the intelligence and morality of the individual citizen, they have even more at stake than any other societies on the excellence of their educational arrangements. Now under Communism these arrangements would have to be made for every citizen by the collective body, since individual parents, supposing them to prefer some other mode of educating their children, would have no private means of paying for it, and would be limited to what they could do by their own personal teaching and influence. But every adult member of the body would have an equal voice in determining the collective system designed for the benefit of all. Here, then, is a most fruitful source of discord in every association. All who had any opinion or preference as to the education they would desire for their own children, would have to rely for their chance of obtaining it upon the influence they could exercise in the joint decision of the community.

It is needless to specify a number of other important questions affecting the mode of employing the productive resources of the association, the conditions of social life, the relations of the body with other associations, etc., on which difference of opinion, often irreconcilable, would be likely to arise. But even the dissensions which might be expected would be a far less evil to the prospects of humanity than a delusive unanimity produced by the prostration of all individual opinions and wishes before the decree of the majority. The obstacles to human progression are always great, and require a concurrence of favourable circumstances to overcome them; but an indispensable condition of their being overcome is, that human nature should have freedom to expand spontaneously in various directions, both in thought and practice; that people should both think for themselves and try experiments for themselves, and should not resign into the hands of rulers, whether acting in the name of a few or of the majority, the business of thinking for them, and of prescribing how they shall act. But in Communist associations private life would be brought in a most unexampled degree within the dominion of public authority, and there would be less scope for the development of individual character and individual preferences than has hitherto existed among the full citizens of any state belonging to the progressive branches of the human family. Already in all societies the compression of individuality by the majority is a great and growing evil; it would probably be much greater under Communism, except so far as it might be in the power of individuals to set bounds to it by selecting to belong to a community of persons like-minded with themselves.

From these various considerations I do not seek to draw any inference against the possibility that Communistic production is capable of being at some future time the form of society best adapted to the wants and circumstances of mankind. I think that this is, and will long be, an open question, upon which fresh light will continually be obtained, both by trial of the Communistic principle under favourable circumstances, and by the improvements which will be gradually effected in the working of the existing system, that of private ownership. The one certainty is, that Communism, to be successful, requires a high standard of both moral and intellectual education in all the members of the community—moral, to qualify them for doing their part honestly and energetically in the labour of life under no inducement but their share in the general interest of the association, and their feelings of duty and sympathy towards it; intellectual, to make them capable of estimating distant interests and entering into complex considerations, sufficiently at least to be able to discriminate, in these matters, good counsel from bad. Now I reject altogether the notion that it is impossible for education and cultivation such as is implied in these things to be made the inheritance of every person in the nation; but I am convinced that it is very difficult, and that the passage to it from our present condition can only be slow. I admit the plea that in the points of moral education on which the success of Communism depends, the present state of society is demoralizing, and that only a Communistic association can effectually train mankind for Communism. It is for Communism, then, to prove, by practical experiment, its power of giving this training. Experiments alone can show whether there is as yet in any portion of the population a sufficiently high level of moral cultivation to make Communism succeed, and to give to the next generation among themselves the education necessary to keep up that high level permanently. If Communist associations show that they can be durable and prosperous, they will multiply, and will probably be adopted by successive portions of the population of the more advanced countries as they become morally fitted for that mode of life. But to force unprepared populations into Communist societies, even if a political revolution gave the power to make such an attempt, would end in disappointment.*

If practical trial is necessary to test the capabilities of Communism, it is no less required for those other forms of Socialism which recognise the difficulties of Communism and contrive means to surmount them. The principal of these is Fourierism, a system which, if only as a specimen of intellectual ingenuity, is highly worthy of the attention of any student, either of society or of the human mind. There is scarcely an objection or a difficulty which Fourier did not foresee, and against which he did not make provision beforehand by self-acting contrivances, grounded, however, upon a less high principle of distributive justice than that of Communism, since he admits inequalities of distribution and individual ownership of capital, but not the arbitrary disposal of it. The great problem which he grapples with is how to make labour attractive, since, if this could be done, the principal difficulty of Socialism would be overcome. He maintains that no kind of useful labour is necessarily or universally repugnant, unless either excessive in amount or devoid of the stimulus of companionship and emulation, or regarded by mankind with contempt. The workers in a Fourierist village are to class themselves spontaneously in groups, each group undertaking a different kind of work, and the same person may be a member not only of one group but of any number; a certain minimum having first been set apart for the subsistence of every member of the community, whether capable or not of labour, the society divides the remainder of the produce among the different groups, in such shares as it finds attract to each the amount of labour required, and no more; if there is too great a run upon particular groups it is a sign that those groups are over-remunerated relatively to others; if any are neglected their remuneration must be made higher. The share of produce assigned to each group is divided in fixed proportions among three elements—labour, capital, and talent; the part assigned to talent being awarded by the suffrages of the group itself, and it is hoped that among the variety of human capacities all, or nearly all, will be qualified to excel in some group or other. The remuneration for capital is to be such as is found sufficient to induce savings from individual consumption, in order to increase the common stock to such point as is desired. The number and ingenuity of the contrivances for meeting minor difficulties, and getting rid of minor inconveniences, is very remarkable. By means of these various provisions it is the expectation of Fourierists that the personal inducements to exertion for the public interest, instead of being taken away, would be made much greater than at present, since every increase of the service rendered would be much more certain of leading to increase of reward than it is now, when accidents of position have so much influence. The efficiency of labour, they therefore expect, would be unexampled, while the saving of labour would be prodigious, by diverting to useful occupations that which is now wasted on things useless or hurtful, and by dispensing with the vast number of superfluous distributors, the buying and selling for the whole community being managed by a single agency. The free choice of individuals as to their manner of life would be no further interfered with than would be necessary for gaining the full advantages of co-operation in the industrial operations. Altogether, the picture of a Fourierist community is both attractive in itself and requires less from common humanity than any other known system of Socialism; and it is much to be desired that the scheme should have that fair trial which alone can test the workableness of any new scheme of social life.[1]

The result of our review of the various difficulties of Socialism has led us to the conclusion that the various schemes for managing the productive resources of the country by public instead of private agency have a case for a trial, and some of them may eventually establish their claims to preference over the existing order of things, but that they are at present workable only by the élite of mankind, and have yet to prove their power of training mankind at large to the state of improvement which they presuppose. Far more, of course, may this be said of the more ambitious plan which aims at taking possession of the whole land and capital of the country, and beginning at once to administer it on the public account. Apart from all consideration of injustice to the present possessors, the very idea of conducting the whole industry of a country by direction from a single centre is so obviously chimerical, that nobody ventures to propose any mode in which it should be done; and it can hardly be doubted that if the revolutionary Socialists attained their immediate object, and actually had the whole property of the country at their disposal, they would find no other practicable mode of exercising their power over it than that of dividing it into portions, each to be made over to the administration of a small Socialist community. The problem of management, which we have seen to be so difficult even to a select population well prepared beforehand, would be thrown down to be solved as best it could by aggregations united only by locality, or taken indiscriminately from the population, including all the malefactors, all the idlest and most vicious, the most incapable of steady

---

[1] The principles of Fourierism are clearly set forth and powerfully defended in the various writings of M. Victor Considérant, especially that entitled *La Destinée Sociale*; but the curious inquirer will do well to study them in the writings of Fourier himself; where he will find unmistakable proofs of genius, mixed, however, with the wildest and most unscientific fancies respecting the physical world, and much interesting but rash speculation on the past and future history of humanity. It is proper to add that on some important social questions, for instance on marriage, Fourier had peculiar opinions, which, however, as he himself declares, are quite independent of, and separable from, the principles of his industrial system.

industry, forethought, or self-control, and a majority who, though not equally degraded, are yet, in the opinion of Socialists themselves, as far as regards the qualities essential for the success of Socialism, profoundly demoralised by the existing state of society. It is saying but little to say that the introduction of Socialism under such conditions could have no effect but disastrous failure, and its apostles could have only the consolation that the order of society as it now exists would have perished first, and all who benefit by it would be involved in the common ruin—a consolation which to some of them would probably be real, for if appearances can be trusted the animating principle of too many of the revolutionary Socialists is hate; a very excusable hatred of existing evils, which would vent itself by putting an end to the present system at all costs even to those who suffer by it, in the hope that out of chaos would arise a better Kosmos,* and in the impatience of desperation respecting any more gradual improvement. They are unaware that chaos is the very most unfavourable position for setting out in the construction of a Kosmos, and that many ages of conflict, violence, and tyrannical oppression of the weak by the strong must intervene; they know not that they would plunge mankind into the state of nature so forcibly described by Hobbes (*Leviathan*, Part I. ch. xiii.), where every man is enemy to every man:

In such condition there is no place for industry, because the fruit thereof is uncertain, and consequently no culture of the earth, no navigation, no use of the commodities that may be imported by sea, no commodious building, no instruments of moving and removing such things as require much force, no knowledge of the face of the earth, no account of time, no arts, no letters, no society; and, which is worst of all, continual fear and danger of violent death; and the life of man solitary, poor, nasty, brutish, and short.

If the poorest and most wretched members of a so-called civilized society are in as bad a condition as every one would be in that worst form of barbarism produced by the dissolution of civilized life, it does not follow that the way to raise them would be to reduce all others to the same miserable state. On the contrary, it is by the aid of the first who have risen that so many others have escaped from the general lot, and it is only by better organization of the same process that it may be hoped in time to succeed in raising the remainder.

The Idea of Private Property not Fixed but Variable

The preceding considerations appear sufficient to show that an entire renovation of the social fabric, such as is contemplated by Socialism, establishing the economic constitution of society upon an entirely new basis, other than that of private property and competition, however valuable as an ideal, and even as a prophecy of ultimate possibilities, is not available as a present resource, since it requires from those who are to carry on the new order of things qualities both moral and intellectual, which require to be tested in all, and to be created in most; and this cannot be done by an Act of Parliament, but must be, on the most favourable supposition, a work of considerable time. For a long period to come the principle of individual property will be in possession of the field; and even if in any country a popular movement were to place Socialists at the head of a revolutionary government, in however many ways they might violate private property, the institution itself would survive, and would either be accepted by them or brought back by their expulsion, for the plain reason that people will not lose their hold of what is at present their sole reliance for subsistence and security until a substitute for it has been got into working order. Even those, if any, who had shared among themselves what was the property of others would desire to keep what they had acquired, and to give back to property in the new hands the sacredness which they had not recognized in the old.

But though, for these reasons, individual property has presumably a long term before it, if only of provisional existence, we are not, therefore, to conclude that it must exist during that whole term unmodified, or that all the rights now regarded as appertaining to property belong to it inherently, and must endure while it endures. On the contrary, it is both the duty and the interest of those who derive the most direct benefit from the laws of property to give impartial consideration to all proposals for rendering those laws in any way less onerous to the majority. This, which would in any case be an obligation of justice, is an injunction of prudence also, in order to place themselves in the right against the attempts which are sure to be frequent to bring the Socialist forms of society prematurely into operation.

One of the mistakes oftenest committed, and which are the sources of the greatest practical errors in human affairs, is that of supposing that the same name always stands for the same aggregation of ideas. No word has been the subject of more of this kind of misunderstanding than the word property. It denotes in every state of society the largest powers of exclusive use or exclusive control over things (and sometimes, unfortunately, over persons) which the law accords, or which custom, in that state of society, recognises; but these powers of exclusive use and control are very various, and differ greatly in different countries and in different states of society.

For instance, in early states of society, the right of property did not include the right of bequest. The power of disposing of property by will was in most countries of Europe a rather late institution; and long after it was introduced it continued to be limited in favour of what were called natural heirs. Where bequest is not permitted, individual property is only a life interest. And in fact, as has been so well and fully set forth by Sir Henry Maine* in his most instructive work on Ancient Law, the primitive idea of property was that it belonged to the family, not the individual. The head of the family had the management and was the person who really exercised the proprietary rights. As in other respects, so in this, he governed the family with nearly despotic power. But he was not free so to exercise his power as to defeat the co-proprietors of the other portions; he could not so dispose of the property as to deprive them of the joint enjoyment or of the succession. By the laws and customs of some nations the property could not be alienated without the consent of the male children; in other cases the child could by law demand a division of the property and the assignment to him of his share, as in the story of the Prodigal Son.* If the association kept together after the death of the head, some other member of it, not always his son, but often the eldest of the family, the strongest, or the one selected by the rest, succeeded to the management and to the managing rights, all the others retaining theirs as before. If, on the other hand, the body broke up into separate families, each of these took away with it a part of the property. I say the property, not the inheritance, because the process was a mere continuance of existing rights, not a creation of new; the manager's share alone lapsed to the association.

Then, again, in regard to proprietary rights over immovables (the principal kind of property in a rude age) these rights were of very varying extent and duration.* By the Jewish law property in immovables was only a temporary concession; on the Sabbatical year* it returned to the common stock to be redistributed; though we may surmise that in the historical times of the Jewish state this rule may have been successfully evaded. In many countries of Asia, before European ideas intervened, nothing existed to which the expression property in land, as we understand the phrase, is strictly applicable. The ownership was broken up among several distinct parties, whose rights were determined rather by custom than by law. The government was part owner, having the right to a heavy rent. Ancient ideas and even ancient laws limited the government share to some particular fraction of the gross produce, but practically there was no fixed limit. The government might make over its share to an individual, who then became possessed of the right of collection and all the other rights of the state, but not those of any private person connected with the soil. These private rights were of various kinds. The actual cultivators, or such of them as had been long settled on the land, had a right to retain possession; it was held unlawful to evict them while they paid the rent—a rent not in general fixed by agreement, but by the custom of the neighbourhood. Between the actual cultivators and the state, or the substitute to whom the state had transferred its rights, there were intermediate persons with rights of various extent. There were officers of government who collected the state's share of the produce, sometimes for large districts, who, though bound to pay over to government all they collected, after deducting a percentage, were often hereditary officers. There were also, in many cases, village communities, consisting of the reputed descendants of the first settlers of a village, who shared among themselves either the land or its produce according to rules established by custom, either cultivating it themselves or employing others to cultivate it for them, and whose rights in the land approached nearer to those of a landed proprietor, as understood in England, than those of any other party concerned. But the proprietary right of the village was not individual, but collective; inalienable (the rights of individual sharers could only be sold or mortgaged with the consent of the community) and governed by fixed rules. In medieval Europe almost all land was held from the sovereign on tenure of service, either military or agricultural; and in Great Britain even now, when the services as well as all the reserved rights of the sovereign have long since fallen into disuse or been commuted for taxation, the theory of the law does not acknowledge an absolute right of property in land in any individual; the fullest landed proprietor known to the law, the freeholder, is but a 'tenant' of the Crown. In Russia, even when the cultivators of the soil were serfs of the landed proprietor, his proprietary right in the land was limited by rights of theirs belonging to them as a collective body managing its own affairs, and with which he could not interfere. And in most of the countries of continental Europe when serfage was abolished or went out of use, those who had cultivated the land as serfs remained in possession of rights as well as subject to obligations. The great land reforms of Stein and his successors in Prussia* consisted in abolishing both the rights and the obligations, and dividing the land bodily between the proprietor and the peasant, instead of leaving each of them with a limited right over the whole. In other cases, as in Tuscany, the *metayer* farmer* is virtually co-proprietor with the landlord, since custom, though not law, guarantees to him a permanent possession and half the gross produce, so long as he fulfils the customary conditions of his tenure.

Again, if rights of property over the same things are of different extent in different countries, so also are they exercised over different things. In all countries at a former time, and in some countries still, the right of property extended and extends to the ownership of human beings. There has often been property in public trusts, as in judicial offices, and a vast multitude of others in France before the Revolution; there are still a few patent offices in Great Britain, though I believe they will cease by operation of law on the death of the present holders; and we are only now abolishing property in army rank. Public bodies, constituted and endowed for public purposes, still claim the same inviolable right of property in their estates which individuals have in theirs, and though a sound political morality does not acknowledge this claim, the law supports it. We thus see that the right of property is differently interpreted, and held to be of different extent, in different times and places; that the conception entertained of it is a varying conception, has been frequently revised, and may admit of still further revision. It is also to be noticed that the revisions which it has hitherto undergone in the progress of society have generally been improvements. When, therefore, it is maintained, rightly or wrongly, that some change or modification in the powers exercised over things by the persons legally recognised as their proprietors would be beneficial to the public and conducive to the general improvement, it is no good answer to this merely to say that the proposed change conflicts with the idea of property. The idea of property is not some one thing, identical throughout history and incapable of alteration, but is variable like all other creations of the human mind; at any given time it is a brief expression denoting the rights over things conferred by the law or custom of some given society at that time; but neither on this point nor on any other has the law and custom of a given time and place a claim to be stereotyped for ever. A proposed reform in laws or customs is not necessarily objectionable because its adoption would imply, not the adaptation of all human affairs to the existing idea of property, but the adaptation of existing ideas of property to the growth and improvement of human affairs. This is said without prejudice to the equitable claim of proprietors to be compensated by the state for such legal rights of a proprietary nature as they may be dispossessed of for the public advantage. That equitable claim, the grounds and the just limits of it, are a subject by itself, and as such will be discussed hereafter. Under this condition, however, society is fully entitled to abrogate or alter any particular right of property which on sufficient consideration it judges to stand in the way of the public good. And assuredly the terrible case which, as we saw in a former chapter, Socialists are able to make out against the present economic order of society, demands a full consideration of all means by which the institution may have a chance of being made to work in a manner more beneficial to that large portion of society which at present enjoys the least share of its direct benefits.

EXPLANATORY NOTES

Principles of Political Economy

5   *pro tanto*: just so much.

8   *the Moravians*: one of the earliest evangelical Protestant sects, originating in the protest movement led by J. Hus (burned at the stake for heresy in 1415) in ancient Bohemia and Moravia (present-day Czech Republic), the Moravian Church (or Unitas Fratrum) established mission communities during the eighteenth century in, among many other places, the American colonies (Pennsylvania and North Carolina) and the West Indies; the sect emphasizes the obligation of each to exert himself to meet the simple needs of the community, and it attempts to foster the requisite communal goodwill through a distinctive 'choir system' that divides the community into separate groups (for example, married people, small children, older boys, and older girls) whose 'natural' affinities will promote voluntary association and mutual co-operation.

the followers of Rapp: George Rapp (1757–1847), the leader of an evangelical Christian sect at Württemberg, he and his followers emigrated to America seeking religious freedom and established a socialist association (the 'Harmony Society') in Pennsylvania as of 1805; local harassment forced the Rappites to leave in 1814 to establish another socialist community at New Harmony, Indiana; but after suffering more persecution, they sold the land and buildings to Robert Owen in 1825 and returned to Pennsylvania, where they established a successful socialist community at Economy (near Pittsburgh); after Rapp's death, the community abandoned its socialist principles, withered away by the 1890s, and is currently maintained as a historical site by the state.

9   *the late revolutions in Europe*: the worker revolts of 1848–9 in France, Italy, Austria, and elsewhere.

Mr Owen and his followers: Robert Owen (1771–1858); a successful cotton manufacturer, he advocated a 'new moral world' of decentralized socialism and also established several short-lived socialist communities in Britain and the United States, including that at New Harmony, Indiana (1825–7).

Published, among other works, *A New View of Society*...
(London, 1813); *Book of the New Moral World*, i–vii (London, 1838–44); and *The Revolution in the Mind and Practice of the Human Race* (London, 1849).

9 *M. Louis Blanc*: Jean Joseph Louis Blanc (1811–82); a fierce critic of competition, he advocated government intervention to gradually establish a decentralized socialism based on the principle (later made famous by Marx) that each should contribute according to his abilities and receive according to his needs. Published, among other works, *L'Organisation du travail* (Paris, 1839), and *La révolution du février au Luxembourg* (Paris, 1849).

M. Cabet: Étienne Cabet (1788–1856); a radical French politician and writer, he became a disciple of Robert Owen while exiled from France during the 1830s, proposed a communist utopia in his *Un voyage en Icarie* (Paris, 1840), and emigrated in 1848 with some followers to America ('Icaria') to establish a communist association at Nauvoo, Illinois (an advance party had already failed miserably to establish a community in Texas); after he attempted to impose a rigid uniformity within the community, he was expelled in 1856, the year of his death; the 'Icarians' subsequently splintered into several factions, some heavily influenced by the writings of Karl Marx, but by the turn of the century effectively dissolved.

10 *St Simonism*: Claude Henri de Rouvroy Saint-Simon (1760–1825); a nobleman, imprisoned during the Terror, he edited a series of radical journals, including *L'Organisateur* (1819–20), and advocated decentralized socialism as the most productive type of economic system known to social science. Published *Du systeme industriel* (Paris, 1821).

Fourierism: François Marie Charles Fourier (1772–1837); defended a decentralized form of socialism in many works, including *Théorie des quatre mouvements et des destinées générales* (Lyons, 1808) and *Le nouveau monde industriel et societaire* (Paris, 1829). Distribution was not perfectly egalitarian under his scheme but instead reflected inequalities of labour, saving, and even talent. Mill encouraged practical experiments with Fourierism as perhaps the most promising form of socialism.

19 *The proportioning of remuneration ... favoured by nature*: for modern discussions of this problem, see, for example, G. Co-

hen, 'On The Currency of Egalitarian Justice', *Ethics*, 99 (1989), 906–42; and R. Arneson, 'Liberalism, Distributive Subjectivism, and Equal Opportunity for Welfare', *Philosophy and Public Affairs* (1990), 158–94.

20 *the Jesuits in Paraguay*: See Bk. I, Ch. XI (*CW* ii. 164–70).

21 *ménages*: households or rooms.

33 *inheritance ab intestato*: inheritance from a person who has died without making a legal will.

34 *legitima portio*: legitimate portion, lawful or customary share.

40 ——*immetata quibus jugera liberas | Fruges et Cererem ferunt, | Nec cultura placet longior annuā*: the quote is from Horace, *Carmina*, Book III, Ode XXIV, lines 12–14. In admiration of barbarian nomads, he says that the 'undivided (literally, unmeasured) fields afford abundant harvests for the whole tribe. Nor does any period of cultivation longer than a year please them'. The nomads annually abandon the fields, leaving the soil in more or less the same condition for others to use.

land . . . is the original inheritance of the whole species: for relevant modern discussions, see e.g. G. Cohen, 'Self-Ownership, World Ownership and Equality', *Social Philosophy and Policy*, 3 (1986), 77–96; and J. Roemer, 'A Challenge to Neo-Lockianism', *Canadian Journal of Philosophy*, 18 (1988), 697–710.

44 *the great measure of justice in 1833*: the Emancipation Act whereby Britain abolished slavery, with compensation to the slavemasters, within the Empire.

brevet: licence.

53 *Catallactics, or the science of exchanges*: the term was proposed by Richard Whately, *Introductory Lectures on Political Economy* (London, 1831). It still occasionally surfaces in modern economic writings, for example, L. von Mises, *Human Action* (New Haven, Conn., 1949). Friedrich Hayek uses the term 'catallaxy' to refer to any spontaneous order such as the market based on exchanges (*Law, Legislation and Liberty*, i–iii (Chicago, 1973–9)).

55 *Mr De Quincey*: Thomas De Quincey (1785–1859); a brilliant literary figure who wrote the sensational *Confessions of an*

Opium Eater, and also dabbled in political economy. Published *The Logic of Political Economy* (Edinburgh, 1844).

59 *a preceding chapter*: Bk. I, Ch. XII.

Dr Chalmers: Thomas Chalmers (1780–1847); preacher, Professor of Moral Philosophy at St Andrews (1823–8), then Professor of Divinity at Edinburgh until his death. Published *An Enquiry into the Nature and Stability of Natural Resources* (Edinburgh, 1808); and *On Political Economy in Connexion with the Moral State and Moral Prospects of Society* (Glasgow, 1832).

64 *the volume of separate Essays*: Mill's *Essays on Some Unsettled Questions of Political Economy* (London, 1844).

74 *Mr Senior*: Nassau William Senior (1790–1864); first Drummond Professor of Political Economy at Oxford (1825–30; elected again 1847–52), he largely wrote the Commission Report that led to the Poor Law of 1834. Also published *An Outline of the Science of Political Economy* (London, 1836).

76 *Mr Tooke*: Thomas Tooke (1774–1858); prosperous businessman born in Russia, expert on price movements and on money and banking policy, a founder (with Ricardo, Malthus, James Mill, and others) of the famous Political Economy Club. Published, among other works, *An Inquiry Into the Currency Principle* ... (London, 1844), and *A History of Prices (1793–1857)*, i–vi (London, 1838–57).

102 *Mr Wakefield*: Edward Gibbon Wakefield (1796–1862); published an edition of Smith's *Wealth of Nations* (London, 1835–9) as well as many works advocating 'systematic colonization' to relieve population pressure and promote growth.

110 *M. de Sismondi*: Jean Charles Leonard Simonde de Sismondi (1773–1842), Swiss historian and political economist, his main economic work is *Nouveaux principes d'économie politique*, i–ii, (Paris, 1819; 2nd edn., 1827).

125 *Mr M'Culloch*: John Ramsay M'Culloch (1789–1864); first professor of political economy at University of London (1828–37). Published *The Principles of Political Economy* (Edinburgh, 1825; 3rd. edn., 1843); and *A Treatise on the Principles and Practical Influence of Taxation and the Funding System* (London, 1845).

Mr Malthus' Essay: T. R. Malthus, *An Essay on the Principle of Population* ... (1798; 6th edn., 1826).

126 *America, in her great civil war*: still the bloodiest war in United States' history, fought from 1861–5, won by the North to preserve the Union and free the African slaves.

129 *the Art of Living*: utilitarianism as Mill understands it. See also *System of Logic*, Bk. VI, ch. XII.

132 *insouciance*: indifference or carelessness.

in loco parentis: literally, in place of parents; in a paternalistic fashion.

136 *the case of the Lancashire spinners and weavers*: during the Civil War, when President Lincoln had imposed a blockade to prevent the Confederacy from exporting its goods (including raw cotton), the British working classes held public meetings to express their support for the blockade, contrary to their own narrow material interests. This sensitivity to the just claims of the North was in marked contrast to pro-Confederacy editorial opinions expressed in several leading British newspapers, including *The Times*. On 31 Dec. 1862, the Lancashire spinners and weavers held a meeting at Free Trade Hall, Manchester, where they resolved to send an address to Lincoln in support of his Emancipation Proclamation (the final version of which was issued on 1 January 1863, after a preliminary version had been announced on 22 September 1862). Lincoln's Proclamation was essentially an executive war measure that freed the slaves in the rebellious Confederate states but not in the slaveholding 'border states' that remained loyal to the Union. Slavery was not abolished under the Constitution until ratification of the 13th Amendment on 18 December 1865. On the Emancipation Proclamation and the 13th Amendment, see J. H. Franklin, *The Emancipation Proclamation* (New York, 1963).

138 *carrière*: career or vocation.

144 *Mr Babbage*: Charles Babbage (1791–1871); Lucasian Professor of Mathematics at Cambridge, first President of Section F (the Statistical Section) of the British Association, an expert on industrial organization and production with a practical interest in technological innovations (his calculating machines are generally considered early versions of the computer). Published *On the Economy of Machinery and Manufactures* (London, 1832).

146 *the Limited Liability Act*: passed in 1855.

151 *tracasseries*: annoyances or harassments.

152 *the 'Co-operator'*: a radical journal devoted to the cause of socialism, published in London and Manchester (1860–71), edited by Henry Pitman.

159 *in limine*: at a gut level.

163 *mala fides*: bad faith, with intent to deceive.

175 *donation inter vivos*: gift exchanged between living persons.

186 *the mobilier*: a tax on movable property such as furniture.

the patente: a licence fee.

195 *reductio ad absurdum*: literally, reduction to absurdity; Mill is disproving a proposition by showing that its implications are absurd.

222 *the separate essay*: 'Of the Laws of Interchange Between Nations', Essay I in Mill's *Essays on Some Unsettled Questions*.

238 *the defaulting states of America*: at various times (for example, during the great panic of 1837 and after the Civil War), various southern states defaulted on interest if not principal owed to their bond-holders, including the British banks.

259 *taille*: a tax on agricultural capital.

intendants and subdélégués: various administrative agents and deputies of the central government.

pays d'états: country estates.

261 *the Court of Chancery*: a court of equity presided over by the Lord High Chancellor, the Chancery Division of the High Court of Justice in England and Wales.

267 *Dr Johnson*: Samuel Johnson; famous eighteenth-century Tory literary figure.

277 *société en nom collectif*: collective association.

société anonyme: a private association (joint-stock company) whose owners share profits and have limited liability in proportion to their capital investments.

commandite: a private company whose profit-sharing owners are of two sorts: managing partners with unlimited personal liability for the debts of the enterprise; and 'sleeping partners' with limited liability.

286 *Mr Carey*: Henry Charles Carey (1793–1879); American social scientist bent on protectionism. Published, among other works, *Principles of Political Economy*, i–iii (Philadelphia, 1837–40); *The Past, the Present, and the Future* (Philadelphia, 1848); and *Principles of Social Science*, i–iii (Philadelphia, 1858–9).

302 *Mr Rae*: John Rae (1796–1872); a much-travelled Scot of various occupations (including medical doctor), his only published work is *Statement of Some New Principles on the Subject of Political Economy* (Boston, 1834), a brilliant critique of Smith in which much of modern capital theory and more is anticipated.

306 *since the passing of the Homestead Act*: the Act, enacted in 1862, provided for distribution of 160 acres of federal land to any settler who paid a $10 fee and agreed to farm for 5 years. More than 100 million acres of public land were distributed before the Act was repealed in 1910.

312 *the famous 'maximum' of the revolutionary government of 1793*: during the Terror, the Maximum was a policy of wage and price controls, applicable at first (as of May) only to grain prices but then later (as of Sept.) extended more generally; for a time, violation of the price controls was punishable by death; the policy was abolished in Dec. 1794.

the Irish emergency of 1847: the famine.

315 *the famous Statute of Labourers*: the 'Statutes of Artificers', enacted in 1380 when the Black Death had caused a steep decline in the supply of labour, controlled wages and restricted mobility of workers.

319 *Professor Fawcett*: Henry Fawcett (1833–84); Marshall's immediate predecessor as Professor of Political Economy at Cambridge (1863–84), Liberal MP for Brighton (1864–84), blinded by a shooting accident at age 25. Published, among other works, *A Manual of Political Economy* (Cambridge, 1863), and *The Economic Position of the British Labourer* (London, 1865).

324 *the laissez-faire school*: those political economists who argue that government should generally leave the private market alone so that competitive forces may work spontaneously.

330 *ensemble*: whole collection.

335 *La société . . . des galères*: society exercised the most unlimited and arbitrary jurisdiction over the manufacturing indus-

try: it used the property of the manufacturers without any scruples; it decided who might work, what things people might produce, what materials they ought to employ, what procedures it would be necessary to follow, what usages people might give to the products, etc. It was not enough to make something well, to manufacture correctly, it was necessary to produce according to the rules. Who does not know that regulation of 1670, which prescribed seizing and nailing to a post, with the name of the makers, any commodities not conforming to the rules just sketched, and which, for a second offence, required the manufacturers to attach themselves there also? It was not a question of consulting the tastes of consumers but of conforming to the whims of the law. Armies of inspectors, commissioners, superintendents, jurors, and guards were authorized to enforce them; they demolished the trades, they burned the products which were not in conformity to the rules: improvements were punished; they fined inventors. They subjected to different rules the manufacture of objects destined for domestic consumption and that of products destined for foreign trade. An artisan was not free to choose the location of his business, his work schedule, or for whom he worked. There exists a decree of 30 March 1700, which limits to eighteen towns the number of places where people might engage in the business of making stockings; a judgment of 18 July 1723 directed the manufacturers at Rouen to suspend their work from 1 July to 15 September, in order to facilitate the gathering of the harvest; Louis XIV, when he wished to undertake the colonnade of the Louvre, prohibited private individuals from employing workers without his permission, under penalty of a fine of 10,000 pounds, and workers from working for the individuals, under penalty, for the first offence, of imprisonment, and for the second, of the galleys.

355 *Poor Law of 1834*: the Poor Law established a central Board to oversee the administration of welfare support for the poor; able-bodied recipients and their families had to work 'indoors', in workhouses where they resided; they were stigmatized by loss of civil rights and strongly discouraged from procreation; disabled recipients were not stigmatized, however, and could receive support 'outdoors'; this welfare policy remained in force throughout the nineteenth century, and, despite the Unemployed Workman Act of 1905, its basic

premisses were not repudiated until the universal social security system was enacted by Labour in the New National Assistance Act of 1948.

Chapters on Socialism

372   *In the great country . . . manhood suffrage prevails*: the 15th Amendment to the US Constitution was ratified and became law on 30 March 1870, suggesting that Mill's draft was prepared after that date. Sect. 1 of the amendment states: 'The right of citizens of the US to vote shall not be denied or abridged by the US or by any State on account of race, color, or previous condition of servitude'. Restrictions 'on account of sex' were not made unconstitutional until ratification of the 19th Amendment in 1920.

the last Reform Act: the Reform Act of 1867. Mill refers to it as a great 'constitutional reform' with crucial implications for the existing laws of property. The Act extended the franchise to include all freeholders and many rent-payers, including those in the boroughs paying at least £10 per year and leaseholders in the counties paying £5 or more per year. As a result, Parliament would now have a stronger incentive to respond to the views of the working classes with 'next to no property of their own' and no good reason to 'support . . . property as it is, least of all . . . inequalities of property'. More extensions of the franchise followed and, by 1918, it was extended to all competent adults at least 21 years of age.

373   *the Reform Act of 1832*: sometimes called 'the Great Reform Act', it got rid of the 'rotten boroughs', redistributed parliamentary seats to newly created boroughs and counties (shires) where substantial numbers of people formerly had no representation, and extended the franchise to the upper middle classes, dooming the old aristocratic party (the 'Tories') to oblivion.

374   *the return to Parliament . . . the working classes*: a united Labour Party was formed in 1906, reorganized in 1918 with a socialist agenda just after the once-dominant Liberal Party had collapsed, and first became the majority party in 1945.

wise foresight, or . . . mankind will be gravely imperilled: it is perhaps needless to add that 'wise foresight' was not exercised anywhere to accomodate the redistributive claims of the working classes. Moreover, 'the future of mankind' really was 'gravely imperilled' largely as a result of the consequent hardening of class prejudices. At an international level, revolutionary socialist doctrines did lead to fascist and totalitarian regimes bent on destroying the existing economic order.

376 *the Labour Congresses and the International Society*: the International Association of Working Men (the First International) was established in London in Sept. 1864. Karl Marx drafted the Inaugural Address and played a dominant role within the Association throughout its eight years of existence. Mill refers to its First and Fourth Congresses held, respectively, at Geneva in 1866 and at Basle in 1869. The Association generally fell apart after the Fifth Congress held at The Hague in 1872, where Marx engineered the expulsion of his anarchist opponent Mikhail Bakunin and his followers. Note that Mill attributes the pure labour theory of value to 'the continental socialists who object to all interest on money, and deny the legitimacy of deriving an income in any form from property apart from labour'.

coup de main: sudden stroke of the hand, quick and unexpected revolution.

377 *La Solidarité, published at Neuchâtel*: during 1870–1, the official organ of the Jura federation of workers (largely small-shop watchmakers), ardent followers of Bakunin (then resident in Switzerland as leader of the anarchist–socialist Alliance of Social Democracy). The paper was edited by James Guillaume (1844–1916). Both Bakunin and Guillaume were expelled from the International at its Fifth Congress in 1872, much to the disgust of the Jura federation (it lodged a formal protest and refused to recognize the expulsions).

379 *persons who have . . . abstract justice and the general good of the community*: on my interpretation, persons who are firmly motivated to maximize an enlightened idea of the general happiness in which lexical priority is given to 'abstract justice' in the sense of equal rights for all members of the community. For Mill's discussion of abstract justice, see *Utilitarianism*, Ch. V.

380 *the very question at issue*: the question is whether the evils listed by socialists are (as they suggest) merely consequences of the existing rules of distribution, or (as many conservatives

suggest) 'necessities of nature'. Mill is drawing attention here
to the practical importance of his claim that rules of distribution are entirely a matter of choice. Evils attributable to the
existing social arrangements may be remedied by reform of
the institutions. But there is no point in trying to remedy evils
which 'flow from physical laws [of production, for example]
which human power is not adequate, or human knowledge
has not yet learned, to counteract'. Note the stringent test he
proposes for concluding that the evil consequences of existing
rules of private property are irremediable. These evils are to
be considered remediable 'until it is shown that any other
state of society would involve an equal or greater amount of
such evils'.

384 *désœuvrement*: unemployment.

a minuter analysis . . . human mind: Mill is here alluding to
what he elsewhere calls 'ethology, or the science of the formation of character' (*System of Logic*, Bk. VI, Ch. V). In his
view, 'nearly all the forms of misconduct' and of bad character observed in a given social context are ultimately consequences of the existing social institutions, including its rules
of distribution. Moreover, given that the institutions themselves are a matter of choice, their existence and stability may
be inferred to depend 'on a backward state of the human
mind'. Ethology as he conceived it remains today an undeve-
loped possibility. But, as he makes clear in the *Logic*, it would
consist of 'middle principles' that connect the universal principles of psychological hedonism to empirical generalizations
specific to a particular institutional context. More specifically,
any theorem of ethology would purport to explain this or that
observed form of conduct or character as an effect of particular social laws and customs, keeping in mind that individual
actions (including the choice to establish and maintain the
social institutions) are ultimately driven by actual (not necessarily enlightened) ideas of utility. Note the residual role
assigned to peculiar 'congenital predispositions' or inherent
'quiddities' in this sort of explanatory framework. Indeed, as
he says in the *Political Economy*: 'Of all vulgar modes of
escaping from the consideration of the effect of social and
moral influences on the human mind, the most vulgar is that
of attributing the diversities of conduct and character to
inherent natural differences' (*CW* ii. 319). For rare and
imperfect examples of what Mill seems to have had in mind

by ethology, see Alexis C. de Tocqueville, *Democracy in America* (1835–40), i–ii, ed. P. Bradley (New York, 1945); and John E. Cairnes, *The Slave Power* (London, 1862).

385 *this system of private war*: an allusion to the Hobbesian state of war.

388 *Sismondi, in his work on Political Economy*: *Nouveaux Principes d'économie politique*, i–ii (Paris, 1819; 2nd ed., 1827).

390 *M. Considérant*: Victor Prosper Considérant (1808–93), leading exponent of Fourier's brand of socialism, his main work is *Destiné sociale* (Paris, 1847).

396 *Book of the New Moral World*: completed by 1844, the book consisted of seven parts, the second of which was published in 1842.

400 *la féodalité industrielle*: the industrial feudal system, that is, a system in which 'comparatively few' capitalist overlords ('immensely rich individuals or companies') exercise virtually absolute power over large pools of dependent workers. Remarkably, Tocqueville also noted that an extraordinarily harsh 'aristocracy of manufacturers' supported by miserable workers was 'growing up' in America. Given the relatively confined role of manufactures in the predominantly agricultural economy of the time, however, he regarded it as 'a monstrous exception in the general [egalitarian] aspect of society'. And yet: '[T]he friends of democracy should keep their eyes anxiously fixed in this direction; for if ever a permanent inequality of conditions and aristocracy again penetrates into the world, it may be predicted that this is the gate by which they will enter' (*Democracy in America*, ii. 168–71).

401 *une baisse continue des salaires*: a continuous decline in general wages, as claimed by Owen, among others.

403 *Socialists . . . have a very imperfect and one-sided notion of the operation of competition*: Mill now takes up and perhaps somewhat qualifies the defence given in the *Political Economy* (Bk. IV, Ch. VII. 7) of the general utility of competition. During the course of his discussion here (pp. 405–8), he concedes in large measure the socialist objection (pressed by Louis Blanc and Fourier) that competition is not the 'best security for quality' in the context of a large-scale dynamic economy where it is difficult for consumers to be sure that any one of myriad middlemen in business for the moment is

of trustworthy character. But he thinks this problem can be remedied by introducing consumer co-operatives to deal directly with established wholesalers or producers without otherwise abandoning 'the existing constitution of property'.

410 *The portion ... which falls to capital merely as capital*: this interest payment is the reward for merely abstaining from present consumption because the savings are invested in a least-risk investment which requires no managerial or entrepreneurial skills from the investor. The investor merely has to wait and is virtually guaranteed of his profit. For Mill's discussion of the components of profit, see *Political Economy*, Bk. II, Ch. XV. 1 (*CW* ii. 400–2).

413 *The Difficulties of Socialism*: this chapter and the next should be read in conjunction with *Political Economy*, Bk. II, Chs. I–II; Bk. IV, Ch. VII. 5–7; and Bk. V, Ch. XI. 11, 15, and 16.

419 *the motive on which [Plato] relied ... worse men*: see *The Republic*, 1. 347, in E. Hamilton and H. Cairns (eds.), *Plato: The Collected Dialogues* (Princeton, NJ, 1961), 596–7.

427 *to force unprepared populations ... end in disappointment*: Mill's warning, unheeded by the revolutionary socialists on the Continent, has been borne out most recently by the collapse of the Soviet Union.

430 *Kosmos*: harmonious social order.

432 *Henry Maine*: Maine (1822–88); an eminent legal historian, Master of Trinity Hall, Cambridge (1877–88), published many works, including *Ancient Law* (London, 1861). Mill is referring to Maine's claim that 'the movement of the progressive societies has been ... distinguished by the gradual dissolution of family dependency and the growth of individual obligation in its place', in other words, 'the movement ... has hitherto been a movement from status to contract' (pp. 168–70).

433 *the story of the Prodigal Son*: see Luke 15: 11–32.

in regard to proprietary rights over immovables ... duration: see also Mill's discussion of various types of sharecropping and cottier systems in *Political Economy*, Bk. II, Chs. VIII–X (*CW* ii. 297–336).

the Sabbatical year: the seventh year. Under Mosaic law, agricultural land was to be left fallow and debtors were to be released from their obligations on the Sabbatical year.

434   *the great land reforms of Stein . . . Prussia*: Karl Freiherr vom
und zum Stein was an enlightened government minister vested
with large powers by King Frederick William III of Prussia
for a brief period (1807–8) during the Napoleonic occupation.
An ardent German nationalist, he was a leader of the reformers who persuaded Frederick William to issue an edict in
Oct. 1807 that emancipated the serfs and introduced a system
of peasant properties as of 1810. Another leader of the reform
movement was Wilhelm von Humboldt, whose work *Sphere
and Duties of Government* (London, 1854) provides 'the grand
leading principle' quoted by Mill at the head of *On Liberty*.
Baron vom Stein was exiled by Napoleon in December 1808
but he returned to play a leading role in the dictator's fall by
1815.

435   *metayer farmer*: a sharecropper who generally contracts directly with the landowner and pays a customary rent equal to
some proportion (usually 50%) of the crop net of expenses.
Mill emphasizes that the proportion is settled by custom
rather than by competition (*Political Economy*, Bk. II, Ch.
VIII).

THE WORLD'S CLASSICS

A Select List

HANS ANDERSEN: Fairy Tales
Translated by L. W. Kingsland
Introduction by Naomi Lewis
Illustrated by Vilhelm Pedersen and Lorenz Frølich

ARTHUR J. ARBERRY (Transl.): The Koran

LUDOVICO ARIOSTO: Orlando Furioso
Translated by Guido Waldman

ARISTOTLE: The Nicomachean Ethics
Translated by David Ross

JANE AUSTEN: Emma
Edited by James Kinsley and David Lodge

**Northanger Abbey, Lady Susan, The Watsons,
and Sanditon**
Edited by John Davie

Persuasion
Edited by John Davie

WILLIAM BECKFORD: Vathek
Edited by Roger Lonsdale

KEITH BOSLEY (Transl.): The Kalevala

CHARLOTTE BRONTË: Jane Eyre
Edited by Margaret Smith

JOHN BUNYAN: The Pilgrim's Progress
Edited by N. H. Keeble

FRANCES HODGSON BURNETT: The Secret Garden
Edited by Dennis Butts

**FANNY BURNEY: Cecilia
or Memoirs of an Heiress**
Edited by Peter Sabor and Margaret Anne Doody

THOMAS CARLYLE: The French Revolution
Edited by K. J. Fielding and David Sorensen

TOBIAS SMOLLETT: The Expedition of Humphry Clinker
Edited by Lewis M. Knapp
Revised by Paul-Gabriel Boucé

ROBERT LOUIS STEVENSON:
Treasure Island
Edited by Emma Letley

ANTHONY TROLLOPE: The American Senator
Edited by John Halperin

GIORGIO VASARI: The Lives of the Artists
Translated and Edited by Julia Conaway Bondanella and Peter Bondanella

VIRGINIA WOOLF: Orlando
Edited by Rachel Bowlby

ÉMILE ZOLA: Nana
Translated and Edited by Douglas Parmée